B.B. KING

There Is Always One More Time

BY DAVID McGEE

Backbeat Books
San Francisco

Published by Backbeat Books
600 Harrison Street, San Francisco, CA 94107
www.backbeatbooks.com
email: books@musicplayer.com   **3 1969 01590 5036**

An imprint of the Music Player Network
Publishers of *Guitar Player, Bass Player, Keyboard,* and *EQ* magazines
United Entertainment Media. Inc.
A CMP Information company

( )
CMP
United Business Media

Distributed to the book trade in the US and Canada by
Publishers Group West, 1700 Fourth Street, Berkeley, CA 94710

Distributed to the music trade in the US and Canada by
Hal Leonard Publishing, P.O. Box 13819, Milwaukee, WI 53213

Text design and composition by Michael Cutter
Cover design by Richard Leeds — bigwigdesign.com
Front cover photo by Jay Blakesberg

Library of Congress Cataloging-in-Publication Data

McGee, David, 1948–
B. B. King : there is always one more time / by David McGee.
     p. cm.
Includes bibliographical references (p. 341), discography (p. 330), and index.

ISBN-13: 978-0-87930-843-8
ISBN-10: 0-87930-843-5 (alk. paper)
1. King, B. B.—Criticism and interpretation. 2. King, B. B.—Discography. 3. Blues (Music)—
History and criticism. I. Title.
  ML420.K473M34 2005
  781.643'092—dc22

                    2005013808

Printed in the United States of America

05 06 07 08 09   5 4 3 2 1

TABLE OF CONTENTS

PROLOGUE

From the beginning, B.B. King heard a bigger blues. A bolder and brassier, if not brasher, blues. A blues that by its big sound evoked the pentimento of life, even as it documented the observable rich patterns and near-palpable roiling emotions of the daily grind. A blues that *sang*, sang in celebration of our every breath, sang in celebration of life lived with a passion—a passion for love; a passion for friendship; a passion for companionship; a passion for truth and fair play in personal politics; a passion, it's true, for the revenge of living well; a passion for...passion.

Born Riley B. King in Mississippi, to Nora Ella and Albert Lee King, the boy felt his soul stirred first by the spiritual messages of the gospel songs he sang in church every week. Then he was moved to make his own music after being transformed by the words and music of Blind Lemon Jefferson and Lonnie Johnson—the former being raw, rhythmically intricate, lyrically dark and brooding blues with a randy streak detailing aspects of the segregated world his audience knew well; the latter marked by its cool urbanity, stylistic diversity, and the artist's innovative guitar stylings—fluid, lyrical single-string runs, unusual chordings, double-note harmonic passages—that had elevated the guitar to the forefront as a solo instrument. (Johnson could play country blues with breathtaking command, step into a small-combo or big-band context and deliver a well-observed slice of city life in a jazz setting, or caress a pop confection—be they his own compositions or covers of popular standards—with appealing, unassailable conviction.) Comforted by the sacred, young Riley's imagination was ignited by the secular, because it told a story he saw unfolding every day, either in the cotton fields or in the community. And somewhere between Blind Lemon Jefferson, Lonnie Johnson, and, later, the exuberant jump blues of Louis Jordan, between the hard life in the Mississippi Delta cotton fields and the joyful world of the Church of God in Christ, he found his own turf—seized it, cultivated it, contoured it so it remained fertile season after season, yielding, ultimately, impressive amounts of legal tender, but, more important, a richness of heart and soul that would form him as surely as the music he absorbed in his youth and reimagined in his adult life.

Chapter 1

DELTA BORN, DELTA RAISED, DELTA SCARRED

"I was born in the great Mississippi Delta, that part of America that someone called the most Southern place on earth. Born on September 16, 1925, on the bank of Blue Lake, between Indianola and Greenwood, near the tiny villages of Itta Bena and Berclair. Daddy was Albert Lee King and named me Riley B. The 'B' didn't stand for anything, but the 'Riley' was a combination. Daddy had lost a brother called Riley, but Daddy also drove a tractor for a white plantation owner named Jim O'Reilly. When Mama went into labor and Daddy went looking for a midwife, O'Reilly helped him find the right woman. O'Reilly was there when I was born and asked Daddy what he was calling his baby boy. Seeing that O'Reilly was a fair and good man, he wanted me to have his name. Years later, when I asked Daddy why he dropped the 'O,' he said, ''Cause you didn't look Irish.'"[1]

Such are B.B.'s fondest memories of his Daddy. Nora Ella and Albert Lee parted company in their son's youth, and years later B.B. would recall that Daddy "only comes into focus when I see him waving good-bye. He's standing still, but me and Mama are moving." Nora Ella took young Riley back to her family in Kilmichael, Mississippi, where various relatives worked on white-owned plantations and, more important, passed on hard-earned wisdom to the impressionable youngster. Crucial to his later development was the counsel of his great-grandmother, a former slave whom B.B. remembers talking about "the beginnings of the blues." She told him that singing helped get the field hands through the long days of picking, that "singing about your sadness unburdens your soul."[2] At the same time, though, the field hands were using the blues to send each other coded messages, warning of the boss's impending arrival. "Maybe you'd want to get out of his way or hide," B.B. says. "That was important for the women because the master could have anything he wanted. If he liked a woman, he could take her sexually. And the woman only had two choices: do what the master demands or kill herself. There was no in-between. The blues could warn you what was coming. I could see the blues was about survival."[3]

 The blues was about survival.

 That initial insight into the power of music would inform one of the most imposing bodies of musical work ever recorded by an American artist. It was a childhood lesson that stuck in a profound way. But his great-grandmother's wisdom was only the beginning of Riley B. King's education. "What mattered most in the Mississippi of my childhood was work," B.B. recalls.[4] He toiled in cotton and corn fields, milked 20 cows a day (ten in the morning, ten at night) on Flake Cartledge's farm. After those morning milkings, he walked some three miles to the one-room schoolhouse that was home to kindergarten through grade 12, all taught by Luther Henson, "who had a powerful influence on my young brain."[5] By his own admission, B.B., who was afflicted with a pronounced stutter, was an indifferent student ("I'd put myself near the bottom"[6]), but not without common sense, an innate intelligence, a curiosity about the world, and a mind ready to absorb his elders' instruction. Luther Henson gave him the blessing of hope, and demonstrated a spiritual resiliency Riley embraced as he cultivated dreams of a better life far from the Delta cotton fields.

 Henson, B.B. says, "had a vision. He'd tell us, 'Y'all see how the white kids have school buses and y'all don't. Well, that's going to change one day. One day soon. Y'all hear about lynchings, where our people are punished for something they didn't do. If the whites wanted to, they could kill every one of us. But there are good men among the whites, just like there are bad men. Crazy people come in all colors. And one day soon the good people will win over the crazy people. One day the courts will listen to our side of the story. And one day the law separating coloreds from whites will be thrown out. Because one thing is certain. No matter how bad things seem now, change is on the way. That's the law of nature. Justice is coming. And justice is a powerful force—more powerful than evil. Justice can't be stopped.'"[7]

 Understanding that the blues is about survival was, in and of itself, too little information; soon enough Riley found the attributes of patience and tolerance essential to getting along, whether he was interacting with whites or blacks. To these cornerstones of a personality yet taking shape was added one more fundamental building block.

"Church was the highlight of the week. Church was not only a warm spiritual experience, it was exciting entertainment, it was where I could sit next to a pretty girl, and mostly it was where the music got all over my body and made me wanna jump. Sunday was the day."[8]

Riley attended the Church of God in Christ ("that means they'll be doing whatever it takes to praise the Lord, making a joyful noise, even talking in tongues"[9]) in Pinkney Grove. There the Reverend Archie Fair commanded his flock's attention with both his biblically charged words and his Sears Roebuck Silvertone guitar, "the one object in the whole church that fascinated me most.[10]

"The body is hollow wood with a cord that plugs into the wall," B.B. remembers. "Its rounded shape and lovely curves remind me of the body of a beautiful girl. I wanna run up and put my arms around the guitar, but I don't dare. I don't know how to play. And besides, here comes the Right Reverend leading the congregation."[11]

When Reverend Fair arrived at Riley's house for supper one day, he was toting his guitar, which he rested on Riley's bed while engaging in fellowship with his host. Sitting there unattended, the instrument was like a mythological Siren beckoning Riley to its side. Knowing—or assuming—the adults were distracted by their conversation and wouldn't be paying attention to him, he eased over towards the bed. "While they're not looking, I reach over and, oh so carefully, touch the wood of the guitar. Just sort of gently stroke her. Touch her strings to see how they feel against my fingers. Feels good. Feels like magic. I wonder, How do you get her to make those sounds? How do you get her to sing?"[12]

These questions were answered in short order, when the Rev caught Riley admiring his guitar. Although "Mama's mad I touched something that don't belong to me," Reverend Fair was more sanguine about the child's transgression. In fact, he encouraged Riley to "touch it," adding, "It ain't gonna bite you."[13]

He showed Riley how to hold the instrument, then how to make a few simple chords and get music out of it. He demonstrated the classic template, a I-IV-V chord progression.[14] To this instruction the Reverend added a bit of wisdom Riley would never forget: "The guitar is a precious instrument. It's another way to express God's love."[15]

Seven years old in 1932, living through a Great Depression he knew nothing of ("The farm was in the country, and the country was cut off from the rest of the state. I didn't know about no stock market crash or Depression"), Riley believed he had found his calling. He began teaching Sunday school to younger kids in church. The Church of God in Christ enriched his spirit in every way. "Church had the singing, church had the guitar, church had folks feeling good and happy; church was all I needed."[16] The boy's enthusiasm and commitment, so evident that B.B. says people regarded him as a "church boy, and I was glad to be seen that way,"[17] convinced his mother and the Reverend that Riley, stutter and all, was on his way to serving God as a guitar-playing preacher. Philosophically and musically, then, seven-year-old Riley B. King had put the finishing touches on a solid philosophical and spiritual foundation.

Enter snuff-dipping Great Aunt Mima, several years Riley's mother's junior, and "young-thinking, the most modern of all my relatives."[18]

Aunt Mima owned a crank-up Victrola and the first collection of records Riley had ever seen, all stacked up neatly next to the record player. Her personal flamboyance aside, Aunt Mima was meticulous in caring for the heavy shellac discs, teaching Riley the delicate technique of placing a record on the turntable and setting the needle precisely on the outer groove. Mission accomplished, Riley sat and watched as the needle tracked into the actual recording. "And then—pow!—those beautiful scratchy sounds flew in my face, cutting right through me, electrifying my soul."[19]

From Aunt Mima's collection of nearly 50 discs Riley cued up recordings by Robert Johnson, Charley Patton, Bumble Bee Slim, and countless others. Two artists in particular leaped off Aunt Mima's turntable and into Riley's marrow: Texas bluesman Blind Lemon Jefferson and the widely traveled Louisiana native Lonnie Johnson. "I liked Robert [Johnson] and all the rest, but those were my favorites."[20] In Jefferson's music he heard sounds "as close to the field shouters as anyone else. He had a big burly voice and put so much feeling into his words until I believed everything he sang. He had power. Like all the great bluesmen, Blind Lemon sang for sinners. When he sang 'Rabbit Foot Blues' or 'Shuckin' Sugar Blues' or 'That Crawlin' Baby Blues' or 'Mosquito Moan,' I moaned along with him. It was like him and his guitar were part of the same being. You didn't know where one stopped and the other started. Blind Lemon was strong and direct and bone-close to my home."[21]

Johnson, on the other hand, "took a minute longer to appreciate than Blind Lemon," but would have by far the more lasting influence on B.B.'s approach to the blues.

"Lonnie was definitely a bluesman," B.B. observed, "but he took a left turn where Blind Lemon went right. Where Blind Lemon was raw, Lonnie was gentle. Lonnie was more sophisticated. His voice was lighter and sweeter,

more romantic. He had a dreamy quality to his singing and a lyrical way with the guitar. Unlike Blind Lemon, Lonnie sang a wide variety of songs. I liked that. I guess he found the strict blues form too tight. He wanted to expand. When he sang 'Tomorrow Night,' probably his most famous ballad, I understood that he was going to a place beyond the blues.[22]

"Blind Lemon and Lonnie hit me hardest, I believe, because their voices were so distinct, natural, and believable. I heard them talking to me. As guitarists they weren't fancy. Their guitars were hooked up to their feelings, just like their voices."[23]

Riley "flat-out tried to copy" Jefferson and Johnson,[24] and even after he was exposed to other formidable bluesmen from his home state—Robert Johnson, Elmore James, Muddy Waters, and others—"no one molded my musical manner like Blind Lemon and Lonnie. They entered my soul and stayed."[25]

But education at Aunt Mima's went further yet. B.B. became transfixed by Bessie Smith, her brief rival Mamie Smith, and Ma Rainey, strong women who sang with such emotional force it "tore off the top of my head."[26] He of course heard gospel; one recording in particular, the Reverend J.M. Gates's "Death's Black Train," had an especially powerful impact on him. He heard the big bands of Duke Ellington and Count Basie, and another light bulb came on: their rhythms, "more complicated than the beat of the blues," fired his imagination.[27]

Not least of all, he heard country music, notably the Singing Brakeman, Mississippi's own Jimmie Rodgers. In a brilliant career spanning only six years from his signing to RCA Victor by legendary talent scout Ralph Peer in 1927 to his death from tuberculosis in 1933, Rodgers forever altered traditional country music, not the least of his achievements being to establish the template for a new, more expressive instrumental sound by including in his 1928 sessions Joe Kaipo, a steel guitarist of Hawaiian ancestry. In 1930 he had engaged in a summit meeting of the highest order in recording "Blue Yodel No. 9" with jazz giant Louis Armstrong on trumpet and Armstrong's wife Lillian on piano. On this outing Rodgers made explicit both the emotional and stylistic links between jazz, blues, and country. A year after the Armstrong sessions, Rodgers went against form again when he recorded in Louisville with a black jug band. Throughout his abbreviated career, Rodgers evinced an uncanny ability to re-invent any song—an original composition, a cover version, or something snatched from the public domain—so that it sounded as if it had been written to serve his singular, multicultural, stylistically eclectic vision. Celebrated as Rodgers was for his evocative vocals (blessed with a plaintive, unadorned tenor voice, he employed what he termed a "blue" yodel for dramatic effect—not the clear, bright, ululating sound stereotyped as Swiss style, but something that suggested an underlying, epic sadness or melancholy) and his stirring original songs, it's his relentless crossing and expanding of music's boundaries that stands as his most valuable contribution.

In the nascent stages of his formulations about what music could be, Riley was moved by Rodgers's expansive arrangements, hearing in them the common links in seemingly disparate styles. Lyrically Rodgers's songs hit home too, telling the same type of hard-luck tales and rejoicing over many of the same twists of fate Riley had heard blues artists singing about: songs of common folk trying to get a leg up in the world, of men and women trying to figure out each other, for good or ill. Years later B.B. would call country and blues "first cousins"[28] and observe that "most of the good lyrics that tell about men and women come from country music."[29] He listened to country music on his dad's radio, "a Zenith that had a battery the same size that you would have in your car today. The battery was about as big as the radio. We used to hear Minnie Pearl, Cowboy Copas, Roy Acuff, and Bill Monroe, too. I could put C-E-G-B♭ together in country music before I could do blues. Long before."[30]

Musically, Rodgers, and eventually most of mainstream country, made a sound signature out of the steel guitar, further fueling Riley's ever broadening sense of music's possibilities. "The country guys just killed me the way they played the slide," B.B. says. "I heard these Nashville guys play that slide—oh, man, I used to be crazy about it and I still am. A guy named Bob Wills and His Texas Playboys had a big orchestra, but he featured violins and they played Western swing music. He had a guy that he called Leon [Leon McAuliffe] that played the slide and he would say, 'Go Leon!' so I started trying to play. Since I couldn't use the bottleneck, I would trill my hand on the string and my ears would seem to say that sounds something like a bottleneck."[31]

Young and impressionable, Riley was absorbing it all: gospel, the music that "got all over my body and made me wanna jump"; hard, acoustic blues from Blind Lemon Jefferson and pop-edged, electrified blues from Lonnie Johnson; the powerhouse declamations of strong-willed, big-voiced blues women; brass, blues, and advanced rhythmic concepts courtesy the Duke and the Count; Jimmie Rodgers singing of everyday lives and adding grandeur to his tales with exotic instrumental support.

This concoction was B.B. King's primordial ooze. Though still years from revealing his own distinctive solo voice, he found that an eclectic approach within the blues framework made sense. In many ways the final piece of the puzzle that was coming together to form B.B. King out of the raw stuff of Riley B. King emanated once more from his own family—specifically, his

mother's cousin, Booker T. Washington White, or Bukka White as he was known.

White periodically dropped in on his cousin's family, always "looking like a million bucks. Razor-sharp. Big hat, clean shirt, pressed pants, shiny shoes. He smelled of the big city and glamorous times; he looked confident and talked about things outside our little life in the hills. He always had a good word and candy for the kids, a real happy-go-lucky guy, joking and stroking everyone with compliments and charms. He lit up my world."[32]

But there was more. Bukka White was a real bluesman, his guitar "as much a part of his person" as his "fancy big-city clothes."[33] Here indeed was a man of style and substance. But the glamorous times he related to young Riley and family were shadowed by a dark personal history all too common to black men raised in the Deep South, in segregation's merciless climate.

Born on a farm in Houston, Mississippi, in 1909, White received a guitar for his ninth birthday. A few years later he got serious about playing the blues after being introduced to and inspired by Charley Patton. Came the Depression and White hit the road, his wanderings taking him all over the South and as far north as Buffalo, New York. Big and strong, he was a skilled enough athlete to make a living pitching two seasons for the Birmingham Black Cats before moving on to Chicago in the late '30s and using his sledge-hammer fists to support himself as a boxer. In the Windy City he established himself with the local blues crowd, befriending the likes of Big Bill Broonzy, and in 1937 was offered a chance to record by Lester Melrose of the Melrose Brothers publishing company, a concern that had been responsible for arranging recording sessions for locally based blues and jazz artists for nearly two decades. He was scheduled to go in for the date immediately upon his return from paying a social call on relatives in Mississippi.

Back in the Delta, he and a friend were ambushed one night by a fellow looking to settle an old score; White, who had come prepared for such an attack, promptly dispatched his would-be assailant with a gunshot to the leg. Arrested and sentenced to two years in the Parchman Prison Farm, he managed to get back to Chicago (either by jumping bail or through the auspices of Lester Melrose) to cut two original songs ahead of his imprisonment in Mississippi. Issued on the Vocalion label, White's first single, "Pinebluff, Arkansas" b/w "Shake 'Em On Down," sold more than 16,000 copies—making it a bonafide hit among "race" records—with the shuffling, slightly bawdy "Shake 'Em On Down" becoming the favored side of the two. A year later Big Bill Broonzy offered an updated version of the song in his own "New Shake 'Em On Down," and several other blues artists covered the original version.

Upon his 1940 release from Parchman, White returned to Chicago to cut some new sides for Vocalion. Writing solidly for two days in early March, he came up with a dozen songs torn from the dark heart of his life—songs about death, imprisonment, duplicitous women, the privations of poverty, and the shiftless, aimless existence of the hobo he had once been. Singing in a deep, quavering voice and pounding hard chords on his guitar or razor-sharp slide lines (with Washboard Sam slapping out percussive support on washboard), White fashioned some of the most vivid imagery and soulful poetry the blues has ever known, work that stands alongside that of Robert Johnson, Skip James, Son House, and Charley Patton as monuments of the Delta style in its deepest form. Few Delta accounts of death's long reach are as harrowing as "Strange Place Blues," White's reflections on his mother's passing. In a voice haunted and disbelieving, he laments, "I thought after my mother was put away/I thought my wife would take her place/But my wife done throwed me away," his tragedy now doubled as he realizes he is completely, utterly alone in the world. In "When Can I Change My Clothes?" he protests the humiliations of a prison regimen designed to destroy every shred of the inmates' dignity in the name of rehabilitation, a theme he plumbed to equally moving effect in "Parchman Farm Blues," wherein he beseeches an unresponsive God to help him overcome the tribulations of his confinement. "District Attorney Blues" finds him inveighing against a legal system that was especially unforgiving of black men's trespasses, a bold statement in 1940. "Fixing to Die Blues" is an interior monolog about death imagined from the deceased's viewpoint, with White's propulsive riffing and stinging slide lines heightening the eerie narrative line.[34]

The distinctive gut-wrenching howl of White's slide work commanded Riley's attention. But however much White's playing impressed the young boy—"he was really raw"[35]—only the slide got under his skin. "I never really wanted to play like him," B.B. told Ted Drozdowski in *Guitar World*, "with the exception of the slide."

Riley did, however, want to emulate White in other ways. "I liked his style. He used to tell me, 'Always dress like you're going to the bank to borrow money.' In other words, don't go around slouchy, lookin' bad and like that. The other kids used to tease me about wearing suits and jackets, but one of the reasons I did was Booker."[36]

First a sound, then a style—both personal and musical—began taking shape, at least conceptually (the child still did not have his own instrument, apart from the primitive diddley bows—a broomstick with a piece of clothesline wire attached at each end—he fashioned from time to time as the parts became available), as Riley took in all the influences and the advice that came as if by Providence, always at the right time, when he needed it most, even if he didn't recognize it as such at the moment. By age ten he had lived a lot of life for his tender years, and had at least the inkling of a future he wanted to explore. With a moral compass defined by his mother, the Reverend Archie Fair, and the Holy Bible, an indefatigable work ethic, and boundless ambition, young Riley did not seem destined for a life of hard labor toiling on the rich earth of the Mississippi Delta.

However many fortuitous turns Riley's life had taken, his tenth year also brought tragic, seismic upheaval: Nora Ella, his mother, died. Blind and struggling to breathe, she left her son this advice on their final parting: "People will love you, if you show love to them. Remember that, son."[37]

Invited into various relatives' homes, Riley decided he would make his own way, not out of any sense of mission, or ambition, but rather out of bitterness over his mother being taken away from him and his family torn apart. "Mama's death cut me off from the world. I had my family once and my family had been destroyed. I'd rather live with the destruction than deceive myself. As a ten-year-old I decided to go it alone."[38]

Flake Cartledge, a "fair-minded and liberal man" who kept "evil forces like the Klan off his land," gave Riley his own cabin in which to live and steady work in the house and in the corn and cotton fields. "I put my grief in hard work," B.B. says. "I hid my pain, a pattern that set me on a course for life."[39]

Back at the Cartledge farm, Riley began his education in the adult world. Working in the fields for long hours, he learned, as he hadn't before, about the economics of sharecropping, how the paltry wages paid for backbreaking work underwrote the plantation owners' opulent lifestyles and perpetuated the sharecropper's misery. He learned, as he hadn't before, that the plantation was a world unto itself, where the black field hands gained a measure of protection from the dangers of the outside world—even the local police recognized the plantation owner as the absolute ruler of his dominion who would mete out his own form of justice if the occasion demanded. But in return for that protection black workers were obliged to stay put. Riley understood that the plantation offered him some security, but, having heard stories from his relatives about the slave days, he came to regard sharecropping simply as a continuation of "the slavery mentality."[40]

Safe though it was, the plantation didn't isolate Riley from the real world. He witnessed angry confrontations between black and white; he endured the humiliation of being considered something less than a second-class citizen. Sometimes the hurt came from his own kind, specifically a cousin who liked to make sport of him for being alone and barely scraping by, never having food waiting for him when he got home from school or anyone around to take care of his daily needs. In a world as economically deprived as the plantation, social status was measured on scales of family and belongings, and by those reckonings Riley truly was poor. As an adult, Riley has never denied the anger he carries with him from these days; it runs deep, ready to ignite in an expressive performance on the order of "Five Long Years," one of his earliest recordings, which is ostensibly about a bad woman who rewards his hard work by throwing him out. But when he growls the lyric, "if you've ever been mistreated/ you know just what I'm talking about," he brings a righteous intensity to those words, an intensity that doesn't quite square with the notion that this anger is fueled simply by a woman's thoughtlessness. Rather, its fury carries the weight of history, a history informed by the violence and soul-bludgeoning hammer of segregation.

Yet the lessons his mother taught persist. If his cousin gained some perverse delight in putting Riley down, then Riley's sense was "never to give that kind of hurt to anyone else. My revenge was to change a bad feeling into a good one. If I'm working with you and I sense you're feeling a little insecure, I try to make you feel great. That's how I get rid of my old hurt. If I don't do that, my hurt grows and makes me mean and vengeful. But if hurt can change to kindness—that's something Mama showed me—the world becomes a little less cruel."[41]

Instead of letting bitterness and anger eat him up, Riley looked on the sunny side, always on the alert for something that would take him to a place in his heart and soul where he felt comforted, happy. Outdoor movies in Kilmichael in the spring and summer provided such occasions. There was always a chance some fetching young girl might welcome his company while the movie played. And when the movies featured heroic cowboys such as Gene Autry and Tex Ritter, and earnest detectives such as Dick Tracy, doing good deeds for the unfortunate, Riley would get lost in their worlds, imagining himself in those roles in real life.

Music served the same escapist purpose: "It took me away," he said.[42]

At age 12, with a payday advance on his $15 monthly salary from Flake Cartledge, Riley began his musical journey in earnest when he paid a man in Kilmichael $15 for a used cherry-red Stella acoustic guitar "with a short neck and a good solid sound."[43]

Riley's relationship with his guitar was intense and intimate from the start. "Couldn't keep my hands off her," he said of his treasured Stella. "If I was feeling lonely, I'd pick up the guitar; if something's bugging me, just grab the guitar and play out the anger; happy, horny, mad, or sad, the guitar was right there, a righteous pacifier and comforting companion. It was an incredible luxury to have this instrument to stroke whenever the passion overcame me, and, believe me, the passion overcame me night and day."

In his own stumbling way, Riley began forging an individual sound from the moment he had a guitar to call his own. Trying to emulate the styles of his heroes Blind Lemon Jefferson and Lonnie Johnson proved frustrating, because "they were so deeply individual that imitation didn't work."[44] The frustration he experienced in his attempts to emulate Jefferson's and Johnson's styles taught Riley an important lesson, though: " … the blues isn't like painting by numbers or following the dots. The blues, I would soon learn, is something you live."[45]

His guitar now his favored confidante, Riley began devoting most of his spare time to learning how to make it sing. For 50 cents he purchased an instruction book from a Sears Roebuck catalog, and began teaching himself the country songs that filled its pages. He didn't care what kind of song he played; anything that taught him how to get music out of that box he was holding was "a learning method; slowly I was reading notes and playing scales."[46]

Gaining fluency on his instrument, and blessed with a sweet, strong tenor singing voice for his age, Riley dug into his first love, gospel music, by teaming with his cousin Birkett Davis, and two friends from school, Walter Doris, Jr., and Dubois Hune, to form a gospel quartet, the Elkhorn Jubilee Singers. Rehearsing diligently to hone their sound, they aspired to cross the propulsive gospel style of the Golden Gate Quartet with the close, smooth, pop-style harmonies of the Ink Spots. All in their early teens, the boys found their voices changing, and the harmonies they heard in their heads proved elusive in fact, despite the church's flock spurring them on with encouraging shouts and hands upraised to touch the Lord's.

Yet at the very moment Riley felt things going his way, his world was upended again. First, his guitar was stolen from his cabin on the Cartledge farm. "I was so heartbroken, it was a long time before I got another," he said. "I didn't want to take another chance of losing something so precious." Then, quite out of the blue, his father returned and took his son to Lexington, where Albert Lee lived with his new wife, three daughters, and a son, and worked driving a tractor on a plantation near Tchula, Mississippi. It would take years for Riley to feel close to his new family and comfortable in the Lexington environment. It was a far larger town than Kilmichael, and Riley's family lived next door to a white family—something Riley had not expected to happen anytime soon. His memories of that time are bittersweet at best. In downtown Lexington, while running an errand for his stepmother one Saturday afternoon, he saw a group of white men hang the body of a dead black man from a beam on the front of the courthouse. He watched in silence, anger consuming him as he saw white people smiling as they strolled by the 19-year-old's limp form. "I feel disgust and disgrace and rage and every emotion that makes me cry without tears and scream without sound. I don't make a sound."[47]

At the Ambrose Vocational High School, he was one of hundreds of students bussed in from the surrounding area, and he had multiple teachers for different subjects. More to the point, he felt out of place socially. "My accent was country, my clothes were torn. Had nothing but one pair of denim overalls. Same clothes I wore to work I wore to school. Other kids, with their clean shirts and nice trousers, talked clearly and expressed themselves well. I was tongue-tied. . . . In my hidden heart I felt over my head."[48]

Though now living in his father's house, Riley found Albert Lee remote and uncommunicative, but not without admirable qualities of which the son took note. "I admire Daddy's guts. He never slacked off work or lied to me or shirked his responsibilities. He dealt with his family from a distance, but was available when needed. Eventually I'd do the same. I don't know whether I was copying him or whether, by coincidence, my work, like Daddy's, simply kept me away. All I know is that in many ways, big and small, I've followed my father."[49]

But there were "precious moments" in Lexington, stolen moments when his musical education flowered anew and the messages in the music comforted his troubled soul. Radio provided an escape route. "Two stations out of Nashville came through loud and clear. WSM played country, and I loved listening to those weeping pedal steel guitars. But it was WLAC that kept me wrapped up in the radio. They played black music. I'd sit enthralled, listening to the original Sonny Boy Williamson, who had a stutter worse than mine and a harmonica style that gave me goose bumps. There were no empty spots between his human voice and his harmonica voice; they were inseparable. Plus his rhythm was so rocking, you'd forget the blues he just gave you a minute ago."[50]

Despite never being entirely comfortable in Lexington or with his new extended family, Riley began to put together a worldview informed by the music he was hearing, the lessons taught in his mother's home, and the conviviality he witnessed between whites and blacks, random acts of violence notwithstanding. Although he was suppressing considerable anger over the shameful treatment of black people in the Deep South, he found the higher ground early on, and began carrying himself with a grace and equanimity that may have seemed arrogant to some, but was in fact an understanding of people black and white sharing the earth as one.

"I wasn't taught to hate white people," he said. "That dead body hanging from the platform broke the heart and wounded the spirit of every black man and woman who passed by. But I suspected that it also hurt right-thinking white people. Both parents had spoken well of fair-minded white people—my namesake, Jim O'Reilly, and Flake Cartledge—so I knew better than to blame a whole race for the rotten deeds of a few. When some blacks talked about whites as the devil, I could see the source of their wrath. I could still see the dead man outside the courthouse on the square. But I couldn't turn the fury into hatred. Blind hatred, my mother had taught me, poisons the soul. I kept hearing her say, 'If you're kind to people, they'll be kind to you.'"[51]

That lesson remained with him the rest of his life and informed his approach to others in and out of the music business, and the personal dignity he exhibited through the years. But only six months into his Lexington experience, Riley found things weren't adding up to a rich life, no matter the wisdom gained: " … living in a ticky household where I was scared of breaking rules; living with an instant family who were really strangers to someone like me, who was deeply shy; going to a school that seemed big as a factory and just as cold; feeling poorer and shabbier than the kids around me; stammering through my lessons; never liking the Lexington that had displayed a dead body in front of the courthouse."[52] Come the early fall of 1938, Riley mounted his bicycle and "sped out of town like a bat out of hell, never to return."[53]

He had one destination in mind: home. Or what he considered home, that being his modest cabin on the Cartledge farm, where he intended to resume his life in the fields among people he felt close to, people he had learned from, people who cared about him, people who made him feel like family.

Arriving at the farm after his two-day bicycle journey, Riley found his little cabin occupied by another tenant. Where to now? Deeper into the Delta, to Indianola, to his great aunt Beulah Belle Davis and her husband John Henry's place, where he would be reunited with his cousin Birkett Davis, who had sung with him in the Elkhorn Jubilee Singers. Riley worked the fields at the Cartledge plantation to earn enough money for bus fare to Indianola, and he was gone again. Cousin Birkett greeted him with commonsense advice: "Cotton pays good down here. Stay around and you can make some money."[54]

Riley's new family worked on a huge plantation owned by Johnson Barrett, a spread estimated by Riley to be "maybe a thousand acres in all." Working the sharecropper's shift, from "can to can't," sunup to sunset, returning in the dead of night to a house eight miles out of Indianola that had three bedrooms, a kitchen, and no electricity, Riley simply buckled down. The privations of the physical space were irrelevant; his kinfolk gave him a stable, loving environment in which he felt valued. In Barrett Johnson he found "a trustworthy teacher,"[55] a reserved man of the Jewish faith who possessed "quiet strength"[56] and who hired as his foreman one Booker Baggett, a black man, "something no other owner would dare do." Another strong-willed, soft-spoken, hardworking male role model, Baggett "knew everything there was to know about planting"[57] and drove a tractor with such authority as to make Riley dream of the day he could take the wheel.

Riley also fell into his first big love affair while on the Johnson farm, when at 14 he swooned over a girl he called Angel. Fell so hard he even began contemplating marriage. It was a short-lived and tragic romance, as Angel and her entire family were killed in a car crash. Devastated, Riley submerged his grief in work.

"I'd get out there, work up a head of steam, and pick like crazy. I'd be excited; it was the culmination of the long growing season and also a feast for the eyes, this world of white blossoms. Around Indianola we had a kind of cotton called Delta Pinelent. The planters liked it 'cause it was good for oil, and the pickers liked it 'cause it carried a heavier seed. More weight meant more money. Me and my cousin Birkett Davis would pick side by side, both of us raw bundles of energy. . . . I did more than work the cotton fields. I helped grow corn and soybeans. I baled hay with a combine pulled by a mule, maybe the toughest job of all . . . I cut wood in a sawmill. I was still a scrawny kid but learned to pick up big logs by leveraging them with thin sticks.[58]

"Work seemed to keep the problems inside my head from getting any bigger. I missed Mama less when I worked; I thought less about Angel and the way she died. Work kept me sane."[59]

Not that music had taken a backseat to any other endeavor, or had lost its power to boost Riley's spirits when things got rough. After he had bought a guitar with $20 he had saved up from work, he joined a gospel group, the Famous St. John Gospel Singers. Riley traded tenor leads with N.C. Taylor, and the two of them worked up some intricate five-part harmonies with the other members of the group, including brothers John and O.L. Matthew and Riley's cousin Birkett Davis. Their inspiration was the Golden Gate Quartet, but they were also paying close attention to the newer approaches of the Soul Stirrers and the Dixie Hummingbirds—"the Hummingbirds had a great guitarist named Howard Carroll and a lead singer called Ira Tucker with a voice as soulful and deep as the Deep South."[60]

The Famous St. John Gospel Singers began performing in local churches—or at least those local churches that would have them. Some churches regarded the presence of a guitar in a gospel group as anathema to the proper, reverential spirit of the worship service and would cancel the Famous St. John group before it had a chance to corrupt their flocks. As usual, the musicians had the last laugh. "To some, the guitar made us look like a rebel group," B.B. recalled. "Later, though, when they saw our music was drawing crowds, they'd reconsider and invite us back."[61]

Amidst his dreams of the Famous St. John Gospel Singers actually becoming famous, Riley found his musical spirit energized and inspired by other sources. He remembers what he calls "ten-cent vendors—a primitive screen attached to a projector that, for a dime, showed three-minute music pieces."[62] The most vivid of these short films starred jazz clarinetist Benny Goodman fronting a big band that featured a black guitarist named Charlie Christian, a visionary who most fully explored the electric guitar's sonic palette. Recording with Goodman's band between 1939 and 1942 (when, at age 23, he died of tuberculosis), Christian redefined the instrument's role in the band context and in the process rendered obsolete the acoustic guitar in the jazz ensemble. Inspired and influenced by tenor saxophonist Lester Young's lyricism, Christian, who played tenor sax also, adopted a similar style in constructing a singular approach to technique, melody, and harmony that brought the guitar out of its supporting role and into the spotlight. To Christian, the guitar was a solo instrument, pure and simple. Sustained legato phrases, improvisations based on the passing chords played between a song's root harmonies, and a tonal style akin to that of a reed instrument were Christian-pioneered innovations that propelled jazz into the modern age.

"On certain songs Charlie Christian soloed in a manner that blew off the top of my head," B.B. recalled. "His technique went beyond my Sears Roebuck instruction books. He took me to a new place; he played and phrased like a horn—a sax or a trumpet—that, in turn, played and phrased like a singer. Any way I looked at it I was in love. Christian played free and fast and swung his ass off."[63]

This was Riley's introduction to swing, and it made a profound impact on his ideas about music, about what a genre's stylistic framework could contain. The diminished chords Christian played "seemed to stretch my ears,"[64] although at that time he could recognize them only as "this unusually gorgeous sequence of notes."[65] Fletcher Henderson's arrangements for Goodman caught his attention too—"the happy play between the trumpets and the saxes, the rhythm riding over and under every inch of the music.

"Charlie Christian was smack dab in the middle of it all, a miracle man doing things to a guitar I never imagined possible. He pointed to a musical world outside Blind Lemon Jefferson and Lonnie Johnson."[66]

Indianola, of all places, turned out to be precisely the right spot for Riley to cultivate a Catholic sensibility about the blues. Church Street, and specifically the Jones Night Spot, was the locus of the action on Friday and Saturday nights. It was an eight-mile walk from the plantation to the club, but walk it he would and spend the entire evening into the early-morning hours peeking in through the slats of the rickety club's walls, watching breathlessly as perfumed women in tight dresses would grind their bodies against the men's, all the while exulting in the exuberant rhythms coming from the bandstand—the bandstand, where Count Basie, with Mr. Five by Five, Jimmy Rushing, on vocals, held forth; the bandstand, where Pete Johnson and Jay McShann (the latter boasting a vibrant young sax player named Charlie "Bird" Parker) brought in boogie-woogie from Kansas City ("some older folks looked down on boogie-woogie as nasty and radical, but I loved its rocking rhythm and amazing technique";[67] the bandstand, where Sonny Boy Williamson (Rice Miller) on harmonica and Robert Jr. Lockwood on guitar got the joint jumping with rowdy, stomping blues shouts.

"As a kid, hanging around Church Street, the presentation of music was so powerful, I couldn't help but jump for joy," B.B. said. "I had discovered art, or truth, or whatever you want to call it; I had seen a light I'd follow forever."[68]

In his determination to follow the light, Riley let nothing stand in his way. He had a notion that the Famous St. John Gospel Singers were good enough to make a living on the road, singing their music instead of working menial day jobs. His mates in the Singers didn't share his optimism, however; they were barely making ends meet as it was, and the thought of leaving their only sure source of income for the uncertain payday of a music career was simply unthinkable. Riley stuck with the group, playing the circuit of churches around Indianola but feeling restless and "stuck."[69]

Purely out of a desire to make more money, he made a trip to Church Street on his own one Saturday night before the action heated up, plunked himself down on a curb, guitar in hand, and began playing gospel songs, belting out "Working on a Building," "I Know the Lord Will Make a Way," "The Old Rugged Cross," all the while earning effusive praise and encouragement from the passersby. But the encouragement Riley was looking for—cold, hard cash in the form of tips for his busking—was not forthcoming. Plan B was in order.

"I strum a little blues I heard Sonny Boy playing last Saturday night at the Jones Night Spot. I remember half the words and make up the other half. Something about my baby done left me and I'm feeling down, Lord knows this here is a mighty lonesome town. Then I start singing how when she loved me, she loved me good; say, when she loved me, the woman loved me good; but now I'm the laughingstock all 'round my neighborhood. Thing about the blues is that blues are simple. You sing one line; you repeat that line; and then rhyme your third line with the first two. They call it the twelve-bar blues 'cause each of those lines is four bars. That's it. In that basic form, though, you can cram a lifetime of stories 'bout the woes and wonders of earthly love. Everything fits into the blues."[70]

Sure enough, some of the same tightwads who had offered only verbal support for the gospel numbers responded to the blues by digging out some spare change to toss Riley's way. Point made.

"That was my first lesson in marketing," B.B. related. "I saw something about the relationship between music and money that I'm still seeing today. Real-life songs where you feel the hurt and heat between man and woman have cash value. I took note. I started coming to town every Saturday and spent my afternoons on that curb, singing as many blues as I could remember—and making up the rest. From one P.M. to nine that night, I might make ten dollars or even more. Confidence made me a better singer, and people tipped bigger when I sang with more conviction. Before long, I might walk that eight miles home with the loud jangle of heavy coins in my pocket. I was astounded, delighted, and determined to keep it up."[71]

Keep up the music he did, and he kept up his work driving a tractor on the plantation, and he kept up with as many part-time paying jobs as he could handle. What he didn't keep up was his schooling. By grade ten Riley was a dropout—with everything else going on in his life, "school seemed like a burden."[72] Despite lingering regrets even today over his lack of education—"I feel like I'm missing a component, a way of understanding the world, that only more schooling could have provided"[73]—in his late teens Riley was brimming with energy for and commitment to his work and his music, which brought him both a sense of fulfillment and a bit of cash to boot. Everything else was superfluous, including book learning.

By now the blues had dug in and taken hold of Riley's soul. Gospel would always have its place in his life—"My mother had filled my heart with a love for a compassionate God. Gospel songs sang of that love"—but the blues continued to light the path into the forbidden world revealed to him on those long Saturday nights of peeping tomfoolery outside the Jones Night Spot.

"When the blues began paying, and when the other St. John Singers still wouldn't go to a big city like Memphis to find fame, I gave the blues even more of me."[74]

All the years wound down to a single, transcendent, life-altering moment for Riley. He had absorbed all he could of Blind Lemon's style, of Lonnie Johnson's, of the great gospel singers he had been listening to since childhood, of the varieties of blues he could hear on the radio and at Jones Night Spot, of the traditional country songs that, like the blues, told stories about people struggling with real-world problems or exulting in a bit of good fortune or real, true love.

Then he heard T-Bone Walker playing "Stormy Monday," and nothing was the same for him ever again. He goes on at length about this moment in his autobiography, and this revelatory passage about a moment that solidified the template of the music that would become associated with Riley B. King could not be better described than in B.B.'s own words, because in them is the essence of the artist who would become the single most important ambassador of the blues in his time.

> When I heard Aaron T-Bone Walker, I flat-out lost my mind. Thought
> Jesus himself had returned to earth playing electric guitar. T-Bone's blues

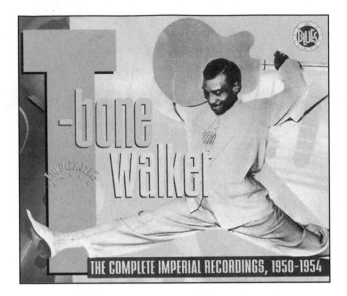

THE COMPLETE IMPERIAL RECORDINGS, 1950-1954

filled my insides with joy and good feeling. I became his disciple. And remain so today. My greatest musical debt is to T-Bone. He showed me the way. His sound cut me like a sword. His sound was different than anything I'd heard before. Musically, he was everything I wanted to be, a modern bluesman whose blues were as blue as the bluest country blues with attitude as slick as those big cities I yearned to see. Later I'd learn that, as a kid, T-Bone had led Blind Lemon Jefferson around Dallas. I liked knowing that two of my idols were linked so tight.

"'Stormy Monday" was the first tune. "They call it Stormy Monday," sang T-Bone, "but Tuesday's just as bad." Yes, Lord! The first line, the first thrilling notes, the first sound of his guitar, and the attitude in his voice was riveting. I especially loved "Stormy Monday"—and still sing it today—'cause it's the true-life story of a workingman. He talks about the weeklong routine, payday ("the eagle flies on Friday"), partying on Saturday, and falling down on your knees and asking the Lord's mercy on Sunday.

T-Bone had a single-string style that, like Charlie Christian's, reminded me of a horn. His blues approach was deadly, but you could tell he knew jazz. Jazz was in his blood. He'd cut off the notes and leave spaces between the phrases that took my breath away. When he played, you felt his personality: edgy, cool, and a little dangerous. His guitar could cut you like a lethal weapon or stroke you like a sweet-talking love letter. And when he sang, he made you feel the story was strictly between you and him.

Mostly, though, T-Bone's guitar had a voice of its own. The voice was high-pitched, sweet, sassy, and sexy as a slinky woman. Just as surely as if he were talking to you, T-Bone spoke through the strings and amplifier attached to his guitar. He was electric in more ways than one. Electricity coursed through my body when I heard the man play. His sound was branded in my head. And his arrangements—a sax or muted trumpet whispering in his ear, a couple of quiet horns repeating a haunting refrain— were models of simple grace.

T-Bone was from Texas, and I didn't get to see him when I was a kid. I studied his pictures, though, and saw that he held the edge of his guitar against his stomach and played with an outward stroke. I held it flat against my stomach. I tried to change to T-Bone's style, but it didn't work. Felt awkward. T-Bone was also a showman, doing splits onstage and playing behind his back, a trick I could never manage. He was a short guy— handsome, sophisticated, and self-assured—who wore elegant clothes. I imagined he lived the life I wanted to live.

Like many guitarists coming up in the late '30s and early '40s, I tried to copy T-Bone's sound. I couldn't. And because I couldn't, I had to keep working until, by accident or default, I developed a sound that became me. I'm not entirely settled with that "me" sound today. See, T-Bone's sound was completely individual. Couldn't be no one but him. It was as much part of him as his liver. I've strived for that feeling. I've heard a sound in my head something like a whining Hawaiian or country-and-western steel pedal guitar. I've attempted to duplicate that twang or vibrato or cry. I've been haunted by it. I've also been haunted by the harmonies I first heard in Reverend Archie Fair's sanctified Church of God in Christ in the hills of Kilmichael. I've tried to integrate all those sounds into my music. But style is a funny thing. If I saw it walking down the street, I wouldn't know it till I heard it. When I heard T-Bone, though, I knew that nothing about guitar blues would ever be the same. I didn't know this man—I wouldn't meet him till years later—but I felt T-Bone Walker leading me into the future.[75]

Walker's style is all over B.B.'s, and the family tree linking the inspiration to the pupil is deep in shared roots. Walker was indeed the "eyes" for Blind Lemon Jefferson in Dallas, and Jefferson had a lasting impact on the Texas-born Aaron Thibeaux Walker. Born in 1910 in Linden, Texas, Walker took up guitar at age 13, his interest fueled by the dynamic stylings of Scrapper Blackwell, accompanist to blues pianist Leroy Carr.

But two other blues giants would exert an even greater sway over Walker's stylistic evolution. One was Lonnie Johnson, whom Walker was able to study during Johnson's frequent forays into the Dallas area; the other, of course, was Blind Lemon. From Johnson, Walker adapted a single-string solo-ing style that he developed into a voice that was direct, evocative, economi-cal, inventive, and tender or tough as the material demanded. Jefferson's sin-gular guitar stylings and lyrical folk poetry left an indelible imprint on the budding artist as well, who absorbed the master's lessons while leading him around the Dallas streets where Jefferson played for tips. More so than Johnson, it was Jefferson's raw, emotional approach that informed Walker's first recordings, "Trinity River Blues" b/w "Wichita Falls Blues," made in 1929 for Columbia, on which he was billed as Oak Cliff T-Bone, Oak Cliff being the section of Dallas where he lived. When that record didn't sell, Columbia dropped him. By that time Walker had a full schedule playing with a group of school friends in the Lawson-Brooks big band, an affiliation that continued until 1936, when he headed west to Los Angeles's thriving R&B scene; his place in Lawson-Brooks was assumed by Charlie Christian, prior to his brief association with the Benny Goodman band.

In 1939, while working with the Les Hite Band, Walker was signed to the fledgling Varsity label and cut "T-Bone Blues," which brought him some attention, although he didn't play guitar on the session. Even so, he was then beginning his early experiments with the newest sonic innovation on the block, the electric guitar, and, along with Christian and a handful of other players, breaking new ground. Signed to the nascent Capitol label in 1942, he made a statement with his early release, "I Got a Break, Baby." Nearly a minute passes at the outset with nothing but soloing from Walker, everything from frisky single-line runs, sustained bent notes, ostinato riffs morphing into screaming three-note chords, and rich, legato phrases to speed-picked single notes cartwheeling one over the other. Then Walker the vocalist enters, casu-al but confident, swinging his phrases with Joe Turner–like assurance. The whole package was there, and from that foundation he would move on to write his name large in blues and R&B history, commanding respect and attention right up to his death in 1975.

After a year with Capitol, Walker jumped the to Black & White label in 1945, upon the rescinding of wartime restrictions on materials used for recording. The 50-plus songs he recorded in a variety of contexts over the next five years are now considered among the most important body of blues work ever committed to tape. In it are contained signposts to B.B.'s warm, single-string lyricism, Albert Collins's blazing, hard-picked attacks, Albert King's hearty but unusually tender voicings—the list goes on and on, encompassing virtually every important guitarist who followed in Walker's footsteps over the next three decades. Moreover, he had the vocal chops to work persuasively in a number of styles. A mid-1949 session produced "Don't Give Me the Runaround," a languorous jazz-pop fusion in the style of the King Cole Trio, sung in a silky, seductive voice that could easily be mistaken for the smoky gray crooning of Cole himself; a swinging bit of Louis Jordan–style small-combo novelty, "I Know Your Wig Is Gone"; and Walker's self-penned Mount Rushmore of a blues song, "Call It Stormy Monday but Tuesday Is Just as Bad." In 1950 Walker joined the Imperial label for what turned out to be a four-year aesthetic extension of the Black & White legacy in its ongoing redefinition of modern blues. In addition to being a touchstone for musicians who came in his wake, Walker was a popular figure with the general public: a galvanic live performer, his club dates across the country invariably drew packed houses, and many of his '40s and '50s singles routinely peaked in the upper reaches of the R&B chart.

For Riley, both a musical and a philosophical foundation were nearly complete. At 17 his life took one more fateful turn on the personal side. After a brief courtship, he married the teenage Martha Lee Denton, from the hill country of Eupora, Mississippi. The two had met in church. Both too young to be admitted to Jones Night Spot, they had instead spent one of their memorable dates doing what Riley loved to do, peeking through the club's slats at the evening's entertainment, which happened to be Louis Jordan. Riley knew of Jordan's music from having heard his music on KWEM radio in West Memphis, Arkansas, but this was the first time he had seen him in person, albeit through a limited field of vision.

"Seeing [Louis Jordan] through the peepholes was incredible," B.B. recalled, "his big bug eyes, his golden alto sax, his strut onstage. He sang 'Knock Me a Kiss' and 'I'm Gonna Move to the Outskirts of Town' and 'What's the Use of Getting Sober When You Gonna Get Drunk Again.' Me and Martha, we were laughing up a storm, tapping our feet, having a great time looking at all the dancing couples dressed to the teeth, smooching and swinging to the music, when I felt good enough to turn to my girl and kiss her. Her mouth against mine was so soft and sweet that the kiss went on a long, long time."[76]

Riley and Martha were married soon after, but as Martha was to learn the hard way, her only co-respondent in life was Riley's music. She may have felt his lips on hers that night outside Jones Night Spot, and Riley was sincere in his affection for her, but the Louis Jordan tunes rocking the joint were a more potent aphrodisiac. In the music of T-Bone Walker and Louis Jordan, Riley heard the sounds of all his musical heroes distilled into an intoxicating brew. And it had his name on it.

Born in Brinkley, Arkansas, in 1908, Jordan got his big break in 1936 when he landed a gig with Chick Webb's popular band, playing saxophone but also serving as one of the outfit's vocalists, although he was clearly secondary in that role to a legend a-borning, Ella Fitzgerald. Playing live, in the studio, and on radio broadcasts whetted Jordan's appetite for more of a starring role, leading to his departure from Webb's group in 1938 and the formation of his first band, Louis Jordan's Elks Rendez-Vous Band, which promptly landed a recording contract with Decca Records and issued its first recordings that year ahead of Jordan retooling his outfit into the Tympany Five. Working tirelessly over the next three years, Jordan and the Five built up a rabid following for their raucous live shows and finally hit it big commercially in 1942. Over the next ten years, more than 50 of Jordan and the Tympany Five's singles became Top Ten R&B hits, with 18 going to No. 1. He was also one of the few black artists then to make a significant dent in the pop market: in the five-year period between 1944 and 1949 he had 19 Top 30 pop hits, nine of these rising into the Top Ten; 1944's "G.I. Jive" topped the pop chart for two weeks in May, and its flip side, "Is You Is or Is You Ain't (Ma' Baby)," topped out at No. 2 for three weeks in July. Among other black musical artists, only Nat "King" Cole, then with his Trio, rivaled Jordan's popularity as a crossover artist. You snuggled to Cole; you kicked out the jams to Jordan. Between the two of them they covered all the bases: Cole's music was dignified, refined, and tenderhearted, even when it swung, and Cole could croon a love ballad with any of the gifted interpreters of his generation. His music every bit as sophisticated as Cole's, Jordan simply let the good times roll, limning in his witty lyrics the comedic situations common to the human experience, engaging in witty, punning wordplay that bounced hipsters' jargon off the King's English, and keeping the rhythm high-spirited, hot, and pulsating, buttressing it all with call-and-response parts, hand-clapping, and sundry verbal exhortations of pure pleasure. In his arrangements were elements of blues, jazz, gospel, classic pop, even Latin harmonic ideas. In the mid-'50s, when his Olympian chart run ended, Jordan had at once laid the foundation for R&B and defined the spirit of early rock 'n' roll. A 1953 recording, "House Party," pretty much summed up Jordan's *raison d'être*: "I want to boogie-woogie all night long/I am ballin' tonight, 'cause tomorrow I may be gone. That's right, baby!" Jordan did the musical equivalent of chewing up scenery on the cut, shouting and laughing through his vocal, urging everybody in the room to bump it up a couple of notches as the horns surged and swung, the sax blared and honked, and the percussion steamrolled everyone in sight. It was good-time music, unabashed in its enthusiasm for rocking and rolling in the most carnal sense, and life-affirming in its upbeat philosophies and sunny outlook.

Shortly after Riley married Martha, with the United States now active in the World War in both the Pacific and European theaters, he was called into the service. He took basic training in Hattiesburg, Mississippi, and felt the sting of racism even while serving his country: white and black soldiers were segregated, and German prisoners of war were treated with more respect than the black G.I.s, who were not protected by the Geneva Convention rules. Through an agreement between the Selective Service and the plantation owners in Sunflower County, Mississippi, Riley was sent back to work the land, driving a tractor, harvesting cotton and soybeans to provide food and clothing for the American fighting forces. Here, on the fertile ground that had provided him sustenance and stability over the years, he witnessed German POWs working the same fields and being treated with more civility than the black Americans. The humiliation he felt seared his memory, scarred his soul.

"We were seen as beasts of burden, dumb animals," he said, "a level below the Germans. To watch your enemy get better treatment than yourself was a helluva thing to endure. . . . As a 20-year-old, fresh out of basic training, I was starting to feel the weight of the system. I felt the injustice. And I felt anger. . . . The pain of the past is hard to describe. But it's there. It lingers for life."[77]

This rage, coupled to a sinking realization of the limited opportunities ahead of him if he stayed put, fueled a fire in Riley that burned with greater intensity as each "can to can't" shift in the fields rolled by. He knew a bigger world was out there.

"I was born on a Mississippi plantation and grew up in the cotton fields," he told David Hinckley in a *Parade* magazine interview from October 20, 1985. "And I enjoyed it while I was there. I just knew I wouldn't want to do it all my life. So I dreamed about the house on the hill and having things like other people had. Not a lot of things, but nice things. An automobile, a family, a few bucks in the bank.

"I couldn't visualize having that if I stayed on the plantation. So I dreamed. And in the end, I worked harder for it than I ever did in the cotton fields."

By this time Martha had miscarried the couple's first child, and Riley's frustration over what he increasingly perceived as a dead-end job, a dead-end life even, was mounting daily. The breaking point came when he parked his tractor at the end of a long day and stood frozen in fear as a post-ignition lunge broke off its smokestack and destroyed part of its manifold. Seeing "hundreds of dollars in repairs, and it was all my fault," he panicked.

Hustling back to his living quarters, he gathered his guitar and all of his $2.50 in pocket money, and lit out for Highway 49 north.

"Don't know what I'm doing except for leaving. I ain't looking back till I get to Memphis.

"Gotta get to Memphis."[78]

Chapter 2

MEMPHIS: ARRIVAL, RETREAT, RETURN

The Memphis that Riley B. King first set eyes on in 1947 was, by some reports, not the same freewheeling city it had been before the Great Depression. Or at least that was said of its most colorful thoroughfare, Beale Street, which began on the Tennessee side of the Mississippi River and ran for 20 blocks eastward. It was a street that harbored both light and dark. Banks and clothing stores and dry-goods stores and pawnshops (most owned by whites) served the community by day. But come sunset, its streets were alive with music and sin. Music was everywhere, in clubs such as Pee Wee's, in grand theaters such as the Palace and the Pastime; and, so it seemed, were gambling and prostitution and violence, especially murder. "In the early decades of this century . . . Memphis was the murder capital of the country, and Beale Streeters did more than their part to secure the title," observed Stanley Booth in his book *Rythm Oil*. "One night in 1909 a saloon keeper named Wild Bill Latura walked into Hammitt Ashford's black saloon, announced that he was going to turn the place into a funeral parlor, and with six bullets shot seven patrons of the establishment, killing five. Beale Street was dangerous. . . ."[1]

But Beale was also the "main street of Black America," according to one wag. It most certainly was a place where whites and blacks mingled peacefully, and where "a black man with a little bit of money in his pocket could shop for clothes or have his hair cut by day and engage in any manner of illicit activity by night without white folks paying much mind."[2]

Central to Beale Street's culture, though, was music. In 1909 Alabama-born W.C. Handy, "the Father of the Blues," set up headquarters on Beale and three years later published his first blues song, "Memphis Blues" (written as a campaign song for mayoral candidate E.H. Crump); in 1914, he published one of the most popular blues songs of all time, "St. Louis Blues." Through the '20s and '30s he wrote and published dozens of blues songs of his own and compiled collections of blues tunes in book form and published them as *Blues: An Anthology* (1926), *Negro Authors and Composers of the United States* (1935), and *Unsung Americans Sung* (1944). One of the most beloved figures in American popular music, Handy died on March 28, 1958, at the age of 84, succumbing to acute bronchial pneumonia. His burial in Woodlawn Cemetery, Bronx, New York, drew some 150,000 people to the funeral route.

Handy's success drew other black musicians to Memphis in general, and to Beale Street in particular. They would play all night, wherever they could find a spot to blow or pick, be it inside a club or outside on the street in or around Beale Park (later renamed in honor of Handy). Where music flourished, enterprising entrepreneurs followed. In 1950 Florence, Alabama, native Sam Phillips, a former radio announcer and engineer, opened a recording studio in an abandoned radiator repair shop at 706 Union Avenue, only a mile or so east of Beale. His slogan—"We Record Anything—Anywhere—Anytime" —was meant seriously, and at the outset Phillips found himself paying the rent by documenting weddings and funerals. But he knew what he really wanted to do, and what he loved. "Negro artists in the South who wanted to make a record just had no place to go," he said. "I set up a studio just to make records with some of those great Negro artists."[3]

In his definitive biography *Last Train to Memphis: The Rise of Elvis Presley*, author Peter Guralnick said Phillips "believed in himself, and he believed— even to the point of articulating it in public and private utterances from earliest adulthood on—in the scope and beauty of African-American culture. He wanted, he said, 'genuine, untutored negro' music; he was looking for 'Negroes with field mud on their boots and patches in their overalls ... battered instruments and unfettered techniques.'"[4]

Six years before he became a Memphis resident, though—only three years before B.B. first set eyes on the Bluff City—Phillips had made his initial visit to the town while en route to Dallas, Texas, with his older brother Jud and other friends for the purpose of attending a sermon by the Reverend George W. Truett. Once in Memphis, Phillips migrated immediately to Beale Street, "to me the most famous place in the South. We got in at five or six o'clock in the morning and it was pouring down rain, but we just drove up and down, and it was so much more than I had even envisioned. . . . My eyes had to be very big, because I saw everything, from winos to people dressed up fit to kill, young, old, city slickers and people straight out of the cotton fields, somehow or another you could tell every damn one of them was glad to be there. Beale Street represented for me something that I hoped to see one day for all people, something that they could say, I'm part of this somehow."[5]

In an oral history posted on the PBS Web site devoted to the network's American Roots Music series (www.pbs.org/americanrootsmusic/pbs_arm_oralh_bbking.html, 2001), B.B. recalled his first trip to Memphis and Beale Street as being like "going to Berlin or Paris or London or someplace," and spoke with awe of the sight of people hanging out on the street, "loitering." "You didn't do that in Indianola!" he exclaimed. "You'd have to be at work, not hanging all over the street." What he learned, quickly, was that "hanging all over the street" was something akin to work for the people who did it. A lot of folks were out there making connections, hoping to get a leg up in some way, no doubt illicitly in some cases, but in others it might be musicians finding a social groove that might pay off professionally down the line.

"Every day on Beale Street to me was like a community college," B.B. said. "I had a chance to learn so much just watching the people. There were famous people that would come into Memphis and they would hang on Beale Street. Some of the great musicians would practice out at Handy's Park or someplace.

"They'd sit out there and I'd get a chance to hear these great people. And I'd only heard their names [before]. [I'd] see them out there practicing—some gambling, some doing other things—but it was a whole way of learning that was new for B.B. King. I tell you I'd never seen a place like it before, and I was in awe of everything."[6]

The music inundating Beale was a glorious sound to Riley's young ears, but an intimidating one as well, because the caliber of the playing was so far beyond his own. "Before Beale Street I thought I was pretty hot stuff," he said. "After Beale Street I knew I stunk. The cats could play rings around me. . . . I'd soon learn Memphis was full of local geniuses."[7]

Of Beale Street's rich history Riley was largely ignorant. He would pick up on its contemporary history fairly quickly and then become an important part of it. But as a young man fresh off the Delta cotton fields and feeling overwhelmed by the big city action ("I was confused. . . . I'd never seen anything like it."[8]) Riley knew only that he needed to find his cousin, Bukka White, who had been living in Memphis for several years.

From one of the local cats Riley got an address for Bukka, who turned out to be his cousin's keeper in the best sort of way. The worldly White's life experiences—from his imprisonment in Parchman to his savvy about the business of music gained from his years of playing in clubs, juke joints, and less savory venues, to his misadventures with women (he was in the process of divorcing a wife when Riley met him in Memphis, and was engaged to another woman at the same time)—had given him, say, a more informed perspective on ground-level survival. Which is not to be flip about White's contribution to Riley's education. However rough-and-tumble his own existence may have been, White was not without discipline, a moral compass, or personal pride. That much was evident in his advice to Riley to "always dress like you're going to the bank to borrow money." When Riley showed up on his doorstep in Memphis, Bukka wasn't about to let his cousin sit around and live hand-to-mouth. "We'd better start thinking about getting to work," he told Riley, by which he meant working for a living, as he did at the Newberry Equipment Company, which manufactured underground gasoline storage tanks for service stations. White got Riley signed on at the plant and advised him sternly, "Don't mess around on this job. Don't be lazy on it."[9] Riley took the advice to heart. He learned to weld, made friends with his co-workers, and became a reliable employee who drew about $60 a week in pay. To supplement this income, he took a second job at the McCallum and Roberts cotton mill, but the midnight-to-8 A.M. shift quickly took its toll on his energy, and he ceased his moonlighting after about two months.

White's blues were in and of themselves educational, at least as they pertained to the notions Riley was formulating about this music he was drawn to, both as fan and as artist.

"I felt something beautiful inside Bukka's soul," he recalled. "Even if I didn't follow his style, I was moved by his sincerity. He loved telling stories, simple stories, and used his blues to tell them. His blues was the book of his life. He sung about his rough times and fast times and loving times and angry times. He'd entertain at a party for two hundred people with the same enthusiasm as a party for twenty. Bukka gave it his all. His music had a consistency I admired. Like all the great bluesmen, he said, *I am what I am*. I wondered if I could be that steady and strong."[10]

In time that question would be answered in the affirmative and then some, but at the time he first pondered it Riley was only eight months out of Indianola, having left behind a confused wife and what he figured was a disgruntled employer. So back to the Delta he went, where he made amends with Martha ("it took us a while to readjust"[11]) and returned not merely apologetic to Mr. Johnson but determined to repay him the cost of the damage to the tractor. Understanding and sympathetic, Johnson rehired Riley and worked out a payment plan to recover the $500 cost of repairs.

Having done the right thing, however, Riley was almost immediately feeling "back in the trap."[12] He returned to his spot with the Famous St. John Gospel Singers but remained the only group member willing to strike out on the circuit in hopes of moving up a few rungs on the gospel ladder to the point where they could survive on the music and leave the cotton fields far behind.

About this time a friend whose time in the military had taken him to France during World War II came back to the Delta with a pack of carefully wrapped 78-rpm discs of some of the most exciting music Riley had ever heard. The chain of influences now added another link in the form of the Belgian Gypsy guitarist Django Reinhardt, who had teamed with violinist Stephane Grappelli to become all the rage of Paris in their combo called the Quintette du Hot Club de France. In the *Rolling Stone Jazz & Blues Album Guide*, John Swenson observed that Reinhardt "had a breathtaking ability to string out melodic lines effortlessly and employ them inside glittering harmonic castles buttressed by daring octave leaps. Reinhardt used the richly melodic folk materials available to him for raw material and played with a distinctive fingering technique due in part to a fire injury that left him with limited use of two fingers on his left hand. His bell-like tone on perfectly articulated single-note runs was a revelation to guitarists who had previously heard the instrument only in a rhythmic context."[13]

"He hit me as hard as Charlie Christian," B.B. said. "Django was a new world. Him and Grappelli swung like demons. The syncopation got me going, but the beat was just the beginning. It was Django's ideas that lit up my brain. He was light and free and fast as the fastest trumpet, slick as the slickest clarinet, running through chord changes with the skill of a sprinter and the imagination of a poet. He was nimble like a cat. Songs like 'Nuages' and 'Nocturne' took me far away from my little place in Indianola, transporting me over the ocean to Paris, where people sipped wine in outdoor cafes and soaked in the most romantic jazz the world has ever known.

"I loved Django because of the joy in his music, the lighthearted feeling and freedom to do whatever he felt. Even if I hadn't been told he was a Gypsy, I might have guessed it. There's wanderlust in Django's guitar, a you-can't-fence-me-in attitude that inspired me. It didn't matter that he was technically a million times better than me. His music fortified an idea I held close to my heart—that the guitar is a voice unlike any other. The guitar is a miracle. Out of the strings and frets comes this personality—whether a blind black man from Texas or a Gypsy from Belgium—of a unique human being."[14]

At the same time, though, Riley was picking up on other musicians who weren't guitarists but who had strong, individual voices on their instruments and played with authority and passion. Saxophonists in particular drew his attention, especially tenor giants Ben Webster and Lester "Prez" Young ("Prez invented cool"[15]), and Duke Ellington's alto sax man Johnny Hodges.

"The great jazz instrumentalists taught me how to sing and interpret a song," B.B. observed. "They showed me how a horn can have as much personality as an actor."[16]

Of the blues artists who were coming of age in his own time, Riley would come to admire Muddy Waters above all others. "Loved his shouting, his songwriting, his wailing guitar. Back in Indianola, we knew he'd gone to Chicago, where he established a whole school that he'd rule for five decades. … No one had Muddy's authority."[17]

Born McKinley Morganfield in 1915 in Rolling Fork, Mississippi, Waters grew up in Clarksdale on the Stovall Plantation. He was raised by his grandmother, who bestowed upon him the nickname Muddy, to which his friends added Waters. Taught by a friend, Waters took up the guitar in 1932, when he was 17. Waters's most direct influences were Charley Patton, Son House, and Robert Johnson. House's sound is heard prominently in Waters's early bottleneck voicings, although on many of the Library of Congress recordings from 1941–42 he is working in the more complex, polyrhythmic style associated with Johnson. A neighbor owned a record player, as did Muddy's grandmother, and through them he was he exposed to the music of Blind Lemon Jefferson, Lonnie Johnson, Tampa Red, Leroy Carr, and other seminal blues artists, further broadening his musical vocabulary. In between "plowin' mules, choppin' cotton, and drawin' water," as he described his duties at Stovall, he began to make a name locally by converting his one-room log cabin home into a juke joint on weekends and providing music, drink, and gambling for the attending revelers.

Folklorist Alan Lomax, heading up a field recording team for the Library of Congress, came to Clarksdale in 1941 looking for Robert Johnson, unaware that he had been dead for nearly three years. Told that the man on Stovall's played a lot like Johnson, Lomax tracked down Waters at home and recorded him performing two songs. Lomax returned the next year and recorded more sides, some with Waters playing solo acoustic; some with Waters and a primitive string band, the Son Sims Four; some with Waters and guitarist Charles Berry. Encompassing 18 sides in all, these recordings, cut in Waters's cabin, are raw, moving, and hint at things to come. One of the 1941 tracks, "Country Blues Number One," is descended musically and lyrically from House's "My Black Mama" and Johnson's "Walkin' Blues." Thus a pattern emerged: Over

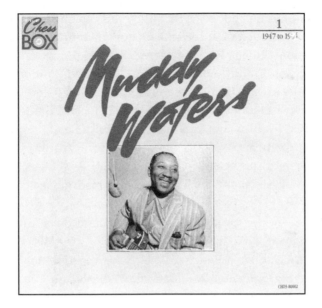

the course of his career Waters would make frequent figurative forays back to the Delta for material, building new songs out of folk tales and fragments of choruses he had absorbed in his youth, adding new and sometimes bolder lyrics to material otherwise decades old. As for thematic focus, Waters's songs were in the Delta tradition of brooding ruminations on death and faithless love, aptly summarized in titles such as "You're Gonna Miss Me When I'm Dead and Gone," "You Got to Take Sick and Die Some of These Days," and "Why Don't You Love So God Can Use You?" Vocally he displays mastery of the nuances of Delta blues singing, but while the stark authority of his voice is commanding, he was not yet the overpowering presence he would become a few years later after relocating to Chicago.

In 1943, Waters packed his belongings in a suitcase and boarded an Illinois Central train, joining the mass exodus of black people out of Mississippi to greater opportunity in the north, Chicago in this case. In the mid-'40s he got his first electric guitar and began working with various combinations of musicians headed by an older Delta-born bluesman, Sunnyland Slim. With Slim and bassist Big Crawford he recorded some unsuccessful sides for the Columbia and Aristocrat labels, the latter a Chicago-based operation run by Polish brothers Leonard and Phil Chess.

In 1948, Waters, now a solo artist, cut two Aristocrat sides in the Delta bottleneck style, "I Can't Be Satisfied" b/w "(I Feel Like) Going Home," which sold rapidly in Chicago and in the South. By this time he was working clubs with a band that included Claude Smith on guitar, Jimmy Rogers doubling on guitar and harmonica, Baby Face Leroy on guitar and drums, and Little Walter Jacobs doubling on guitar and harmonica. This configuration, which later included Elgin Evans on drums, began recording in 1950 and developed the hard-driving sound of modern urban blues on "Louisiana Blues," "She Moves Me," "Honey Bee," "Still a Fool," and "Long Distance Call." "Louisiana Blues" was significant for being Waters's first recording to feature Little Walter's amplified harmonica and his first national R&B hit; also, it was the single that established the Chess label, which had been formed in early 1950 after the brothers Chess bought out their Aristocrat partner.

Leonard Chess was producing Waters in these days, and his lack of musical training worked to his and the artist's favor. Like Waters, Chess went on instinct and feel. He close-miked Waters's voice, so that it was bold and out front of the raging band; ditto for Little Walter's amplified harp, which was virtually a searing, soulful second voice. In 1954, bassist Willie Dixon penned three songs for Waters that became major R&B hits and, over time, acknowledged blues masterpieces—"Hoochie Coochie Man," "I Just Want to Make Love to You," and "I'm Ready." That same year saw pianist Otis Spann and drummer Fred Below (replacing Elgin Evans) join Waters, and the band develop such rhythmic innovations as stop-time patterns and a driving back-beat that quickly found their way into other artists' songs. Waters was surrounded by great musicians, and in Dixon and Chess he had the support and advice of two studio-savvy mentors, one an artist himself, the other a technician, both of whom understood where this music was headed and knew how to get it there.

B.B. was "agitated" by the variety of music he was hearing and the exotic places it was coming from, "different rhythms reflecting exciting changes in people's lives."[18] Postwar America saw enormous, even cataclysmic changes in everything from science and technology to civil rights to popular entertainment. With the rise of mechanization, sharecropping was in its death throes, and blacks were migrating *en masse* out of the South to the industrial areas of the North, which promised better-paying factory work and a more tolerant racial atmosphere.

Riley was getting ready to join the exodus himself, but not to Chicago. "I was never tempted by the Windy City," he says.[19] Rather, he was beckoned only partway, back to the city of his dreams, only a few miles up the highway from Indianola, a world apart from the one he'd known all his life, but one in which he saw a future before him: back to Memphis, to its history, to its community, to its embrace of music and artists of all stripes; back to its local geniuses, who in time would have to admit one more to their club.

In late 1948 Riley set out for the Bluff City (Martha was left behind with assurances that her husband would send for her later), riding north on the back of a grocery truck and helping with loading and unloading along the way. But he intentionally overshot his mark and crossed the Mississippi into West Memphis, Arkansas. There, he tracked down Sonny Boy Williamson No. 2 at radio station KWEM (Sonny Boy had recently defected from KFFA in Helena, Arkansas, and its fabled "King Biscuit Time" show). Stuttering, and quaking inside, he asked for a chance to sing a song on Sonny Boy's show. The brawny bluesman, who had been alone in the studio playing his harmonica when Riley approached him, glared at the lad ("he seemed to resent the interruption," B.B. recalled[20]), then dryly suggested he play something.

Launching into a version of Ivory Joe Hunter's "Blues at Sunrise," Riley performed it flawlessly, to his own surprise, and won an approving nod from Sonny Boy, who invited Riley to perform at the end of the program—with one stipulation: "Just be sure you sing as good as you did just now."[21]

Riley did precisely as he was told, and the upshot was a number of favorable calls from listeners. A pretty good start got better almost immediately, when Sonny Boy realized he had double-booked himself for gigs that night. He offered Riley his gig at the 16th Street Grill in West Memphis and told him to ask for Miss Annie, the proprietor.

To Riley's continuing good fortune, Miss Annie had heard him on the radio and liked his style. She told him she would turn off her jukebox during his show, "'cause the ladies like to dance to a live man."[22]

Riley was beside himself: those fine-dressed, slow-grinding ladies he used to watch through the slats of the Jones Night Spot would now be dancing to his music. As if he needed more inspiration, there it was.

"For the first time I played for dancers, played for these ladies who moved so loose and limber that I played better than I'd ever played before. Might have messed up my musical measures or screwed up a lyric or two, but, baby, the beat was there. And these people—all these young people, people no older than me—they loved that beat. They'd forgive me whatever mistakes I made."[23]

When it was all over, Miss Annie offered him a steady job, six nights a week at $12 a night, providing he could get a radio show like Sonny Boy's and mention the 16th Street Grill on the air.[24]

Now, to Memphis. Now, to the new radio station he had heard about from cousin Bukka, with the call letters WDIA, "something new" in radio, as B.B.

observed, "blacks talking black to other blacks on the air."[25] On Union Street, in the heart of downtown Memphis, he located the station. His first look at it was from the street, where he saw, through a plate glass window, disc jockey Nat B. Williams, Memphis's first black DJ, working his shift. Riley motioned to Williams, who beckoned him inside. He told Williams he wanted a job on the air, and Williams summoned one of the station's owners. Although WDIA catered to the black community, its owners were two white men, Bert Ferguson and John R. Pepper. Ferguson questioned Riley about his experience, then station manager Don Kern popped in as Riley auditioned with a Louis Jordan tune. The men liked what they heard, but Ferguson wanted to know if Riley would be comfortable being a pitchman, like Sonny Boy, for one of the station's sponsors, an alcohol-laced tonic called Pepticon that was purported to cure practically any known ailment. Not only was Riley willing to pitch for Pepticon, he made up a jingle for it on the spot and got the job. He went on the air that afternoon, working the 3:30 P.M. to 3:40 P.M. slot, touting Pepticon, and performing Louis Jordan's "Somebody Changed the Lock on My Door" and "Buzz Me, Baby."

Riley's Pepticon show proved popular enough with listeners that he was given a second slot, from 12:30 to 12:45 in the afternoons, and from time to time he filled in for the disc jockey Maurice "Hot Rod" Hulbert on his *Sepia Swing Club* show. Apart from the radio shows and his regular gigs at Miss Annie's, he supplemented his income by picking cotton across the river in Arkansas, where he could make almost triple what he was paid in Mississippi. But WDIA, which had built a 50,000-watt transmitter, was occupying more and more of his time, to Riley's great satisfaction. On weekends he capitalized on the popularity of his Pepticon show by going out on with a company salesman and singing his jingle on the back of a flatbed truck.

Finally, he was fully vested in the WDIA disc jockey family when a nickname was bestowed on him and he became known on the air as the Beale Street Blues Boy, which soon mutated into Bee Bee, and at last to simply B.B. Riley receded into history, as far as the public was concerned, but the gritty experiences he carried with him in his journey out of the Delta—the anger and the fear as well as the tolerance, the sense of fair play, and the good manners and good humor—were permanently imprinted on his soul. B.B. and Riley B. King were never far apart.

But now there was hope, tangible hope, that the dream of a career making music would be realized. In an interview with *New York Times* reporter Bernard Weinraub ("Spinning Blues into Gold, the Rough Way," March 2, 2003), Robert Gordon, author of *It Came From Memphis* and *Can't Be Satisfied:*

The Life and Times of Muddy Waters, pinpointed Pepticon as the key moment in B.B.'s career. "He realized he had the charisma and personality to win people over," Gordon said. "He translated that later into sales of his records. He sold himself. People liked having B.B. King in front of them. He was acceptable and accepted."[26]

Indeed. B.B., emulating the folksy manner of one of radio's top stars, Arthur Godfrey, looks back and says he developed "a believable on-air personality. I was just me. I like to say I played everything from Bing Crosby to Lightnin' Hopkins. . . . Generally I soft-pedaled myself as a deejay. Didn't ego trip. I tried to please the public while, at the same time, educating myself on the new music."[27]

Equally important, he was gaining an on-air education in showmanship that he would carry onto the stage and into the recording studio. In an interview with Rob Bowman and Jerry Richardson for *The Black Perspective in Music* ("A Conversation with B.B. King, King of the Blues," 1989), he said his radio experience "taught me my technique, it taught me things about either too loud or not loud enough, even playing as well as singing, it taught me a little bit about projection, how to get an audience to listen; you know you have the imaginary audience when you are sitting in front of the microphone, you don't see them, but you know they are there, then there are times when you figure that they aren't there. That helped me a lot."[28]

His musical education, though, was informed by his own history. As a child he had absorbed the country blues of Blind Lemon Jefferson, which he regarded as "the backbone of the music." He heard the blues "modified and modernized by artists like Lonnie Johnson. And then came T-Bone, with his slick single-note styling that copped the cool attitude of jazz without losing a lick of soul. At the end of the 1940s, it felt like black music was on fire. And sitting in the broadcast booth at WDIA, I felt all the warm, beautiful heat."[29]

In his autobiography, B.B. enumerated the artists whose music was blessing him with that "warm, beautiful heat." In the roiling cauldron of postwar American popular music, B.B. took special note of a select few musicians whose approach he would measure against his own, adapting an instrumental or vocal tic from this one, noting another's distinctive flair whether it be musically, sonically, or sartorially. In the end, all of these artists made an impression on B.B. at a time when he was still figuring out his own voice.

Speaking to Rebecca West in *Blues On Stage* (April 20, 2000), B.B. explained that the process of picking up pointers from other artists that he then refines in his own way is one that continues on to the present day. "I admire those people whomever they may be," he said of artists who have caught his attention over the years, "but I think to myself, 'That's not me.' So if I can get a little bit of that—some musicians might use the word 'steal,' but I don't use the word 'steal,' but 'borrow' a little taste of this, a little taste of that, I could put it in here and it would sound all right for me, but I wouldn't do it exactly like that person did it."

More than that, as he explained, he simply had given up on trying to copy other artists—"my fingers were too stupid and my mind refused to work that way"—and focused instead on developing his own instrumental voice. He found the key to what he was seeking in the lonesome moans of the pedal steel guitars he heard on country and western recordings. That sound had appealed to him immediately upon first hearing it in his younger years and now it was about to become the springboard for one of the most distinctive sound signatures in blues history.[31]

"That cry sounded human to me," B.B. noted of the pedal steel's allure. "I wanted to sustain a note like a singer. I wanted to phrase a note like a saxist. By bending the strings, by trilling my hand—and I have big fat hands—I could achieve something that approximated a vocal vibrato. I could sustain a note. I wanted to connect my guitar to human emotions. By fooling with the feedback between my amplifier and instrument, I started experimenting with sounds that expressed my feelings, whether happy or sad, bouncy or bluesy. I was looking for ways to let my guitar sing."

Singing, he added, is "the most basic musical act. . . . To me singing is like talking. If it ain't natural, it ain't right.[32]

"As time went on, I tried to link my singing voice with my guitar as best I could."[33] In the beginning B.B. did this by simply strumming the guitar as he sang. But as he became more proficient on one instrument—his guitar—he developed an approach with his other instrument—his voice—that made both more effective.

"He never played while he was singing," noted Peter Guralnick. "When the vocal was over, the guitar was introduced to play single notes that extended the vocal line. He made use of the treble end of the scale for dramatics in a way quite different from John Lee Hooker or Muddy Waters or traditional blues singers."[34]

B.B. himself summed up the style succinctly: "Both sounds—guitar and voice—were coming out of me, but they issued from different parts of my soul."[35]

As Guralnick sees it, B.B. "almost single-handedly introduced the blues to white America" owing to "the urbanity of his playing, the absorption of a multiplicity of influences, not simply from the blues, along with a graciousness of manner and willingness to adapt to new audiences and give them something they were able to respond to."[36]

The "multiplicity of influences" Guralnick noted gained in number as the 1940s wound down and B.B. prepared to step onto a larger platform for his music. These were not all household names, even in the black community (although most were), but all were distinguished by their distinctive sound signatures.

Texas-born Charles Brown had emerged from Johnny Moore's Three Blazers and would go on to write and record numerous upper-level R&B chart singles—nine in 1949 alone—including two No. 1s in 1949's "Trouble Blues" and 1951's "Black Night." Meanwhile, a Christmas song he wrote and recorded with the Three Blazers in 1947, the melancholy "Merry Christmas, Baby," was becoming a seasonal classic, charting every year in the first three years after its release. While "Drifting Blues" is regarded as his signature song, "Merry Christmas, Baby" has lived on in numerous cover versions, by far the most powerful being Elvis Presley's tour de force of blues vocalizing.

"You didn't know what you liked more, his piano playing or silky vocals," B.B. said of Brown. "He also had amazing technique. I loved the idea he could play Bach but preferred blues. Fact is, you could hear a little Bach in Charles Brown's blues."[37]

Roy Brown, B.B. observes, "had a big-throated, full-throttle way of singing, and a vibrato that went right through me. As a singer, he had balls."[38]

Brown melded the cry of the blues to the fervor of gospel, then tossed in a dash of Bing Crosby–style crooning. His signature sound—shouting, wailing, relentlessly rhythmic—bridged the hard-charging R&B of the late '40s and early '50s and early country- and blues-influenced rock 'n' roll. Recording in New Orleans in the late '40s, Brown played a key role in the development of Crescent City rock 'n' roll in addition to influencing B.B. and contemporaries of his such as Bobby "Blue" Bland.

In an era with no shortage of potent blues balladeers, Nat King Cole stood apart, especially for B.B., who took more than musical direction from the man with the smoky gray voice. Born Nathaniel Adams Coles in 1919 in Montgomery, Alabama, the young Nat grew up in the gospel world, playing piano and organ as a child in a Chicago church presided over by his father, the Reverend Edward James Coles, after the family moved there in 1923. Much like the young Riley B. King spending Saturday nights peeking through the slats at Jones Night Spot to see the rhythm and blues and jazz greats of the day in performance, young Nathaniel could be found outside the Grand Terrace Cafe, eating up every note of the jazz performances going on inside,

particularly those of his idol, the formidable jazz pianist Earl "Fatha" Hines. In the mid-'30s, after disbanding his own group, Cole joined his older brother Eddie's band, Eddie Cole's Solid Swingers, and appeared on that group's early recordings before striking out on his own again.

He wound up in California, knocking around from club to club, his career in low gear, until he got what he thought would be his big break. In 1937 he formed a trio with guitarist Oscar Moore and bassist Wesley Prince (later replaced by Johnny Miller) and was booked into Los Angeles's Swanee Inn for a four-week run. Six months later the Trio was still packing the Swanee and the club owner had elevated him to royalty by billing him as "King Cole." Signed to Decca in 1940, the King Cole Trio cut 16 sides, all unsuccessful commercially at the time, but revelatory in retrospect. These recordings showcase both the Trio's engaging instrumental approach and its lead vocalist's skill in negotiating a range of material. The swinging dialogs between the musicians set up solo passages that are models of tasty economy, with the bass settling in steady at the bottom as Moore constructs deft, lofting lines built on octave chords and legato single-string runs modeled after Charlie Christian's. All the while Cole comps gently behind him, then steps forward for a solo turn that invariably surprises in its combination of chordal leaps, arpeggio runs, and minimalist, impressionistic right-hand fills. As a vocalist, Cole had already perfected the smooth delivery that served him so effectively when he moved towards pop-oriented jazz in later years. Rather than breathtaking range, he developed an impeccable sense of phrasing; like all masterful vocalists, a bent note here or a subtle change in timbre there communicated worlds in the way of deep feeling and point of view. Warm, sensitive, convivial, his voice remains one of the most wondrous instruments in all of American music. What Nat gained later in his career as the hits on Capitol piled up (86 singles and 17 albums in the Top 40 between 1943 and 1964) would provide another model for B.B. as he got established on the blues circuit: broad-based appeal that transcended all boundaries of race, age, gender, and musical preference.

"Nat was a case unto himself," in B.B.'s estimation. "His jazz trio was the epitome of taste, musicianship, and serious swing. The musicians knew Nat was the next great piano player after Art Tatum and Earl Hines. His technique was a miracle of economy. And when he romped, watch out!... The ease of Nat's approach is the root of his genius. That ease could apply to anything— piano jazz and, later on, pure pop singing. His image also influenced me. Nat was a fashion plate. Wore those pinstriped suits with matching silk ties and handkerchiefs. He was a singing star who dressed as clean as the chairman of the board of General Motors. As I was emerging as a public personality of my own, image was important. I looked to certain role models—Duke Ellington was another figure of great stature and impeccable dress—who epitomized class." And, he noted, he could add Billy Eckstine ("a flashy dresser") and T-Bone Walker ("too cool for words") to his pantheon of clotheshorses whose personal style influenced his own.[38]

"I wanted to be cool," he said. "I was a kid from the country trying to lose the stink of manure. I didn't look like a star. In fact, I never would. Even today I'll walk down the street and get lost in the crowd. But back then I was determined to follow those entertainers who'd developed a sense of style and dignity. Being a bluesman carried a stigma, both from blacks and whites. I fear that's true even today. A bluesman is supposed to be some guy slouched on a stool, a cigarette hanging from his lips, his cap falling off his head, his overalls ripped and smelly, a jug of corn liquor by his side. He talks lousy English and can't carry on a conversation without cussin' every other word. Ask him about his love life and he'll tell you he just beat up his old lady. Give him a dollar and he'll sing something dirty. He's a combination clown and fool. No one respects him or pays him no mind.

"I resented that. Still do. That's why looking to role model musicians was so important. They told the public—and ambitious entertainers like me—that blues-rooted music could be presented with the same class as grand opera."[39]

These then were the sum total of B.B. King's personal and professional makeup as he entered 1949: musical influences from a wide range of black artists and a narrower range of white artists in country and pop. From certain of the black artists he took indelible lessons in style and appearance and public demeanor that were a perfect fit on a young man who had been raised to be respectful, well mannered, and tolerant without overlooking the harsh realities of the segregated society he was trying to negotiate. He knew how to work a crowd, he knew how to be effective on the air, his work ethic was admirable, and as a musician he knew exactly what he was then and what he wanted to be in time. This fateful year would be life altering and, for an instant, life threatening, but would loom large forevermore in B.B. King's legend.

In December B.B. played a date in Twist, Arkansas, a small town about 35 miles northwest of Memphis. Not a club, this, but rather a large room in a private house, kind of a makeshift juke joint. The only heat emanated from a garbage pail in the middle of the floor, half-filled with kerosene. At some point during the night, in the midst of what B.B. has described over the years as a rockin' good time ("... couples get to jitterbugging, snake-hipping and trucking," he remembers[40]) a fight broke out between two men, whose scuffling upended the garbage pail, spilling burning kerosene across the floor, "spreading an incredible river of fire."[41] In a frenzy, the assembled throng, B.B. among them, surged toward the only exit. Once outside, though, he realized he'd left his guitar in the house. As the house was consumed in flame, B.B. knew he couldn't sit by and let his guitar be reduced to cinders—he couldn't afford to buy a new one, for starters. Without hesitation, he rushed back into the inferno, grabbed the guitar neck, and tried to hustle back out. A wall collapsed behind him as he leaped out the exit, "just missing my ass and my guitar by a couple of inches."[42]

Outside, he heard someone comment that the men were fighting over a woman named Lucille, who worked at the house.

Lucille.

"I decided right then and there to christen my instrument Lucille, if only to remind me never to do anything that foolish again," B.B. said.[43]

There have been many Lucilles over the years—17 as this is written, the current one being a Gibson model ES-355 solid-body, which has been the Lucille of choice for the past 26 years, its predecessor being the Gibson ES-335 arch-top; before he bought his first Gibson, B.B. played pretty much any brand guitar he could afford, including Fender, Gretsch, and Silvertone. He's so identified with Gibson now that the guitar manufacturer has honored him by marketing a B.B. King model Lucille guitar.

But specs don't tell the story of the B.B.–Lucille relationship. Just as

Charles Foster Kane told his despairing wife, "My dear, your only co-respondent is the *Chronicle*," so has B.B. forged an intimate relationship with his instrument that even he admits rivals the pleasure he gets from a living, breathing partner of the opposite sex.

"I've turned to Lucille for comfort and relief," he says. "Just to pick her up and stroke her settles me down. Some folks like sitting by waterfalls or meditating in rose gardens. Some people pop pills to relax or hike up mountains. I sit down with Lucille. I put her on my lap and wait until some happy combination of notes falls from her mouth and makes me feel all warm inside. With the possible exception of real-life sex with a real-life woman, no one gives me peace of mind like Lucille."[44]

The locus of B.B.'s life now was WDIA and the Beale Street culture, which to him were one and the same. Blacks and whites commingled on Beale, and whites were as much a part of the WDIA audience as blacks. B.B. has referred to the station and the street as "islands of understanding in the middle of an ocean of prejudice."[45]

At this juncture B.B. was making some key musical connections in pushing his career forward. One of the finest bands in town was headed by Tuff Green, and his combo included Phineas Newborn, Sr., on drums, the teenage Newborn sons, Phineas, Jr., and Calvin, on piano and guitar, respectively, and Ben Branch on saxophone. The senior Newborn, from Jackson, Tennessee, was a respected veteran of the fertile Memphis music scene who had come to town with his wife Rose near the start of the Depression. After the birth of Calvin, their second son, the family had moved to within shouting distance of Beale Street, where Phineas found regular work as a drummer. One of his steady gigs was drumming at the Palace Theater's notorious Midnight Rambles, late-night, adults-only fare featuring wild music, bawdy jokes, and scantily attired dancing girls, all rolled out to the delight and titillation of an interracial audience. One of the popular bands Phineas played with was Memphis native Jimmie Lunceford's Chickasaw Syncopators. Phineas was invited to join the Syncopators at one time but declined, his aim being to form a family band with his talented sons. Phineas, Jr., was a prodigy as a piano player and became the most acclaimed of the two sons strictly for his virtuosity; Calvin carved out his own local legend as a flamboyant showman and resourceful guitarist. The eldest Newborn son astounded B.B., who regarded him as "more than great. . . . a genius who could play Chopin and Mozart when he was only a child. Folks were calling him the new Art Tatum."[46]

A lasting friendship was born when B.B. met a promising young blues singer from the Memphis area, Robert Calvin Bland, who became known as

Bobby "Blue" Bland, circa 1957 —
the quiet storm of postwar blues.

Bobby "Blue" Bland. Born near Memphis in 1930, Bland received his first lessons in direct, heartfelt singing while a member of various church groups in town; in the late '40s he took to Beale Street and began honing a singular vocal approach out of the gospel, blues, and early R&B that had become his artistic touchstones. Bland didn't, and doesn't, have a big, powerful voice. Rather, his was the quiet storm of postwar blues—forceful and determined in a macho kind of way on uptempo numbers, but with an underlying tenderness that could put the hurt in a ballad to a degree that, of all his contemporaries, only B.B. himself approached. Along the way, he developed the earmarks of a master stylist as well in his subtle use of nuance to suggest deeper feelings roiling below the surface of his dignified demeanor. In time he also developed a signature vocal tic, a kind of choking sound he called "the Squall" that was his version of a shout—except that Bland sounded like he was trying to dislodge something from his throat. Not the most pleasant of vocal affectations, "the Squall," Bland insisted, drove the women wild. One of his longtime female fans, Maurice Prince (who was the proprietor of the Los Angeles–based Maurice Snack 'n' Chat restaurant), described Bland's music as "sexy blues" that women found most appealing. "Men would come out to see B.B.," she said, "but the women would flock around this guy because he would sing kind of quiet and come out with these sexy notes. He was softer than B.B.—

you had to kinda listen, and that got under your skin. When Bobby would sing something, it was more like he was talking directly to you."[47]

Although Bland's artistic growth was far from complete when he cut his first sides at Sam Phillips's Memphis Recording Service in 1951, he sounded every bit the assured vocalist, recording in his hometown backed by musician friends from Roscoe Gordon's band. A year later he was signed to the Houston-based Duke label, teamed with players unfamiliar to him (Johnny Board and His Orchestra), and lost nary a step—in fact, Board brought a big, ambitious sound to Bland's sessions by way of a prominent horn section and an organist and vibraphonist whose embellishments lent the arrangements a jazz feel, inspiring even richer-textured performances from Bland. Such was the genesis of a signature style that embraced not only florid, emotionally charged blues (and borderline pop) ballads but also hard-driving blues and jump blues orchestrations, extending a tradition pioneered in the '30s by Big Joe Turner and the boogie-woogie cats from Kansas City. In 1955 he began recording in Houston with a small orchestra led by trumpeter-arranger Joe Scott, who in the years ahead would assume a critical role in the sound and sensibility peculiar to Bland's music. The early years produced some power-ful music—in 1956 a wrenching torch number, "You or None," rendered with Percy Mayfield–inspired cool sensuality, and an explosive performance on "Time Out" (also from '56) in which he charges into his high register and wails like a Sonny Boy Williamson harmonica solo—but his breakthrough would not come until 1957, with a shuffling bit of R&B clairvoyance in "Farther Up the Road," notable for the incendiary dialogue between Bland, lusting for revenge, and guitarist Pat Hare firing off portentous-sounding four-bar riffs around him before launching into an angry, serpentine solo attack. Upon its release the song bolted up the charts, and stayed at No. 1 for two weeks that August. At the same time "Farther Up the Road" was intro-ducing Bland to a larger audience, the song was also establishing a unique storytelling style, not exclusive to Bland but employed most effectively by him on many of his most memorable sides. Bland begins his tale in progress and proceeds to hurtle towards a denouement while scattering minute details of the story's first act, in effect shifting the time line to create drama around key sentiments such as "farther on up the road / someone's gonna hurt you like you hurt me." From this point forward, Bland's Duke recordings were notable for the diversity of their arrangements and the singer's imaginative vocal stylings. Whether he was shouting over a pulsating, horn-driven, Ray Charles–style arrangement ("Close to You," from 1960) or crooning sensitively on a moody, lilting ballad ("Two Steps from the Blues," again 1960), he was believable and affecting. One of the most frequently charting R&B artists of all time (ranked No. 11 in *Joel Whitburn's Top R&B Singles, 1942–1988*), Bland also has several top-notch albums to his credit, and one indisputably monumental one, 1960's *Two Steps from the Blues*, one of the most powerful R&B albums ever recorded. From the raw-boned confessional blues of the opening title song to the final, touching "I've Been Wrong So Long," Bland constructs a concept album devoted to intimate reflections on love and longing so personal and atmospheric it comes off as R&B's answer to Sinatra's brilliant forays into thematic unity, *Only the Lonely* and *In the Wee Small Hours*.

B.B. makes no bones about his regard for Bland's artistry. "He's my favorite blues singer," he states. "Man can sing anything, but he gives the blues, with his gorgeous voice of satin, something it never had before. He lifts the blues and makes them his own. I got started a little before Bobby, but when he came 'round Beale Street, I loved having him sit in with those little bands of mine. Bobby was one of the joys of Beale Street."[48] (He was also, in addition to an occasional member of the band, B.B.'s chauffeur and valet at various points.)

The "little bands" B.B. put together to tour around Tennessee, Arkansas, and Mississippi—and to play on the air at WDIA—were comprised of musicians whose paths he had crossed in Memphis. These included drummers Earl Forrest and E.A. Kamp, pianists Ford Nelson and John Alexander, Jr., and saxophonists Solomon Hardy, Richard Sanders, and Herman Green.

In his book *Bluesland*, blues authority Pete Welding quotes B.B. talking about this period as being a time when he was meeting "guys who are now very big in the jazz field. George Coleman, who [later] was with Miles Davis. Herman Green, who was with Lionel Hampton, was with me for a time, and so was George Joyner, the bassist."[49]

The musician who would emerge as most famous from this bunch did so for all the wrong reasons. He was a gifted piano player named John Alexander, who came out of the loose confederation of local musicians who played together around town as the Beale Streeters and numbered B.B. and Bobby "Blue" Bland among their membership. As Johnny Ace, Alexander, signed to the Duke label, had several R&B hits in the early '50s, and then cut "Pledging My Love," a velvet-smooth R&B ballad that hit the Top 20 and might have made Ace a crossover star if it hadn't made him a legend first. When it was released in 1955, Ace was dead, having expired on Christmas Eve of 1954 after losing a game of Russian roulette backstage before a show that evening at Houston's City Auditorium.

Now almost always accompanied by a band, B.B. was forced into a necessary degree of discipline in his playing in that he was no longer one man with a guitar, able to wail all night on his own terms without regard for song structure, tempo, or even dynamics, save for his own emotional investment in a song and how he conveyed that to his audience within the context of his story. It was a pivotal moment in B.B.'s development. The raw, unfettered acoustic Delta blues he had grown up with would always be a profound experience spiritually as well as musically for fans and musicians alike, but had never become much of a commercial force outside the black market. In contrast, Louis Jordan and T-Bone Walker, with their electrifying combos, pointed the way to crossover acceptance and, presumably, the material comforts that came with it. On his journey out of the Delta to the big city of Memphis, B.B. never lost his love for Blind Lemon Jefferson and Lonnie Johnson. But he took note of the evolving blues scene as new styles emerged, and began the process of sculpting his own voice out of the seminal influences of his younger years, long before anyone had ever heard of the Beale Street Blues Boy.

However, once he began playing with a band, and in a band, he had to rein in his tendency to take the song wherever his mood suited him. That is to say, he learned he had to keep time, and this was no easy feat. As he told Pete Welding, "We worked together, but they didn't always like it, because my timing was so bad. My beat was all right—I'd keep that—but I might play 13 or 14 bars on a 12-bar blues! Counting the bars—that was out! These guys would hate that, because they had studied, but all my musical knowledge was what I'd got from records. I tried to play it right, but I ended up playing it my way."[50]

B.B.'s haphazard sense of time frustrated one of his mentors as well. Robert "Jr." Lockwood also had been raised in the Delta, and had been taught as a youngster to play guitar by Robert Johnson, who lived with Lockwood's mother on and off over a period of years (the actual number is in dispute, although Lockwood himself insists it was nearly ten years). Lockwood was still a teenager when his path crossed that of the second Sonny Boy Williamson, and the two played together around the Delta for a couple of years before Sonny Boy wandered off. They reunited in 1941 and were featured on the inaugural "King Biscuit Time" broadcast from Helena's KFFA. B.B.'s history with Sonny Boy dated back to those nights spent outside Jones Night Spot, glimpsing the forbidden world. He'd seen Sonny Boy (né Rice Miller) performing and understood why "they didn't call him King of the Harmonica for nothing. . . . he was a big dude who blew the blues out of that sucker until there was nothing left to blow. He played sitting down, using his feet like a drum—stomping loud and hard—shouting and inhaling and exhaling on his harp like his life was on the line." Almost as impressive was the guitar player, "who made the guitar cry and scream."[51]

Lockwood, he said, "was the first dude I ever heard play 'One O'Clock Jump' and make the guitar sound like the whole Basie band."[52]

As an occasional member of B.B.'s touring band, Lockwood found his patience tested by the leader's casual relationship with meter. In fact, "B.B. didn't have no sense of time," Lockwood stated unequivocally in an interview with Peter Lee in *Guitar Player*. "I was working with him as a sideman all over Arkansas and Tennessee. He had a horn player, a drummer, me, and him. I tried my best to teach him time, but I think that I—it was hard for him to understand. When I got ready to leave, B.B. had a contract with somebody who was going to record him, and I told the man to put eight pieces with him and he would have to listen to the band! So the man put eight pieces with him. . . ."[53]

Lockwood put it more bluntly in an interview published as part of a B.B. King tribute in *Living Blues* magazine (May–June 1988). "His time was apeshit," Lockwood said. "I had a hard time trying to teach him."[54]

In that same issue, B.B. didn't dispute Lockwood's claim and admitted that in their time together "he taught me a lot." But, he added, "he used to get mad at me because he'd say, 'You'll never play nothing.' He'd beat me on the hand and say, 'Man, how come you play like that?' I'm paying him, but he'd smack me. But he's my friend and I love him. And a lot of things he said to me made so much sense."[55]

All of this tutelage, and all the lessons he had learned about life and music, were directed at one goal, as far as B.B. was concerned, and that was to get on record. In 1949 the timing was right. In the heady years immediately following America's triumph in World War II, small record labels began popping up all over the map, challenging the hegemony of the three majors—Columbia, RCA, and Decca—by scouting out those artists whom the majors had deemed uncommercial or had simply overlooked. At the turn of the decade this meant mostly black artists, and aggressive independents—such as Los Angeles–based Specialty, run by Art Rupe, Lew Chudd's Imperial label, and the Bihari brothers' Modern Records; the Ertegun brothers' Atlantic Records out of New York; and Leonard and Phil Chess's Chess Records, out of Chicago—were combing the nation for unclaimed talent. All of these labels, and more, would find what they were looking for, and then some, when rock 'n' roll opened previously segregated airwaves to R&B artists that appealed to the new music's emerging teen audience.

In 1946 in Nashville, former CBS broadcaster and Grand Ole Opry announcer Jim Bulleit had founded Bullet Records in response to learning that jukebox operators were rabid for more country records. Bullet Records would launch the recording careers of country legends-in-the-making Ray Price, Pee Wee King, and Chet Atkins, among others, and only a year after it opened for business it crossed over to the pop side with a vengeance: Nashville-based pianist-composer-bandleader Francis Craig's 1947 Bullet single "Near You" logged an astonishing 17 weeks at No. 1 on the pop charts, becoming both the first major pop hit on an independent label and the theme song for "Mr. Television," Milton Berle. Bulleit branched out into R&B with his Sepia subsidiary, but he was forced out of the operation in 1948 and replaced by Overton Ganong, a former Memphis resident.[56]

B.B. asked WDIA owner Jim Ferguson if he could cut a record in the radio station's studio. That was fine with Ferguson, but WDIA, not being a label operation, had no means of releasing or distributing sound recordings. How B.B.'s sides got to Bullet remains open to speculation. (In his autobiography, B.B. asserts that Ferguson "put me in touch with a man with a transcription firm in Nashville that made commercials: Jim Bulleit. Bulleit also owned Bullet Records, a small operation, and decided I was ready."[57] All fine and good, this, but it doesn't account for Bulleit no longer being at the label.) The direct link would seem to be, as Colin Escott suggests in a liner essay accompanying the Ace Records four-CD retrospective of B.B.'s early recordings, *The Vintage Years*, that Ferguson contacted Ganong and sealed a deal for B.B.

WDIA technical manager Don Kern served as engineer and producer for B.B.'s first session, cutting the artist and his studio band on an acetate disc in Studio A. To back him, B.B. assembled not his usual touring musicians, but a lineup of formidable Memphis hands, led by bass player–bandleader Tuff Green and also including brothers Thomas and Ben Branch on trumpet and tenor saxophone, respectively; Sammie Jett on trombone; Phineas Newborn, Sr., on drums, and his sons, Phineas, Jr., and Calvin, on piano and guitar, respectively. (Ben Branch, who went on to be the bandleader for the Operation Breadbasket movement begun by Martin Luther King, Jr., and Jesse Jackson, entered the history books as the last person to speak to King before the civil rights leader's assassination on April 4, 1968.)

No evidence has ever surfaced of Bullet having any kind of option or right of first refusal on B.B.'s services beyond the two singles the label agreed to release.

First Recordings

"Miss Martha King" b/w *"When Your Baby Packs Up and Goes"*
August 1949, Bullet 309

"Got the Blues" b/w "Take a Swing with Me"
October 1949, Bullet 315

B.B.'s first recordings, all original songs, hardly signal the emergence of a modern blues giant, but neither are they as inconsequential as some critics have contended. What's missing from the four Bullet releases is any distinctive guitar work by B.B.; Calvin Newborn asserts that he plays the opening riff in "Miss Martha King"—a pair of standard descending blues scales, an ascending run back up the neck, and a terse thematic statement before the band eases in. B.B. was still a few years away from employing his guitar as a complement to and extension of his singing voice. As for the singing voice itself, it's still unformed, albeit expressive. This is the young B.B., singing in a high and keening timbre, and though he had absorbed the styles of plenty of great singers at this point, he tears through these four songs with little variation in pace, seeming more focused on volume than on subtlety and nuance. As a blues shouter, he's impressive enough for a youngster, though swagger is about all he's offering.

B.B. may be the titular artist here, but his band steals the show. "Miss Martha King" features a sultry sax solo from Ben Branch over Tuff Green's solid walking bass line (with Calvin Newborn offering a reprise, barely audible, of the opening descending scale run), and later a languorous trumpet solo by Thomas Branch ahead of B.B.'s closing verse. The jump blues "When Your Baby Packs Up and Goes" is keyed by a sparkling instrumental break featuring a sputtering sax solo by Branch, and a rousing bit of barrelhouse piano from Newborn, Jr., that gives way to a blustery trumpet solo courtesy Branch again. On the jump blues "Take a Swing with Me," Branch steps out with another lively sax solo. However standard this fare was for its day, though, B.B.'s use of brass and reed instruments reflects his vision of a bigger blues presentation à la Louis Jordan and is a harbinger of the distinctive sound signature he would eventually trademark.

Of the four Bullet-issued sides, the one on which the vocal and instrumental elements mesh most effectively—and surely would have caught the ear of any talent scout—is the mid-tempo blues "Got the Blues." At the piano, Newborn, Jr., employs an arsenal of effects, from comping chords to right-hand trills to slip notes to tasty glissandos, and engages the blaring horns in a spirited, low-down dialog. This would all be for naught, though, were B.B. not singing with impressive conviction and deep feeling. This, his most thoughtful early vocal, finds him injecting short falsetto swoops at the end of lyric lines and exhibiting a more rhythmic sense of phrasing, putting into action some of the techniques he learned as a gospel singer—especially melisma (singing the same syllable over a series of notes)—in service to his woeful lament.

Lyrically, B.B.'s mean-woman blues themes are unremarkable, standard blues fare, but at the very least his writing shows him conversant in the form and style of songwriting the blues audience responded to. At age 24, though, it appears he wasn't ready to take that audience anywhere but to familiar places. He certainly had enough profound life experiences, and enough street sense about him, to be more daring lyrically, in the style of cousin Bukka White, for example (without the prison time), but he chose the safe road of every man's blues, that being woman trouble.

"Miss Martha King" then becomes the most revelatory of the Bullet sides. The first lyric B.B. sings—"I'm sittin' here thinkin' / thinkin' 'bout Miss Martha King"—echoes the opening lyric of his musical hero Blind Lemon Jefferson's "Match Box Blues" ("I'm sittin' here wond'rin'…"), and then moves along to an avowal of his love for the woman. By the second verse, he's singing about her running around and treating him wrong, a charge he reiterates in the closing third verse.

This, as it turns out, is hardly a fictitious scenario, but the characters have been reversed. In fact, it was B.B. who was running around, rarely denying himself the carnal pleasure women would offer him after a show. (In 1949 he had fathered a child by a woman in Indianola, and over the years would father 15 children by 15 different women and financially support them all.) "That was something new and wonderful in my life," he said of the distaff side's affection for him. "I liked that feeling. It wasn't the reason I played music, but it was a side benefit I couldn't always pass up."[58]

"'Miss Martha King,'" he said, "reflected some of the stress in our marriage. Despite our troubles, I loved that good-hearted lady and wanted her to hear it in song."[59]

The Bullet singles didn't sell, though, and an enlightened B.B. ("I thought if you made a record, that was it. I found out that was *not* it."[60]) returned to his disc jockey job at WDIA, returned to playing the juke joints in the immediate area, and, when money was dwindling from those endeavors, returned to the cotton fields.

From the Inside: B.B.'S First Session_____

An Interview with Calvin Newborn
"B.B.'s the only somebody I've ever known
that hasn't changed a lick since I first met him."

Only 16 years old when he was called in to play on B.B.'s King's first recording session, Calvin Newborn, like his father Phineas, Sr., and brother Phineas, Jr., went on to become a highly regarded jazz musician. Now 71 years old and living in Jacksonville, Florida, Newborn remains active in music—at the time of this interview he was putting the finishing touches on a new album for the Memphis-based Yellow Dog Records label—and as an evangelist for Noni Juice, a miracle cure-all from Tahiti that he represents as a distributor. A repository of colorful tales from the postwar Memphis music scene, he knows how to answer a question by filling in the context for his interlocutor. His take is, well, his take. For example, several B.B. discographers believe Newborn did not play on the first B.B. session for Bullet, but rather came in for the second round of recording. This despite Newborn's forthright assertion of his role on "Miss Martha King"—and if each and every statement doesn't square with the research, it's still beyond dispute that he was present and accounted for at the dawn of a monumental career. Attention must be paid, and respect accorded.

Do you recall what you were told when you were called in to do the B.B. King session? Did you get the word from your father that you were going to work on that?

Probably it was my father, because he knew B.B. He introduced me to B.B. and asked B.B. to take me down to Beale Street to pick me out a guitar to learn on. B.B. took me down to Nathan's Pawn Shop and picked me out a big, black hollow-body guitar. I always did like hollow-body guitars; y'know, it was a nice box.

What kind of guitar was it?

I don't remember the brand name. All I remember is it was a big, black guitar with a round hole, and I got it and I wanted to take classical guitar, 'cause I had taken two years of piano. I started taking piano lessons at the age of eight; my brother was nine. And I took piano for a couple of years; well, not a couple of years, but I was in the second grade book when I decided to let my brother have the piano. I must have been ten years old, something like that. Then my dad asked B.B. to take me down and pick me out a guitar, because I told them I wanted to play guitar. Then he took me down to Nathan's Pawn Shop and picked me out this guitar and I bought it for five dollars. Yeah, I had won the amateur show at the Palace with my brother. My brother was on one end of the piano, and I was on the other end of the piano, playing the boogie-woogie on the bottom; but I was already a showman by then, 'cause my dad always told me you had to give the people something to see plus something to hear. So I was dancin' and singin' "'Hey Ba-Ba-Re-Bop!'" See, I was too young to be singin' what I sang, but my brother and I had seen the Midnight Ramble. We walked all the way from Orange Mound and saw the Midnight

Ramble when we were, I guess I was about five or six then. We saw the Midnight Ramble one Saturday night, and man, that did it for me as far as show business. A stage show and they was cussin' and everything, and naked women. You know I was excited.

Being so young, how did you get into a show like that?

Well, we went early—well, not too early—went early enough to pay our way in to see the movie, and when the lights came on we got down up under the seats till the lights went out. And when the lights came back on, two little heads, with eyes as big as teacups, saw the stage show.

So you didn't sneak in. You paid your way in.

Oh, yeah. Yeah, we did. Nobody paid us any mind no way; we got out, we ran all the way home. But, you know, what I was saying was I won five dollars playing "Hey Ba-Ba-Re-Bop!" with my brother playing the top of the piano and I was playing the bottom and dancin' and singin'. I sang, "Your mama's on the bottom / Your papa's on top / Your sister's in the kitchen / Hollerin', when they gonna stop / Singin' hey ba-ba-re-bop." Lionel Hampton had a hit with that at that time; it was a big hit. And my dad was playin' with Hampton. When he came home off the road with Hamp he said, "Lionel Hampton got a Polly parrot he taught how to sing 'Hey Bop-a-Re-Bop.' I know one of y'all can sing." My brother wasn't fixin' to sing nothin'. So I was the one that sang "Hey Ba-Ba-Re-Bop" and he played the stuff out of the top end of the piano while I did all the clownin' on the bottom. We won first prize, five dollars. Rufus gave each one of us a five-dollar bill. And that's what I bought that guitar with.

Now did B.B. give you lessons on that guitar?

He gave me my first lesson. It wasn't no lesson; he just sit down and started playing.

You just watched him.

Yeah, I just watched him. B.B. was a natural. He could sing already and he just played what he sang. But B.B. really didn't know very much at that time. I wanted to study classical guitar but the only classical guitar teacher in town wouldn't teach me; he told me I'd run the rest of his students away; you know how it was back then. So I just wrote the guitar headquarters and got me some books. I could already read piano music, so I taught myself; so I'm a self-taught guitar player. B.B. taught himself too; he didn't know how to read, but he taught himself how to sing and play a few chords behind what he sang. But he couldn't sing too well and play too at the time. So that's why I got on the record date, I guess, 'cause I was playin' that boogie-woogie bottom. Well, B.B. had a little trouble back then recognizing when the end of the chorus was over. He might sing 13 bars, y'know. But by the time we got in the studio B.B. was singing 12-bar blues good.

So is that you playing that boogie-woogie riff that opens "Miss Martha King"?

Yeah, that's me. That's me playing that boogie-woogie riff.

What do you recall of B.B. in the studio at that time? Was he comfortable? Did you sense he knew what he was doing?

Well, B.B. was always a humble fellow. He's the only somebody I've ever known that hasn't changed a lick since I first met him. He's still the same B.B. He's always been very humble. He didn't say much, he just took care of business, you know.

I suppose you and your brother were the least experienced musicians there. B.B. had some seasoned talent around him on that date. What was your father's role in the studio?

He was in charge of things, because my dad knew the business inside out and he liked B.B. because B.B. was like him. They were both naturals. My dad couldn't read either, but he could play anything. So they were both naturals and they got along fine. Dad, he was the leader. He'd tell everybody. My brother, I think that's why they didn't let him play very much, because they were lookin' for the raw talent sound, and my brother was so far ahead of everybody else, he was playing too much piano.

He had a great solo on "Got the Blues." A really strong solo.

Yeah, but I think he was playin' a little bit too strong [*laughs*]. They didn't want no strong playing. [Author's note: This is a reference to B.B.'s first session for the Modern label, at the Memphis YMCA, when Jules Bihari sent Phineas Newborn, Jr., home and in his place hired Ike Turner to play piano on the recording date.]

Those sessions with B.B., what was the mood in the studio?

Well, y'know, B.B. is so easygoing. Everything went smooth except I do remember my dad and my brother had a little disagreement, you know what I mean? I think Sam Phillips probably mentioned what a good beat he played. Junior called it the shuffle and [my father] called it the mash. And Junior might have said, "Shh—"—he didn't get the word out before my dad smacked him upside the head. He couldn't stand for nobody to cuss him. And that was a curse word—"shhh"—you know. So my brother was pissed off during the whole session because my dad called what he played a mash and my brother called it a shuffle. I think my dad really was, I think that was his beat, that boogie shuffle, I think he started that thing; he called it the mash. Anyway, but he never got recognition he deserved for the drummer that he was. He was a hell of a drummer. I know Art Blakey knew how good he was.

When I got to New York Art Blakey and I used to get together all the time, and he'd always want to play with me, because he knew my dad.

I'm sure B.B. knew exactly what he was getting when he called him in for the session.

Oh, yeah. Well, they had played together before too. My dad knew B.B. well then. You know, he was by the house, and that's when my dad asked B.B. to take me down on Beale. But I didn't know who B.B. was till after that. Then I used to hear him over the radio—"Pepticon sure is good / Get it any way that you could." Fact, I just wrote a song, I can't advertise it too much. I just took me a shot of Noni Juice and man, it got me feeling good. That Noni Juice is real and natural, it's good. And it heals everything. It reminded me of when B.B. used to sing that Pepticon song. So I wrote a song to it. Maybe it's time for me to get known, you know. Start making some greenbacks. Lot of people getting rich selling that Noni Juice.

I've never heard of Noni Juice.

Well, you've heard of it now.

Where do you get it?

Well, you order it. I'm a distributor myself. I bought a case, drank that up. It's really amazing how good it is. I don't try to sell it, I'm not trying to sell it to you, but it's something that everybody should want because it's good for any kind of ailment that you have. It fights cancer; it lowers high blood pressure—in fact I'm sayin' all that in the song. And it comes from Tahiti, and it grows in that pure soil, that good soil. It's a fruit that I know the Creator put here for us to use for our ailments. What it does, a doctor has proved—I've got tapes and things where you can see what it does—you know, if your cells are deteriorating, are germy, it runs away the bad cells and puts good ones there. It creates good cells in your body. It's good for any system—your respiratory, digestive, for your whole immune system. It's amazing; it's amazing fruit. You could almost call it a drug because it fights germs better than alcohol, better than anything I know. I was bitten by a few mosquitoes the other day, and I went to a store and spent six dollars almost for some multi-bacterial stuff. And I put that on there but I'm still scratchin' and turnin' red. And shoot, man, I put some Noni Juice on the mosquito bites and overnight it was gone. And I could feel it going away. I could feel them germs runnin' from that Noni Juice.

So you can drink this and put it on your skin too?

Yeah, you drink it and they've got it, even made it in candy now. They got candy and they got salve you rub on your skin. Nineteen ninety-six was when they discovered it. And a lot of doctors recommend and they've been talkin' about it and there's a lot of people testifyin' about how good it is. It's a miracle drug, man; it's something I believe God put here for people who want to be healthy. And health is our most precious asset.

Let me ask you one final question about B.B. Knowing him as long as you have, have you been surprised at how he's been able to sustain his career? And by the level of popularity he's achieved?

No, I'm not. I knew B.B. was gonna be successful because he was so humble. So easygoing and he loves what he's doing. And people love somebody who is that way. Everybody loves B.B. Instances like when he used to play at the Club Paradise in Memphis, my mother and my whole family would want to go see B.B. and it was no problem. He knew my mother and he recognized her. So she would never have a problem—"Come on in, Mrs. Newborn." She could go back in the dressing room or wherever. He was just a nice person. I knew that was gonna take him a long way. It's just that he did struggle a long time out there on the road. Musicians can be hard to handle sometimes. That's why I never really wanted my own group [*laughs*]; I always played with somebody, and I was always their problem. B.B., he always kept some musicians who admired him and respected him, always kept somebody to take care of whatever needed to be taken care of. The people who started out with him, they were like a family, you know. I think his humility is what made me know he was gonna go far. He had no ego, he had no inferiority complex like a lot of musicians do when they can't read. B.B. always wanted to, he told me, "Man, I wish I could play like you." In New York, I never will forget it. He and the guitar player out of Texas, Gatemouth Brown, he and Gatemouth was sittin' together listenin' to me and man, he said, "Calvin, I wish I could play like you!" And I said, "B.B., I wish I was makin' half the tax you pay." [*Laughs.*] But B., I loved him. I just wrote a song for him, a tribute, a blues to him. I played this blues in Memphis at the Club Handy, he was celebrating a birthday and I played "King of the Blues" for him. It's a Slide Hampton blues that I love because it's different from the average blues. I put lyrics to it. "I saw a picture in a frame / and didn't know what was its name / Looked at it again / I knew that it was Riley King, a man who paid a lot of dues / It was B.B., the king of the blues / He picked bales of cotton / Plowed fields behind a mule / He drove a tractor / Walked miles in the rain with his guitar / To sing the blues over radio airwaves / Beale Street Blues Boy never changed, stayed the same / B.B. King, the king of the blues." It's a blues, but it's a different kind of blues. And if he would hear me play it, B.B. would jump straight up in the air!

You know, a lot of musicians don't realize, if you learn how to read you're not limited. And a lot of them, 'cause a lot of them think it's better if they don't

B.B. in 1948, performing in WDIA's studio,
Memphis.

learn how to read too, you know, but I just hate to hear youngsters tell me—
and they're out there on the road making a whole lot of money playing rock
'n' roll. And they'll ask, "Calvin, should I learn how to read music?" It makes
me angry, because they don't know that if you can't read, you're limited to
what you can play. But I don't know, we're always looking for a soft way out.
In fact, well, anyway, B.B. is one of the few people that I know, one of the few
musicians that I know, that hasn't changed; he's still the same. Of course
there's a lotta musicians that hasn't changed, but they've been assholes all the
time [*laughs*] with a chip on their shoulders. He's always been a nice person.
He's a good man, I love him.

Chapter 3

THE MODERN AGE

Despite their commercial failure, B.B.'s two Bullet singles generated more positives than he could have imagined. For starters, he remained a disc jockey—moreover a disc jockey for WDIA, the station that had cut the deal with Bullet, which assured his singles of good airplay and the artist a higher profile as a local personality. Being on record also allowed him greater leverage in negotiating a higher personal appearance fee with club owners. In the grand scheme of things, the most important upshot of his brief tenure on Bullet was that his singles came to the attention of the Bihari brothers—Saul, Jules, Lester, and Joe—at Modern Records.

The brothers had started out servicing jukeboxes before launching Modern in 1945 to take advantage of the post–World War II boom that had brought to California a sizable migrant population from the South, Southwest, and Midwest, and with them a demand for entertainment—jukeboxes for the clubs and restaurants, records for the home. Right out of the box Modern saw good sales on recordings by R&B singer–piano player Hadda Brooks, including a No. 4 R&B hit in 1947 with "That's My Desire." As was the custom at the time, the Biharis began looking around for sources from which to buy master recordings to release on Modern—in Texas, they found the Gold Star label, from which they leased recordings by Lightnin' Hopkins and Harry Choates, and the Blue Bonnet label, whence came Smokey Hogg. Modern's first No.1 R&B hit came in 1948 with Pee Wee Crayton's "Blues After Hours," followed the next year by a succession of hits by John Lee Hooker (his monumental No. 1 "Boogie Chillen'"), Lightnin' Hopkins, Little Willie Littlefield, Jimmy Witherspoon, Floyd Dixon, and

Saunders King. In an industry growing fertile on the strength of independent labels giving black artists an opportunity denied them by the majors, Modern became a model of smart signings coupled to visionary business practices. As John Broven notes in his article "B.B. King's Record Company," in the booklet accompanying Ace Records' (U.K.) essential four-CD box set of B.B.'s Modern recordings, *The Vintage Years*, the Biharis not only understood the nature of the R&B market, but also had in place "a first-class distribution system, an acute awareness of the jukebox industry and the growing importance of disc jockeys, and at various times were self-sufficient with their own in-house studios and record pressing plants. Their publishing company, Modern Music, was to be a veritable cash cow."[1]

In 1950 the Modern roster had grown to the point where distributors were balking at taking on so many releases from one label. The Biharis responded by forming a subsidiary, RPM. They also launched a series of long-playing albums, each at a $2.85 price point, and were also moving confidently into the new 45-rpm format for singles. "The Biharis were close to the cutting edge of recording software," Broven notes.[2]

That same year Jules Bihari went on record with a statement that augured well for Modern's artists, and especially for B.B. King. In an April 28, 1945, *Billboard* magazine announcement of Modern's first releases, mention is made of Jules saying that "the releases he has made up this time allow the musicians full range of interpretation. They play what they want and how they want. . . ." Trusting the artists was not unusual at this juncture in time, but for an artist like B.B., who was still configuring his myriad influences into a distinctive style, having free rein to express himself artistically was crucial to his development. With this philosophy guiding them, the Biharis were building an enterprise in which art and commerce coexisted fruitfully.

In the summer of 1950 the Biharis came to Memphis on a talent scouting expedition. In January of that year Sam Phillips had opened the Memphis Recording and Music Service on Union Avenue and soon began recording local blues and R&B artists and leasing out their masters to independent labels. Phillips understood the broad-based appeal of the music black artists were making ("I knew whites surreptitiously listened to the blues," he said[3]) and was convinced that Memphis was a hotbed of talented artists waiting for a chance to get on record. He had a larger mission as well, and he knew that if his conscience steered him properly he would do the good deed he was setting out to do, and have a viable business as well.

"My work was not only to cut hit records, but my purpose was to simultaneously try to get acceptance for the artistry of black people, and hopefully then we would have more people that would get interested in listening to black music," he said. "The Atlantics and the Chesses and the Checkers and all of that, they were tryin' to do the same thing to a certain extent, but I knew what it took to get it. I knew where it needed to break out first, and that would be the South."[4]

How the Biharis found B.B. is where the trail goes cold. John Broven writes that the brothers "were introduced" to the artist, without identifying by whom. Sebastian Danchin, writing in 1998, suggests it was WDIA technical manager Don Kern who sent the Bullet records to the Biharis. In the Ace box set booklet, Colin Escott claims the Biharis heard about B.B. during a visit to WDIA, and asserts that Don Kern did indeed give them an acetate of B.B.'s recordings.

One person who apparently wasn't involved in all this was Ike Turner, who has frequently been cited as the go-between, given that he was working for the Biharis as a talent scout in the area. Sussing this out is not easy, because B.B. has both asserted and denied Ike's involvement.

In a 1982 interview with Sebastian Danchin, B.B. said he met Ike before either one of them had ever recorded, in Clarksdale, Mississippi. "Then I didn't see him anymore until he was recording, and so was I. And he then was associated with the people I started to record with later, which was the Bihari brothers, but Ike never did have anything to do with me."[5]

But in his autobiography, published in 1996, B.B. recalled an incident in Clarksdale when Ike sat in with his band, "played piano and made us sound a whole lot better. Whatever little money I got, I gave some to Ike, who seemed to appreciate it."[6] B.B. adds, "And [Ike] remembered me. I say that because when I was contacted by the Bihari brothers ... I learned Ike was their talent scout. He'd mentioned me."[7]

However, Ike told Colin Escott that in 1950 he was based in Clarksdale and didn't bring his band to Memphis until the following year, and then at B.B.'s urging.[8]

The other suspect in this mystery would be Sam Phillips, who by his own admission tipped off the Biharis to the relatively unknown but promising artist who was also a WDIA disc jockey. In an interview with John Broven for the Ace box set, Phillips said he knew the brothers "indirectly" through Memphis disc jockey Dewey Phillips. He claimed that B.B. and another promising Memphis blues artist, Roscoe Gordon, had cut some demos for him, "and I was very interested in doing some things for them." Speaking to the Biharis on the phone, he offered to send them four sides he had cut on each artist; if they were interested, Phillips said, he would set up sessions with the artists when the brothers came to town. The parties later shook hands on an agreement to give Modern first shot at any artists Phillips discovered and recorded.

Upon meeting the Biharis, B.B. was immediately impressed, especially with Jules, whose demeanor and perspective reminded him of Flake Cartledge. "He was more a buddy than a boss," B.B. said of Jules, who "didn't show the prejudice or reserve of many white men of that era. He hated segregation and paid it no mind, crossing the color line like it wasn't there. We'd go to Beale Street, hanging in clubs, listening to music, eating chili, chewing the fat. Jules gave me confidence. After hearing my blues, he said I was an artist with a future. No businessman had told me that before. I was motivated to justify his faith in me, and for the next decade or so I recorded for his company under the Modern or RPM or Kent labels."[9]

Between late 1949 and 1951, B.B. cut 11 sides at the Memphis Recording and Sound Service, 10 of which were released on singles. He was accompanied on these recordings by many of the musicians he had played with for years, as well as the newer acquaintances who had joined him for the Bullet recordings. As indicated in the Ace box set, these included Bill Harvey, Solomon Hardy, Richard Sanders, Billy Duncan, Ben Branch (tenor saxophone), Hank Crawford (alto saxophone), Fred Ford (baritone saxophone), Nathaniel Woodard (trumpet), Sammie Jett (trombone), Phineas Newborn, Jr., Ford Nelson, Johnny Ace, Ike Turner (piano), Calvin Newborn (guitar), James "Shinny" Walker, Tuff Green, George Joyner (bass), Phineas Newborn, Sr., E.A. Kamp, Earl Forrest, Ted Curry (drums), Onzie Horn (vibraphone).

The First Modern Sessions, Recorded at Memphis Recording and Sound Service, 1949–1951 _____

"Mistreated Woman" b/w "B.B. Boogie"
September 1950, RPM 304

"The Other Night Blues" b/w "Walkin' and Cryin'"
December 1950, RPM 311

"My Baby's Gone" b/w "Don't You Want a Man Like Me"
March 1951, RPM 318

"B.B. Blues" b/w "She's Dynamite"
June 1951, RPM 323

"She's a Mean Woman" b/w "Hard Working Woman"
August 1951, RPM 330

Commenting in the Ace booklet on the spirited "B.B. Boogie," Colin Escott posits that the lively recording—marked by frantic, driving instrumental work by Calvin Newborn on guitar, his brother Phineas, Jr,. on piano, and Newborn *père*, Phineas, Sr., laying down a percussive cacophony on drums—reveals more about Sam Phillips's ambitions than it does B.B.'s. That's true of most of the sides recorded under Phillips's aegis. He clearly felt he had stumbled onto something in 1951 when an Ike Turner session, featuring Ike's cousin Jackie Brenston on lead vocal, yielded a massive No. 1 R&B hit in "Rocket 88" (a propulsive, roaring jump blues modeled after Jimmy Liggins's "Cadillac Boogie") that in later years Phillips would insist was the first rock 'n' roll record; being a savvy entrepreneur, he set out to capitalize on a winning formula. "B.B. Boogie," Tampa Red's "She's Dynamite," and "Hard Working Woman" share "Rocket 88"'s intensity and roiling rhythm, and B.B.'s Roy Brown–influenced shouting is urgent and personable all at once—an irresistible call to the party. "Hard Working Woman" pumps ferociously thanks to a raucous workout on the 88s, stop-time figures throughout the arrangement, a steady-rollin' boogie beat, a bleating sax solo, and a chorus echoing the refrain back at B.B. "She's Dynamite" is even more revealing: the piano soloing is all indefatigable, amphetamized energy; the distorted, howling guitar and the hard-blowing sax are playing at tonal extremes; and B.B. is riding herd over it all with a swinging, shouting vocal. Any one of these wild workouts ought to have had a "Rocket 88"–like chart impact, but none did. Nor did any of the well-executed ballads—the walking blues "Mistreated Woman," the yearning "The Other Night," the low-down lament "Walkin' and Cryin'"—or the fanciful rhumba-inflected blues "My Baby's Gone." The latter is noteworthy, though, as the earliest indication of B.B.'s willingness to try out new styles within a blues framework, all in the name of seeking a hit.

Despite their commercial failure, these are good recordings, in step with and even ahead of the times in some cases, especially "She's Dynamite," a sizzling performance in the "Rocket 88" mold that sounds like a harbinger of something new. If all the other Phillips-directed recordings are fairly standard fare for the times, "She's Dynamite" has the unquantifiable ingredient that elevates it onto another plateau—the bristling energy of Phineas Newborn, Jr.'s piano soloing remains startling to this day, as do the incendiary guitar and sax. But it might have been less a record than it was, and is, had B.B. not stepped up with a driving vocal fully expressive of an ebullient personality, conversational yet rhythmically propulsive and, finally, a plain delight to experience as a listener—this is a fellow you'd want to get to know. With this, B.B. more than hinted at the captivating, and smart, vocalist he would become. His performance draws you in, has that intimate, person-to-person quality common to great singers, makes the listener seem part of the artist's inner circle. In short, it summons a community to the artist, whose shared values are echoed in the lyrics and expressed in the singer's emotional, nuanced delivery. "She's Dynamite" was a great leap forward for B.B., but beyond showing up on some local charts it made no more commercial impact than any of the other singles emerging from the Union Avenue sessions.

Ace Records A&R consultant John Broven, who assembled *The Vintage Years* and consequently immersed himself in B.B.'s music, assesses the recordings made with Sam Phillips as "very intriguing because they show a talented artist who is clearly feeling his way. I think the main problem was that there wasn't a hit song there, so it's either basic boogie blues or basic slow, 12-bar blues, which really didn't set the songs apart from the pack, apart from 'She's Dynamite,' which sort of had that pre–rock 'n' roll sound. But it's very interesting to see B.B.'s guitar style start to develop a little bit tentatively at times. The musicians were from that jazzy blues Memphis school. Vocally B.B. had a very sweet voice, as you could hear even at that stage, but it hadn't quite clicked. But it all came together later on '3 O'Clock Blues,' which I think is an amazing record."[10]

Although B.B. speaks of being in the recording studio as if he approached it with some trepidation, Phillips found him "a little more at ease" in the sessions owing to his experience in the WDIA studio. As for the artist's comportment, Phillips regarded B.B. "to a great extent" as a black Elvis "insofar as demeanor and humbleness, and just a sweet guy. He came in, he was just somebody that you could easily work with and we did. I did not feel with B.B. that I'd have a lot of trouble being able to work my psychological magic."[11]

In those early sessions, Phillips observed B.B. to be an artist still in search of a style and not using his voice to its fullest potential. "I would question the sameness in his voice sometimes because B.B. has got an unbelievable natural ability in his voice to capture your attention. I can't say that he has a voice that is totally distinctive like Howlin' Wolf's, but at the same time it wasn't long until everybody knew a B.B. King record instantly. The turning point was '3 O'Clock Blues.'"[12] (Phillips also told Broven that B.B. didn't play guitar and sing at the same time—"he couldn't play guitar and sing. It's just one of those things."[13]) In a remarkable passage in the Broven interview, Phillips waxes eloquent on how he made do with the limited gear of the time and pinpoints the ultimate goals of his approach to recording. Carl Perkins said that Phillips's Sun releases "always had a little roar about them,"[14] and that would appear to be not an accident but a purposeful philosophy. From his

Sam Phillips, circa 1957.

own experience in radio, Phillips had an advanced understanding of sound and electronics and how the latter could affect the former, both negatively and positively, in the marketplace. And Sam Phillips was nothing if not marketplace-savvy.

"I loved working with untried, unproven talent—black and white," he told Broven. "I love sound. What I had in equipment, I made it do. Back then, I could make dubs that were adequate for anything except a master. With recording, you have to capture what's in that studio. Then you've got to transfer it to where you can get the frequency responses that you need for the proper loudness—not overdo it and distort it, beyond intended distortion [*laughs*]. All those things are fascinating to me until this very day. My equipment was what I could afford, and when I got a 350 Ampex tape recorder, man I tell you, then I was able to buy another one shortly after that. I did my own thing, I could do it with what I had, it was no big thing to overcome. My equipment and I understood each other."[15]

To Phillips, being on intimate terms with his equipment meant being able to get a leg up on the competition for sales and jukebox play, not merely by making better records, but by making different records, experimenting with new approaches and encouraging sensibilities that were "fantastically different," whether the genre be country, the blues, or gospel. This, he said, "was a challenge of a lifetime for all my energies."[16]

Phillips's memories of working with B.B. seem too detailed to be the work of a fevered imagination, but B.B. himself, on one occasion, disavowed having any contact with Phillips in the studio. In a radio interview that took place in the year 2000, and now posted on writer Spencer Leigh's Web site as "An Audience with the King" (spencerleigh.demon.on.uk/bbking/htm), B.B., when asked about his Memphis sessions, remarked, "Coming from Mississippi, I had never been in a recording studio before. The company I was with [Modern] knew about [Sam Phillips's] studio, but most of the things we did on remote things, on portable Ampex recorders. We did '3 O'Clock Blues' at the YMCA. It was all one-track mono, but they were starting to talk about hi-fi. My company told Sam Phillips that anytime I had something to record to go ahead and let me do it and send them the bill. Some people think I was once with Sam, but I wasn't. And I didn't record with him. I recorded with an engineer and for most of the things I didn't have a producer—I am the one who produced them."[17]

So many particulars of this statement are accurate that the assertion "I didn't record with [Sam Phillips]" is indeed a puzzlement. Ampex recorders were the standard at that time; "3 O'Clock Blues" was indeed recorded at the YMCA; everything was recorded in one-track mono, but stereo was on the horizon; Phillips's deal with the Biharis was as B.B. stated it; B.B. was never signed to Phillips's label; and B.B. is on record as saying he was in charge of his early sessions—in fact, in his autobiography he singles out Jules Bihari for special praise for the latitude he gave his artists in the studio.

"Jules had a good feel for black music, but no expertise in the studio," B.B. says. "He essentially left it up to me. He felt I could write my songs and tell other musicians the sound. I did have some ideas. For example, I did a version of Tampa Red's 'She's Dynamite' all sped up and rocking. I wanted to be blue, but I wanted to be modern. I wanted my energy to get all over the song. I had good support on all of my early efforts. I loved having the Newborn men behind me—Papa Phineas on drums and his boys Junior on piano and Calvin on guitar. Nothing as good as family."[18]

(Discussing the Biharis' musical savvy, Broven noted that Joe was raised in New Orleans in the '30s and absorbed the Crescent City's fertile blues and jazz music, "so that did give him a feel for the music, possibly more than his brothers." When the family relocated to Los Angeles, the Bihari brothers immersed themselves in the L.A. club scene, which became a talent pool for them after they launched the Modern label. "Don't think one can say they were total novices," Broven said. "There was something they imbued within themselves from that great West Coast musical scene. And the other thing was that Jules was a jukebox operator and had been in the '30s and '40s, and this I think gives you tremendous insight into what's happening musically. They obviously spotted what was happening in black music, and what was in demand for this music wasn't being satisfied by the major labels.[19])

But then B.B. says he "felt good recording over at Sun Studios, owned by Sam Phillips. Jules told Sam to give me time whenever I came up with material. In the early '50s, I'd work there often. Sam served as engineer."[20]

Without a direct answer from B.B. himself, perhaps the distinction here is a semantic one. When B.B. says he never recorded with Sam, but that he worked with an engineer, perhaps he meant to say Sam Phillips was never in a producer's role but rather an engineer's—and he was the engineer B.B. worked with on the sessions at the Memphis Recording and Music Service.

At any rate, B.B. did record at 706 Union Avenue, and it's implausible that Sam Phillips would not have been there in those early years. Jack Clement, who eventually became Phillips's in-house producer-engineer (he steered some of Johnny Cash's more adventurous recordings and wrote a couple of the gems himself as well), did not join the company until 1956.

Moreover, as Broven pointed out, the acetate masters of B.B.'s early recordings (Ace Records now owns the Modern Records archive for Europe; P-Vine has it for the Far East, Virgin for the U.S.) bear the Memphis Recording and Sound Service label, "so there's no doubt that if Sam wasn't there, he had to be involved." Broven also noted that when asked to discuss his work with B.B., Phillips agreed, but only after he had taken time to review the recordings, "and it was only after Sam had actually studied them that we held the interview. So in other words, it wasn't as if he was going to speak off the top of his head. He really did want to study it and absorb it and therefore make sensible comments. And I have to say I was very impressed."[21]

Broven's take on B.B.'s statement that he never recorded with Sam supports the notion that it was a semantic issue with B.B., who "may have seen the Biharis, who were there, as the people he was recording for. But there's no doubt that Sam was there. Sam was strictly a one-man operation in those days. I read it as B.B. saying he'd never recorded for Sam Phillips as a Sun artist. But yes, he more than likely saw Sam as just the engineer and the Biharis as who he was recording for."[22]

Even the Biharis' break with Phillips is open to argument, or at least to differing points of view as to its cause. The Biharis' version is that Phillips reneged on their handshake deal to give Modern right of first refusal on his discoveries by selling "Rocket 88" to Chess Records in Chicago (which released it in April and saw it top the chart in June, a development that could not have pleased the Biharis), and placing both Roscoe Gordon and Howlin' Wolf with Chess after sending their demos to the Biharis. In his essay for the Ace box set Colin Escott notes, "The result was that the Biharis had no further dealing with Phillips until the mid-'60s when they recorded Little Richard at Phillips's new studio."[23]

Phillips's version suggests the Biharis kept acetates he had sent them without compensating him for his work, all in abrogation of their agreement. With that breach, Phillips then went to Leonard Chess with his latest masters, including "Rocket 88."

Despite what went down at his studio only two years after the falling-out with the Biharis—when, in quick succession, Elvis, Carl Perkins, Johnny Cash, Roy Orbison, and Jerry Lee Lewis showed up at 706 Union Avenue and changed the course of American popular music—even Phillips regretted the missed opportunity of working with an artist as promising as B.B. "There is no doubt I would have loved to have worked more with B.B.," Phillips told Broven. "I would guarantee you that we would have had some interesting things that would have developed. He probably served himself well staying with the blues at the time, but we might have done it a little differently."[24]

"3 O'Clock Blues" b/w "That Ain't the Way to Do It"
December 1951, RPM 339

"She Don't Move Me No More" b/w "Fine Looking Woman"
April 1952, RPM 348

The Making of "3 O'Clock Blues"
"I wanted to put my own hurting on that beautiful song."

The break with Phillips meant the Biharis needed a new place to record in Memphis. For the next year they would make good use of their tape recorder's portability, setting up sessions at the local YMCA on Lauderdale Street (where Joe Bihari draped blankets on the walls for sound reinforcement), at Tuff Green's house, and at various other exotic spots in and around Memphis.

One of the songs B.B. brought in for his first YMCA session was one he had long admired, Lowell Fulson's "3 O'Clock Blues," which had been a minor hit in 1948. The Oklahoma-born Fulson's guitar style, like B.B.'s, was shaped dramatically by T-Bone Walker's approach, whereas his vocal technique owed much to the graceful swing of Charles Brown and the precision cool of Billy Eckstine. Fulson began recording for the Swingtime label in 1946, cutting big-band sides that made their way into the blues canon over the years, including two, "3 O'Clock Blues" and "Every Day I Have the Blues," that became landmarks for B.B. An avid fan of Fulson's music, B.B. had tirelessly promoted his music at WDIA, and reputedly was the only disc jockey playing Fulson's records on the air in 1950.[25]

B.B.'s version of "3 O'Clock Blues" begins with a bold, distorted upper-strings run that curls back in on itself as the horns pump softly in the background. When B.B. enters wearily lamenting, "Now here it is three o'clock in the morning," the emotion in his voice, the sense it imparts of a man completely drained emotionally, is gripping. This is not a transformed B.B. King—there had been intimations of this sort of vocal prowess in some of the earlier recordings—but it is a B.B. King who has essentially put all his vocal tools together. The slight tremble in his voice when he sings the second line, "Can't even close my eyes," paints an aural portrait of total despair, and then he soars into his husky upper register to moan, "Oooooohhhhh, three o'clock in the mornin', baby," and suddenly he has upped the ante like he never has before on record: B.B. is totally enveloped in his character's low-down blues, his voice imparting abject loneliness. In the background the band drones, staying low profile—now and then Ike Turner's piano is heard in a brief, tinkling right-hand run before it recedes again into the ensemble drone—and between verses B.B. looses Lucille for a tart run of notes before he returns to the narrative. In the instrumental break, he takes a serpentine solo, the notes coming in flurries and then in hard-picked single notes, and B.B. is feeling it to the point where, in the midst of his solo, he shouts a hearty entreaty, "Come here, baby!"

Mood, as Colin Escott points out in the Ace booklet, has a lot to do with the appeal of "3 O'Clock Blues." Certainly the stark, plaintive, unadorned notes from B.B.'s guitar and the band's low, dark drone, and that sprinkling of tinny notes from Ike Turner's piano, create a noirish ambiance and sustain it through the entire three minutes, three seconds. But the mood is heightened by the forceful personality in B.B.'s singing. Sounding by turns desperate, anguished, and lonely, he infuses every line with character in a way that had been suggested but never fully realized in his earlier recordings. He's so in command, in fact, that he even steps out of character after he sings the lyric, "I'm going down to the bowling ground," and says to the listener, "That's where the mens hang out at," a nifty dramatic device designed to bring the listener into B.B.'s confidence and win him or her over to his point of view.

(B.B. has never explained this almost surreal line about the "bowling ground," or why it's a place where "the mens hang out at." In his original version, Fulson sings, "I'm gonna jump outta boat and drown," so perhaps the explanation for B.B.'s colorful interpolation is that he simply misunderstood what Fulson was singing.)

In Arnold Shaw's book *Honkers and Shouters*, Joe Bihari recalled the YMCA "studio" as being "a large room with an out-of-tune upright piano." At the same session that yielded B.B.'s "3 O'Clock Blues," Bihari also cut sides by Roscoe Gordon, Johnny Ace, Bobby "Blue" Bland, "and possibly Ike Turner." Bihari, though, was unhappy with Newborn, Jr.,'s work on piano. "It just wasn't happening," he told Shaw. "During the break someone started playing piano. I said, 'That's what I want to hear,' so I paid off Phineas, and Ike Turner finished the session."

B.B. himself has a vivid recollection of his career-making session. As he sang, he thought of how much he loved Fulson's version, "but how I wanted to put my own hurting on that beautiful song. For reasons I can't remember, we recorded in an empty room in the YMCA on Lauderdale and Vance. We used two Ampec [sic] reel-to-reel tape recorders, and of course it was recorded mono with no editing. Make a mistake and start over. We did it in two takes. Richard Sanders and Billy Duncan were on saxes, Johnny Ace on piano [Author's note: B.B. contradicts Bihari's account], and Earl Forrest on drums. … I give lots of room to Lucille, who's featured as much as me.

"I can feel Lucille coming into her own; she's finding her soul. At the start of the song she grabs your attention and she also solos in the middle. At the conclusion I sing, 'Good-bye, everybody, I believe this is the end … you can tell my baby to forgive me for my sins.' The mood is sad as suicide. To me, it's pure blues with the only two voices, mine and Lucille's, trading laments. It sounded sincere to me. I know it sounded good to Jules Bihari 'cause he released it as my seventh single. The others didn't go anywhere. This one went to the top."[26]

Indeed. Released in December 1951, "3 O'Clock Blues" found a nationwide audience quickly; by February 2, 1952, it was sitting atop the *Billboard* R&B chart, where it stayed for five weeks; in toto, it had a 17-week chart run. Everything was set up for B.B. to complete his long journey out of the Mississippi Delta, out of the privations of poverty if not the humiliations of segregation and racism, and into a fruitful life as a musician and entertainer.

B.B.'s fulfillment as a musician wasn't translating to harmony in his private life. Eight years of marriage to Martha ended in 1952, when she filed for divorce. Frustrated and left lonely by B.B.'s ever-quickening touring pace, and jealous of the adoration female fans showered on her husband, Martha had had enough. And B.B. couldn't blame her. "There was more disappointment than bitterness," he said. "I still loved her and cherished her ways. But I couldn't stay home and, as our disagreements increased, I couldn't stay faithful. The road became more than a distraction; it became my life."[27]

"More disappointment than bitterness" would be the most accurate characterization of B.B.'s next divorce, from WDIA, in 1953. The station had been good for B.B. in more ways than he could have imagined when he joined it, but he had been good for it, too. In pitching the cure-all elixir Pepticon, he had proven himself an effective on-air salesman; eventually, his persuasive personality attracted the attention of Lucky Strike cigarettes, which began running 15 minutes of spots on B.B.'s show, thus paving the way for other national advertisers to come onboard.[28] Sebastian Danchin's research indicates that WDIA led all other independent radio stations in the '50s in numbers of national advertisers, an achievement related directly to the drawing power of the Beale Street Blues Boy. But in a bit of well-intentioned deception, WDIA overplayed its hand with Lucky Strike and lost the account. With B.B. on the road so much of the time, it became impossible for him to keep up his live broadcast schedule. So the station began airing prerecorded shows, trying to create the illusion that B.B. was in the studio doing his thing, which worked beautifully until a Lucky Strike rep found out that B.B. was in fact working off-site, prompting the advertiser to sever its contract with the station. B.B. and station management came to a mutual but respectful parting of the ways, and he was replaced on the air by his buddy Rufus Thomas, who in turn used his WDIA platform as a springboard to national success as a recording artist and performer.

In the years immediately following his breakout with "3 O'Clock Blues," B.B. acquired the accoutrements of a successful touring attraction, namely booking agents with clout, bandleaders and arrangers with experience and smarts, and money, lots of money by his standards at the time.

With the help of local promoter Robert Henry, B.B. signed on with Universal Attractions in New York City, which paired B.B. with Tiny Bradshaw's 18-piece big band (B.B.'s band was taken over by Johnny Ace) and set out to book B.B. into the nation's four most prestigious venues for black artists—the Howard Theater in Washington, the Royal in Baltimore, the Apollo in New York City, and the Regal in Chicago. On national tours his paydays rose to $2,500 a week after starting at $1,000 a week, the latter being a staggering sum in his experience, the former almost incomprehensible.

Unsurprisingly, even the *über*-disciplined B.B. King found himself intoxicated by his suddenly fat wallet. He spent money on women, he spent money on clothes, he spent money on jewelry (one purchase he was proud of: a ring with the initials B.B. set in diamonds), he bought a white Cadillac, and he indulged a growing fondness for gambling. "I ... made money, lost money on gambling, pawned jewelry, stopped gambling, got the jewelry out of hock, and started all over again."[29] Self-indulgence didn't cloud B.B.'s thinking completely: he took some of his largesse and bought his father a 147-acre farm outside Memphis. B.B. envisioned that one day it would provide sanctuary for his entire family: "I suppose I was dreaming how one day we all might live on the farm. As long as there was a King, he or she would have shelter and food."[30]

When he wasn't on national tours performing in front of Tiny Bradshaw's band, B.B. was back home playing one-nighters, often with Bill Harvey's band backing him. A local legend among Memphis musicians, Harvey was, in B.B.'s estimation, "the George Washington of Memphis musicians ... a brilliant bandleader and arranger and tenor saxophonist." Working with Harvey was "a thrill and an education. Like Luther Henson, Bill was a patient teacher. He could have written me off as a know-nothing newcomer, but he gave me respect and, even more importantly, taught me to respect my talent."[31]

In 1953 and 1954, B.B., backed by Harvey's seven-piece band, toured ceaselessly as "B.B. King Featuring the Bill Harvey Band," booked by Don Robey's Houston, Texas–based Buffalo Booking Agency. Robey was a black businessman with a tough reputation who later bought and operated the Peacock label, its roster dotted with formidable artists such as Bobby "Blue" Bland, Johnny Otis, Johnny Ace, Big Mama Thornton, and others. In a record industry dominated by white owners, Robey was among the pioneering black entrepreneurs who paved the way for Berry Gordy, Jr.'s Motown and Sam Cooke's SAR labels. (And, on a less illustrious note, B.B. King, who in his career has twice founded, and quickly dispensed with, two labels, Blues Boy Kingdom in 1956 and Virgo in 1968.)

Nineteen fifty-five brought B.B. to another pivotal point in his life in music, when ill health, stemming from excessive drinking, forced Bill Harvey into retirement. Although he would never stop learning from others as his career progressed, B.B. knew his apprenticeship was over: it was time to put together his own touring band, it was time to heed a call he had been hearing to be independent, not to rely on someone else for his livelihood. Driven, as always, by the circumstances of his raising, he returned to Memphis, where he consulted with a financial expert and then made his move: after assembling a band, he bought a bus for touring purposes.

B.B. onstage at the Trianon Ballroom, Chicago, in 1963.

"My goals were to try to make a name and try to make some money," B.B. said. "I was born on a plantation and things weren't so good. We didn't have any money. I never thought of the word 'poor' 'til I got to be a man, but when you live in a house that you can always peek out of and see what kind of day it is, you're not doing so well. And your restroom is not inside the house. I always wanted something better. So when I put the first band together, I thought that things would be better 'cause I had seen people that were doing better."[32] With a few more hit singles behind him, B.B.'s rate went up and he was able to add more pieces to the band, eventually touring with a 12-piece group that included brass. His fondness for the big-band sound was now realized in his live shows as well as on record.[33]

"I've had a band ever since," B.B. said. "In my prejudiced opinion, the B.B. King bands have been good, giving me that snap I need, playing a mix of jazz and blues that sets the right tone for my show. The horns give me the harmonies I first heard in church, and the rhythm section locks me into grooves that satisfy my soul. My bands have also instructed me. Dozens of musicians, many of them far better than me, have passed through."[34]

"It just caught the atmosphere of the time."

John Broven on the breakthrough of "3 O'Clock Blues"

In listening to the Bullet recordings and the first recordings at Sun, could you have seen "3 O'Clock Blues" coming, given the development?

I couldn't, no. I think it's a record that Sam Phillips wouldn't have made. The song originally came from Lowell Fulson, so it was an established song. I think Colin Escott made a very good point in the [Ace] booklet in that it didn't have a hook, but it was all mood. And it just caught the atmosphere of the time. And there's that phrase, I don't have it exact, about "the boys down at the bowling ground." I have asked B.B. and his manager what does that mean, and I really haven't got a clear answer. But it's just one of those things that just comes out of nowhere. Maybe that's the hook of the song!

I'm impressed by the maturity B.B. shows on that recording, given what we had heard up to that point. It's almost like night and day to me. And I just don't know where it came from, that he was suddenly that guy on "3 O'Clock Blues." You wonder, Is that just the way it happens? That suddenly the switch goes on and you have this remarkable performance that doesn't seem to have a precedent in his previous recordings?

It's such an important record. Not only did it make No. 1, but it stayed in the charts for four, five months. It was a genuine hit, in other words. It was not hype. It just sold and sold and sold. So, yes, a really important record.

Two other important things about that record. It was recorded at the YMCA and was not state of the art by any means, and I think that in a funny way contributed to that recording. It's got this muddiness that added to the atmosphere. I think it's fairly well accepted that Johnny Ace was the pianist on the initial takes of the song, which unfortunately don't survive. But then Ike Turner came in and provided the underpinning on the piano. It's very interesting, isn't it, that Joe Bihari, and possibly B.B., we don't know, realized it wasn't working? It almost happened by accident. It's not as if they had something which they did know was going to happen and wasn't working and would be rejected if Ike hadn't come in and rescued them.

The story is he sent Phineas Newborn, Jr., home because he was dissatisfied with his playing. Which seems to have been given credence by Calvin saying his brother was "playing too much" at the sessions.

Right! Well, whether it was Newborn or Johnny Ace is still open, but Ike Turner did come in to save the day.

Chapter 4

PRE-ALBUM SINGLES:
AN ARTIST REVEALED

Between December 1951 and the end of 1958, when his first Crown album appeared, B.B. released 41 singles on the Modern subsidiary, RPM, which was formed in 1950 in response to distributors complaining to the Biharis that they couldn't handle all the releases coming from Modern. In 1953 the brothers had formed the Crown label as a singles line, eventually to evolve into a budget album label; Lester Bihari, with brother Joe helping out with the gift of Elmore James as an artist, launched the Meteor label in Memphis in 1952 and later introduced a country line under the Flair imprint, which evolved into a major R&B player. During that time B.B. had almost as many misses as hits—three consecutive singles bombed after the mammoth, chart-topping success of "3 O'Clock Blues" in late '51; four consecutive singles failed to chart following the 1953 No. 4 R&B hit "Please Hurry Home"—but when he made the charts, it was usually with a significant impact. Seventeen of these singles charted, some were double-sided hits, all but six were Top Ten R&B entries (in fairness, this number also includes his first two visits to the pop charts, with the June 1957 single, "Be Careful with a Fool" [No. 95], and the September 1975 item "I Need You So Bad" [No. 85], which perhaps should not be considered failures at all, given the discs' significance as B.B.'s first crossover chart recordings), four of them were No. 1 singles. He went from recording at the carpet-covered walls of the Memphis YMCA and in Tuff Green's acoustically dubious home to working in professionally outfitted facilities in Houston and Cincinnati as well as the Modern studios in Culver City, California, and, the state-of-the-art Capitol Studios in Los Angeles. In most cases, his hits found a permanent place in his repertoire—

it's the rare B.B. aficionado who can claim to have seen a full set of his in which he does not perform "Every Day I Have the Blues" or "You Upset Me, Baby" or "Sweet Little Angel"—and many of the misses have their intriguing moments that defy explanation as to why they weren't hits. Then there are B.B. oddities, fleeting, strange moments that reveal an unflattering side of his personality—either that or he's simply suspending his own moral code in order to give the audience what he thinks it wants to hear; or maybe, in the context of the times, he thinks he's being funny. On "That Ain't the Way to Do It," the flip side of "3 O'Clock Blues," near the end B.B. advises that if your woman's not doing right, "beat her three times a day and whup her late at night," articulating a strain of violence not uncommon in the blues but startling in the context of B.B.'s gentlemanly demeanor. Another such instance occurs in his reworking of Big Jay McNeely's "There Is Something on Your Mind" on 1993's *Blues Summit* album, when he advises an aggrieved man to extract payback with a baseball bat. In the original, unissued 1956 version of "Why I Sing the Blues," now available on the Ace box set, B.B. offers a caustic view of marriage, describing the wife as offering "the affection of a servant, the kindness of a slave, and the love of a dog," all the while being unfaithful to her mate. In a recording career spanning nearly 56 years as this is written, these prehistoric attitudes towards women and violent responses to marital strife are exceedingly rare, which makes them all the more jarring. What to make of it? The record shows 15 children by 15 women, two marriages resulting in two divorces (no cruelty or abuse charged by the former spouses, however), and a pronounced drive, if his autobiography is to be believed, for carnal knowledge of any woman he goes out with. Ultimately, it's safe to say that over the years B.B. has enjoyed the company of many women, in and out of bed, and the record shows only honorable conduct on his part (he has supported financially all of the children he has sired). Perhaps it's telling that when he re-recorded "Why I Sing the Blues" in 1969, he recast it as a powerful and scalding political statement about the unconscionable treatment of African-Americans through history rather than a misogynistic screed. In his later years, he continues to sing about bad luck in love affairs and bad women, but minus the harsh invective aimed at the distaff side in his younger, more impetuous years.

But there are more important things going on in B.B.'s pre-album singles than his unfortunate lapses into sexism. By far the key event of these years was the Biharis' hiring in 1954 of Maxwell Davis as a staff arranger-producer-musician-bandleader. Davis was a formidable figure in the West Coast music R&B scene, having accompanied live and on record the likes of Charles

Brown, T-Bone Walker, Johnny Moore and the Three Blazers, and Amos Milburn (for whom he arranged the signature hit "Chicken Shack Boogie"). He began working with B.B. in the studio, remained at his side through the entire tenure with Modern, and stayed on through the early '60s after B.B. signed with ABC-Paramount.

"His strength lay in his ability to create an easily recognizable ensemble sound that could also be subtly adapted to the personality of each artist it accompanied," Sebastian Danchin opines in assessing Davis's impact on B.B.'s development. "In King's case, this was all the easier because the musicians who worked with him onstage also came into the studio, directed by Davis and playing his scores. Another of his trademarks was the prominence given to sax players in the Coleman Hawkins mold, who always found a way to slip in a rasping solo between two verses."[1]

In his autobiography, B.B. is even more explicit about what Davis contributed to his music, referring to him as "the man most responsible for my best work," praising him for being able to "write, think, and adapt," and likening him to his childhood mentor, Luther Henson—"a loving teacher."[2]

More to the point, the always nattily attired, handsome Davis ("he looked like Nat King Cole and dressed just as sharp") knew how to take the ideas B.B. heard in his head and turn them into vibrant musical arrangements. "Maxwell had a sound—lean, clean, the perfect complement to my blues," B.B. said. "I'd come in from the road with a tape of something I was writing, and within minutes Maxwell would punch out a chart that expressed the soul of the song. He amazed me. He always left room for Lucille, understanding so well how she and I worked together. He wrote a chart of 'Every Day I Have the Blues' with a crisp and relaxed sound I'd never heard before. I liked it so well, I made it my theme. . . . Maxwell Davis didn't write majestically; he wrote naturally, which was my bag. He created an atmosphere that let me relax."[3]

To Escott, writing in the Ace booklet, B.B. succinctly summarized the difference between his two important musical mentors. "Bill Harvey, great musician that he was, didn't take the time with me that Maxwell did. Maxwell would school you a bit on what he'd do. He'd make you talk, tell him what you had in mind and you'd make a beautiful marriage."[4]

"Every Day I Have the Blues" is a good case study of Maxwell's style. The arrangement is as B.B. described: lean, clean, relaxed, with plenty of room for some jaunty single-string commentary from Lucille that meshes beautifully with the swinging horn section. Then B.B. comes in vocally, using all his tools, from straightforward, conversational crooning to a high, crying register that dips down into a throaty moan. On the instrumental break, the symmetry between the pounding drums, the swaying horns, and the stinging guitar solo is breathtaking in its conception and execution. A Memphis Slim recording from 1948 that was never a hit for Slim, "Every Day I Have the Blues" was a slow grooving 1950 hit for Lowell Fulson that influenced B.B.'s approach, but its best-known version was by Count Basie, with big-voiced Joe Williams singing lead. Basie had a hit with it twice, the last time coming in 1955, the same year B.B.'s version peaked at No. 8 on the R&B chart (its B-side, "Sneaking Around [with You]," peaked at No. 14). According to Colin Escott, Slim was unperturbed by the failure of his recording of his own song: "The composer royalties ... were sufficient to buy a Rolls-Royce with which to squire himself around Paris." The session was recorded at Capitol's old studio on Melrose Avenue, which Joe Bihari insisted had "a better sound" than the company's new studio in its striking new tower in downtown L.A. "We jacked B.B.'s guitar straight into the board, so it sounded a little different."[5]

The previous fall, October 1954, had seen B.B. hit No. 1 again, with another magnificent Davis arrangement on "You Upset Me Baby," a song inspired in part by Amos Milburn's "Hold Me Baby." A bright, buoyant shuffle, the song announces itself with the horns blasting a sputtering series of ascending chords, followed by a stop-time figure that sets the stage for Lucille to enter with a swinging, top-strings response before she's joined by the entire orchestra. B.B. alternates between crying out the verses and almost speaking the title refrain, which he articulates as "you upsets me, baby," very matter-of-fact in his tone, adding a humorous edge to a song that seemed to be praising his woman's virtues, especially those of a physical nature (the song opens with B.B. reciting her measurements), but in the end finds him either intimidated or threatened by her beauty, yet another nuance to consider in considering B.B.'s mindset vis-à-vis the female of the species.

A key record for B.B. came with the August 1952 chart-topping success of "You Know I Love You," his fourth RPM single following "3 O'Clock Blues"—and his first chart record of any kind in the wake of his breakthrough success. Puzzling, this, because it's not as though the other singles were puny performances. A well-traveled jump blues, "Shake It Up and Go" offers a blazing rhythm track, frenetic sax work by, presumably, Richard Sanders, a spiky, propulsive guitar solo by B.B., and an engaging, party-down vocal. A Doctor Clayton song, "Gotta Find My Baby," has some spirited guitar work by B.B. as well as his earnest vocal to recommend it. "Some Day, Somewhere," a reworking of Lowell Fulson's "Midnight Showers of Rain," is a low-down blues lament with an impassioned, pleading vocal from B.B. supported by his

In a trade photo published in 1954, B.B. is flanked by Modern Records co-founder Joe Bihari (left), influential Los Angeles disc jockey Hunter Hancock (near right) and an unidentified onlooker. Hancock is presenting B.B. with an award commemorating the success of his previous seven RPM releases. At the time of this photo, B.B.'s current RPM single was "Love Ya Baby" b/w "The Woman I Love."

own steely lower-strings soloing. By far the most interesting of these recordings is the B-side of "Shake It Up and Go," Muddy Waters's "It's My Own Fault, Darlin'" (aka "It's My Own Fault"). The officially released single is distinguished by B.B.'s electrifying soloing, which makes more dramatic use of short, clipped phrases and bends than he had to date, and with the imaginative pianist Lloyd Glenn stepping up with some evocative piano accompaniment. A more compelling performance of this song was never released commercially, but is available on the Ace box set.

Recorded at Tuff Green's house in Memphis, it gets off to a fiery start with a rush of heavily distorted chording on B.B.'s part, and then, discreetly, a vibraphone surfaces (apparently played by Onzie Horne, a WDIA music director who would go on to become an arranger for Isaac Hayes), adding a dark, chiming effect to the arrangement. Then B.B. comes in vocally, crying almost at the top of his range, singing looser and freer than he ever has in the studio to date and shouting encouragement to the band on the instrumental break. The version released on RPM single 355 is more polished and more restrained in every way—an admirable professional recording—but the raw intensity of the session at Tuff Green's house works on a gut level that wouldn't be so manifest on a B.B. King record until 1963, when he was taped live at Chicago's Regal Theatre.

"You Know I Love You" is a showcase for B.B. the crooner, as his guitar is not audible, if he's playing it at all. But the horns' steady hum and Ike Turner's piano, with its languorous, rolling right-hand fills, establish a sensuous ambiance for B.B.'s plaintive plea to a woman who's left him heartbroken and still very much in love with her. Singing sweet and tender, B.B. ascends most elegantly into a poignant near-falsetto in the chorus, his misery nearly palpable. The sincerity of his reading of the lyric "When night begins to fall / I wish I could hold you in my arms" surely struck a responsive chord with his female fans who dreamed of their own beaus articulating such romantic yearnings.

Despite its title, B.B.'s next No. 1 single, 1953's "Please Love Me," was not a sensitive ballad, but a big, bold jump blues keyed by a fierce, raw Elmore James–style slide effect, except that B.B. couldn't play slide—as Escott points out in the Ace booklet, B.B. clearly had perfected his perpendicular-to-the-neck vibrato by this point, as his solos employing this effect are jolting.

In mid-'56 a new song entered B.B.'s standard repertoire and remains there still. "Sweet Little Angel" made its way to B.B. via the original version written and recorded by Louise Bogan in 1930 and subsequently reinterpreted by Tampa Red and, in 1949, by Robert Nighthawk, the latter recording being the inspiration for B.B.'s version. Titled then as "Sweet Black Angel," it underwent a lyrical transformation in B.B.'s hands, although the suggestive opening sentiment, "Got a sweet little angel / I love the way she spreads her wings," survived intact, and the story goes on to recount the object of B.B.'s affection always giving him more than he asked for—a $20 bill when he asked for a nickel; a whiskey still when he asked for money for a drink of liquor—until the twist at the end, when he reveals that he's not sure she's really in love with him. Two versions of the song were recorded, the hit single track being cut at a radio station in Little Rock, Arkansas, featuring B.B.'s down 'n' dirty road band in an arrangement that spotlights a pulsating horn line, steady-rolling piano soloing, and B.B.'s taut treble runs. Those runs are in the version released on his first Crown album, *Singin' the Blues*, but they're better developed and smoothly integrated into the arrangement, which is more sedate—bluer, in a word—than the road band's version. The horns stay almost muted here, pumping steadily but with subtlety in the background, an ideal complement for the ambitious guitar soloing, which incorporates single-string runs, flurries of speed-picked notes on the lower strings, and some utterly piercing string bending that leaves a howling note hanging in the air for a split second before resolving into another run of notes. Also, B.B. altered the original ending to close on a positive rather than uncertain note: in response to inviting his woman to "go out and have a good time," she buys him a Cadillac Deville. Of course, the simpatico arrangement, with all the elements properly dispersed in their universe, is by Maxwell Davis.

"He Had That Knack of Communicating Through His Lyrics"
A Conversation with John Broven

When you get an overview of the pre-album singles era in B.B.'s career, what do you hear about him as an artist in terms of his big three attributes—the songwriting, the singing, the guitar playing?

This is very important. It's interesting that immediately after "3 O'Clock Blues" the next three records just bombed, nothing happened to them at all. It wasn't until "You Know I Love You" came along that the momentum was restored. Everyone talks about "3 O'Clock Blues," but "You Know I Love You" was a very important record because it restored him as a chart act. You have to remember in those days that the records were important because artists earned their money by playing gigs and by touring. B.B. was known as a touring artist, and in a sense needed these regular hit records to keep him at the top of the pole. So I think "You Know I Love You" is important from a hit point of view in restoring that momentum, but it also shows, I think, a very underrated side of B.B., and that's the quality of his singing. This is almost a blues ballad, a nice melody, but it showed the sweet side of his singing, and already, for such a young artist, maybe he was showing that maturity.

When I did research for the B.B. box, I thought it would be nice to get the viewpoint of one of his fans. I spoke to Bobby Hebb's sister in Nashville, who I'd known had been to B.B. concerts in the '50s. It was quite interesting to get a woman's perspective, if you like. She said every show they attended they wore white gloves, hats, dressed to the nines, it was like going to church. It was like a fashion parade. But the other thing was it was like B.B. was talking to them, and it was the lyrics of the songs that were important. A song like "You Know I Love You" had that immediate sentimental impact. Another one was "Did You Ever Love a Woman." You can just imagine the women in the audience would be screaming and shouting. So he had that knack of communicating through his lyrics. And I put that knack to him starting off as being a disc jockey. To be a good disc jockey, which he clearly was, you had to have that ability to communicate, so that helped him to appreciate what was required to get to an audience, and he translated that to his songs.

That's a good point. In looking back over B.B.'s songwriting, how much of his skill can you attribute to that period where he was a disc jockey, listening to records and how they were constructed and the language of those records" He was fluent in the blues idiom as a writer, very early on; maybe not on the Bullet recordings, but there's a couple of passages even on those songs that are interesting. When he gets to recording with Sam Phillips and into the Modern era, the singles era, there's some phrases that really jump out. And it's not like he had a lot of book learning. He had learned how to write a blues song, how to write a ballad, how to write a jump blues.

The other interesting thing about songs is that it really wasn't until we got into the box set that we saw how many of the songs had blues roots. A lot of them were derived from other artists' songs, particularly those of Doctor Clayton, an artist whose time had been and gone; they were forgotten figures. And yet B.B. obviously knew them through the disc jockey days and remembered their records. Certainly Doctor Clayton, I don't think there's any doubt at all, in the higher register influenced B.B.'s vocal style very much. So yes, there's lots of things about that WDIA disc jockey era that are really fundamental to B.B.'s greatness. He was also a great listener, wasn't he? And skilled at interpreting what he heard and actually developing that into his own style.

Do you hear in those singles a steady arc of growth through those years?

I think he was very lucky. After the Sam Phillips recordings, he was finding his way and he had "3 O'Clock Blues" and then immediately he had to go out on the road. That's when he really left Memphis, when "3 O'Clock Blues" put him on that Southern circuit. The band he went with was Bill Harvey's Orchestra. You know Bill Harvey, I know Bill Harvey, Bobby Bland knows him, Junior Parker. But he's one of the great forgotten heroes, really. The musicianship that Harvey was able to provide gave B.B. that kick-start and all of a sudden it took him out of that routine, 12-bar blues and gave his music a bit of swing sensibility, jazz sensibility, with a strong rhythm section behind him. So he was lucky, I think, with Bill Harvey, and then of course Maxwell Davis came into the picture, and he worked steadily with B.B. throughout the Modern era, right through the albums, and even came back and did some work with him on ABC. He just gave that sophisticated sound that showed how sophisticated an artist B.B. really was. He and Maxwell just meshed perfectly.

I believe that from a young age B.B. heard a bigger blues for himself. Bill Harvey was one step on the road to realizing that sound in a live setting. But in the studio, if B.B. himself is to be believed, Maxwell Davis was able to translate the ideas B.B. wanted to express musically, and then add his own touch, especially with the horns.

Very much so. It's interesting going back to the big band, and to re-emphasize—I really got this from talking to George Coleman, who was with B.B.'s band and went on to play with Miles—just how big a jazz town Memphis was, and B.B. was part of that. Of course he had his roots in Mississippi with the down-home blues and the gospel, of course, and it all meshed together. I suppose it could have gone either way, but I think what Maxwell Davis did was to put B.B. in a very sophisticated environment that he could just react to. Listen to one of my favorite songs, "Sweet Little Angel." It's a traditional blues song, but B.B. just somehow turned it into his own song with the band. But what's interesting about that recording is that it was a minor hit, but it wasn't the version with Maxwell Davis's band; that only appeared on the Crown LP. The single version—both of them are on the box set—was recorded on location with his road band. The difference is quite alarming in a sense. The one with the road band is fairly crude; it wasn't the smooth outfit that Maxwell Davis had with those great musicians.

Chapter 5

THE CROWN ALBUMS

Even though B.B. King became a prolific album artist during his tenure with the Biharis—12 LPs released between 1957 and 1963—the singles market was still robust and, in the case of a musician whose liveli-hood rested on him remaining a solid draw as a touring act, vital to B.B.'s prosperity. B.B. King coming to town with a new hit single under his belt was a combination that kept his booking agency busy and consequently kept B.B. and his band in greenbacks.

In 1958 B.B. had a No. 9 R&B hit with a beautiful ballad, "Please Accept My Love." In a style typical of the era, it features B.B.'s plaintive vocal way up front, supported by the Vocal Chords' feathery, overdubbed background hums, with his single-string soloing buried way down in the mix. Vocally, B.B. gives a mag-nificent performance, pouring emotion into his readings, rising into a near-falsetto at the end of lyric lines, stretching out syllables to create tension, and overall projecting a deep connection to the lyrics' emotional content. Recorded two years after B.B.'s lush 1956 love ballad "On My Word of Honor" (No. 3 R&B), "Please Accept My Love" shares the earlier single's heightened romanti-cism, lovely orchestral arrangement, and pop-ish vocal chorus. ("On My Word of Honor" was co-written, pseudonymously, by the Platters' producer, Buck Ram, and was eventually released by the Platters, whose version charted lower than B.B.'s as an R&B item but was a Top 20 pop hit.) But its standout quality is a mesmerizing vocal performance by B.B. that once again underscores not only his superior technical command as a vocalist, but also the degree to which he could meld a conscious stylistic approach to pure, unadulterated feeling, com-municating a belief in the words he was singing to a degree that hit listeners right where they lived, immersing them in his passion while skillfully masking the careful thought he had given to the song's narrative arc.

"Please accept my love," as a sentiment, had quite a bit of resonance for B.B. in 1958. He had fallen in love again, deeply so, with eighteen-year-old Sue Carol Hall, whom he had met during a gig at her mother's nightclub, Club Ebony, in their native Indianola. Despite the burden of being a single parent, she had attended college and was well read. Her lively intellect struck a chord in the semiliterate B.B. She took an interest in his business affairs and counseled him to take his obligations to the IRS seriously and to keep better records of his financial transactions. "Like her mama, she had a good head for business and wasn't afraid to show her ambition," B.B. said.[1] That ambition included going on the road with B.B., a notion he found "a little intimidating. The road, after all, was my private territory, where I'd always done what I wanted. The road was my turf."[2] But Sue didn't want to stay home and wait for her man to come back from the grind. "I want to be your wife and be with you wherever you are. I love you, B," she told him.[3]

In June of 1958, at B.B.'s insistence, the couple traveled to Detroit, to be married by his favorite preacher, the Reverend C.L. Franklin, father of the future Queen of Soul, Aretha Franklin, in a ceremony at the Gotham Hotel attended by a couple of witnesses, with drummer Sonny Freeman, "my mainstay for 17 years," at B.B.'s side.[4]

Touring with Sue's child proved difficult, though. Less than a year after their marriage, she told B.B. she wanted to relocate to Southern California, which, after little thought, B.B. agreed to do. His father had moved his family to the Golden State earlier, so B.B. purchased a house near Albert's, in South Pasadena, a Los Angeles suburb. The living was easy, the weather mild, the family close by, and the music and recording businesses only a short drive down the freeway.

As Sebastian Danchin observes, "For a rootless person like [B.B.], owning a home symbolized both social success and a happy family life. Since his divorce from Martha, he had been content to live in apartments in Memphis, spending his money on clothes, instruments, and transport for his band, not to mention indulging his passion for gambling. With the Los Angeles house, he was finally allowing himself to think of his own needs, and giving tangible shape to his rise in the world; in ten years, an orphaned farmworker from Mississippi had become famous, made a career for himself, and started a family. He seemed unstoppable."[5]

"Please Accept My Love" would become a concert evergreen for B.B., as would his next hit single, the No. 2 R&B hit from 1960, "Sweet Sixteen, Pt. 1."

Penned by Atlantic Records co-founder Ahmet Ertegun and recorded for Atlantic in 1952 by Big Joe Turner, this production builds from a whisper to a triumphant shout, with Lucille way up front co-starring with B.B.'s vocal— truly a complementary voice to his own, as B.B. has always described her— and alternating between terse single- or double-note expressions of concern or speed-picked, multiple-note subtextual runs. The horns ease in on the second verse and sway gracefully until the finale starts and the whole affair takes flight, morphing into a full-bore revival, complete with a gospel call-and-response finale that has B.B. shouting his closing lyric line to the point where his voice is figuratively into the red, almost cracking.

When B.B. King albums started appearing in 1957, with the initial release being a powerful compilation of previously issued singles titled *Singing the Blues* (its awe-inspiring lineup of tunes included "Please Love Me," "You Upset Me Baby," "Every Day I Have the Blues," "3 O'Clock Blues," "You Know I Love You," and "Sweet Little Angel," among others), the long-player was issued as part of Modern's budget series on the Crown label, which retailed in some areas for as little as 99 cents. The packaging contained little information—no personnel listings; generic gee-whiz liner notes that were reprinted on several other albums or were dispensed with altogether in favor of a list of available Crown releases—but did not skimp on cover art, which was uniformly striking. The Biharis favored dark, bold colors, eye-catching typefaces, and, for the most part, appealing photos of B.B. captured in relaxed poses, usually with Lucille in his arms or at his side, and sporting a winning smile on his handsome face. The *King of the Blues* album featured an inspired bit of design showing a wispy plume of smoke rising from the cigarette between B.B.'s fingers and forming a slight haze over the album title.

By this time in his career B.B. already had a mountain of songs to his credit as a writer. Some, as previously noted, were artful rewrites of earlier blues songs (which in some cases were rewrites of rewrites of an original song from antiquity); others were wholly original ideas on B.B.'s part. Only rarely did he work with a true collaborator, but hardly any of the songs bear a sole Riley B. King composer credit; rather, most are co-writes attributed to King–Jules Taub, King–Joe Josea, King–Sam Ling—all pseudonyms for the Biharis, who, in a common business practice that has not entirely disappeared in the music industry, took co-writing and publishing credits, and thus, according to Colin Escott in the Ace booklet, some 75 percent of the royalties that would normally have accrued to B.B. alone. To this B.B. had only a rhetorical but sarcastic comment to make to Escott, to wit: "I never met 'Taub' or 'Josea.' How could they write with me?"[6]

B.B. was even more perturbed by his albums being released on a budget label, sales of which were below the radar of the trade magazines' chart reporting. Despite the albums selling impressively, they never made a dent in the charts. "They went for 99 cents," B.B. complained to Escott. "*Billboard* didn't recognize them. We got no recognition at all. That's what made me want to leave."[7]

His dissatisfactions with the business side of his music making didn't deter B.B. at all in the studio during these years. With Maxwell Davis ever present and fashioning their wondrous arrangements, B.B.'s Crown albums feature some extraordinary music. And by this juncture B.B. is so accomplished in all the aspects of his artistry—guitarist-singer-songwriter—that even an ill-conceived project such as *Twist with B.B. King* (the title alone is a dead giveaway as to its intent to capitalize on a current dance craze, and the music is suitably shallow) contains within its grooves occasional moments when B.B. asserts himself to a degree that jolts the proceedings out of their doldrums. In addition to Davis being on his team, B.B. also had an impressive lineup of musicians spurring him on the album sessions, some of whom he had been using since 1954 and who were as respected in the jazz world as they were in R&B. Among these were pianist Lloyd Glenn, whose lengthy résumé included a productive stint with B.B.'s idol, Lowell Fulson; the redoubtable tenor saxophonists Plas Johnson and Bobby Forte; Jewell Grant on alto sax; Jake Porter on trumpet; Red Callender (a towering figure in the history of jazz bass, he had recorded in the '40s with Nat King Cole, Charlie Parker, Louis Armstrong, and Erroll Garner, among others, and owned the distinction of turning down offers to join both Duke Ellington's Orchestra and the Louis Armstrong All-Stars) and Ralph Hamilton on bass; and drums manned by either Sonny Freeman, Jessie Sailes, or New Orleans legend Earl Palmer.

These LPs afforded B.B. and Maxwell Davis, sometimes at the Biharis' urging, to address current musical trends, always in search of the elusive hit. By the time B.B. became an album artist, rock 'n' roll was all the rage, and to black artists such as Little Richard, Fats Domino, and Chuck Berry, as well as numerous black vocal groups, the new musical craze had broken down some long-standing and emotionally charged barriers. "Race records," recordings by black artists marketed solely to black communities, were about to be consigned to history; the emerging teen pop culture had embraced music of no color but rather of sound, style, and attitude. For B.B., however, the critical distinction was that his music remained true to the blues and the blues audience. Its lyrics dealt with adult themes—the Everly Brothers could fret in song about staying out too late on a date in "Wake Up, Little Susie," but when someone didn't come home on time in a B.B. King song, bad things, sometimes life-altering things, happened. In a 1957 interview with *Hit Parader* magazine, B.B. made no bones about where he stood with respect to the rock 'n' roll audience. "We don't play for white people," he said. "Of course, a few whites come to hear us on one-night stands, but they are so few we never run into segregation problems. I'm not saying we won't play for whites, because I don't know what the future holds. Records are funny. You aim them for the colored market, then suddenly the white folks like them, then, wham, you've got whites at your dances. That's what happened to Fats Domino, [but] we don't play rock 'n' roll. Our music is blues, straight from the Delta. I believe we'll make it on that."

Time has proven him right, but at that point the Biharis were concerned about diminishing sales tallies for blues records. They suggested B.B. try something that came natural, such as ballads in a contemporary vein. He and Davis would take a stab here and there—sometimes with spectacular results, as with the moving, doo-wop-styled "I Love You So" on his third Crown LP, 1959's *B.B. King Wails*—but would always return to the blues fundamentals. That pattern has repeated itself throughout B.B.'s career—test the water, then get back to the blues (when funk began to take hold in the '70s B.B. experimented with wah-wah guitar on some album tracks, a disastrous move that didn't last long). "B.B. wasn't really selling to white audiences," Joe Bihari told John Broven. "With the ballads we were trying to get him into something else because we weren't selling blues."[8]

"The Biharis wanted to sell records," B.B. acknowledged, "but they didn't pressure me to do rock 'n' roll 'cause at the time I was still selling a lot of records, according to my standards. Forty, fifty, sixty thousand. Quite a few went eighty, ninety, hundred thousand."[9]

B.B.'s Crown albums are accessible only through Ace Records' ambitious reissue program. The label has undertaken to reissue all 12 Crown releases, and as this is written in September 2004, six of those dozen albums are back on the market, with another slated for release in November 2004 and another in the spring of 2005. In the States, Virgin, which has U.S. rights to the Modern recordings, has done a mediocre job of exploiting that treasure trove, confining itself to compilations of mostly familiar 1950s recordings, but it does have an important two-fer CD available featuring the first two albums, the towering *Singin' the Blues* and *The Blues*. The Ace packaging is far superior, with the album covers reproduced in brilliant color, the original liner notes reprinted when applicable, full release information (including dates of release, catalog numbers, 45 rpm releases by title and catalog number, and chart hits) and liner notes by John Broven that fill in the history of the album in the context of B.B.'s career and then-current musical trends.

A cursory look at the available titles is telling. These projects were proving grounds for the artist, who willingly tried his hand at new styles and at the same time stayed firm with the blues and, indeed, sought to expand the idea of what the blues could be, with the able assistance of Maxwell Davis and his crack musicians. In addition, the Ace reissues provide a broader context for the album cuts by containing an additional eight bonus tracks not on the original album but recorded near the same time as the album cuts, so that it's possible to come away with a clearer sense of where B.B. was headed stylistically at the time in question.

Singin' the Blues/The Blues

Flair/Virgin, 1991

As noted earlier, 1957's *Singin' the Blues* might well have been titled *Greatest Hits, Vol. 1*, for the inclusion of so many of B.B.'s career-establishing monuments, including "3 O'Clock Blues," "Please Love Me," "Every Day I Have the Blues," and "You Upset Me Baby." John Broven summarizes it best: *"Singin' the Blues* is almost a perfect compilation of the greatest hits of the time. I don't think any of the compilers since have come up with a better collection of songs than the Biharis came up with at the time. It's just one of the greatest compilations. And also it had a fabulous cover, showing B.B. in that checked jacket that he still talks about."[10] *The Blues* doesn't boast as many momentous tracks, but it does capture King and his stellar studio band in peak form on uptempo rousers ("Ruby Lee"), slow blues grinders ("Fast Day"), and breakneck boogie-woogie straight from the Kansas City school ("Boogie Woogie Woman," fueled by Willard McDaniels's boisterous piano solos).

B.B. King Wails

Crown, 1959; Ace, 2003

B.B.'s third Crown album was released in the wake of his R&B hit "Please Accept My Love." At a moment when the trend in blues, jazz, and pop was towards small combos, B.B. is heard here backed by a full, robust horn section (likely from his road band at the time, according to Broven's liner notes, which would include Johnny Board blowing a hearty tenor sax). The grinding opening track, "Sweet Thing," is a thinly disguised reworking

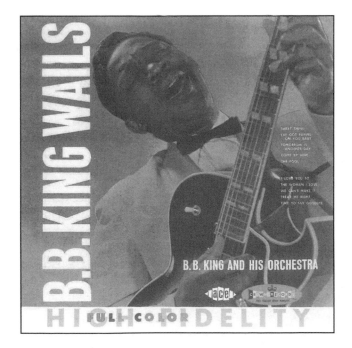

of "Sweet Sixteen," its opening lyric echoing the latter's "When I first met you baby," but continuing on with "you were just out of school," thus establishing the female's age as surely as "you were just sweet sixteen." Elsewhere the self-explanatory "I've Got Papers on You Baby," a boisterous jump blues, finds Maxwell Davis conjuring up a driving arrangement, ebullient horns, and multiple stop-time figures for added effect and B.B. checking in with a couple of tasty guitar solos to complement a hard-charging vocal that justifies the album title. The uptempo love ode "Come By Here" has a folk melody and a non-chorus structure reminiscent of the folk song that must have inspired it, "Kumbaya." In what surely was an intentionally humorous touch, the blues love ballad "The Fool" starts out as a typical song of its type, until suddenly, to jarring effect, a muted trumpet emerges, and returns at other points in the song, always blaring a mocking retort to B.B.'s impassioned pledge of love, as if to emphasize that the singer's devotion is, indeed, foolish. If "The Fool" suggests a jaundiced view of love, not so the beautiful doo-wop–influenced ballad that follows it, "I Love You So," a song that would have been ideal for any of the white or black group harmony outfits of the day. Here, though, the harmony parts are replaced by smooth, lilting horn lines and a robust, droning sax buttressing and punctuating B.B.'s sensitive crooning. It all works up to a stupendous closing crescendo that finds B.B. signing off with a soaring reading of the title sentiment, then shouting, "I mean *you*, baby!" The bonus tracks include a previously unissued blues ballad, "Yesterday," with an evocative arrangement weaving delicate flute lines through the melody. An unissued, unremarkable take of "Why I Sing the Blues" is here, and the disc closes with B.B.'s overdubbed vocals on tracks recorded by members of the Count Basie and Tommy Dorsey orchestras, with arrangements by Maxwell Davis. The Basie track is a somewhat restrained take on "Every Day I Have the Blues," B.B. handling the lyrics at a more deliberate, reflective pace than he did on his original recording; the latter is a sprightly, classic pop rendition of Dorsey's 1941 No. 4 pop hit, "Yes Indeed," which featured vocals by the great pop stylist Jo Stafford and the song's composer, Sy Oliver. Neither Basie nor Dorsey were present when their orchestras cut these tracks, and the Dorsey number features an uncredited female vocalist.

B.B. King Sings Spirituals

Crown, 1959; Ace, 2004

This long-awaited reissue is, arguably, the most valuable of all, as it represents the only gospel album B.B. has ever recorded to date—odd, given his

deep immersion in gospel as a child and the pronounced gospel feel in his singing. That Ace has performed a most valuable service in reissuing this album is borne out by the spirit and emotional commitment B.B. brings to these recordings. Backed by a standard church band of organ, piano, drums, and bass, and singing with either (or both) the Charioteers (a Los Angeles–based quintet that had recorded for the Riverside label in 1944) and the Southern California Community Choir (the original album credited the SCCC as the accompanying vocal group, but an overdubbed Kent single [No. 392, "Precious Lord" b/w "Army of the Lord"] acknowledged the accompanying vocalists as the Charioteers; the consensus at Ace is that both groups are likely present on the album, at different times). That said, the performances get the job done—this is spirit-raising music of a higher order. Thomas A. Dorsey's evergreen "Precious Lord" is given an appropriately stately treatment, whereas "Swing Low Sweet Chariot"/"Rock Me Lord" are rocking, hand-clapping exhortations, and "Jesus Gave Me Water" is infectiously celebratory. The band (with some inspired soul contributing bracing blues piano runs on "Save a Seat for Me") backs the singers solidly (and B.B.'s overdubbed Lucille is heard crying at the start of the string-enriched "Precious Lord"). B.B.'s singing is impassioned and thoughtful throughout, as might be expected of an artist so steeped in the gospel tradition and respectful of the songs' messages. His sophisticated approach to the lyric lines of "I Never Heard a Man" betrays more than a passing familiarity with Sam Cooke's rhythmic phrasing, and the song's swaying arrangement may well have been the inspiration for the Ray Charles hit "(Night Time Is) The Right Time." On "Save a Seat for Me" he delivers a wailing, blues-drenched reading that is positively jaw-dropping in its sustained intensity. And nothing in the B.B. catalog really prepares a listener for the fury and passion unleashed in his vocal scorching of "Army of the Lord"— working at the very limits of his vocal range, his voice takes on a throaty quality that makes him sound less like B.B. King than, say, Julius Cheeks of the Sensational Nightingales. A glorious sound it is, arising from performances of such conviction and passion that a thorough understanding of B.B. King as an artist is impossible without this album.

My Kind of Blues

Crown, 1960; Ace, 2003

An album that ages like fine wine and was powerful in its day as well, *My Kind of Blues* is the closest studio approximation of how B.B. must have sounded in some of the joints he played around the Memphis area with his small combo (granted, by 1960 he was a much more accomplished player and vocalist than he was in the '40s and early to mid-'50s, but the repertoire and approach are surely similar). The interesting backstory of this LP is that it was recorded in 1958 in the Chess studios in Chicago, when a disgruntled B.B. was pondering bolting Modern for a label that would not only pay him more, but would sell his albums at full price and place greater emphasis on packaging and marketing. The Biharis worked out a deal with Leonard and Phil Chess to buy the masters of those sessions, and with B.B. to bring him back to the Modern fold. The Chess sessions were then issued on Crown as *My Kind of Blues*. Backed by only pianist Lloyd Glenn, bassist Ralph Hamilton, and drummer Jessie Sailes, B.B.—true to the album title—essays eight of his favorite blues tunes and throws in a couple of his originals as well. The Ace reissue also contains eight bonus tracks recorded in the same style. The single version of Muddy Waters's "My Own Fault" is here (originally released in 1960 as the B-side of "Shake It Up and Go"), and B.B. took this occasion to pay homage to another of his idols, Peter Joe (Doctor) Clayton, on three Clayton-penned numbers, including the slow, mournful blues "Hold That Train"; "Please Set the Date," with a chugging arrangement and a melody reminiscent of Bill Doggett's huge instrumental hit from 1956, "Honky Tonk (Parts 1

& 2)"; and a pleading, mid-tempo version of the playful "Walking Dr. Bill." The latter B.B. puts over with a marvelously nuanced vocal that features shouting passages, some high-pitched hollers (à la the good Doctor himself), and some melismatic touches on key lyrics. (An overdubbed take of "Walking Dr. Bill" and an alternate take of "Hold That Train" are among the bonus tracks.) Glenn's tinkling piano support and a weary vocal by B.B. lend Cecil Gant's "Understand" a country flavor (B.B. rewrote this song as "Blues Man" on his 1998 Grammy-winning album, *Blues on the Bayou*); the stomping rhythm, swinging guitar solos, and carefree vocal bring a gospel feel to Sleepy John Estes's "Someday Baby"; Robert Petway's "Fishin' After Me" (aka "Catfish Blues") is an engaging shuffle with gospel overtones, with Sailes sounding like he's having the time of his life driving the whole affair down the road and B.B. playing the role of a jilted lover to the hilt. A bonus track, Ivory Joe Hunter's "Blues at Sunrise," alternates between dreamy passages and shouted choruses, with a beautiful B.B. guitar solo featuring soft, sustained notes rife with melancholy. A similar easygoing arrangement with dramatic interludes characterizes a sturdy treatment of Charles Brown's "Drifting Blues." All in all, *My Kind of Blues*, so aptly titled because it brings together songs by a multitude of artists whose work influenced B.B.'s style and sensibility, has a singular intimacy among the albums in B.B.'s catalog; never again would he enter a studio with such a spare lineup or record such stripped-down arrangements. Coming in 1960, though, the minimalist nature of the album illustrated how far B.B. had traveled—his guitar solos are marked by impeccable choices and showcase a superb use of dynamics and phrasing for effect, and the tools at his command vocally are even more impressive in a milieu that allows him greater latitude in playing a role. *My Kind of Blues* is the masterpiece of the Crown albums, and ranks with the best work in B.B.'s catalog.

King of the Blues

Crown, 1960; Ace, 2003

On his second album release of 1960, B.B. returned to the bigger sound Maxwell Davis and orchestra could provide for a long-player devoted large-ly to sensitive blues balladeering. If anyone hadn't taken notice yet, this album was a showcase for the masterful singer B.B. had become. On its orig-inal ten tracks, and the Ace reissue's additional eight bonus tracks, his expert deployment of sensuous, deeply felt phrasing, tonal shading, and melisma bespeak a heightened mastery of the nuanced vocal techniques that infuse a song with blood and heart. Perfectly attuned to the narratives' dramatic arc, Davis's arrangements are a powerful, intelligent complement to B.B.'s per-formances. The moaning horn line on "Long Nights (The Feeling They Call the Blues)" could not have been better cast to augment B.B.'s heartfelt vocal and tart guitar solos. The lush, poignant ballads "I'll Survive," "I'm King," and "If I Lost You" spotlight Davis's smart, imaginative horn charts, designed to lay on the hurt the songs describe, just as the driving arrange-ments of stompers such as "Good Man Gone Bad" lend those numbers some jet-age thrust. The bonus tracks include a striking reprise of "3 O'Clock Blues" notable for the interplay between organ, piano, and saxophone as B.B. delivers an emotion-wracked vocal and Lucille sends up wailing protests of her own. Whispering discreetly in the background, so much so that it's bare-ly audible, a saxophone becomes an indispensable element of the foreboding sound of Sonny Boy Williamson's (John Lee Williamson) "Million Year Blues," reworked and retitled "When My Heart Beats Like a Hammer," a ter-rific small-combo take on this warhorse. Overdubbing to update the sound, the Biharis issued a single version of Big Maceo's "Worried Life" in 1970 to capitalize on B.B.'s success with "The Thrill Is Gone." Cast as a hymn, with a somber, rumbling organ way out front and a female chorus moaning gospel-style chants that echo B.B.'s vocal lines with heartrending harmony, it

rose to No. 48 on the R&B chart, not a bad showing at all for the little label that could.

Easy Listening Blues

Crown, 1962; Ace, 2004

The title of B.B.'s all-instrumental tenth Crown album is not inappropriate, as it contains a fair share of mellow jams; but with the addition of some searing bonus tracks, it becomes quite a hot outing indeed. Notice the date—B.B. was already signed to ABC-Paramount at the time of release, indicating that this material was recorded, as John Broven points out in his liner notes, "in mammoth sessions over one or two days at the end of 1961 with a view to stockpiling masters prior to [B.B.'s] departure to ABC. The use of a small combo meant there was no need for intricate arrangements or extensive studio time." Broven believes the Biharis were inspired to cut an all-instrumental album on B.B. as a response to the success of an upstart blues picker from Texas, Freddie King. Inspired by B.B., Muddy Waters, and T-Bone Walker, Freddie had developed a style that was forceful and aggressive, blues picked hard (with a plastic pick on his thumb and a steel one on his forefinger, an

unusual technique he picked up from Muddy Waters's guitarist Jimmy
Rogers) on heavy-gauge strings. But he also possessed a keen sense of phrasing and an unerring feel for using space to heighten the effect of his solos. He
had a major hit in 1961 with "Hideaway," a rocking instrumental built on a
Hound Dog Taylor boogie and incorporating quotes from Jimmy McCracklin's
"The Walk" and Henry Mancini's "The Peter Gunn Theme," and he possessed
a restless drive to find new modes of expression within the blues framework.
B.B. would not experience similar success solely as an instrumentalist, as the
songs on *Easy Listening Blues* seemed less in tune with rock 'n' roll–era propulsion than with immediate postwar small-combo jump blues, even if the
Biharis tried to cash on in a current dance craze by retitling the song "Hully
Gully" as "Hully Gully Twist." Nevertheless, on the easy-listening cuts the
playing is relaxed and engaging, the mood languorous, and there's rarely a
track lacking captivating dialog between B.B.'s guitar and Lloyd Glenn's personable piano. One of two rarities here is a previously unreleased version of
"Boogie Rock," dubbed from a pristine 78 owing to the disappearance of the
master tape. With B.B. attacking a treble-strings boogie pattern with gusto
(actually, not unlike Freddie King) and Glenn joining the fray with an arpeg-

giated jig of a piano solo, Maxwell Davis steps in about midway and blows a ferocious sax solo amidst a wildly pumping horn arrangement. On the other hand, a more sedate "Talkin' the Blues" (which was discovered only during the research for this reissue; it was indicated as an "unknown" track in the Modern archives) features a breathtaking B.B. guitar workout rife with expressive artillery: sustained bent notes; slides and razor-edged, serpentine single-string runs; and double-string riffs comprise the colorful soloing B.B. contributes over Glenn's dramatic piano parts. He's either rolling off a right-hand riff or pounding an ostinato when B.B. takes flight ahead of a soaring Maxwell Davis–arranged blast of song-ending horns. Over a lively boogie riff led by Davis's bleating sax in "Three O'Clock Stomp," B.B. fashions a rhythmically compelling bottom-strings solo, setting the stage for Davis's gruff, protesting sax solo. Things proceed to an agreeable fadeout on a song with a bit of New Orleans flavor in its sound and style. Not a major entry in B.B.'s catalog, this album, but in terms of charting B.B.'s development it shows how disciplined he was in the small-combo lineup and features some of the most scintillating blues guitar-piano set-tos of its day.

Blues in My Heart

Crown, 1963; Ace, 2004

B.B.'s eleventh LP and first of two 1963 releases might well be seen as the vocal follow-up to the all-instrumental *Easy Listening Blues*. Like its predecessor, *Blues in My Heart* largely features slow blues shuffles and some assured vocalizing in a mellow mode. Plas Johnson is onboard to add some smoky sax solos and late-night ambiance; Maxwell Davis contributes some church-style organ fills here and there. Lucille is in full expressive voice but saying only what needs to be said—over the course of an album B.B.'s soloing had never been as consistently economical as it is here. And for a crash course on the proper and dramatic use of dynamics, the cut "I Need You" is the required textbook, as B.B. spins out both full potent lines and delicate fading runs on the upper neck. What has emerged as the key song here is "Downhearted," by Jane Feather, wife of the prominent jazz critic and producer Leonard Feather. Originally recorded by Johnny Moore's Three Blazers, it too is done at a steady, stately pace, its groove punctuated by B.B.'s stinging runs and wailing, sustained notes and Plas Johnson's beefy sax commentary. In 1964 B.B. re-recorded the song for ABC-Paramount with Sid Feller producing, Maxwell Davis updating his arrangement with more propulsion from the horn section, and B.B. investing his vocal with far more outrage than can be detected on the laidback original. Retitled "How Blue Can You Get," it became and remains a fixture in his live

shows, where the slow boiling fury he conjures during the litany of outrages he cites against his lover ("I bought you a ten-dollar dinner / you said thanks for the snack / I gave you seven children / and now you wanna give 'em back") gives way to a full-throated, gravelly shout at the end and a guaranteed eruption of applause and supportive cheers from the audience, all these years later.

B.B. King (later retitled The Soul of B.B. King)

Crown, 1963; Ace, 2003

On its face, B.B.'s final budget-priced album for the Biharis' Crown label would seem to have a couple of strikes against it from the outset. That is, its original ten tracks were recorded not only at different times, but in different eras. Some come from sessions recorded in late 1952 in Houston, with B.B.'s first bandleader, Bill Harvey, in charge. Others are of more recent vintage, including Maxwell Davis–produced sessions cut in 1959 and 1961. In terms of context, the earliest songs were laid down at the dawn of R&B's entrance into the mainstream and at the moment gospel music was entering what is widely regarded as its golden age, and rock 'n' roll was still a half-decade away from altering the universe. The later recordings were made when the rock 'n' roll pioneers were

either struggling, reinventing themselves, or had died, whereas R&B had firmly taken root in the mainstream and was about to birth a new baby called soul music. When he recorded with Bill Harvey in 1952, B.B. was still a year away from experiencing his first hit single and was still an artist developing a distinctive style; by the time of the 1961 sessions, he had become a steady presence on the R&B charts, had even sneaked into the lower regions of the pop charts, and was recognized by his peers for his gifts as a guitarist and vocalist. As for the blues, apart from the emergence of important artists such as Muddy Waters, Howlin' Wolf, and Freddie King, the span of years represented on these album tracks saw no change commercially for the genre: the music business still considered it "race" music made largely by black artists for the black community. At the time Crown released *B.B. King*, bluesmen, according to John Broven's reissue liner notes, "were either dusting off their acoustic guitars to join the folk-blues coffeehouse set, or resurrecting themselves as hip soul brothers," while B.B. "stuck to his chitlin' circuit blues roots."

Considering the span of time represented by the recordings assembled for *B.B. King*, the album is remarkably seamless. A listener coming to it with no knowledge of the recording history might consider the big-band swing of

"Sundown" to be dated, or retro, but only in the context of contemporary sounds and styles, not because it seems out of place here. A driving boogie instrumental, "Boogie Rock" (aka "House Rocker"), has a timeless quality that renders its recording date irrelevant; the Davis-produced blues ballad "Come Back Baby" (aka "Can't We Talk It Over") is another for-the-ages performance marked by a beautiful, pleading B.B. vocal, a mesmerizing, wailing sax solo from George Coleman, and right-there piano commentary courtesy Connie Mack Booker. The bonus tracks include homages to Sonny Boy Williamson II via a steady-rolling version of "Eyesight to the Blind," to Walter Davis and the ever-reliable Tampa Red on the swaying, sax-pocked ballad, "Green and Lucky Blues," and to Elmore James with a furious rendition of "Dust My Broom," keyed by an exuberant, shouting vocal by B.B. and some righteous guitar protestations. Although lacking a theme or mood to bind it together à la *My Kind of Blues* and *Easy Listening Blues*, *B.B. King* boasts admirable virtues in the quality of the singing and playing. Broven put it best in concluding his reissue liner notes by observing that despite the eclectic nature of the tune stack, "the compilation does stand up well musically, emphasizing yet again B.B.'s remarkable consistency throughout his 12 years with the Modern Records stable."

"He may have come out of the country, but he certainly is very sophisticated."
John Broven on the Crown Albums

When you listen to the Crown albums, do you hear a more ambitious approach than was typical of that time? Or are they very typical of the time, other than B.B. trying out a lot of different styles?

I think, first of all, the first Crown album, *Singing the Blues*, is almost a perfect compilation of the greatest hits of the time. . . . But then, I guess you could say the first concept album was the spirituals one, wasn't it? I haven't spoken to anyone about what the reaction was to that album, because at that time blues, gospel—ne'er the twain shall meet. Whether B.B. got any adverse reaction to that, I don't know. I haven't asked him.

Did B.B. resist the Biharis' efforts to get him more in step with the trends in mainstream music, especially rock 'n' roll?

I think he was very compliant. But if you look at his first two Top 100 hits, one was "Be Careful with a Fool," a straight-four ballad, and "I Need You Bad," those have nothing to do with rhythm and blues at all. Another famous record is "Bim Bam," which had a chanting female chorus. It's a record that B.B. says he hates. But that record is a great favorite with the young jivers in England—if you go to a rock 'n' roll club, don't be surprised if you hear "Bim Bam," and it fills the dance floor. It's got a terrific rhythm, just perfect for jiving, and a great sax solo by Plas Johnson. In effect it's a very commercial record. Now, I don't call that a bad record. So yeah, the Biharis were trying ballads, they were trying doo-wop— "Sneaking Around" and "Please Accept My Love"—and spirituals.

What's your sense of B.B.'s awareness of trends outside of the blues, and his need, if any, to respond? From time to time he seems to acknowledge a trend musically, and then move on with the blues, never trying too hard to capitalize. That pattern wasn't restricted to the Modern era; in the '70s, once he had finished the ride with "The Thrill Is Gone" and his sales had fallen off, he tried some funk stuff, playing wah-wah guitar, and it was fairly awful. He got back on track when he hooked up with the producer Stewart Levine, who took the essence of B.B. King, coupled it to the Crusaders, and made everyone notice B.B. again, fans and booking agents alike.

And extending that, he really hasn't followed up *Riding with the King*, has he? And that's when he went back to doing a basic blues record and sold about five million.

Why do you think that he never acknowledged the world outside of his own music to any great degree?

Throughout all of this, he's kept on the road and doing almost like traditional shows. He almost hasn't acknowledged his album projects to any great degree. When he made those albums with the Crusaders, onstage he was still playing the blues. I attribute this, again, to his background as a disc jockey who was so open to different sounds. Another thing I noticed, when I interviewed him, was what an intelligent man he is. You can just see it in his eyes. He may have come out of the country, but he certainly is very sophisticated. And it's that supreme intelligence that has enabled him to be a great guitar player and to absorb everything that's gone on around him. Other than his disc jockey work, the other thing that's important is that B.B. is renowned as a record collector. So it just didn't stop with what he was hearing on the radio or what was on the charts at the time. He certainly used to go into Dovell's jazz record shop in London and buy the place out! So he was a fan as well.

Are there Crown albums that stand out for you? I love My Kind of Blues. *Do you think we'll ever hear B.B. like that again?*

That's a classic. And no, I don't think we'll ever hear him like that again. That's just a magical record in every sense. The artwork, to start with, is stunning in my opinion, as all of them are. But they just had the right feel in the studio. I think Lloyd Glenn contributed a lot to that record with his piano, and then B.B. was stretching out on guitar. It was just a great coming together. It's my favorite. And then *Singing the Blues*, of course, with its collection of hits. Those two really stand out. You have to remember that the Crown label was a budget label, and it's a mass-marketing exercise. As we say in the booklet, we quote B.B. that he wasn't very happy with it. His main complaint was that budget albums weren't reviewed in *Billboard* or *Cash Box*. And the reason why was because there was so many of the damn things. There's just no way that the trade magazines could cover everything.

And didn't he get a lower royalty rate, because they sold for 99 cents or so?

That's right. That was the other thing that manifested itself as time went by—"My five percent or whatever is not what Muddy's getting." But B.B., I'm sure he knows but won't admit it, that the Crowns did him good. First of all, they were priced right for his fans. And the Biharis did have a great rack-jobbing operation; his LPs were everywhere. So from a PR point of view, the Crown albums got his name around. And it wasn't like it was shoddy artwork. The pressings were a little bit suspect, but the artwork was terrific. On the whole the compilations hold up pretty well. The whole Crown era was very interesting. I tend to think overall those Crown albums were a benefit to him. Certainly that's how we in Europe were first aware of B.B. because the singles hadn't been released there. But in the early '60s the import stores started to bring in the Crown LPs, and they could do it because they were budget priced and obviously the exchange rate and so on made them affordable—the LPs were priced no more than an average home product. All of a sudden here was this B.B. King album, and a lot of people were buying it under the radar, so to speak. Now the LPs were seeping out not only throughout the U.S. but certainly throughout Europe as well. That helped build up B.B.'s stature.

Chapter 6

"AIN'T NOTHING BUT A BUSINESS"

.B.'s thirteen-year association with Modern was mostly smooth, owing to the great trust that existed between the artist and the Bihari brothers, but B.B. did press his case for a better contract by threatening to bolt a couple of times. One such revolt occurred in 1953, when he agreed to a deal with Don Robey's Peacock label but signed with Modern after the Biharis offered to pay him $2,000 more than Robey had offered. As noted earlier, B.B. and Chess flirted with each other in 1958, until the Biharis again moved in with money and retained the artist and some recordings, including those that comprised the Crown album *My Kind of Blues*, and a single, "Recession Blues," a bit of social commentary released on the Kent label, which had supplanted RPM in 1958 and would continue to issue B.B. singles until its dissolution in 1972.[1]

With the Biharis failing to shape B.B. into a mainstream artist who could deliver the rock 'n' roll teen market—and, most important, the buying power it wielded and for which every pop label lusted—B.B. began looking at other possible musical homes. He considered, again, moving to Chess, but Willie Dixon, a blues giant whose songwriting, bandleading, and producing artistry were virtually without peer in his generation and had paid big dividends for the label, warned him away. "B.B. King once asked me about coming to Chess in the early 1960s when him and Chess were just about to get together," Dixon wrote in his autobiography. "I told B.B., 'Look, you'd be doing the wrong thing if you worked for Chess,' and he didn't get with him. I don't know whether I was the cause of it, but I knew damn well what Chess was doing to everybody else. Why the hell should you get on the same boat?"[2] (An eloquent defense of

Phil and Leonard Chess's accounting practices is offered in Nadine Cohodas's *Spinning Blues into Gold: The Chess Brothers and the Legendary Chess Records* [New York: St. Martin's Press, 2000]. The Chess brothers assert that many of the artists who have claimed they were cheated out of royalties over the years failed to mention that they were regular recipients of loans from the company when money got tight, or that their loans were repaid through deductions from royalties. In short, there are two sides to every story, and the Chess brothers, like most of the small-label entrepreneurs of the time, were willing to give when there was need, but also expected to get back as well.)

Taking the savvy Dixon's advice to heart, B.B. turned next to an early idol who had since become a good friend, Louis Jordan. Invited to Jordan's house in Phoenix, Arizona, B.B. told of his divided loyalties—he felt beholden to the Biharis for giving him an opportunity, but at the same time his dream of reaching a larger audience with his music seemed fruitless in light of Modern's limited resources and vision. Jordan listened and then showed B.B. something he had never seen before: a royalty check for $100,000, from Decca Records. "The bigger the company," Jordan said, "the better your chance of getting these royalty checks. The big companies are more accountable than the small ones. Remember, B—it's a business. Ain't nothing but a business."[3]

Other labels were vying for B.B.'s attention, but the relatively young ABC-Paramount label most piqued his interest. Founded in 1943 as a television network to challenge CBS and NBC, ABC had merged with Paramount Pictures in 1955 and in that same year had unveiled its own record label, ABC-Paramount. Catering to the teen pop market, the label had its share of hits early on: George Hamilton IV's maudlin 1956 single, "A Rose and a Baby Ruth," had risen to No. 6 on the pop chart, and a year later Hamilton returned with a Top Ten single in "Why Don't They Understand." Its meal ticket, though, was an ambitious, pushy teenage lad of Canadian extraction, Paul Anka, whose self-penned debut single, "Diana," had gone to No. 1 pop in mid-1957, inaugurating a near three-year run of hit singles that regularly landed in the chart's upper regions, including another No. 1 (for four weeks) in 1959 in "Lonely Boy" and two other No. 2 singles in '59 and 1960, "Put Your Head on My Shoulder" and "Puppy Love," respectively. Ironically, Anka, when all of 15 years old, persuaded Joe Bihari to record him. One single was released, but when Jules Bihari declined to offer Anka a contract, the upstart Canadian approached ABC.

However, it was not the teen idols that caught B.B.'s attention. Rather, it was ABC-Paramount's new focus on developing a solid R&B roster, starting with the 1960 signing of Ray Charles away from Atlantic. Lloyd Price, who

Lloyd Price, circa 1952.

had scored several hits on Specialty in the early '50s, had led the label's charge into the R&B-to-pop crossover arena with his 1957 hit "Just Because," a Top 30 pop single originally released on a label Price had launched upon his discharge from a four-year army stint and picked up for national distribution by ABC-Paramount. His next pop hit was even bigger—a No. 1 single in 1959 in the form of a lyrically toned-down version of the old folk tale about a vicious gambler, "Stack-O-Lee," retitled in Price's version as "Stagger Lee" (even in its sanitized form, Stagger Lee still shoots his rival Billy). Adding pop elements to his sound in the form of a smooth background chorus singing over a pumping R&B horn section, Price exuded good vibes in his vocal attack: "Stagger Lee" was an ebullient, dance-inducing frolic. The result was his first and only pop chart–topper. The follow-up "Where Were You on Our Wedding Day?" took the same upbeat approach to a touchy subject—in this case, a bridegroom abandoned at the altar—but peaked at No. 23 pop. Undeterred by this tepid showing, Price regrouped with a vengeance. With the horns and the chorus goosing him along, he offered up a joyous love ditty extolling his beloved's most endearing quality in "Personality," and returned to the Top Ten again, this time spending three weeks at No. 2 before dropping off. "I'm

Gonna Get Married" followed its predecessor's upbeat formula and became Price's third Top Ten pop single of the year, rising to No. 3. He made three more appearances in the Top 20 in 1959–'60.

B.B. was no Lloyd Price, though. He was a bluesman; he wasn't going to sing bouncy pop confections about teen love and teen misery. Ray Charles was more the model, and when he went No. 1 in 1960 with a sumptuous, orchestrated rendition of Hoagy Carmichael's "Georgia on My Mind" and came back a year later to top the chart with a bit of raw, blistering roadhouse R&B in the form of the Percy Mayfield–penned "Hit the Road, Jack," B.B. got religion. He also got some sage advice from another veteran, Fats Domino, who had ended his productive stay at Imperial (where his record sales had rivaled Presley's) to sign on at ABC-Paramount. Fats (who had played piano on Lloyd Price's first Specialty hit, "Lawdy Miss Clawdy," a No. 1 R&B single) told B.B., "You need a good company with good distribution. You don't want a company that'll put you on the shelf." (Not incidentally, Fats proffered some additional advice, often unheeded by the lustful B.B., to wit: "Keep your standards up. Certain things you gotta avoid, like fooling with women you really don't know anything about."[4])

Fats also instructed B.B., "'If you're going to be recognized in the record business, you have to at least have a company that is recognized. Like if you've sold a million copies of a record or an album, it should be certified."

"And as we were [with the Biharis], it would never be," B.B. explained. "And he was quite right, because we sold many, many records. But I never did see any certifications, even though I had two or three gold records that they gave me. But I never saw anything that was legitimately documented. So I went to ABC."[5]

In addition to having the infrastructure lacking at Modern, ABC-Paramount had another inducement to offer in the form of a $25,000 advance tendered by its president, Samuel Clark.

But as John Broven discovered in his research for the Ace box set, B.B.'s unhappiness with Modern may have been ex post facto. Apparently B.B. offered the Biharis a chance to match ABC's offer, "so the inference is that really he wasn't that unhappy with the Biharis anyway," Broven says.[6]

To Broven, Joe Bihari revealed that Jules refused to match the ABC offer simply because he felt the money could be better spent elsewhere. "By now they had this thriving budget LP business, but also, to accommodate that, they had invested in this large pressing plant," Broven noted. "Jules's theory was that he didn't want to spend $25,000 on one artist, even though it was B.B., when he could spend that on equipment and on improving the pressing plant facilities. That was the reason behind the Biharis' decision. So in other words, B.B. was very gentlemanly about it and gave the Biharis a chance to match the offer. My impression from Joe was that if they had matched that offer, B.B. would have stayed with them.

"Another point that shows there couldn't have been that much bitterness was they clearly arranged several sessions before the ABC-Paramount contract came into effect. They basically were storing up material to enable them to continue to release their Crown LPs after the fact. They could only have done that with B.B.'s cooperation. One doesn't know what sort of incentives they gave B.B. to do it, and so on and so on."[7]

Thus the quiet end of the Modern/RPM/Crown/Kent era in B.B.'s life in music. Whatever his frustrations with the Biharis and their operation, he left behind a formidable body of work that has largely stood the test of time. Moreover, he had been adventurous in taking chances with the staid form of the blues, using the lessons he had learned from listening to a broad range of musical artists to sculpt a sound signature for himself that remained true to the blues' eternal verities but suggested a broader definition of what the music could be when an artist dared to venture beyond accepted boundaries. He had written many of his own songs, establishing himself as a major blues writer fluent in the basic idioms and eminently capable of coining arresting phrases and telling a story with an individual flair. He was already recognized as a distinctive guitarist, and would prove even more influential in the years to come as new generations of blues musicians, especially in England, would adopt and adapt his techniques in reshaping '50s blues styles for the rock audience of the '60s. Succeeding generations picked up that ball and ran with it into the present day, and B.B. himself has been a gracious champion of young upstart guitarists indebted to his style, such as Jonny Lang and especially Kenny Wayne Shepherd. As a vocalist, he had proven himself a persuasive stylist as well, one who could belt a blues with conviction, or caress a ballad lyric, whether it be a lament or a love testimonial, with nuance and sensitivity and no small degree of sensuality—when the occasion demanded, he could be as seductive as Percy Mayfield or as hearty (and hardy) as Jimmy Rushing.

He joined ABC-Paramount with newfound confidence, brimming with enthusiasm, well prepared and eager to make his move into the mainstream, to bring his blues to the crossover audience he knew was out there waiting for it.

Brother Ray had done it. Why not B.B. King?

Chapter 7

DRIFTING BLUES

n 1962 the black music landscape was on the verge of a cataclysmic upheaval and with it an equally remarkable ascension into the popular culture mainstream. At once black artists' music celebrated the conceit that life, liberty, and the pursuit of happiness were self-evident truths; demanded that those truths apply to them; and voiced the rising anger of a people not merely denied their constitutional rights but also punished for asserting them. Soul music was taking root, born in the church and in the street; reflecting sensibilities and values equally informed by rural and city life experiences; as gritty and down-home as gospel and blues yet as tuneful and tenderhearted at times as finely crafted classic pop.

It flowered in Memphis, at the Stax studio in a converted movie house on McLemore Avenue, where an integrated group of musicians went from playing fraternity parties and local dives to crafting a horn-enriched fusion of rock 'n' roll and rhythm and blues, and exporting it with astounding success to the rest of the country—indeed, the world. From Memphis it filtered southeastward, to the unlikely burg of Muscle Shoals, Alabama, where an eccentric and colorful bunch of rhythm-crazed white musicians and songwriters developed their own take on "the Memphis Sound" and began churning out hits with regularity at Rick Hall's Fame studio, backing artists from as far away as Detroit (Aretha Franklin's first, epochal session, which yielded "[You Make Me Feel Like] A Natural Woman") and as close to home as ... home (native son Percy Sledge). It flowered in Chicago, spearheaded by the visionary Curtis Mayfield, a poet who was soul incarnate; it flowered in another mutation in Detroit, where at Berry Gordy, Jr.,'s Motown label a smart, integrated group of inspired musicians, writers, and performers fused soul and pop into an infectious, celebratory sound that was embraced by young white teens as was no other black music before it.

Giants emerged from these creative cauldrons—Smokey Robinson, Marvin Gaye, Otis Redding, Aretha Franklin, Solomon Burke, Sam and Dave, the Temptations, for a start—as well as a host of other inspired artists who may have grabbed the brass ring only once (à la Jimmy Hughes, with "Steal Away") or who, for reasons ranging from personal instability, bad habits, or the luck of the draw simply could not sustain a career beyond an initial, incandescent hit or two (James Carr, supremely gifted but troubled and erratic, may be alone in hitting this trifecta). Apropos the temper of the times, though, four artists in particular stood out, for both the advanced ideas informing their art and the examples they set in empowering themselves as businessmen.

Born in Barnwell, South Carolina, in 1933, James Brown rose from a hard-scrabble childhood marked by economic deprivation, petty crime, and incarceration in county jail and juvenile work farms to become one of the most dynamic entertainers and adventurous musical minds in American popular music. Schooled in the gospel tradition as a member of the Gospel Starlighters quartet, he entered the secular world when the quartet renamed itself the Flames and converted to the gospel of R&B. Signed to Syd Nathan's Cincinnati, Ohio–based King label, the Flames' (billed on disc as the Famous Flames) first record, an urgent, surging gospel-drenched plea titled "Please Please Please," was released in early 1956 and rose to No. 6 on the R&B chart. Clearly the dominant figure in the group, Brown soon and forever after received top billing on disc and on the road. After floundering commercially for nearly two years, and changing his band's lineup as well, Brown topped the chart in December 1956 with "Try Me," which also crossed over into the pop market, making an appearance in the lower reaches of the Top 50 chart. This success launched him into the upper tier of the black entertainment market, earning him gigs at New York's Apollo Theatre, the Howard in Washington, D.C., the Royal in Chicago, and the Uptown in Philadelphia as he built a growing following in the Northern states to go along with an ever more fervent fan base down South.

He continued to have fair-to-middling chart successes; in manager-agent Ben Bart he found a mentor who counseled him to maintain discipline in his professional and personal affairs, and was a dutiful steward of Brown's finances. Brown also picked up a powerhouse band along the way, its immediate effect being to liberate him onstage in developing a show he said would be designed to "give people more than what they came for—make them

James Brown at the Apollo, New York, in 1963.

tired. . . ."[1] A master showman, Brown introduced into his live act a dramatic set-closing ritual he lifted from the professional wrestler Gorgeous George. Having danced and shouted himself to exhaustion, Brown, drenched in sweat, on his knees, would be gently cloaked in a cape, helped to his feet and, with the aid of an assistant, led slowly toward the wings. Suddenly, off came the cape and then came Brown rushing back to the mic for one final, apocalyptic surge of emotion. "Everywhere [Brown] went it created pandemonium … " observed Peter Guralnick in *Sweet Soul Music*.[2]

Since 1956, Brown had worked the market steadily, constantly refining his stage presentation for maximum polish and visceral impact, maintaining a steady flow of new recordings, and missing no opportunity to promote himself as "The Hardest Working Man in Show Business." His Olympian moment occurred in 1963 with the release of his self-financed *Live at the Apollo* album. "A commercial and artistic turning point in the history of James Brown and Southern soul music," according to Guralnick,[3] the album logged more than 14 months on the chart, peaking at No. 2, finishing the year as the No. 32 album, an unparalleled feat for an R&B LP. "It also established James Brown once and for all not only as the premier R&B box office attraction of his time but as an artist with untapped potential for crossover success …" Guralnick noted.[4]

The success of *Live at the Apollo* added fuel to the blaze always burning beneath James Brown. His 1965 Top 30 pop single "Out of Sight" introduced the advanced notion of rhythm as melody, almost entirely dispensing with chord changes and instead generating forward momentum via what the critic Robert Palmer described as "plenty of trick rhythmic interludes and suspensions."[5] Between August 1965 and August 1967, he notched his first four Top Ten pop hits, all of them as forward-looking in their musical architecture as they were consciously crafted to inspire a sheer visceral response in his fans' loins: in 1965 came "Papa's Got a Brand New Bag Part 1" (No. 8 pop, No. 1 R&B for eight weeks) and "I Got You (I Feel Good)" (No. 3 pop, No. 1 R&B for six weeks); in 1966, "It's a Man's Man's Man's World" (No. 8 pop, No. 1 R&B for two weeks); and in 1967, "Cold Sweat—Part 1" (No. 7 pop, No. 1 R&B for three weeks). His success was so sweeping, and his fans' affection for him so fervent, that his every utterance on race, civil rights, politics, or any issue of the day was headline news. Politicians vied for his endorsement; athletes, movie stars, and celebrities of every stripe sought his company. At one time he owned three radio stations, the first black American to do so, and other accoutrements of his success included "a fleet of cars, a $713,000 black Lear Jet, and a Victorian-styled castle in Queens, complete with moat, drawbridge, and a Black Santa Claus on the lawn."[6]

Ray Charles was the visionary whose work defined and redefined the genre and then was studied, and widely imitated, by other artists, black and white. In addition, he demanded control of his art: when he jumped from R&B powerhouse Atlantic to R&B nonentity ABC-Paramount, it was less for money than for ownership of his master recordings. He would also found his own label, Tangerine, and, with Sid Feller, would direct his own recording sessions.

Raised in Greenville, Florida, Charles had come on the scene in shameless emulation of his idols, Nat King Cole and Charles Brown. His first recordings, for the Downbeat (later Swingtime) label, in 1950 find him affecting both Cole's and Brown's smooth, silky delivery, working in the same supper-club groove, and even sporting a guitarist, Gosady McKee, who played in the style of the King Cole Trio's superb Oscar Moore. In 1952 Atlantic purchased Charles's contract from Swingtime and encouraged him to explore some fresh approaches. The right mix took a while to coalesce, but over the years Charles found his own voice—a voice that came not from late-night soirees but from the gritty, down-home church of his youth and that swung with assurance and personality to burn. To powerful effect, he melded it to arrangements incorporating sweeps of gospel-influenced shouting, harmonizing, and call-and-response exchanges; driving rhythms and a soft spot for sweet-natured

Ray Charles, circa 1962.

love songs and American pop antiquities such as Stephen Foster's plaintive "Swanee River," which in 1957 became "Swanee River Rock (Talkin' 'Bout That River)" in Charles's propulsive, jet-age rendition. (That Charles was striking a chord, though, should have been evident a year earlier, when Elvis Presley covered Charles's driving blues, "I Got a Woman," on his first RCA album.) It finally came together for him in 1959, with a sizzling bit of R&B-cum-gospel testifying titled "What'd I Say (Part I)," a No. 6 pop single.

"Working with jazz musicians (including Milt Jackson of the Modern Jazz Quartet), [Charles] helped to bring jazz out of the abstract improvisations and random rhythms of bop, back toward what Charles Mingus, Horace Silver, and Bobby Timmons talked of as 'the roots,' 'funky music,' 'soul,'" observed British music historian Charlie Gillett in *The Sound of the City: The Rise of Rock 'n' Roll*. In Gillett's view, Charles's early ABC recordings found him exercising a powerful personal style. "His best records ('Hit the Road, Jack,' in particular) were among the best he ever did, intense feeling tinged with humor, economical, imaginative musical arrangements, and strong lyrics."[7] In sound, in style, in spirit, Ray Charles, with his big bands and expressive female backing singers, one foot firmly planted in the gospel sound, the other in the big beat of rhythm and blues, sent a message in his music that convinced B.B. he could flourish creatively at ABC.

Sam Cooke was another case. He fused all the elements that characterized '60s soul music, and put an indelible stamp on the style. As a 19-year-old, he was the star attraction of gospel's most popular group, the Soul Stirrers, whose venerable lead singer, R.H. Harris, had taken Cooke under his wing and given valuable instruction in style and comportment. Cooke took it from there: once he was in front of audiences, the word got out and soon hordes of adoring teenage girls were flocking to the Soul Stirrers' shows, worshipping the young Adonis more than the word he was espousing. Nevertheless, his gospel recordings, from a 1951 take on Thomas A. Dorsey's "Peace in the Valley" to his self-penned beauty, "Touch the Hem of His Garment," and monuments such as "Jesus Gave Me Water" and the old Baptist hymn "Were You There," were vivid, gripping performances, the very best gospel had to offer. In 1956 he went solo but stayed with Specialty, the Art Rupe–owned, L.A.-based label for which the Soul Stirrers recorded, and released a secular single, "Lovable," under the *nom de disc* Dale Cooke so as not to offend his gospel followers. Released from his Specialty contract in '57, Cooke signed with the Keen label (founded by Bob Keane, who went on to discover and produce Ritchie Valens, most notably). Cooke's first Keen single, the lilting love ballad "You Send Me," had a three-week run atop the pop charts in 1957. That success begat an eight-year skein of hits that included 28 Top 40 pop singles and 30 Top 40 R&B entries.

At Keen from '57 through mid-1960, Cooke recorded light, upbeat, pop-influenced material, barely revealing of the artist's deep immersion in gospel and R&B. When he signed with RCA in 1960, and subsequently gained control of his work, Cooke went back to the source, to gospel and blues, for inspiration and depth. Many of the songs from this period are built on the life experiences he understood as a black man in a segregated world in upheaval, and spoke as directly to his black audience as had his music with the Soul Stirrers. There was always room for a bright, soaring love song such as "Cupid" or a double-edged dance tune on the order of "Having a Party," but Cooke also covered harder blues such as the Howlin' Wolf–Willie Dixon co-write "Little Red Rooster" and sophisticated classic pop on the order of the Gershwins' "But Not for Me" and the Sammy Cahn–Jimmy Van Heusen classic "All the Way." His first significant record in a tougher vein was 1962's "Bring It On Home to Me," a soulful plea enlivened by an urgent gospel call-and-response section featuring Cooke sparring with his accompanying vocalist Lou Rawls as if they were back in church working the congregation up to full lather.

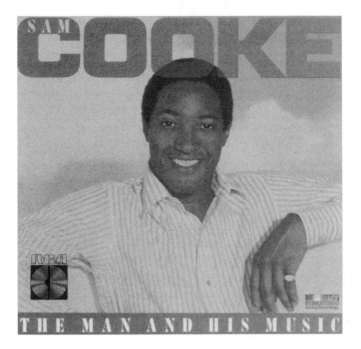

Cooke's move to the pop field laid the foundation for modern soul music, not only in his forward-looking blend of gospel, pop, and R&B, but also in his songwriting, which revealed a burgeoning social conscience informed by gospel's shouts of struggle, peace, and freedom. For Cooke, the political was personal, as he embraced the ideal of self-determination at the ballot box and in the wallet. To that end, he assumed command of his career both as an artist and as a businessman. Thanks to the skills of the accountant who became his manager, Allen Klein, Cooke gained creative control of his music, past and present, and moved aggressively to shape a future that would enable him to realize his artistic vision. He formed his own label (SAR/Derby), music publishing firm (Kags Music), and management company, and set out to be as much a factor behind the scenes as he was in the spotlight. "My future lies more in creating music and records than in being a live performer," he told *Billboard* magazine in 1964. That same year he also told the British publication *Melody Maker*, "Real gospel music has got to make a comeback," a prediction he did his best to make come true at SAR, where he made gospel, mostly through the Soul Stirrers, the cornerstone of the label.

In 1964, Cooke was shot to death in a Los Angeles motel by a woman who claimed he had attacked her. The next year saw the release of what is widely regarded as his finest hour on record with his song "A Change Is Gonna Come," a No. 31 pop single that has taken on a life far greater than any chart position could reveal. Attuned to the temper of the times—after a president had been assassinated; after chief of police Bull Connor had sicced his dogs and trained his hoses on black protesters in Birmingham, Alabama; after newly elected Alabama Governor George Wallace had intoned "segregation now, segregation tomorrow, segregation forever" in his 1963 inaugural address; after Governor Wallace had stood in the doorway at the University of Alabama to block the admission of black students; amid the ongoing horrors in Mississippi—"A Change Is Gonna Come" was a somber, determined message, in keeping with the Movement's early embrace of Gandhian pacifism, that communicated the certainty of a new day dawning even as Cooke's world-weary vocal accepted the truth of a long, hard journey ahead.

At B.B.'s new professional home, ABC-Paramount, the Impressions, led by a formidable writer-guitarist-producer in Curtis Mayfield, had reached the Top 20 of the pop chart in 1961 with an ethereal bit of soul titled "Gypsy Woman," and starting in 1963 went on a near two-year run of Top 20 singles that found Mayfield increasingly embracing the genre in Sam Cooke fashion, as a pulpit for social and spiritual commentary. The Impressions embodied the sweet side of soul. When they mated their soothing gospel harmonies and Mayfield's plaintive falsetto cries to one of Johnny Pate's subtle but rhythmically gripping arrangements, the message became not polemic but inspirational, memorable, and moving.

On the blues front, Freddie King, as noted earlier, had already made his mark with "Hideaway" and was moving on when B.B. made the jump to ABC. Another powerful new guitar slinger was on the horizon in the form of Indianola, Mississippi, native Albert King (no relation to B.B., Albert changed his surname to King from Nelson after hearing B.B.'s "3 O'Clock Blues"). He shaped a singular style of blues guitar that echoed Elmore James and Robert Nighthawk in its ferocious razor-edged assault, but was also distinguished by steely single-string lead lines, muscular phrasing, and a tender heart à la Lonnie Johnson and T-Bone Walker. Tuning to an open E-minor chord, King, a lefty, played the guitar as strung for a right-handed player, but upside down, and executed jaw-dropping string bends by pulling down across the fretboard until he reached *la note juste*. Disdaining flash, King was about solidity—basic, straight-ahead, indefatigable drive minus filigree or ostentatious displays of technique. A big, strong man, he seemed never to tire but rather to gain steam as the night wore on. In the early '50s King had recorded for Parrot, but only started to gain some notice in the blues world with a move to the Little

Milton–founded Bobbin' in 1959. There he turned out some raucous sides that found him blazing away on guitar in front of a jump band outfitted with a saxophone section and a piano player, thus laying the foundation for his startling breakthrough the next decade. A 1961 single, "Don't Throw Your Love on Me So Strong," became a national R&B hit, but a one-shot. Frustrated, King moved to the East St. Louis–based Coun-Tree label. Working with a quintet (complete with organ), King cut four sides, released as two singles, that garnered some solid airplay in the Midwest and created a demand for King on the concert circuit. Two years later he jumped at an offer from Memphis's Stax label and made an immediate and lasting impact on blues history. For more than two decades, while under contract to Stax and Tomato, he delivered a remarkable number of high-quality albums that adhered to no formula save that of remaining adventurous within the context of an identifiable sound signature.

In Chicago Muddy Waters and Howlin' Wolf were still going strong, especially the latter; Buddy Guy was a few years away from finding his individual voice as a guitarist, and harmonica virtuoso Junior Wells, who had replaced Little Walter in Muddy Waters's band, was cutting some interesting solo efforts but not yet gaining much momentum on his own.

Nineteen sixty-two also saw the emergence of a new stud in the Texas blues guitar pantheon in Albert Collins, whose spitfire single "Frosty" sold a million copies. A master of dynamics, Collins had been taught the blues basics by a cousin and by Lightnin' Hopkins, who taught him to play in E-minor and D-minor tunings. Playing with a capo on the seventh and eighth frets of his guitar, Collins achieved a high-pitched, biting tone that became one of the most familiar sound signatures in modern blues and an important influence on younger blues and rock players coming up then.

Such was the lay of the land in 1962 when B.B. signed his ABC-Paramount contract and banked $25,000. Immediately he began to understand what Fats Domino had been telling him about an organization with more resources at its disposal. He found ABC to be "a different world," where recording techniques were sophisticated beyond any he had experienced. With the development of better recording consoles and improved tape and tape-editing equipment, he learned that the best bits from different performances could be spliced together to make a finished, seamless take. "That gave me more confidence," he said. "Didn't worry so much about making mistakes 'cause mistakes could be fixed. Basically, though, it didn't change much else, since I still record a song in relatively few takes."[8]

Easing B.B.'s transition, Maxwell Davis stayed on as his arranger, and B.B. would soon enter into a fruitful partnership with staff producer/arranger Johnny Pate, early mentor to the Impressions. ABC, B.B. said, "put money in the charts and hired the best musicians around. I also teamed up with a lyricist, something new for me, and with Fats Washington wrote 'My Baby's Comin' Home' and 'Slowly Losing My Mind.' I was starting to feel a new zip in my music and couldn't help but be encouraged. Maybe I'd start selling better."[9]

Unfortunately, B.B.'s optimism was short-lived. Encouraged on the one hand that the label "started to think in terms of B.B. King becoming a major force in the music business," he was dismayed to find that the terms of that goal meant something other than "the blues singer and blues guitarist that he had been." Arriving for a session for his ABC debut album, *Mr. Blues*, produced by Sid Feller (Ray Charles's studio alter ego) and Clyde Otis, he learned he would be accompanied by "18 strings! They had voices! Now that's frightening!"[10] His fears proved well founded. Not that yearning love ballads such as "Young Dreamer," "On My Word of Honor" (which had been a No. 11 R&B hit for B.B. in 1956), and the tender "Guess Who?" (a 1959 hit for Jesse Belvin) were inferior songs, but the lush, string-rich orchestrations and pop-styled vocal background choruses were outdated. These cuts sounded like mid-'50s recordings in feel and performance; however, the same approach to Lonnie Johnson's "Tomorrow Night" works fabulously if the point was to make it into a dreamy paean to lovestruck anticipation, as it was. On the other hand, the blues ballad "By Myself" benefits from Belford Hendricks's low-key pop arrangement, which keeps B.B.'s crying vocal front and center, the better to spotlight an impassioned reading. Lucille doesn't make a significant appearance until the third cut on the first side, "Chains of Love," rising up out of a wash of saxophones and trumpets before B.B. comes in crooning in front of Maxwell Davis's swaying, horn-driven arrangement. Lucille isn't heard again until the end of the song, when B.B. cuts loose with a rapid flurry of descending notes before the orchestra signs off with a chordal blast. The Maxwell Davis–arranged "Blues at Midnight" is more like quintessential B.B., with its plaintive vocal supported by pungent retorts from Lucille and a gritty horn arrangement; the same could be said for another Davis arrangement, "Sneakin' Around," which in its original version had been a No. 10 R&B hit for B.B. in 1955. This rendition is done at a more deliberate pace than the original, and B.B. approaches it in a sedate mood; when he sings, "Oh, I'm so tired of sneakin' around with you," he sounds like he's had all he can take of the deception enveloping him. The album closes with a boisterous Maxwell Davis arrangement of "I'm Gonna Sit In 'Til You Give In," a song later cited by B.B. as evidence of him speaking out, albeit obliquely, on a current issue. With the civil rights movement heating up in the South, a favored tactic of black protesters had been to occupy all the seats at whites-only lunch counters. Although the song is about waiting for a woman to give it up, its lyrics suggest a comment on the times. Over stop-time blasts of tenor sax, B.B. declaims, "Ever since the world began / men have received the right to live from God above / but there is only one right that you can give / that is the right for me to have your love." Later in the song he makes reference to riding "that freedom train." It's hardly a protest song, and the bright, bouncy Davis arrangement would seem at odds with the gravity of the situation out in the streets, but as the first inkling of a growing social conscience in B.B., and of his responsibility as an artist to speak out, "I'm Gonna Sit In 'Til You Give In" is a tentative step forward. The violent images that had been burned into his mind's eye in his youth remained vivid, and the indignities still endured by blacks were never very far from being visited on him personally. Although he felt like an outsider when soul music took hold in the '60s, he endorsed and embraced its message.

"As the decade wore on and the civil rights movement spread, the music became tougher and prouder. Made me proud," he said. "The '60s were filled with beautiful soul because black people were more vocal about the respect we wanted and the good feeling we had about ourselves. The politics seeped into the music, and the politics were about life-affirming change. I liked all that."[11]

B.B.'s instinct about his ABC debut was on the mark: *Mr. Blues* appeared to have had the effect of driving away his core blues audience without adding any new pop fans to his base. For almost two years neither Kent nor ABC saw any chart action on B.B.'s singles. Matters improved slightly in 1964, when B.B. re-recorded "Downhearted," which he had cut in his final sessions for Kent the year before, and retitled it "How Blue Can You Get." The song has gone on to have a long and treasured life in B.B.'s live repertoire, but the 1964 single barely made it into the Hot 100 pop chart, peaking at No. 97—but that was progress, ending a drought that began in 1962 with the release of his Kent single "Gonna Miss You Around Here" b/w "Hully Gully Twist," which rose to No. 17 R&B. Since that time, ten consecutive B.B. singles (nine on Kent, one on ABC) had failed to chart. A follow-up to "How Blue Can You Get," a somber ballad titled "Help the Poor" (not a social statement, this, but rather a self-pitying plea for a woman's love), made a fleeting Top 100 appearance too, peaking at No. 98, and a third ABC single, "Never Trust a Woman" b/w "Worryin' Blues," topped both of its predecessors by rising to No. 90 pop.

B.B.'s final Kent sessions came back to haunt ABC in 1964. Whereas his new label was attempting to recast him for the mainstream market, the Biharis continued to let B.B. do what he did best, resulting in a consistently higher quality of music from the artist on Kent than on ABC. None of the Kent recordings was better than the languorous shuffle "Rock Me Baby." Its cool temperament and after-hours ambiance were captivating. B.B. only made it better with a casual, warm vocal, gently swinging but intimate, almost conversational at points, and a little commentary from Lucille in the form of a discrete ostinato riff and a low-key solo (he even misses a note at one point, hesitates for a split second, then picks up in time like nothing had happened) playing off a steady rolling piano. (The piano player's identity is uncertain; the Biharis insist it was Maxwell Davis, but others have claimed it was Jimmy McCracklin or Lloyd Glenn.[12]) The song had deep roots historically, being based on Arthur "Big Boy" Crudup's "Rock Me Mama" from 1945 but more directly related to Li'l Son Jackson's 1951 recording, "Rockin' and Rollin'." Muddy Waters did his part to immortalize it with his own tough version in 1956, but B.B.'s was the more significant recording, both commercially and aesthetically, for what it said about the artist who was formed at Modern Records and whom ABC was trying to reinvent, for all the wrong reasons.

Johnny Pate knew better. Perhaps inspired by the astounding public response to James Brown's *Live at the Apollo*, Pate decided to record B.B. in a live setting, with his stellar road band backing him, playing for his audience, and finally capturing on tape everything that was special about the bluesman the label couldn't figure out.

Live at the Regal _____

ABC, 1965; MCA, 1997
Recorded in Chicago, November 21, 1964
Produced by Johnny Pate
Introductions by disc jockeys Pervis Spann and E. Rodney Jones

Musicians
B.B. King: guitar, vocals
Kenny Sands: trumpet
Johnny Board, Bobby Forte: tenor sax
Duke Jethro: organ
Leo Lauchie: bass
Sonny Freeman: drums

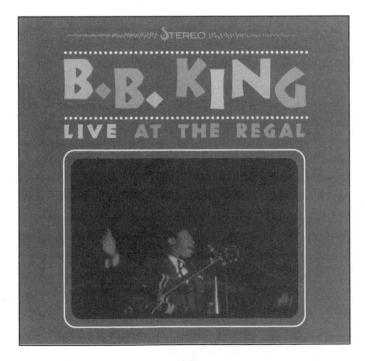

Songs
"Every Day I Have the Blues" (2:27) (Peter Chatman)
"Sweet Little Angel" (4:15) (B.B. King–Jules Taub)
"It's My Own Fault" (3:25) (John Lee Hooker)
"How Blue Can You Get" (3:00) (Jane Feather)
"Please Love Me" (2:55) (P. King–J. Taub)
"You Upset Me Baby" (2:20) (B.B. King–Jules Taub)
"Worry, Worry" (6:21) (P. Davis–J. Taub)
"Woke Up This Mornin'" (1:42) (B.B. King)
"You Done Lost Your Good Thing Now" (4:10) (V. Spivey–R. Floyd)
"Help The Poor" (2:35) (Charlie Singleton)

The occasion for the live recording was a show at Chicago's Regal Theater, a venue B.B. had played "hundreds of times before"[13] and that boasted an illustrious history dating back to the post–World War I era. Over the years it had attracted the finest blues, soul, jazz, and pop artists on the circuit, from Bessie Smith to Duke Ellington to Ella Fitzgerald to Aretha Franklin and Curtis Mayfield. Doubling as a movie house, the Regal presented a show mixing music and film several times a day, starting in the afternoon and running into the evening hours.[14] B.B.'s exceptional road band featured Duke Jethro on piano and organ ("playing a whole mess of blues"[15]); Leo Lauchie on bass; Kenneth Sands on trumpet; Johnny Board and Bobby Forte (the latter "proving himself one of my all-time great sidemen"[16]) on tenor saxes; and on drums the human power station named Sonny Freeman. Additional support was provided by the Regal's house band, directed by trumpeter King Kolax, a veteran of the swing era. B.B. didn't necessarily need the extra instruments Kolax's band provided, but its reeds and brass supplied the fuller sound B.B. preferred and did their part to add to the incendiary nature of the proceedings.

Recorded on a Saturday night, November 21, 1964, *Live at the Regal* captures B.B. in two sets, the first introduced by Pervis Spann, a popular disc jockey at Chicago's WVON, the second by another disc jockey, E. Rodney Jones. Only ten songs are performed, but the synergy between the musicians onstage, and between B.B. and his fervent admirers in the audience, is electrifying and immediate—from the first notes of what had become his standard concert opener, "Every Day I Have the Blues," the audience is in heat for the star. At points youthful female voices can be heard screaming—the first taut notes of B.B.'s guitar solo on "Sweet Little Angel," the set's third number, elicit wild shrieks from the distaff side—and male voices shout encouragement ("Tell us, B!") when B.B. gets into preacher mode to pass along some hard-earned life's wisdom. The song selection reaches back to the Modern era for what amounts to a night built on greatest hits—"Sweet Little Angel," "It's My Own Fault," "How Blue Can You Get?," "Please Love Me," "You Upset Me Baby," "Woke Up This Mornin'," "You Done Lost Your Good Thing Now," "Worry, Worry," with "Help the Poor" being the lone title from his ABC term.

"On this next tune, while we're reminiscin' here," B.B. announces, "I would like for you to pay attention to the lyrics. Not so much for my singin' or the band, 'cause I think they're wailin' out there. How about a big hand for 'em? Give 'em a big hand! Thank you. But now we're going way down an alley; *way* down an alley. I'd like to play a little bit"—and here he breaks into a sweet, crying solo that elicits screams from the females in the audience. Then he soars into a hearty reading of "How Blue Can You Get" that blends hoarse, throaty gospel shouts with tender crooning passages, all of it building up to the litany of grievances against his ungrateful woman, and finally exploding into an anguished shout of "I gave you seven children / and now you wanna give 'em back!" The audience goes wild—before the horns start pulsating and B.B. brings it home with an urgent query, "Babeeee ... how blue can you get??" Which immediately gives way to the scorching, Elmore James–like chording that opens "Please Love Me." The song is done at a breakneck pace, clearly a challenging tempo for B.B., who has all he can handle to keep pace. But he does, and the tension between the band's drive and B.B.'s urgency is exhilarating. Throughout the set, B.B.'s warm rapport with the audience is remarkable. He makes them shout and scream, they make him laugh during his between-songs patter. The ease with which he addresses a roomful of strangers betrays the intimate bond between the artist and his loyal fans, their shared understanding of each other's lives, and an appreciation of their common language, whether it be spoken or in the lyrics of the songs B.B. offers. Willie Dixon once observed that "the blues is about life; if it ain't about life, it ain't the blues," and the audience–artist dynamic evident on *Live at the Regal* proves Dixon's elegant theorem.

The live album would become something of a time line in B.B.'s catalog over the years, each new one revelatory of where his journey had taken him; of his growth as an artist; of his self-imposed obligation to represent the blues with dignity and decorum but with passion too; of his understanding of himself as an internationally recognized public figure who took the blues abroad and, like Louis Armstrong before him, came to be seen as not only the music's ambassador, but his native land's ambassador without portfolio.

In its day, and over subsequent years, *Live at the Regal* was and has been regarded as a pinnacle moment in B.B.'s career, he in his prime, with a great band, a devoted and vocal audience, and delivering bravura performances of his canon's monuments. Throughout the '60s a number of obscure bluesmen, including Delta giants Son House and Skip James, had been rediscovered by young white blues aficionados, who were greeting these elder statesmen like messiahs returned in coffeehouses, at festivals, and on college campuses all over the United States. With the release of *Live at the Regal*, B.B. too joined the ranks of the "rediscovered." He, however, had never been away, had never been off record, had never forsaken the road. Hence, his puzzlement both at the praise heaped on the record and on his welcome back.

"The critics went a little wild," he said of the reaction to the *Regal* album. "Called it my best ever. A bunch of writers talked like they were 'rediscovering' me. But I didn't know I had disappeared, didn't know I'd been hiding. I thought I'd been out there night after night, year after year. Some of the writers described *Live at the Regal* like I was playing way over my head. Well, I ain't one to argue with praise. I like and welcome praise whenever it comes my way. Go on and heap on the praise. But I also know I got to keep my head about me. And even though the live album was cool, I've probably played hundreds of better concerts than the one taped at the Regal. But who am I to argue with critics?"[17]

His misgivings aside, B.B.'s timing with *Live at the Regal* could not have been better in terms of enhancing his public profile. The Beatles had landed on U.S. shores in February 1964, and the Liverpool quartet's all-consuming popularity had opened the door for other British bands to conquer the States with an energized style built on the foundation of early American rock 'n' roll, country, blues, and R&B they had learned off imported recordings. A number of these bands boasted guitarists who were steeped in the blues, especially B.B. King's blues, and in interviews they were quick to praise his work, which had the effect of enlightening a new generation—one too young to have participated in the blues revival of the pre-Beatles '60s but fully invested in the British Invasion sound and respectful of its roots and the trailblazers whose artistry informed the new sensibilities. John Lennon said he wished he could play guitar like B.B. King. Eric Clapton, already a demigod among British blues aficionados while still a young member of John Mayall's Bluesbreakers, rarely gave an interview without praising B.B. King. "So I knew I mattered to some young musicians," B.B. said. "That gave me hope."[18] The Beatles' chief rival for teens' affection, the Rolling Stones, were far more immersed in the blues than the Fab Four—they had started as a blues band, whereas the Beatles were always more inclined towards rockabilly, early rock 'n' roll, skiffle, British dance hall styles, and classic pop than straight-ahead blues. "Keith Richards and Mick Jagger were scholars of black music," B.B. noted. "I think they felt the same way I did—that bluesmen deserved a wider audience. Through sheer conviction on their part, they helped introduce that audience to B.B. King."[19] In addition to these nominally rock 'n' roll bands from across the Atlantic, America had some youthful, homegrown blues acolytes of its own, more purist in their approach than their British counterparts, immensely talented, and quick to honor the giants who came before them.

"I was increasingly grateful to a whole school of new blues players who kept calling me by name," B.B. said, citing the gifted harmonica player and bandleader Paul Butterfield, along with guitarists Mike Bloomfield (who started in Butterfield's Chicago-based band), Elvin Bishop (another Butterfield protégé), and Texas-born and -raised Johnny Winter, who, B.B. said, "acted like my press agents. I believe their only motive was love."[20]

With the new breed praising his work at every turn, and *Live at the Regal* an acknowledged masterpiece, B.B. found the mid-'60s rife with bountiful prospects. Or so it seemed. In fact, though, 1966 could hardly have been worse for him offstage. The glow of the No. 2 R&B, No. 72 pop single in "Don't Answer the Door, Pt. 1," and two other mid-charting R&B hits on Kent ("Eyesight to the Blind," a Sonny Boy Williamson cut from the *Mr. Blues* album, b/w "Just Like a Woman," which peaked at No. 31); "I Stay in the Mood" b/w "Every Day I Have the Blues," which peaked at No. 45) faded with the escalating troubles in the bluesman's personal life. In addition to having his second tour bus stolen and never recovered, the Internal Revenue Service placed a $78,000 lien on his income, which forced B.B. to stay on the road, a debacle he said "cooked my goose."[21] That decision apparently was the last straw for Sue, to whom B.B. had made a promise to reduce his touring schedule in order to spend more time with her.[22] According to biographer Charles Sawyer, Sue, possessing some business sense (educated at UCLA, she was described by B.B. as "an expert in finance"[23]), had offered to straighten out her husband's financial and business affairs, but B.B. declined her assistance for reasons unexplained publicly but presumed to have something to do with the ego of a man of a certain age raised in a certain place at a certain time unwilling to accept a woman's assistance on the professional front. Sue responded by filing for a divorce, which B.B. did not contest.

"She was fed up with my lifestyle and disgusted that I'd broken my promise to stay home," B.B. said. " . . . In a contest between her and the road, Sue reasoned the road would win. And rather than reason with me anymore, she turned it over to a lawyer. . . . I lost Sue. I lost this wonderful woman, and I'm still singing the song that says, 'It's my own fault, baby.' When we were married, I was so convinced it was a lifetime thing, I even bought us adjoining plots at Forest Lawn Cemetery. That was a dream I had to bury. But at least the suit got settled with no mudslinging. We got divorced and, after a few years, we could even go back to being friends. There's no lady I respect more."[24]

Blues Is King

Bluesway, 1967
Recorded in Chicago, November 5, 1966
Produced by Johnny Pate

Musicians
B.B. King: guitar and vocal
Kenneth Sands: trumpet
Bobby Forte: tenor saxophone
Duke Jethro: organ
Louis Satterfield: bass
Sonny Freeman: drums

Songs
"Introduction" (:19)
"Waitin' On You" (2:29) (B.B. King–Ferdinand Washington)
"Introduction" (:49)
"Gambler's Blues" (5:12) (Arranged by B.B. King–Johnny Pate)
"Tired of Your Jive" (3:32) (Janet Despenza–Johnny Pate)
"Nightlife" (4:48) (Willie Nelson)
"Buzz Me" (4:13) (Danny Baxter–Fleecie Moore)
"Don't Answer the Door" (4:10) (Jimmy Johnson)
"Blind Love" (3:33) (B.B. King–Joe Josea)
"I Know What You're Puttin' Down" (3:36) (Louis Jordan–Bud Allen)
"Baby Get Lost" (4:00) (Leonard Feather)
"Gonna Keep On Loving You" (3:46) (B.B. King)

If *Live at the Regal* would be, forevermore, B.B. King's defining live moment, then 1967's *Blues Is King* would be his most notorious. Not that the album generated much attention when it was released, or has come under undue scrutiny since. But this small club date, also recorded in Chicago, this time at the International Club, on November 5, 1966, and steered by Johnny Pate, is the purest, rawest, primeval B.B. ever captured on tape, but hardly the most flattering portrait of the artist. The sound is hollow, the audience is close-miked (jewelry can be heard clattering when the audience applauds),

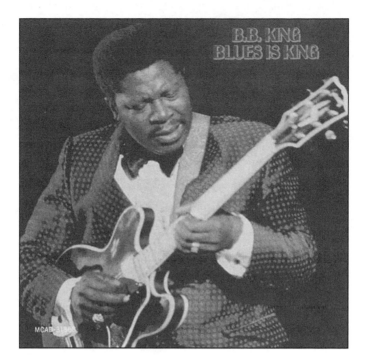

and B.B.'s usual engaging between-songs patter is almost nonexistent. Following the sturdy shuffle of "Waitin' On You," B.B. introduces his band—a quintet featuring mainstays Bobby Forte on tenor sax, Duke Jethro on organ, and Sonny Freeman on drums, now rounded out by Kenneth Sands on trumpet and Louis Satterfield on bass—and then offers a straightforward greeting to the audience: "Yes, ladies and gentlemen, we're so happy to have you with us. We're gonna do our best to try to move you tonight. If you like the blues, I think we can," and with that he rips into a piercing, single-string run, sustaining one note to the point of feedback, and then drives the song to a bruising crescendo, stops for a split second, and returns with a burst of distorted chording preceding his vocal entrance. So begins a B.B.–Pate arrangement of "Gambler's Blues." From that point, other than "thank you," little is heard from B.B. until he kicks off the ninth track on the disc, "Blind Love," by announcing, "If you've been with us a long time, you might remember this one." (Indeed. B.B. cut the song for RPM in 1953, and apart from his own sizzling guitar solo, its most striking feature was the conga played by Charles Crosby, quite an unusual touch for a blues record at that time.)

Long before "Blind Love" comes around, though, B.B. has served up a new persona—not the smooth, gracious host heard on *Live at the Regal*, the very epitome of suave egalitarianism, but rather the street Blues Boy, angry, domineering, jealous, ill-tempered, spiteful, sarcastic, and unpolished. Seven of the ten songs depict women as duplicitous and philandering, and, true to the lyrical content, B.B. expends most of his vocal energy growling and shouting his harsh indictments. He is deeply invested in the emotional content of these lyrics and drawing freely from an ample reservoir of righteous indignation or personal invective when he addresses the women in his songs. Even the jaunty set opener, "Waitin' On You," closes with him ordering his woman to "come on in here / and don't let it happen again," meaning don't ever come home late from a night out. The moody "Gambler's Blues" sees love as risky business, a gamble, a proposition, a game of give and take, and advises that experience has taught him "that love proposition stuff's a fake."

"Tired of Your Jive" rails against a two-timing woman ("you think I don't see what you do behind my back"); bright and bouncy, greeted by whoops from the audience, "Buzz Me" opens with a lengthy instrumental passage featuring Duke Jethro in full Jimmy McGriff mode during his lively organ solo, then finds B.B. appealing to a woman to call whenever she's ready for his true love, a rare instance here of genuine heartfelt affection. In keeping with the tenor of the narratives, the warm feelings of "Buzz Me" turn frosty with the onset of saxophonist Jimmy Johnson's "Don't Answer the Door," B.B.'s most recent R&B hit. This is an irate missive from a man who demands a woman stay in her place at home, alone, when he's not there—and he means alone. Don't let your sister in, most definitely don't let your mother in, and if you get sick, "you just suffer 'til I get home / I don't want no doctor in my house." An unforgiving, harsh screed, "Don't Answer the Door," with B.B. singing blues as deep as any he had ever articulated on record before—his low moans at the end of verses are chilling, sinister moments—is as disconcerting as the anger fueling his performance is unsettling. The slow blues arrangement of Louis Jordan's "I Know What You're Puttin' Down" is in mellow contrast to B.B.'s aggressive shouting, railing against a woman who comes home early in the morning dressed in new clothes she wasn't wearing the night before when she went out to "a dinner, show, and a dance." Calling her a "clown," B.B. advises harshly, "I know what you been puttin' down." Get caught up in the lyric and it's easy to miss a nice, temperate trumpet solo from Kenneth Sands wafting through the soundscape. Similarly, some smooth, sensuous punctuations courtesy Sands and tenor sax man Bobby Forte lose some of their emotional ballast in the wake of B.B.'s snarling at a "two-faced woman" who treats him "like a fool." He must advise, however, that "anytime I'm ready / I can tell you, baby, get lost!" At the end of the song, urging her to come back, he adds, provisionally, "but I got to be the boss."

Only a stirring, low-down treatment of Willie Nelson's "Nightlife" and the sweet-natured album closer, "Gonna Keep On Loving You," break the mean-woman blues cycle. B.B. doesn't approach "Nightlife" with any country or pop affectations; rather, he shouts it out as a surging R&B ballad, allowing Forte to wail away on tenor sax and Jethro to fill in the gaps with rich, gospel-flavored washes of organ chords, and pitching in with a tart guitar solo of his own. Quite distinct from the weariness with which Nelson and Ray Price approached it in their recordings, B.B., a well-seasoned road warrior, strikes a defiant pose when shouting, "The nightlife ain't no good life / but it's my life," as if to make it not a self-pitying lament, but a statement of purpose, a moment of self-definition that he embraces without qualification.

Coming a year after the divorce that had wounded him so deeply, *Blues Is King* revealed the hurt inside that B.B. simply did not share with his public, except in song. The misogynistic strains evident from time to time in his earlier songs were presented here as all-consuming. B.B. knew how to play the aggrieved male convincingly by this time, but where his stance had once been mitigated by humor, now it seemed as if he were eaten up by recrimination and rage. It was not a winning strategy, this startling transformation from sophisticate to bully. New ideas were in order, even if *Blues Is King* was, from a strictly musical standpoint, B.B. in peak form, and memorably so.

The following year, 1967, found him back in the studio for two new albums, each one coming at the blues from a slightly different vantage point. From the fairly straightforward contemporary blues defining the appropriately titled, Johnny Pate–produced *Blues on Top of Blues*, two successful singles emerged in 1968: "Payin' the Cost to Be the Boss" not only rose to No. 10 on the R&B chart, but peaked at No. 39 on the pop chart, making it B.B.'s first crossover success; also in 1968, "I'm Gonna Do What They Do to Me" charted lower, at No. 26 R&B and No. 74 pop, but even so, two inklings of crossover potential in the same year were cause for, if not celebration, at least optimism.

Lucille

ABC Bluesway, 1968
Produced by Bob Thiele
Engineer: Jim Lockert

Musicians on "Stop Putting the Hurt on Me," "Rainin' All the Time," "You Move Me So," "I'm with You," recorded December 18, 1967:

B.B. King: vocal and guitar
Maxwell Davis: leader and organ
Lloyd Glenn: piano
David Allen: bass
Irving Ashby: guitar
Jessie Sailes: drums
Cecil McNeely: sax
Bob McNeely: sax
John Ewing: trombone
Mel Moore: trumpet

Musicians on "Lucille," "Watch Yourself," "No Money No Luck," "I Need Your Love," "Country Girl," recorded December 20, 1967:
B.B. King: vocal and guitar
Maxwell Davis: organ
Bobby Forte: tenor sax
Lloyd Glenn: piano
David Allen: bass
Irving Ashby: guitar
Jessie Sailes: drums

Songs
"Lucille" (10:10) (B.B. King)
"You Move Me So" (2:10) (B.B. King)
"Country Girl" (4:20) (B.B. King)
"No Money No Luck" (3:45) (Ivory Joe Hunter)
"I Need Your Love" (2:15) (W. Spriggs)
 "Rainin' All the Time" (2:52) (B.B. King)
"I'm with You" (2:39) (B.B. King)
"Stop Putting the Hurt on Me" (2:55) (B.B. King)
"Watch Yourself" (6:00) (L. Gross, G. Kerr, S. Barnes)

In December 1967 B.B. returned to the studio with Bob Thiele, a producer-arranger-writer with an impressive jazz résumé, for what amounted to an effort to get the best out of both of B.B.'s incarnations: five of the nine cuts (recorded December 20, 1967) teamed him with a sextet including Maxwell Davis on organ, Bobby Forte on tenor sax, Lloyd Glenn on piano, David Allen on bass, Irving Ashby on guitar, and Jessie Sailes on drums; on the other four cuts, recorded in a single session on December 18, 1967, a nonet provided the backing, its members numbering Davis, Glenn, Allen, and Ashby, plus a horn section comprised of Mel Moore on trumpet, John Ewing on trombone, and on baritone saxes, Cecil and Bob McNeely, brothers of '50s R&B stalwart Big Jay McNeely.

Lucille is B.B.'s most conscious effort yet to kowtow to radio, as five of the songs clock in at under three minutes, and one, the cheery, sing-song "You Move Me So," barely cracked the two-minute mark at 2:10. Ironically, the cut that has endured on into legend is the opening ten-minute-ten-second monologue in song that gave the album its title. In liner notes penned by *Jazz & Pop* magazine blues editor Sheldon Harris, Thiele related the genesis of "Lucille," the song: "It was during the taping session. We were taking a break when I noticed B.B. doodling on the guitar. He was idling through some runs and started to tell me the story of 'Lucille.' I grabbed the switch, signaled the engineer, and flipped him on live."

Harris observes: "And so the story of Lucille, B.B. King's talented Gibson guitar, was unfolded in just one take just as Thiele heard it: free, honest, extemporaneous, a duet that weaves and reminisces for well over ten minutes. It's told in a talking blues style, slow and excitingly fluid, with lacy guitar work accenting King's thoughts. Of hearing a man talk to his instrument. Of hearing it answer."

Harris's description is apt. With affection, and serving up a small portion of ham on the side, B.B. relates the story of his and his guitar's blues odyssey, and the common bond he feels with the beloved Gibson. "If I could sing pop tunes like Frank Sinatra or Sammy Davis, Jr.," he offers at one point, "I don't think I could do it, because Lucille wants to sing the blues." As B.B. reflects on Lucille's virtues—from literally being a lifesaver to staying true to the blues—Lloyd Glenn bolsters the background with some rolling fills at the piano. In the midst of one solo, B.B. exclaims that he hears Lucille crying out with "a little Mahalia Jackson." Towards journey's close he cuts loose with a high, piercing run of notes, and Maxwell Davis sneaks in with some supportive organ fills to bring it all home.

"Lucille is real," B.B. points out in the liner notes. "When I play her it's almost like hearing words, and of course, naturally I hear cries. I'd be playing sometimes and as I'd play, it seems like it almost has a conversation with me. It tells you something. It communicates with me." Later he adds: " … the one thing that I'm concerned about today is to make Lucille sound even more like singing … more in the style of my singing."

Lucille boasts no small number of B.B.'s scintillating guitar solos, but they're so subtly woven into the ensemble playing that the album seems more a showcase for his vocals and this band than for his guitar. On "You Move Me So," the nonet pumps outs a pop-blues keyed by a stout horn chart and an uncredited female chorus shadowing the verses with their own exuberant shouts, as B.B. delivers a delightful, upbeat vocal tailored to put across the song's pop flavor. The small-combo, mid-tempo blues of "Country Girl" and the slow blues of "No Money No Luck" map into B.B.'s strengths as a blues vocalist—the sheer power of the voice coupled to an unerring sensitivity to the storyline, resulting in an immediacy that springs from the deep connection B.B. feels to his material. "I'm With You" rolls out a striking Maxwell Davis arrangement on a B.B.-penned mid-tempo blues, its distinctive markers being David Allen's prominent bass line and bursts of ascending horn lines building the tension before Lucille's tender, pleading solo provides release. Another stimulating Davis arrangement fuels "Stop Putting the Hurt on Me," in which an upper-register horn line is given ballast by the simultaneous low drone of the McNeely brothers' saxes. The album closes with a six-minute, hard-driving small combo workout on "Watch Yourself," with B.B. swinging comfortably into a mock-threatening vocal, part shouted, part spoken, aimed at an untrustworthy woman. The band meshes beautifully here, with Glenn surfacing on piano for a lively fill now and then, Forte making his sputtering presence felt on tenor sax, Davis's organ burbling underneath it all, and the rhythm section of Allen on bass and Sailes on drums never giving an inch as it powers the enterprise forward. Throughout, B.B. has plenty of room for a series of galvanizing T-Bone Walker–style guitar sorties.

A noble experiment with which to close out 1967, *Lucille*, released in 1968, yielded no charting singles whatsoever.

Chapter 8

MANHATTAN TRANSFER

Nineteen sixty-eight would inaugurate a momentous two-year stretch in B.B.'s life and career. In the wake of decisions he made during this period, things changed for B.B., usually for the better, onstage and off, in his business matters and in the recording studio. In a real sense it was as pivotal a time as when he made his first fateful trip to West Memphis.

First, he closed the door on a painful parting with Sue by leaving the house they once shared in California and relocating to New York City. It was a smart move on its face, given that B.B.'s booking agency (the Shaw Agency) and label were based there; but there were also advertising agencies, major radio and TV networks, and the entire infrastructure of the music business—all avenues that might lead to a more profitable career if properly exploited.

Upon getting settled in New York, he set out to dump his manager, Lou Zito, and to persuade an accountant friend of Zito's, Sid Seidenberg, to guide his career. Seidenberg worked for a major Manhattan firm with a show business focus and had already been called upon by Zito to help with B.B.'s tax situation. In addition, B.B. and Seidenberg had both been stationed at Camp Shelby at the same time in 1954, but had never met owing to the army's segregation policy. Initially B.B. approached Seidenberg requesting he look into Zito's bookkeeping practices, the artist feeling that monies due him were not making their way into his account. But Seidenberg reported back not only with a clean bill of health for Zito (although he apparently expressed some misgivings about Zito's management practices[1]) but with news that B.B. actually owed Zito in the neighborhood of $10,000.[2] Impressed by Seidenberg's blunt but honest appraisal, B.B. asked the accountant to manage him. Initially reluctant—"I knew what a manager is and I don't like this business. I didn't like what they did to people, most of the managers. I was not crazy about what their ethics were"[3]—Seidenberg finally agreed when B.B. bought into a five-year plan the accountant detailed, its ultimate aim being to make the artist a household name, stateside and abroad, with all the benefits that would accrue from such recognition.

"With Sid, everything started to change," B.B. recalled. "Sid had vision. He saw way down the road. He said, 'B, we're going to initiate five-year plans. We'll project ahead and see where we want to be five years from now. It's all about expanding your market, getting your music to people who don't know about B.B. King.'"[4]

Seidenberg set out to get B.B.'s gambling habit under control by urging he write a check to himself whenever he needed gambling money so "you'll see exactly what you're doing."[5] He got him signed on with the powerhouse Associated Booking, whose Joe Glaser had been the architect of Louis Armstrong's international success. This major big building block in the plan to broaden B.B.'s market was followed a year later by another, when Seidenberg landed his charge in commercials for AT&T, Pepsi-Cola, and Axion soap powder.[6]

Seidenberg then applied his five-year plan to renegotiating B.B.'s contract with ABC and getting the label to agree to put more energy into treating B.B. as a crossover artist and promoting his albums as such. He also got B.B.—or rather his music—into the movies when producer Quincy Jones hired him to do three songs for the soundtrack of the film *For the Love of Ivy*, starring Sidney Poitier and Abbey Lincoln.

In New York B.B. had found an apartment on Manhattan's Upper West Side, at 10 West 66th Street, right off tony Central Park West and across the street from Central Park itself. "I was ready to live where I'd never lived before," B.B. said, "in the center of the most exciting city in the world."[7]

Four other singles released that year (including a pairing from the *For the Love of Ivy* soundtrack, "The B.B. Jones" b/w "You Put It on Me") failed to chart at all, underscoring a serious issue developing in his nascent relationship with ABC. B.B. loved working in the studio with Maxwell Davis— "Maxwell could read my soul and interpret my sound"[8]—but the producers hired by the label were strangers to him and his modus operandi. Davis, "even though he had the better musical mind," gave B.B. the lead in the studio, trusting the artist to be the best judge of his own performance.

"In the '50s I was in charge; in the '60s I was produced," B.B. said. "ABC put me with producers I didn't know. Because these producers brought me songs, I wrote less in the '60s. There was no need to create my own material. Besides, the '60s was the age of the producer. Record companies felt like producers, not artists, knew how to get hits, and getting a hit—a genuine, across-the-board hit—was something I'd never had. So I accepted the situation."[9]

B.B.'s resentment was well placed. One producer he worked with even brought in another guitarist to supplant him on an album session. But in 1969, before he could rebel against it, his willingness to go along with the program finally paid dividends.

Unbeknownst to B.B., ABC was then harboring an in-house producer who was eager to work with him, not simply for the prestige of the gig, but because he believed his ideas would energize the artist commercially and stimulate him creatively. He would take the essence of B.B. King's music—especially the guitar—and surround it with fresh approaches to the ancient tones of the blues. His bold approach would prove vital to the realization of Sid Seidenberg's grand plan and to B.B.'s ambition to sing the blues for as many people as his and Lucille's voices could reach.

B.B. in 1967 trading licks with Eric Clapton and Oklahoma-born Elvin Bishop. The young guitarists who emerged in the first wave of the British Invasion in the mid-'60s, and their American contemporaries, often paid homage to B.B.'s influence in their interviews. With his career foundering at the time, B.B. said the praise from this new generation "gave me hope."

Chapter 9

REBIRTH

ill Szymczyk had joined ABC the same year B.B. had moved to New York. His production credits included the Boston band Ford Theater, but foremost on his mind was that the label's roster included B.B. King. ABC president Larry Newton became the target of young Szymczyk's persistent requests to be assigned to produce the King of the Blues.

"I kept hounding Larry Newton," Szymczyk recalls. "After my hounding him for a couple of months, he finally acquiesced and said, 'All right, B.B.'s coming back to town next week. We'll set up a meeting and if he says it's okay we'll let you do it.' And that's how it happened."[1]

For Szymczyk, born in Muskegon, Michigan, on February 13, 1943, this was the fulfillment of a dream at a young age. His path had taken him from Michigan into the Navy where, he says, "They crammed about two and a half, three years of college electronics into a six-month period and rammed it down our throat." The crash course suited Szymczyk fine, because he'd been interested in electronics since childhood. For part of one memorable summer of his youth he worked at a celery farm to earn $90 to buy a Sears tape recorder. "The minute I got the ninety bucks, I was done working," he says. "I went and got my tape recorder and started taping anything and everything I could."

He also befriended the disc jockeys at a nearby easy-listening radio station, and in return for fetching them coffee they would give him all their DJ copies of rock 'n' roll records. Armed with this free motherlode, Szymczyk became the DJ of choice at school dances.

For Szymczyk, the turning point in his youth came in the late '50s, some three or four years prior to his 1960 enlistment in the Navy. To his steel bed-

Producer Bill Szymczyk in the studio with B.B.: "We were having fun."

springs he had attached a self-built crystal radio set. However, even with an antenna he describes as "monstrous," he could pull in only one frequency. But it was a good one: Nashville's R&B powerhouse, WLAC—the same WLAC that, years earlier, had transfixed a young Riley B. King.

"It was nothing but R&B. Blues and R&B," he says. "It was [disc jockeys] John R., Gene Noble, and those guys. I was hooked. 'Cause I had never heard anything like that up in Muskegon, Michigan. John Lee Hooker! Howlin' Wolf! Lightnin' Hopkins! Jimmy Reed! B.B. King! I got hooked. And I started sending away for the Midnight Blues Special—'You get 99 records for $4.98! Send your money now!'"

After more than three years in the Navy, Szymczyk was discharged in February 1964. He settled in New York City, where he had been accepted at both the New York Institute of Technology and New York University. Through a friend he landed a summer job as a maintenance worker at Dick Charles Recording, a demo studio. One of the first sessions he witnessed was a date booked by Carole King and Gerry Goffin, who were then in the midst of a prodigious run of hits (including four No. 1 singles) of classic magnitude such as the Shirelles' "Will You Love Me Tomorrow," Little Eva's "The Loco-Motion," Bobby Vee's "Take Good Care of My Baby," the Phil Spector–produced Gene Pitney hit "Every Breath I Take." Even schlockmeister Steve Lawrence had topped the chart on the strength of a Goffin–King tune, "Go Away, Little Girl."

Having found his calling, Szymczyk said adieu to academia and made the studio the focus of his further formal education. In the late fall of '64 he left Dick Charles for a position at Regent Sound Studios, "a real studio" with a four-track recorder that was the facility of choice for numerous R&B acts—Szymczyk names Jerry Ragovoy and Van McCoy as two artists who had a significant impact on him during the Regent years—and one that wanted him to engineer master recording sessions. Here he notched his first producer credit, on an album by Harvey Brooks titled *How to Play Electric Bass*.

During that time, he was collaborating with a friend, writing songs, and producing their demos. "We actually did sell a couple, so I was, quote, a producer. Nothing ever happened, no success, no airplay, no nothing, but I was now a producer."

Meeting and working with Ragovoy led to a job at Ragovoy's own new studio, the Hit Factory (which was to become one of the legendary recording facilities in New York in the '70s). Otis Smith, the sales manager and de facto A&R chief at ABC Records, would cut acts there, and Szymczyk wound up producing one of them, his name long lost to history but memorable to Szymczyk because "he really wasn't very good, and I started going, 'Well, I think you oughta do this' and 'I think you oughta do that' and 'Why don't you tell this guy to do that?' and actually producing the session. Otis saw this and he sent more things my way. And I wound up semi-producing some things. Finally, in 1968, he said, 'Do you want to be a real producer and take an A&R job?' That's when I switched from being an independent engineer to being an actual record producer."

Taking the job at ABC in October 1968 also meant Szymczyk took a $400-a-week pay cut, but the loss of income was immaterial. "It was a matter of, do I want to be an independent freelance engineer and make $800 a week, or do I want to take this job and make $300 a week? That's another of those week-end-long decisions. On Monday I took the gig."

Szymczyk wasn't simply going through the motions and making production an academic exercise. He was developing an aesthetic, the end result of having grown up with the music of rock 'n' roll pioneers and having been waylaid by the R&B wafting over the airwaves out of WLAC. As the '60s wore on, he looked to two producers in particular as best embodying his own ideals with regard to sound: Tom Dowd in America (Dowd had more engineering than producer credits, but his contribution to so many important, enduring recordings makes the distinction between the two roles irrelevant), and Glyn Johns in England. "The Beatles stuff, the Who, the Stones that Glyn Johns was doing, and then all the Atlantic stuff and the Stax/Volt things Tom was doing.

And I was thinking, You get a combination of those two and you'll have something."

On Dowd's recordings, Szymczyk was moved by what he calls "unbridled funk. I kept hearing all these stories about him, what an electronic genius he was. Atlantic was the first major label to get an eight-track machine, and I couldn't even conceive of that at the time. ABC was still stuck in four-track land."

Glyn Johns floored Szymczyk with "the overwhelming rock majesty of the records he made. It was unreal. It was, 'How the hell do they do that over there?' Looking back now, there were many people doing it, but he was the guy who stuck out in my mind."

One final element would come to define the Szymczyk style: his delicate, nuanced use of strings, which would come into play most effectively on the sessions with B.B. From engineering Van McCoy–produced dates at Regent Sound, Szymczyk had been witness to McCoy writing string charts that he describes as "just sweet," and then absorbing McCoy's lessons in using horns and strings together.

Essentially, then, when Szymczyk badgered his way into a shot at producing B.B. King, he brought with him a solid understanding of the music history of his time, a deep immersion in the technology of sound recording, and a philosophy of producing and recording rooted in a sense of how the most exciting music of the day was being captured in the studio.

Live & Well

ABC, 1969

" ... the most important blues recording in many years." —*Down Beat*

Produced by Bill Szymczyk
"Live" engineer: Phil Ramone
"Well" engineer: Joe Zagarino
Re-mix engineer: Bill Szymczyk
Horns arranged by Johnny Pate

Musicians
B.B. King: guitar
Sonny Freeman: drums
Lee Gatling: sax
Val Patillo: bass
Patrick Williams: trumpet
Charlie Boles: organ

"Well" Session
B.B. King: guitar
Paul Harris: piano
Hugh McCracken: guitar
Herb Lovelle: drums
Gerald Jemmott: bass
Al Kooper: piano

Songs
"Live" Session
"Don't Answer the Door" (6:13) (J. Johnson)
"Just a Little Love" (5:16) (B.B. King)
"My Mood" (2:42) (B.B. King–V.S. Freeman)
"Sweet Little Angel" (5:13) (B.B. King–Jules Taub)
"Please Accept My Love" (3:20) (B.B. King–S. Ling)

"Well" Session
"I Want You So Bad" (4:17) (B.B. King)
"Friends" (5:36) (B.B. King–Bill Szymczyk)
"Get Off My Back Woman" (3:16) (B.B. King–Ferdinand Washington)
"Let's Get Down to Business" (3:35) (B.B. King)
"Why I Sing the Blues" (8:37) (B.B. King–Dave Clark)

B.B.'s first experience with his new producer proved to be an inspired outing, one half of it live, one half a studio session. Using his road band, B.B. went into famed New York City jazz club the Village Gate, offered up the usual live touchstones and also introduced a couple of new tunes (one actually was based on an earlier B.B. recording) into his standard repertoire. "Ladies and gentlemen, it's blues time," the emcee announces to the audience as the record begins. "We would like for you to prepare yourselves, get yourselves together, get yourselves in the frame of mind to dig the King, that is the King of the Blues! Mr. B.B. King!" After a shouted "Thank you!" B.B. hits a series of stinging notes, lets them hang there, and comes back softly picking single notes, hard-picking a flurry here, then settling back in quietly as the band vamps behind him. The music builds again, B.B. attacks the strings with gusto, lets a sustained note ring out, then cuts loose with a flurry of hard-picked notes and forceful chording as the band gathers steam behind him. It all comes to a head, cools down, and B.B. shouts, to rousing applause, "Woman I don't want a soul / hanging around my house / when I'm not at home. . . ." So begins a stirring performance of "Don't Answer the Door," albeit less volatile than the version preserved on *Blues Is King*. Next B.B. introduces what he calls "a new thing for you. This is a brand-new tune. A brand-new tune—the *band* don't know it, *you* don't know it, and *I* don't know it either. But we gonna try it. Are you ready for it? Let me get a little more nerve. Got to get the groove going, y'know. You begin to feel the groove? Yeah, it sounds all right to me. So we're gonna try it." The ensuing "brand-new tune" is "Just a Little Love," which in fact was based on B.B.'s 1957 Modern recording, "Early in the Morning." As a live piece it's effective—B.B. gets the audience into a call-and-response echoing his plea, "All I want / is a little bit of love," and the band pumps away between verses as B.B. spices the action with his taut soloing before returning to his pulpit to work the audience into an uproar again.

The revelatory piece on the "Live" side is the third cut, an instrumental titled "My Mood." At 2:42 it's little more than an interlude in the live show, but what B.B. does instrumentally makes it momentous. It's as if he intended to pay homage to all the guitar masters who influenced his style, as he employs delicate single-string runs à la Lonnie Johnson, double-stops from the T-Bone Walker arsenal, and pull-offs, glissandos, sliding notes, embellishments, and a closing run that summon echoes of a multitude of titans from Bukka White to Charlie Christian to Django Reinhardt. Influenced by jazz, enamored of jazz, but never well versed in its technicalities, B.B. here delivered a statement that was historically resonant and sufficiently complex to impress the hardcore jazz students and critics, but ultimately was rich enough in human qualities—tenderness, melancholy, yearning—to make it an aural evocation of a troubled heart. It has both chops and soul to recommend it.

The song's closing crescendo is followed by applause, and after barely taking a breath, B.B. is sounding the first searching, melancholy notes of a lengthy instrumental intro to "Sweet Little Angel," originally the A-side of his No. 6 R&B 1956 RPM single (and B-side of his non-charting Kent single from 1960 featuring "Woke Up This Morning" as its A-side). The song builds, the band starts to roar, especially the horns, but B.B. doesn't try to match their intensity; rather, his restrained single-note soloing makes for an effective contrast to the drama inherent in the music behind him.

"Oh, boy, thank you," B.B. says a bit breathlessly at the end of the song as the applause rises. "We would like to do this one from us. This is a dedication to all of you individually. I wish I could come out and shake everybody's hand, but since I can't, I would like to sing this one just for you. Please pay attention to the lyric in this song. It's titled 'Please Accept My Love.'" With this he closes out the "Live" side with the classically styled R&B ballad originally released as the A-side (b/w "You've Been an Angel") of Kent single 315 in 1958, a No. 9 R&B chart entry (it was also the B-side of his 1963 ABC single "How Blue Can You Get"). The first half of the song is a pure slow gospel showcase, B.B. singing sensuously and deeply, sounding at times like both Billy Eckstine and Bobby "Blue" Bland, caressing the sweet lyric of devotion as the drums, bass, and organ play discreetly in the background. At midpoint, though, the horns let out a wail, the rhythm section starts kicking, the organ vamps become more pronounced, and just as suddenly it all recedes again, for a stop-time measure that B.B. fills with a shouted "I'll—I said I'll / end my life to be with you," before the entire band blasts out a final booming chord, as B.B. hits two loud distorted chords on his guitar before the closing downbeat. Otherwise the guitar is almost absent from this performance, but no matter: B.B.'s vocal performance needs nothing from Lucille to make it more potent or more affecting, and in fact Lucille's silence allows listeners a chance to appreciate B.B. as a crooner on intimate terms with nuance, phrasing, and texture. His gritty soul shouts at the close of the song pack even more of a wallop for being so unexpected an emotional explosion, coming as they do in the wake of a reading rich in restrained expressiveness—so rich it inspires lustful shouts in some female audience members.

In his liner notes, Szymczyk wrote, "There was something else I wanted to try, and the more we talked about it, the more excited B.B. became. We got together what I consider to be some of the best young blues musicians in the country and locked ourselves in the Hit Factory for two nights. The results of those two nights are the 'Well' side of this album. The music is all B.B. King but in a slightly different surrounding. There's an incredible amount of energy that's lacking in a lot of blues music today."

When Szymczyk discussed the album concept with B.B. the producer indicated he wanted to bring in "some young, aggressive musicians, not necessarily black, and see what happened. [B.B.] was open to the idea." The dream team included (on two cuts) Al Kooper on piano (a friend of the producer's dating to the mid-'60s when Szymczyk had produced some demos for Kooper), the increasingly in-demand studio guitarist Hugh McCracken, drummer Herb Lovelle, King Curtis's bass player Gerald Jemmott, and a virtual unknown piano player on the other three cuts, one Paul Harris. Szymczyk had worked with all of these musicians before and knew what he was getting.

For the horn arrangements, Szymczyk reached out to Johnny Pate, who came onboard without any rancor. "Johnny was very happy to do the horn charts," Szymczyk said. "It wasn't a 'you took my gig' deal. He was very friendly. He was a real mellow guy, very professional, very low-key. We only worked on this particular album. Like I said, I didn't want him to feel like I'd aced him out of a gig or anything like that."

From B.B.'s opening solo on "I Want You So Bad"—a mix of triplet flurries and pungent single notes, some bent, some trilled—a couple of things are evident: the mood of this side is something special—it's languorous but charged; there's a tension in the air, but a captivating mellowness too. As the song progresses, Jemmott's bass percolates along, Pate's horn section surges gently in and out of the soundscape, Kooper delivers a lively, angular piano solo, and drummer Herb Lovelle keeps the beat solid. B.B. gives an object lesson in how Lucille is an extension of his voice; even after repeat listenings it seems like Lucille is singing all the way through, when in fact B.B. is laying down one of his most powerful recorded vocals, full of feeling and yearning for a woman he just has to have—"someone like you, baby / someone like you, I ain't never had" he moans at one point.

The moody instrumental "Friends" follows, kicked off with an unaccompanied B.B. solo flight on guitar that sets the tone with its melancholy single-note run marked by slides, pull-offs, and bent notes before the band eases in behind Lovelle's steady, stately rhythm. With B.B.'s ferocious chording driving the mood, the song motors into a higher gear, then B.B. cruises along with a delicate fading run of single notes; McCracken then pulls alongside him with an interesting solo in which B.B.'s single-note forays are echoed and interspersed between robust chords. Paul Harris adds buoyant piano commentary that wends its way back to B.B. again, who takes the proceedings into fadeout with a series of slashing, distorted chords and single notes mirroring and expanding upon the song's opening run.

Sequenced back to back, "I Want You So Bad" and "Friends" form a dynamic, moody couplet, an unusual touch coming at the start of the side, when something uptempo might have been expected in one of those positions. Placed as they are up front, the songs seem to signal the serious intent of the studio sessions, as if B.B. wanted everyone simply to sit and listen to what he had to say instead of hitting the dance floor immediately. However much water that theory holds, the next two songs, "Get Off My Back Woman" and "Let's Get Down to Business," want to take you higher. A classic study in mean-woman blues, "Get Off My Back Woman" is a funky, horn-enriched workout in which B.B. sends a bossy, ambition-challenged woman on her way ("you can catch yourself another ride, baby / somewhere further down the road," he declaims towards the end). "Let's Get Down to Business," on the other hand, is an infectious jump-blues invitation to carnal pleasure (or what *Seinfeld*'s George Costanza would call "make-up sex"), with B.B., making no bones about his delight in seeing his woman come back to him, suggesting a remedy to cure what ails them both and punctuating the verses with syncopated soloing that evokes a satisfied mind.

B.B.'s co-writer on "Get Off My Back Woman" was an obscure musician named Ferdinand "Fats" Washington. In his landmark biography of B.B., *The Arrival of B.B. King*, author Charles Sawyer identifies Washington as B.B.'s "only real collaborator," a man who was called upon strictly to compose lyrics. "From time to time when B.B. was composing and had in mind a particular sentiment he wanted to express and felt blocked," notes Sawyer, "he would telephone Fats Washington and together they would work out the idiomatic expression; in this way B.B. came to crystallize key phrases like 'If you can't do any better, I'd better get me somebody else that will,' and titles like 'Waitin' On You' [first heard on *Blues Is King*] and 'Get Off My Back Woman.'"[2]

This is all prelude, though, to one of the most powerful moments on any B.B. King album, when he takes a song he originally recorded in 1956 and dramatically recasts it with a compelling social message. Co-written with his song plugger friend Dave Clark, "Why I Sing the Blues" (originally recorded for Kent but unissued until it surfaced on a 1987 Ace Record compilation titled *Across the Tracks*) was a jaundiced look at marriage done to a swaying, big-band arrangement. In the first verse, B.B. implored the listener to consider what he's saying from a different point of view: "say that you are me instead of you." In the next verse he suggests the wife will always have "someone else whenever you are out of sight" and follows that assertion with a harsh characterization of the woman providing "the affection of a servant, the kindness of a slave, the love of a dog." After a taut guitar solo, B.B. signs off with a seeming non sequitur: "I might not have lived right all of my life / but, people, believe me, I have tried." Perhaps the strains in B.B.'s own marital life had poisoned his attitude towards the institution, or towards women, and perhaps the bluntness of his and Clark's lyrics explain why the song was never released in its day. Whatever the reason, "Why I Sing the Blues" was, in its original incarnation, nothing more than a dyspeptic, in-your-face take on connubial bliss.

Not so in 1969. Retooled and reconsidered within the context of frightful times for African-Americans, the version of "Why I Sing the Blues" B.B. brought to this session was his most forceful, scalding statement ever about the black experience in America. It aligned him with the great soul artists who were speaking out in their own distinctive voices about the temper of the times. It was angrier than Sam Cooke's "A Change Is Gonna Come" (1965); forceful pamphleteering on a par with James Brown's 1968 hit "Say It Loud— I'm Black and I'm Proud (Part 1)"; and, in its implied refusal to accept the status quo, a striking contrast to Curtis Mayfield's spiritually based appeals for bridging America's racial chasm as expressed in the Impressions' "People Get Ready" (1965), "We're a Winner" (1968, orchestration by Johnny Pate, a Top 20 pop hit and No. 1 R&B hit), and 1969's "Choice of Colors" (also a No. 1 R&B hit). The ferocity of his vocal and guitar attacks underscored, and perhaps revealed for the first time to some, the depth of his pain and anger as a black man scarred by history, intolerant of injustice, and dismayed by the problem's pervasiveness. "When I first got the blues / they brought me over on a ship / men was standing over me / and a lot more with a whip / and everybody wants to know / why I sing the blues," the song begins. He goes on to bemoan the privations of ghetto life ("I've heard the rats tell the bedbugs / to give the roaches some") and the lack of educational opportunities for young blacks; sings with palpable disdain of an entrenched attitude in the workplace that blacks were "born to lose"; wails about a blind beggar being thrown in jail "for what crime?"; discourses on a trip uptown where he finds "everyone got the same trouble as mine / everybody got the blues," and is even told by a woman that he hasn't been around long enough to have the blues.

B.B. begs to differ. A bit more than three minutes into the song, he works a slight variation on the recurring refrain, "I've been around a long time / I've really paid my dues." He shouts: "I've really, really paid my dues / I ain't ashamed of it, people / I just love to sing my blues," but this time he adds a few syllables to the word "love" to invest it with an ironic attitude, the subtext of which is, "Yeah, he's a credit to his race," the very phrasing of the line designed to give anyone listening closely pause to consider what he's really saying.

The song is driven relentlessly by Jemmott's florid bass patterns and Lovelle's propulsive drumming; B.B. interjects a stinging guitar solo, blending hard-picked single notes and soaring bent notes. At the 5:15 mark he says, "One more time, fellas," and sings the verse about the blind beggar, and at 5:40 queries, "Can we do just one more?" Another verse, seemingly improvised, follows ("a lady said, 'You haven't been around long enough'"), which takes the band to the 6:04 mark, when B.B. calls out again, "One more time," kicking off a near-two-minute instrumental dialog marked by a discursive B.B. solo embroidered by all manner of bent notes, pull-offs, trills, soft-picked single-note punctuations, and glottal chording, but also an active second voice in Jemmott's pulsing bass line and, not least of all, Paul Harris's ebullient right-hand flourishes on the keyboard. Finally, at the 8:10 mark, B.B. lets out a hearty laugh. "That's all right, fellas!" he exclaims, and as the song fades out he exclaims again, "That's all right, fellas!"

It's a priceless and telling B.B. moment: a song so filled with pain and anger culminates in a joyous jam with everybody getting equal time. On the one hand, B.B. had spoken his piece and held nothing back. From 1949 to this moment in the studio in 1969, he had never so boldly revealed his feelings as a black American, had never let the sublimated rage of his formative years surface so unequivocally. All the hurt, even the anger, fueling his deepest blues performances was always in the context of a failed romance, or disappointment engendered by faithless women, or regrets over his own shortcomings as a man—but that man could have been black or white or any other race. Not this time. This commentary was a broadside aimed squarely at racism in America, an eyewitness report from ground zero. B.B. never went out on the stump to promote his views on race as an issue, and "Why I Sing the Blues" didn't inaugurate an outpouring of socially conscious songs. But it did indicate his sense of race as a political and social issue. There are no good guys in the song, whether they be police, politicians, slave masters, or social workers, and he describes a broken system in desperate need of overhaul. What B.B. is most explicit about here, however, is his right, if not obligation, to speak out. Consider the time frame. In 1963, B.B.'s friend, civil rights activist Medgar Evers, was assassinated in Mississippi; in 1968, Martin Luther King, Jr., also a friend of B.B.'s, was assassinated in Memphis. While some blacks and some performers voiced their support of a more aggressive, even violent response*, B.B., whose mother made a virtue of tolerance and patience, had no truck with the militants. "I couldn't buy their program," he said. "I understood rage, but I was a practical man. Practicality told me that brutal force wouldn't bring victory. Besides, brute force didn't correspond to the feelings of my heart. My heart wanted change, wanted respect. I didn't need to bust anyone's head open. The men I respected most were doers, not talkers."[3]

As the civil rights movement heated up in the '60s, untold numbers of black lives, mostly those of black men, had been taken by murderous racists at loose (and seemingly above the law) in the South, especially in Mississippi, the focal point of the movement's efforts. That B.B. King's soul would be pierced by these events should come as no surprise; that he would be so fearless in bringing a politically charged message to his music perhaps did.

But then consider the closing instrumental jam among black and white musicians, and the good feelings propelling it—the dialog between the black and white musicians is so engaging and energizing it causes B.B. to burst out laughing. Without reading too much into the interracial lineup Szymczyk had assembled—the producer wasn't looking to make a social statement; he simply wanted to give B.B. a musical challenge—the good feelings attending the endgame of this most unflinching critique of the other America, circa 1968, also reflected the values B.B. had embraced in his youth.

"I held Medgar and Martin both to my heart when, later in my career, some militants called me Uncle Tom," B.B. said. "That hurt, but it didn't destroy me. I felt I was doing all I could by bringing people together through music. I had a clear picture of courage, and it had nothing to do with style or muscle or hip political slogans. You didn't have to be a genius to realize brute force wouldn't work. Mama always talked about kindness and self-respect. Daddy was about work, about feeding his family. In my mind, the two go together. Respect requires work. Medgar Evers and Martin Luther King worked fearlessly so our people could realize respect. That's why they died. And why they live on."[4]

---

* In 1966, in Oakland, California, six young men led by Huey P. Newton and Bobby Seale formed the Black Panther Party, dedicated to "the revolutionary establishment of real economic, social, and political equality across gender and color lines" (www.marxists.org/history/usa/workers/black-panthers/).

Live & Well: *The Studio Sessions*

A Conversation with Bill Szymczyk

How did B.B. relate to the new musicians he hadn't worked with before?

Very well. Very well. He's real easy to work with. And the guys I put with him, they were in awe. Everybody was like, "Oh, man, we're working with B.B. King!" There was a mutual admiration thing going on.

In the Live part at the Village Gate, did you just sort of set up and let it roll?

That was pretty much it. I hired Phil Ramone to engineer it. How cool is that, huh? That was, okay, we'll record the show and we'll pick twenty minutes' worth and we'll pick five, six tunes, whatever.

It was five.

Five tunes out of what he did. Some of the things he'd already recorded live before, so we just took the newer ones and used those. And I mixed them.

A technical aspect of this, miking for a live event as opposed to B.B. in the studio. Was there anything different about that?

Not really. You pretty much close-mike everything. The only difference is you put up a couple of mics for the audience, and that's really about it.

Now when you got into the studio sessions, how much pre-production did you do?

Absolutely none. We all showed up. And B would have the song and he'd play it, and everybody involved would work on the arrangement. We did the whole side in two nights.

Why did you record the Well side at the Hit Factory?

I was the first engineer there when Jerry Ragovoy opened it and hired me to come and be his engineer. So I had a hand in building it, I knew the room, knew what it sounded like, how everything worked. I was real comfortable. It was like my home studio at the time.

And what kind of gear were you working on then?

It was an eight-track machine, a Scully eight-track, a custom board with rotary faders, with maybe 10, 12 inputs, one or two compressors, some electronics, LA-2s, and that was about it, really. A few Pultecs.

Of the musicians you brought in, Paul Harris, the piano player, really stands out on this record and on a couple of other B.B. records too.

Paul Harris I met back when I was engineering at Regent Sound. I got into quite a long two-year groove of doing folk acts during the day and R&B acts at night. A guy named Arthur Gorson, who managed folk acts like Phil Ochs and Tom Rush and a duo named Jim and Gene, David Blue, and people like that, he started using me to record a bunch of his acts. And he brought this preppy-looking piano player from Long

Island in, and he could just play his ass off. He became my favorite keyboard player. So when I was putting the band together, it was either going to be Al or Paul. And I wanted Al, Al wanted the job in the worst way, but the very first night he got into some kind of spat with the drummer, Herbie Lovelle, and he developed this monstrous headache, and he says, "I gotta go home." So I immediately called Paul, and Paul was there the next night and Paul was there from then on.

How many cuts is Al on?

I think he's on two. He is on the first one, "I Want You So Bad," and "Get Off My Back Woman."

The song "Why I Sing the Blues" is very interesting. It's about eight and a half minutes long. If anyone didn't know it before B.B.'s autobiography was published, they learned from that book that B.B. harbors strong resentments over the way black people have been treated in this country, stemming from his own experiences growing up poor in the Delta, seeing some of the outrages firsthand, and being the target of some of them through the years. And he's admitted to carrying around the anger and rage he felt over these injustices, but he's rarely addressed them explicitly on record. And he does nothing but address them explicitly in this song. What were you thinking when this was rolling out?

I was ecstatic. I said, "This is a smash!" First of all, it's a very aggressive record. Gerry Jemmott's bass line is just right in your face. And Herbie's backbeat—oh, it was a great session. It was the last thing we cut for those two days. I smelled single right away. So that was like, Oh, boy, we're on to something here. Needless to say, it wasn't eight and a half minutes long. I did some serious editing on that boy.

Did you ever discuss the song with B.B. or did he say anything in advance about it?

Not really. He'd just bring the tunes in. I remember when he brought that song the second night, Herbie and Gerry were going, "Yeah, that's it!" They were the black guys in the band. And Paul and Hugh and I were right behind B.B. going, "Tell it! Tell it like it is!" The reason it's so long is that the band wouldn't quit. That was one of those takes where everybody knew we had it, but everybody just kept going. And I wasn't gonna stop 'em.

Was B.B. improvising verses at some point?

I think near the end he was. I mean, he'd come in with like sheets and sheets of paper with lyrics on them. He'd be shuffling them in front of him, but I do think he may have made up a few of those verses on the fly at the end of the song.

Yeah, towards the end there's an instrumental part and he comes back in with a verse that sounds to me like he's making it up on the spot. Something about the rhythm of the line that struck me as being improvisational.

Yeah, well, we were having fun.

Completely Well_____

ABC Bluesway, 1969; reissued on MCA, 1998
Production and sound: Bill Szymczyk
Arranged by: Everybody
Strings and horn arrangements: Bert "Super Charts" DeCoteaux
Recorded at the Hit Factories: East and West
Recording engineers: Joe "Ears" Zagarino and Bill Szymczyk
Mastering: Lee Hulko and Incredalathe—Sterling Sound

Musicians
B.B. King: guitar and vocals
Herbie Lovelle: drums
Paul Harris: piano, electric piano, and organ
Hugh McCracken: guitar
Gerald "Fingers" Jemmott: bass

Songs
"So Excited" (5:34) (B.B. King–Gerald Jemmott)
"No Good" (4:35) (F. Washington–B.B. King)
"You're Losin' Me" (4:54) (F. Washington–B.B. King)

"What Happened" (4:41) (B.B. King)

"Confessin' the Blues" (4:56) (J. McShann–W. Brown)

"Key to My Kingdom" (3:18) (Maxwell Davis–Joe Josea–Claude Baum)

"Cryin' Won't Help You Now" (6:30) (B.B. King)

"You're Mean" (9:59) (B.B. King–G. Jemmott–H. McCracken–P. Harris–
   H. Lovelle)

"The Thrill Is Gone" (5:30) (Roy Hawkins–Rick Darnell; originally credited to
   Arthur H. [Art] Benson–Dale Pettite)

Note: On the CD issue of *Completely Well*, the songs "Cryin' Won't Help You Now" and "You're Mean" are linked on one track instead of standing as individual cuts as they do on the original vinyl release.

The good feeling of the "Well" sessions carried over a few months later when Szymczyk reconvened the same lineup of musicians (sans Al Kooper) for the album that would be titled *Completely Well*. The concept, as the producer explained it to the artist, was simple: "I just wanted to do a whole 'Well' session and [B.B.] was definitely for it."

For the tune stack, B.B. brought in a new number, a mournful R&B ballad he had written titled "What Happened"; a driving, funky album opener he co-wrote with Gerald Jemmott, "I'm So Excited"; the Jay McShann–Walter Brown blues classic "Confessin' the Blues," which he had covered previously as the title song of a 1966 ABC album; an exhilarating, uptempo love song penned by Maxwell Davis that B.B. was on his way to making into a classic, "Key to My Kingdom"; a sizzling collaborative effort with all his musicians titled "You're Mean"; a Roy Hawkins song he had long admired but had never figured out how to adapt to his style, "The Thrill Is Gone"; and "You're Losin' Me" and "No Good," two numbers co-written with Ferdinand "Fats" Washington. "Key to My Kingdom" and "Cryin' Won't Help You Now" were the old warhorses of the repertoire. The former had been recorded by B.B. in 1957 as the A-side of RPM single 501 b/w "My Heart Belongs to You"; the latter, cut initially in 1956 as the A-side of RPM single 541 (b/w "Sixteen Tons"), had peaked at No. 15 R&B in its first incarnation before a second single was issued, also RPM 451, with a different B-side ("Can't We Talk It Over") that didn't chart at all.

In essence, *Completely Well* picks up where *Live & Well* left off, with the extended jams that made "Why I Sing the Blues" an eight-and-a-half-minutes-plus experience of bold social commentary buoyed by equally heated instrumental dialogs. At 3:18 "Key to My Kingdom" is the album's shortest song, by a minute-plus; four others clock in at more than four and a half minutes, and two of those are only seconds shy of five minutes; two songs, including "The

Thrill Is Gone," are five and a half minutes in length; "Cryin' Won't Help You Now" is six and a half minutes and segues without pause into a 9:59 workout on "You're Mean," making for an uninterrupted 16 minutes and 29 seconds of vocal and instrumental pyrotechnics. Frequently during the instrumental passages, B.B. is shouting encouragement to his bandmates, or laughing, or cracking wise (as "Cryin' Won't Help You Now"/"You're Mean" fades out, B.B. can be heard joking, "Damn, what you all tryin' to do, kill me?"). Everybody, ultimately, gets their quote in, B.B. both vocally and instrumentally.

According to Szymczyk, B.B.'s enthusiasm became part of the show of the sessions, but it was inspired by the musicians' exuberance. "He got really jazzed by these guys because they were so aggressive and they were good, and they pushed him," Szymczyk said. "Whereas, to be honest with you, his road band a lot of times would just do it by the numbers. They'd done the song a million times and it would be by rote. Whereas the guys I put him with, they'd never played the songs, obviously, because we were doing head arrangements on the date, and they were just digging the hell out of the fact that they were playing with B.B. King, and B.B.'s getting off."

In Alan Govenar's 1988 book, *Meeting the Blues*, which is quoted extensively in Sebastian Danchin's *"Blues Boy:" The Life and Music of B.B. King*, B.B. offers an explanation of why this and all his other sessions with Szymczyk were so productive: the producer's hands-off approach, trusting the artist to know how the music should be made, imbued him with a sense of freedom he hadn't experienced with ABC. "His ideas reminded me of the old Bihari days," King said of Szymczyk. "He wouldn't interfere with you while you were recording. Don't misunderstand me. I know this was a different time, and some of us need coaching. I'm one, but only to a point. Allow me to express me as I am. Let me play as I do. Don't say, 'Sound like this person,' or 'Do you remember hearing the record of so-and-so?' Well, that kind of attitude makes me not want to be on record because I like to be myself.

"Bill Szymczyk was a young producer and he understood me, one of those types that brings out the best in you. . . . "[5]

Some critics have been put off by the amount of time given over to the jamming passages on this record, but time has proven Szymczyk and B.B. correct in their approach. *Completely Well* has aged gracefully, because the sum of the parts adds up to a more than satisfying whole. Instrumentally, B.B. has plenty of room to shine in the context of extended dialogs with other players: his single-string run in the album opener, "So Excited," mirrors the ebullient mood of his upbeat vocal; his second break on "You're Losin' Me" features a beautiful sustained note that hangs suspended in the air for a second before

B.B. picks up the groove again and jets the song forward, and he repeats that feat as the song fades out. On "No Good" and "What Happened," his melancholy soloing heightens the blue mood, and its lack of any pronounced flourishes or embellishments—leaving those more to the swaying horns and to Paul Harris's tinkling piano commentary in "What Happened"—underscores the sadness he expresses lyrically in two ballad treatments of love gone wrong. Hugh McCracken's feisty wah-wah guitar solo in "So Excited" adds a touch of funk to the proceedings; and Paul Harris, on organ and piano, stands out on almost every cut, whether he's getting low-down and bluesy on the ballads or digging in to support and spar with B.B. on "Cryin' Won't Help You Now"/"You're Mean," his stylistic touchstones being both blues and honkytonk on this variegated, syncopated journey.

Despite the number of instrumental highlights on *Completely Well*, in the end B.B.'s vocal performances, among his finest over the course of an entire album, carry the day. "So Excited" was not only a lively opener, but B.B.'s upbeat attitude and rhythmic phrasing elevate the proceedings to an infectious, joyous plane; no wonder the song became a staple in his concert repertoire in the years ahead—the positive message and the funky groove are irresistible. On the other hand, "No Good," which follows the fireworks of "So Excited," is riveting precisely for the unalloyed hurt informing B.B.'s ceaseless, intense growling as he delivers the accusatory lyrics—B.B. gives no quarter here in putting down an unfaithful woman; there's nary a hint of mercy or forgiveness in his tone, but rage to burn. In contrast, the other slow blues, "What Happened," is as deep a lamentation as "No Good" is a screed; the sorrow in his measured rhetorical questions at the outset—"what happened / to that beautiful smile? / the one that you gave me / any time we were face to face?"—says everything about a man utterly devastated by his lover's change of heart. The questions persist, none designed to have an answer, but all framed to suggest the magnitude of his loss, until the blues enveloping B.B. finally overwhelms him. At the end, there is still no hope for reconciliation or even a sense that the singer is ready to move on. He is paralyzed by the blues. Again, conversely, his approach to "Key to My Kingdom" is strictly upbeat and life-affirming—the best way to describe B.B.'s singing here is to say he sounds positively lovestruck as he tells of "the thrill of your kiss" and the satisfaction he gets from being with his woman.

Apart from "The Thrill Is Gone," the song that resonated for B.B. on this album was "Confessin' the Blues." His strutting vocal and the steady grooving arrangement honored the original version by Jay McShann's redoubtable Kansas City outfit featuring vocalist Walter Brown. As a youth hanging outside Jones Night Spot, he had seen McShann and Brown perform the song (with a young Charlie "Bird" Parker on alto sax) one night, and the experience made its mark.

"All I knew was that this form of jazz mixed with blues made me happy," B.B. said. "Hearing Walter Brown sing 'Confessin' the Blues' and 'Hootie Blues' got me high."[6]

(As an interesting side note, in his liner notes for *Completely Well*, Ralph J. Gleason pointed out that "Confessin' the Blues," in addition to being a big hit for McShann, was also the song Chuck Berry sang when he made his first public appearance, in an assembly at his East St. Louis high school, and that the McShann version featured Charlie Parker's recording debut.)

That *Completely Well* has not always received high marks from the B.B. cognoscenti may have something to do with the final song on the album, "The Thrill Is Gone," seeming Olympian when compared to the performances preceding it. From Herb Lovelle's first stuttering drumbeat and Lucille's plaintive entrance with a single, wailing note, it feels like there's something at stake here. The band eases in—Jemmott plucking dark, ominous notes, Harris conjuring eerie, brooding chords from the organ, McCracken filling in the gaps with robust top-string runs—and B.B. cries out, "The thrill is gone / the thrill is gone away," and already he's deep into the feeling, stretching out the word "away" to the point where it sounds like he's near tears. After the first verse, a little more than a minute into the song, strings rise mournfully in the background, and down in the mix cellos play an "Eleanor Rigby"–like passage that is at once elegant in execution yet sinister in mood, the dark underbelly of a captivating, multi-layered string arrangement that delivers both light and dark textures. The light is not illusion—despite the pronounced, near-palpable pain in this narrative account of a woman whose malfeasance spelled a bitter end to a love affair, the lyric asserts that the man will press on, lonely, "free from your spell" but secure enough in knowing he is a "good man" to wish his betraying paramour well as she goes her solitary way. For the final 2:20 of the album cut, B.B. plays a tart, stinging extended solo as the strings and cellos sustain their foreboding dialog, rising and falling as Lucille sings her sad refrain then backs off while the band vamps behind him, as Harris's spooky organ fills flesh out the soundscape.

In the end, "The Thrill Is Gone" promises majesty at the outset and delivers it throughout. B.B.'s soloing is frills-free for the most part, a case study in the emotional potency of a well-considered, soulful, single-string attack, and his vocal, summoned from the deepest well of his gospel heart, also is a marvel of austere embroidery, its power coming simply from an extra syllable added at the end of a lyric line, or a piercing blue note that speaks volumes about a broken heart. The band plays as a tight, restrained ensemble; and the strings, despite their prominence in the arrangement, are subtly employed, entering almost at a whisper in the first verse, then ascending as the cellos gain intensity, but pulling back again for the song's closing instrumental section. All is restraint here, whether it's in B.B.'s soloing, or in his deliberate rendering of the sad lyric, or in the string section's subtle washes of sound, or in the band's low-profile supporting role. All of these factors working together add up to something greater than the sum of the parts, lending "The Thrill Is Gone" the incalculable, unquantifiable X factor of a classic performance.

"The Thrill Is Gone" was written and originally recorded in 1951 by B.B.'s Modern labelmate Roy Hawkins and peaked at No. 6 R&B. Arranged and produced by Maxwell Davis, Hawkins's version begins with Davis's screaming sax solo and settles into a straightforward, prototypical '50s blues ballad. Hawkins's husky, low-down vocal is buttressed by Willard McDaniel's righteous piano accompaniment, he giving the right-hand keys a rigorous workout, and by Davis, stepping out in mid-song for a blaring solo that settles into a more introspective mode before Hawkins returns to close out the story. As opposed to B.B.'s approach to the lyric, Hawkins sounds, depending on the listener's point of view, either utterly defeated by or emotionally disconnected from the events he describes; whereas B.B. transcends his pain and moves on with his life, dignity intact even as he is consumed by loneliness.

Roy Hawkins was a prolific writer, and his Modern singles found a home on the R&B charts in the late '40s and early '50s, including several in the chart's Top Ten. Over one two-year period he was Modern's biggest moneymaker. Born in Texas in 1904, he had been discovered by producer Bob Geddins playing at a club in Oakland, California. Geddins owned a studio in Oakland and released records locally on his own Cava-Tone and Down Town labels; if he saw good sales on one of his releases, he would lease the masters to larger indies. Hence Hawkins's path to Modern, for which he began recording, with Geddins at the helm, in late 1949. (Another of Geddins's artists, Jimmy McCracklin, has gone on to carve out one of the more important blues careers of his time.) As if living out the despair he wrote of so often, Hawkins, then newly signed to Modern, was injured in a car crash that left one of his arms paralyzed. Nevertheless, in 1950 he had his first major hit with "Why Do Everything Happen to Me," which is credited to Hawkins as a writer, although Geddins has claimed credit for writing the song.[7] The single peaked at No. 3 on the R&B chart in early '50 and had a 19-week chart run. Both B.B.

(Kent single 301, 1958; reissued in 1965 on Kent as the B-side of the single "Just a Dream") and James Brown (for Federal) later covered the song. In 1950 Modern teamed Hawkins with producer Maxwell Davis; "The Thrill Is Gone" was their first session, but after a promising start the single faltered, although Jules Bihari later claimed sales remained strong in certain markets even after the single was off the charts. Eventually Hawkins, a heavy drinker according to Geddins,[8] dropped out of the business. Little is known of his later years, but he did live to see B.B., Memphis Slim, James Brown, and Ray Charles cover his songs. He died on March 19, 1974, in Los Angeles County.

B.B. had never forgotten Roy Hawkins or "The Thrill Is Gone." "Something about the song haunted me," he said. "It was a different kind of blues ballad, and I carried it around in my head for many years. I'd been arranging it in my brain and even tried a couple of different versions that didn't work. But on this night in New York when I walked in to record, all the ideas came together. I changed the tune around to fit my style, and Bill Szymczyk set up the sound nice and mellow. We got through about 3:00 A.M. I was thrilled. Bill wasn't, so I just went home.

"At 5:00 A.M. Bill called and woke me up. 'B,' he said, 'I think "The Thrill Is Gone" is really something.'

"'That's what I was trying to tell you,' I said.

"'I think it's a smash hit,' Bill added. 'And I think it'd be even more of a hit if I added on strings. What do you think?'

"'Let's do it.'"[9]

For the string overdubs, Szymczyk called in veteran arranger Bert DeCoteaux. "Back when I was engineering other peoples' R&B stuff, he had done a bunch of things I admired, so when it came time to do a string chart, I called him immediately," Szymczyk said. "I really liked the way he worked; I liked his charts." (DeCoteaux would become a major disco arranger as the '70s wore on, but his résumé also included producing and playing keyboards for Albert King, and producer credits with Z.Z. Hill, Marlena Shaw, the British pub rockers Dr. Feelgood, the Main Ingredient, and Cissy Houston.)

According to Szymczyk, B.B. had gone on the road after the session but returned for the string overdubs. "I remember him being there," the producer said. "He loved it. He was smiling all the way through it."

As for B.B.'s account of the session, Szymczyk offers a constrasting recollection. For starters, he claimed it didn't happen in a 24-hour period, nor was his reaction to the song unenthusiastic. "I was ecstatic with the cut when we were doing it in the studio, so I'm not quite sure where he gets that it wasn't getting it for me, because I was over the top," he said. "I distinctly remember throwing my hands up in the air, I was so happy, when we were doing the fade and saying, 'Oh, this is so cool!' And it was maybe the next day—I don't think it was two hours later, but the next day I called him up and said, 'Look, I really want to put strings on this record.' And he was somewhat reticent at first, in my recollection. But he said, 'Yeah, okay,' in essence saying, 'You haven't fucked up so far, so go ahead on.' I think we put the strings on maybe a week later."

In Szymczyk's view the success of the *Live & Well* and *Completely Well* studio sessions was no mystery: "The main thing I did was hire the right guys. That to me was the key to that whole two-album session—get the right guys and then get out of the way."

In the studio, the producer found B.B. "real happy with everything. He was in his element, he was being himself, but he was doing it with some new, energetic guys. And I don't think we ever did more than two, three takes on anything. We'd maybe do one, go in and listen to it, make a couple of comments and then go out there and do one or two more and that would be it, usually."

B.B. said DeCoteaux's strings made "The Thrill Is Gone" "irresistible." Black radio stations were on the single right away, but it soon crossed over and made pop station playlists around the country too. It had a long chart run, peaking at No. 15 pop (No. 3 R&B). It became, as B.B. said, "the only real hit of my career" and his first Grammy-winning record.[10]

"The song was true to me," B.B. says, noting that "'The Thrill Is Gone' is basically blues. The sound incorporated strings, but the feeling is still low-down. The lyric is also blues, the story of a man who's wronged by his woman but free to go on with his life. Lucille is as much a part of song as me. She starts off singing and stays with me all the way before she takes a final bow."[11]

The success of "The Thrill Is Gone" brought far more lucrative and lasting benefits than a Grammy, though. As Charles Sawyer recounts in *The Arrival of B.B. King,* the single's success resulted in a wholesale change in B.B.'s itinerary. Suddenly the chitlin' circuit gigs were supplanted by appearances at prestigious jazz clubs and rock halls such as the Fillmores West and East and the Boston Tea Party. College concerts became a staple of his touring schedule and, according to Sawyer, "B.B.'s regular stints in college gymnasiums from Boise to Chapel Hill solidified his new career by exposing him night after night to the young affluent whites that comprise the broad base of America's middle class."[12] During this period of transition he also made his first appearances on network TV, with a guest shot on "The Tonight Show" (invited by comedian Flip Wilson, who was the guest host that night, although Johnny Carson later invited B.B. back several times when he was in his regular seat at the host's desk) and on shows hosted by Mike Douglas,

David Frost, and Merv Griffin. In 1970 he opened ten dates on the Rolling Stones' American tour; toured Australia in 1971; embarked on a 45-day world tour in 1972; undertook an African tour sponsored by the U.S. State Department; toured Europe several times; and, according to Sawyer, experienced success "even in Israel, where the legendary Ella Fitzgerald had not succeeded." He went all across America, playing theaters in the round to what Richard Nixon called "the silent majority"—older, white, middle-class Americans—and finally got his shot in Las Vegas, sharing a bill with Frank Sinatra (with Sinatra's approval) at Caesars Palace. According to B.B., a weary Ol' Blue Eyes greeted him cordially in his penthouse at the end of one night's sets and proffered both wine and women, two items that were plentiful in the penthouse. "I didn't take advantage of his generosity," B.B. said of Sinatra's offer, "but I believe it was sincere."[13] B.B. later appeared at the Dunes before signing a three-year contract with the Las Vegas Hilton.

A year later, Szymczyk, having relocated to Los Angeles after ABC shut down its East Coast operation, rendezvoused with B.B. at the Record Plant, for sessions that would yield not another "The Thrill Is Gone" in terms of a career-altering hit single, but an album that matched B.B. with a new cast of top-flight musicians. One, Carole King, only a year away from releasing what would become one of the best-selling albums of all time, *Tapestry*, was already established as one of the preeminent rock 'n' roll songwriters of her generation. Another was veteran session man-bandleader-songwriter-arranger Leon Russell, then on the cusp of extraordinary success as a solo artist in the early '70s. Rounding out the session was the redoubtable veteran string and horn arranger Jimmie Haskell, who had produced and arranged Rick Nelson's great recordings in the '50s and '60s. The result was one of the most cohesive and stirring studio albums of B.B.'s entire career.

A remarkable review of the single "The Thrill Is Gone" appeared in the April 2, 1970, issue of *Rolling Stone*, penned by J.R. Young. In typical Young fashion—no one before or since has written reviews quite like Young—the piece tells the story of two friends, Phil and Bud. Fraternity brothers at an unidentified Oregon school, they are on a drive one night when Phil reveals that once, on that very same winding mountain road, he tuned in a radio station broadcasting from the late 1940s.

> "Not a recording of great moments or anything like that, but the real thing," Phil said. Bud frowned again but Phil nodded and went on, "I mean I think that somehow that radio wave or beam in its outward movement collided with something that reflected it back and somehow the car receiver picked it up and broadcast it."

Bud is puzzled by this, and recalls another story Phil told him: that someone had pictures, almost a film, of Christ on Calvary. The pictures had been discovered buried, wrapped in a parchment tube. What it was, so Phil's story went, was a series of rabbit retinas. Someone had lined up a row of rabbits facing the cross and then chopped their heads off in quick succession. The final retinal imprint was somehow made permanent in each eye, and thus, when all the retinas were lined up, there was a pictorial study of Calvary. The story had bothered Bud for a long time.

The review cuts to 1970, the present day, and Bud hasn't seen Phil since 1964. But Bud finds himself back traveling on the mountain road where Phil claimed to have picked up the late '40s broadcast.

Bud pushed the button of his radio and waited for some music, but he got only static. He remembered how hard it was to pick up anything in the mountains. He slowly turned the tuning knob. Nothing but static ... until slowly the dial seemed to ease into and lock on a strangely haunting tune, a lonely guitar rising somewhere from the past, and then a full and plaintive voice.

The thrill is gone

The thrill is gone away

There was something about it, an unknown quality conjured up from the past that told Bud something, a song for long driving nights in the dark mountains, calm and clear as the lush strings rolled gently under the full white moon above and the silver road ahead. It moved on endlessly, soothing his mind, and Bud thought that, yes, here it was again, a single beam from out of the sky, vibrational energy, a wave again trapped before beginning its second stellar flight, and he found himself taking deep breaths, trying to inhale it all, the sinuous and sharp strings, the fragile tones, and that voice ... that voice.

It slowly began to fade, and Bud reached for the volume and tried to keep pace with the dying sound, but he couldn't hold it. It still fell away as Bud reached full volume. And then the sound was lost altogether. Bud thought he had lost the beam.

"Crap," he muttered.

"AWRIGHT, BABY ... B.B. KING AND THE THRILL IS GONE." The radio suddenly boomed at an incredible volume that almost knocked Bud's head off. "AND WE GOWAN TO DA NEWS BABY AT TWELVE THUTY TWOO." Wolfman Jack from San Diego and the news was today's news, and the beam was just as powerful, not interstellar, and Bud then snapped the radio off in half a second and sat quite still for a few moments, still slightly shaken, his ears ringing.

Then he smiled and rapped the steering wheel with his knuckles. "That Phil," he laughed. "What a card."

Indianola Mississippi Seeds _____

ABC Bluesway, 1970; MCA, 1989

"I've never made a perfect record, ever. Although I'm not ashamed of any of them, there's always something that I could have done better. I know the critics always mention *Live and Well* or *Live at the Regal*, but I think that *Indianola Mississippi Seeds* is the best album I've done artistically."—B.B. King, *Blues Guitar*, July 1993

Produced by Bill Szymczyk
Strings and horns arranged by Jimmie Haskell
Recorded at the Record Plant, Los Angeles
Engineers: Bill Szymczyk and Gary Kellgren
Assistant engineers: Llyllianne Douma, Mike Stone, and John Henning
"Go Underground" recorded at the Hit Factory, New York City; Joe Zagarino, engineer
Mastering: Bob MacLeod, Artisan Sound Recorders

Songs and Musicians

"Nobody Loves Me but My Mother" (1:26) (B.B. King) B.B. King: piano and vocal

"You're Still My Woman" (6:04) (B.B. King–Dave Clark) B.B. King: guitar and vocal; Carole King: piano; Bryan Garofolo: bass; Russ Kunkel: drums

"Ask Me No Questions" (3:07) (B.B. King) B.B. King: lead guitar and vocal; Leon Russell: piano; Joe Walsh: rhythm guitar; Bryan Garofolo: bass; Russ Kunkel: drums.

"Until I'm Dead and Cold" (4:45) (B.B. King) B.B. King: guitar and vocal; Carole King: piano; Bryan Garofolo: bass; Russ Kunkel: drums.

"King's Special" (5:30) (B.B. King) B.B. King: lead guitar; Leon Russell: piano; Joe Walsh: rhythm guitar; Bryan Garofolo: bass; Russ Kunkel: drums

"Ain't Gonna Worry My Life Anymore" (5:18) (B.B. King) B.B. King: guitar and vocal; Carole King: piano; Bryan Garofalo: bass; Russ Kunkel: drums

"Chains and Things" (4:52) (B.B. King–Dave Clark) B.B. King: guitar and vocal; Carole King: electric piano; Bryan Garofalo: bass; Russ Kunkel: drums

"Go Underground" (4:02) (B.B. King–Dave Clark) B.B. King: lead guitar and vocal; Paul Harris: piano; Hugh McCracken: rhythm guitar; Gerald Jemmott: bass; Herb Lovelle: drums

"Hummingbird" (4:36) (Leon Russell) B.B. King: lead guitar; Leon Russell: piano and conductor; Joe Walsh: rhythm guitar; Bryan Garofalo: bass; Russ Kunkel: drums; Sherlie Matthews, Merry Clayton, Clydie King, Venetta Fields; angelic chorus

From the start it's apparent this is no ordinary B.B. King album. The first 1:26 is occupied by a track on which B.B., alone at the piano, wails and moans a gospelized version of "Nobody Loves Me but My Mother." His piano playing is florid—notes raining down on one another, a busy right-hand trill here, a bluesy slip-note passage there, alternately evoking the church and the after-hours joint—and his singing is both powerful and nuanced: the line "nobody loves me but my mother" is delivered with a soulful cry, whereas the punch line, "and she could be jivin' too," is sung softly, his phrasing betraying the bittersweet insecurity at the root of this blues and suddenly conjuring a near-palpable sadness.

At the 1:25 mark, though, B.B. abruptly stops playing and queries, impatiently, "What I wanna know now is what we gonna do?" And immediately Lucille answers with a resounding retort that leads into a surging, moody blues, "You're Still My Woman," marked most prominently by a steady-rolling piano solo and a sweet wash of strings.

The template thus constructed, B.B. and his studio partners proceed to inject it with human qualities and fuel it with scintillating musical discourse. For Szymczyk, *Indianola Mississippi Seeds* saw the full realization of the ideas he had advanced so fruitfully on *Completely Well*. Saying that the former works better than the latter, despite "The Thrill Is Gone" launching B.B. into a higher orbit commercially, is an exercise in hairsplitting, both albums being well conceived and masterfully executed. But on balance, *Indianola* has more of the elusive stuff of art—call it soul, call it the human touch, call it the voice of experience (in life and in music)—that elevates a recording project onto a plane where it touches listeners organically, where the music is understood as much spiritually as physically or intellectually.

The mainstays of this group of players assembled by Szymczyk were prominent young session hands Bryan Garofalo on bass and Russ Kunkel on drums, both of whom the producer had used on other projects. Three cuts feature on rhythm guitar Joe Walsh (then of the Szymcyzk-signed and -produced James Gang, which preceded Walsh's solo career, which in turn preceded his long-term tenure with the Szymczyk-produced Eagles). Four of the nine cuts feature Carole King on piano. Szymczyk had first laid eyes on her at the outset of his career, when he was a maintenance worker at Dick Charles Recording in New York and watched her and Gerry Goffin cutting demos. The two had kept in "semi-touch" over the years, according to Szymczyk, who knew from eyewitness experience that the young and gifted Brooklynite played "great blues piano," and figured that having her on the sessions would simply be "cool." Thus in addition to her daunting résumé as a songwriter, and with what she would go on to achieve as a solo artist, Carole King entered the B.B. story with the distinction of being the first female musician to play on one of his albums.

Leon Russell came to the session with commanding credentials himself. Born (1942) and raised in Oklahoma, he had started his career at age 14 playing in nightclubs in Tulsa; in high school his was by far the best band in a town with a thriving musical scene, so much so that for two years Jerry Lee Lewis spirited the group away to back him on the road. In the early '60s he relocated to Los Angeles and became one of the town's first-call guitar and piano players. The extraordinary group of musicians he often played with in the studio came to be known as the Wrecking Crew, and its members included a hotshot young guitarist from Arkansas named Glen Campbell and a drummer well versed in myriad musical styles named Hal Blaine. Russell's extensive studio credits included work on the Beach Boys' *Pet Sounds* album, piano on Jan and Dean's "Surf City" single, and numerous credits on Phil Spector–produced sessions, and he had arranged and played on several sparkling Snuff Garrett productions of hits for Gary Lewis and the Playboys. He was a superb bandleader and musical director, accomplished and stylish on guitar, bass, and piano, a first-rate songwriter, and a marvelously effective singer whose lazy Southern drawl and marble-mouthed phrasing betrayed his deep immersion in blues and gospel at every turn. When called in to work on *Indianola Mississippi Seeds*, he was approaching his solo breakthrough: within a year he would release his second solo album, *Leon Russell and the Shelter People*, on his own Shelter label, lead Joe Cocker and the Mad Dogs and Englishmen's wild ride, and almost steal the show from George Harrison, Bob Dylan, and Eric Clapton at the Concert for Bangladesh. On record and on the concert stage, he was one of the early '70s' top draws. His song "Hummingbird," which was the final, towering cut on his debut album, got a powerhouse treatment by B.B. as the closing track on *Indianola*.

Apart from "Hummingbird," the album's other eight songs were all written by B.B., or by B.B. in collaboration with Dave Clark. With Clark he delivers the album-opening mid-tempo blues "You're Still My Woman"; a multi-layered nightmare blues, "Chains and Things"; and an uptempo funk workout with a downcast theme ("I can't be a winner because I was born to lose"), "Go Underground." The songs credited to B.B. alone reveal a writer ever more confident of his message, ever more lyrical in his use of language, ever bolder in baring his soul.

On "Ask Me No Questions," a strutting blues with a country feel, in the midst of a stirring guitar-piano dialog between B.B. and Paul Harris (whose jubilant soloing blends influences across the Southern precincts, from Nashville to Memphis to New Orleans, in a most remarkable performance), B.B. first complains about a woman's indifference to him ("you just love me when you wanna / and you think it oughta be all right with me") and winds up not kowtowing to her but making a stand, dignity dented but intact: "You can love me if you want to / or keep playing the field / because I know if you don't love me / I know there's somebody else who will." In the slow blues ballad "Until I'm Dead and Cold," another B.B. original, he sings the lyric with the conversational subtlety and open heart of a Percy Mayfield, and what he's written for himself to sing is not the usual bluesman's lament or devotional, but rather a mature expression of love in its fullest form—he sings of a woman who is "more than a lover to me" and identifies her as a "companion," a "friend," "a part of me." As the narrative unfolds, the surprising twist revealed is that all of his expressions of commitment appear to be directed at a woman who in fact has left him. He, however, does not dismiss her with any macho bluster or revenge scenarios, but instead vows to love on to the end: "What's done is done / but you know I just can't stop loving you / I'll tell you the truth, I'll love you more, baby / And I'll keep on loving you until I'm dead, until I'm dead and cold." A lilting solo by B.B. follows and the song concludes with a hearty blast of horns.

"I call it 'King's Special.' The reason I do is because I got the idea of a train. But I want it with a beat, so a person can dance to it if they want to." So goes B.B.'s spoken intro to the instrumental "King's Special," a five-and-a-half-minute ride with B.B. and Joe Walsh on guitars and Leon Russell at the piano. B.B. and Russell engage in a perky set-to little more than halfway through the number, trading short, deliberate phrases, raising the tempo and gradually lowering it—the locomotive trundling along, up and down peaks and valleys, but always moving forward—until the fadeout begins with B.B. striking a robust double-string chord that evokes the sound of a train whistle before executing a rapid, descending top-string run as the whole enterprise chugs to a halt.

A plush carpet of strings introduces "Ain't Gonna Worry My Life Anymore," but it's quickly rolled up for a funky jam punctuated by a raucous Russ Kunkel drum solo that moves B.B. to say, "That's beautiful, man!" It all ends at the 1:42 mark, and B.B. laughs and says, "That's good, that's good. I just felt like doing something." Then he announces, "Okay, here's another one," and cuts out on a bright run before the band kicks in on a jump blues powered by the redoubtable rhythm section, a bleating sax, pumping horns, a fleet-fingered B.B. solo, and Carole King, working the length of the keyboard at a lightning-fast clip as B.B. contributes gospel-style lyrics. Finally the whole enterprise elevates until the ensemble workout mutates into a smooth, ascending wash of strings at fadeout. Carole King then re-enters with an ominous, repeating triplet figure on electric piano, Lucille signaling B.B.'s vocal entrance by spitting out a terse, single-string run of foreboding notes. Then B.B. unburdens himself of a deep, dark blues that gains added tension when the strings start rising, and keep rising, until they're screaming in tandem with B.B.'s litany of misfortune. In this lyric scenario, everything and everyone is a conspirator in skulduggery, from the people on the job to a coldhearted, wrong-doing woman to a "slave-driving" boss. "I can't play the losing game," B.B. moans; near the song's end, his lament is, "Ain't got no money to buy a ticket / and I don't feel like walking no more." It's a rare blues that B.B. writes in which he casts himself as having no hope, and possibly suicidal, but "Chains and Things" is one, and the dramatic production touches reflect a man whose reality is splintered.

An odd thing happens at the 3:38 mark: as the arrangement moves into a crescendo, B.B. hits a wrong note. He spends a couple of bars working himself out of the dilemma, and eventually falls back into sync with the strings as the song hits an explosive apex. A number of writers have caught this slip, but B.B.'s best explanation of himself was published in an interview in *Blues Guitar*'s July 1993 issue. Speaking to writers Tom Wheeler and Jas Obrecht, he cuts off the comment, "There's a very unusual melody line near the end of 'Chains and Things' on *Indianola Mississippi Seeds*," with a *mea culpa*: "I made a mistake. Now you're getting all my secrets. My bandleader and I have laughed about it many times, but I made a mistake and hit the wrong note and worked my way out of it. We liked the way it sounded, so we got the arranger to have the strings follow it. They repeat the phrase the way I played it. If you've got a good take going and then hit one wrong note, you don't ever want to stop, so I was in the key of A♭, and when I hit [hums E, D♭, E♭, E♭], which is number 5, 4, 5, 5, we just got the rest of the band to follow along."

After the emotional turmoil of "Chains and Things," the lighthearted funk of "Go Underground" is a welcome breather. A carryover from the *Completely Well* sessions, the song's whimsical lyric finds B.B. complaining about a woman who doesn't appreciate his ministrations and signing off each verse with "I think I'll do like a mole and move underground." The track is a nice jam, its most remarkable aspects being Hugh McCracken offering a song-length wah-wah guitar solo and, notably, a sprightly honky-tonk-flavored piano solo by Paul Harris.

Clearly the album's showcase, "Hummingbird," like "The Thrill Is Gone," closes out the disc and even has strings entering at about the same juncture of the song as they do in "Thrill." Jimmie Haskell's strings are dramatic but subtle, ascending and descending delicately in the verses, then becoming more pronounced in the chorus and jittery, anxious in the instrumental breaks.

B.B.'s crooning vocal is modulated, with emphasis placed on the beginning of a lyric line and then softening seductively towards the end and rising proud in the chorus, when it's supported by the strings. At the 3:14 mark, with B.B. declaiming in full gospel lather, really wrecking the house, in soar the female voices dubbed the Angelic Chorus—Sherlie Mathews, Merry Clayton, Clydie King, and Venetta Fields—and the band matches their soul-shaking fervor. Kunkel is pounding the drums so hard it's easy to imagine his whole kit in shreds by the end of the song; Russell is working feverishly on the length of the keyboard, punctuating his chording with robust glissandos; and B.B. can be heard deep in the mix in an extended single-string run. The gals keep wailing, the band keeps blasting … and then it all fades out gently, the storm subsiding and leaving a bracing calm when the last note whispers its exit. "Humming-bird" is a powerful exercise in both tenderness and triumphant spirit, and the ensemble's energy, power, and commitment form a beautiful, moving aural assault that evolves into a full-out Southern Baptist revival meeting.

(Russell, who was the conductor on the session, employed some similar devices in his own version of "Hummingbird" on his first solo album. He opened, however, with a stark, top-strings taste of Delta blues guitar followed by a series of stabbing piano chords ahead of his growling vocal entrance. As the rest of the band settles in behind him, the organ rises in the chorus, a fleeting whirl of synths flits by, and that mesmerizing Delta blues lick is reprised in the gathering calm before Russell returns for another verse. Following a stop-time measure at the end of the third verse, Russell's own Angelic Chorus [comprised of Clydie King, Merry Clayton, and Bonnie Bramlett] cuts loose with some gospel belting of their own, crying, pleading "Don't fly away—away." At that point the Russell track sounds like a Rolling Stones cut circa 1968's *Beggars Banquet* and 1969's *Let It Bleed*, and perhaps that's no coincidence: the Stones' drummer Charlie Watts and bassist Bill Wyman are guests on Russell's album, and Merry Clayton wrote her name large in Stones history with a searing vocal performance on "Gimme Shelter," *Let It Bleed*'s first cut.)

A single, "Chains and Things" b/w "King's Special," peaked at No. 6 R&B and at No. 45 on the pop chart; a second single, "Nobody Loves Me but My Mother" b/w "Ask Me No Questions," did not chart at all. Nevertheless, *Indianola Mississippi Seeds* is a remarkable artistic achievement, strictly top-drawer in its mix of excellent songs, in the musicians' drive to take everything to another level, and especially in B.B.'s powerful vocal performances both as a balladeer and as a blues shouter. With this album, more so than with *Completely Well*, B.B. King had arrived, in Charles Sawyer's formulation, as a fully realized artist in the studio and out.

Indianola Mississippi Seeds:
The Studio Sessions
A conversation with Bill Szymczyk

Ayear after Completely Well *you cut* Indianola Mississippi Seeds, *a great record and the one B.B. says is his best artistic effort. As with the previous two albums, you put together an interesting cast of characters for these sessions.*

You see, I had to put another band together, because I was living in L.A. at the time. I had found Russ Kunkel and Bryan Garofolo. I had done some sessions when I had first got there and they were young guys, up and coming, and I had worked with Walsh, because I had found him in the James Gang and signed him. The very first session I ever saw was a Carole King–Gerry Goffin demo, and she was playing piano and singing the demo. I became a huge Carole King fan. We kept semi–in touch and I had seen her around, and I just thought it would be so cool, because I know she plays great blues piano. So I call her up and said, "Carole, would you like to play on a B.B. King album?" It was an instant "You bet!" So when I got in the studio the very first day, one of my favorite stories is, I said to B, "B.B. King, I'd like you to meet Carole King. Carole King, B.B. King. Perhaps you're related!" They loved it.

Jimmie Haskell, your arranger, had done monumental work in his career, especially for Ricky Nelson in the early days. That was an inspirational stroke to bring him in. His touch with strings is impeccable.

Yeah. Once again, when I moved to L.A. I had to get a new arranger. I had heard a couple of things he had done for Steve Barri, who was my boss. I heard some of his charts and hired him. And he became my Bert DeCoteaux on the West Coast. He's a mild-mannered sweetheart of a guy. He would do anything. He was great. We actually later on tried to make an album with him, with guest vocalists and stuff, but it got slaughtered by the record company. That was after I left. He'd tell us all the Rick Nelson stories, and I'd tell him the B.B. King and James Gang stories. And then we'd lie to each other.

Carole King is playing piano on four of the nine cuts. Throughout this record, including the cuts that Leon's on and the one with Paul Harris, it strikes me that you really allowed the piano players to be heard almost as a duet with B.B. They're very up front on these recordings. Which is good because they're all great piano players. Was that the design?

I think it turned out that way because of the caliber of player that I got in all three of those. And the fact that there isn't someone for B to play off of other than the piano player. The rhythm guitar player, maybe, whether it be Hugh McCracken or Joe Walsh, but in some cases there was no other guitar player, and it would be, Who do you play off? You play off a great keyboard player. And also they didn't take the shine off B's thing.

There's a genuine and ongoing dialog between these instruments. It happens on Completely Well *with Paul Harris, but it's really pronounced on this one. Of course you've got an all-star lineup of piano players.*

I got lucky that way. Leon, I called him specifically because I wanted to do "Hummingbird" with B.B. I'd heard that song on Leon's album and I went nuts for it.

The other interesting thing on here is right at the beginning, and it's the shortest cut on the album. That would be B.B. alone at the piano doing "Nobody Loves Me but My Mother," a singular moment on B.B.'s records. How did that happen?

It was after the session was over the first day; that was the first Carole King and B.B. and Bryan and Russell session. And we were packing up and there was this tack piano over in the corner, and he was saying something like, "I play a little piano too." And [Carole] said, "Oh, really?" And he sat down and I immediately whipped a mic on it and got it down. It was like an afterthought. And then I told him I wanted to put it on the record and he said, "Oh, no, no, no, you can't do that. I don't play piano!" I said, "You do now. It's too cool not to be on the album."

This one was recorded at the Record Plant in Los Angeles. What kind of gear were you on at this point?

I can't remember the name of the board. One thing they did have that was odd was a one-inch 12-track machine, one of the very few MCI 12-tracks ever made. I think we did it on that, but that only lasted about 20 minutes. And we went right to 16 tracks.

You used Gary Kellgren as a co-engineer, one of the co-owners of the studio.

Yeah, he would do the tracks for me. Gary and I started out back at Dick Charles, like three months apart from each other. He was there about three months ahead of me, out of the Air Force. He was on his way to Europe to write the Great American Novel, and I was on my way to school to learn how to do television, and neither one of us made it.

Live in Cook County Jail _____

ABC LP 723, 1970
Production and sound: Bill Szymczyk

Musicians
B.B. King: guitar, vocals
John Browning: trumpet
Louis Hubert: tenor saxophone
Booker Walker: alto saxophone
Ron Levy: piano

Wilbert Freeman: bass
Sonny Freeman: drums

Songs
"Introduction" (1:50)
"Every Day I Have the Blues" (1:43) (P. Chatman)
"How Blue Can You Get" (5:09) (J. Feather)
"Worry, Worry, Worry" (9:57) (D. Plumber–J. Taub)
Medley: "3 O'Clock Blues" (Lowell Fulson) / "Darlin' You Know I Love You"
    (6:15) (J. Taub–B.B. King)
"Sweet Sixteen" (4:20) (J. Josea–B.B. King)
"The Thrill Is Gone" (5:31) (Roy Hawkins)
"Please Accept My Love" (4:02) (B.B. King–S. Ling)

Bill Szymczyk's final B.B. production had significance beyond most live albums. *Live at the Regal* was now accepted as the gold standard of live blues albums, and no one seems to have gone into this project with the idea of topping the Regal show. Nonetheless, there was a purpose to these proceedings recorded on September 10, 1970, and it wasn't simply to cash in on the live-album craze that had been jump-started by Johnny Cash's *Live at Folsom Prison*. B.B. was there to deliver hope, to bring some light to the daily drudgery of the 2,117 inmates, most of them black, some of them women. "The prisoners saw King's visit as an all-too-rare recognition of their humanity," noted Sebastian Danchin in *Blues Boy: The Life and Music of B.B. King*.

Szymczyk lined up a remote recording truck from Location Recorders, whose owner, Aaron Baron, recorded the show and gave Szymcyzk the tapes to be mixed. The repertoire was heavy on slow blues and genial hosting by B.B., who took a few minutes in the middle of "Worry, Worry, Worry" to advise the inmates on the proper way to treat their woman or man, including advice to the men not to beat on their women, and for both sides to recognize that "men are God's gift to women" and "women are God's gift to men." It's a classic bit of bluesman as evangelist and soothsayer. Otherwise, his balladry on "Darlin' You Know I Love You" and "Sweet Sixteen" is sensuous and heartfelt, and the sincerity of his closing sentiments before he winds up the show with a romantic crooning take on "Please Accept My Love" is an affecting wearing of the heart on the sleeve before a tough crowd.

To Tom Wheeler in the September 1970 issue of *Guitar Player*, B.B. explained that when he told the ABC brass he was going to do a show at the notorious Cook County Jail in Chicago, he was advised to take along the press and some recording equipment.

"When we got there we found that about 70 percent to 80 percent of the people in there were black or of other minority races and very young, in their teens or early twenties," B.B. told Wheeler. "The press interviewed a lot of these people and found out that some of them had been there like a year almost and hadn't even come to trial. They were just there, arrested, and they stayed there, couldn't afford bail. So the press really blew it up, man, they really worked with it that next day. I felt that was good, so the people on the outside could know what was happening behind the wall."

His activist instincts stirring, B.B. took it a step further. "I told them that from then on I would be glad to donate my services anytime they wanted them. I felt that the more I went in and played and the press went with me, the more we could let the people out there know. I feel that a lot of the judges and the people who arrest those fellows and put them in there don't even know what it looks like. I felt that if we kept it up long enough, some of these people would probably be invited to go in and see for themselves, and that might make them think a little bit different. Don't get me wrong. I don't think that when a guy does something wrong he shouldn't be punished, but if he does it as a human being, he should pay for it as a human being."[14]

By 1998, when Sebastian Danchin's book was published, B.B. had been true to his word and then some, having performed more than 50 free prison shows over the years. In March 1972 he teamed with attorney F. Lee Bailey to establish the Foundation for the Advancement of Inmate Rehabilitation and Recreation (FAIRR), an organization that grew out of B.B.'s conversations with inmates who told him "it wouldn't be so bad to spend ten or fifteen years someplace if they knew that they would have something to depend on when they got out. They told me, B.B., if we could get guitars, if we could get books, if we could just get something we could work with—and this hurt me so bad, thinking about a guy having to stay in a place for ten or fifteen years, and *nothing*, you know. I would probably be in prison today if it hadn't been for some folks caring about what I was doing."[15]

Live at Cook County Jail marked the end of B.B.'s career-altering two-year journey with Bill Szymczyk. It ended not as the result of any creative differences or some other kind of professional or personal falling-out, but because the moving hand of God scared Szymczyk out of his wits and out of California. In February of 1971 Los Angeles was rocked by an earthquake, and eight days later, Szymczyk says, "I lived in Denver and had no job. I quit. I couldn't relate to earthquakes. I had about a month to finish up three or four things that were in progress. I finished those up and, man, I was gone. So I obviously wasn't working for ABC anymore."

Szymczyk did quite well on his own, as he wound up behind the board on the Eagles' rise to superstardom. Along the way he developed a pragmatic philosophy of production that continues to serve him well: "I'm not a musician; I don't play anything. I listen. And I think that's helped me over the years because I don't favor any one thing. If I was a guitar player, I might favor that. If I was a keyboard player, I might favor that. But I've always believed in listening. And my whole way of producing is to listen and react. Don't go in with a preconceived notion, listen to what the artist is doing and react to that and make it better."

Today Szymczyk lives in self-described semi-retirement in Little Switzerland, North Carolina. In his house is a 24-track studio ("analog—can you believe that?"); he mulls over offers and picks and chooses what appeals to him. He's worked with a local singer-songwriter, and as of this writing was preparing to produce a few cuts on a new album by Los Angeles–based Dishwalla. "A little bit here, a little bit there," he says with complete contentment. "I'm having a heck of a time."

B.B. King in London

ABC/Dunhill, 1971; MCA Special Products, 2001

Produced: Ed Michel and Joe Zagarino

Recorded: Olympic and Command Studios in London, June 9–16, 1971, and modified at the Village Recorders and the Record Plant in Los Angeles and the Hit Factory in New York.

Knobs, buttons, slides and switches: Zags, with the engineering assistance of Baker Bigsby, Andrew Hendrickson, Pete Booth, Chris Kimsey, Rufus Cartwright, Phillip Holland, Lee Kiefer, John Stronach, Joe Veneri, Tom Brown, and Eddie James

Songs and Musicians

"Caldonia" (4:00) (F. Moore)

B.B. King: guitar and vocal; with Jim Price and Ollie Mitchell: trumpets; Chuck Findley: trombone; Bobby Keys: tenor saxophone; Bill Perkins: baritone saxophone and clarinet; Duster Bennett: harmonica; Gary Wright: organ; Rick Wright: electric piano; Peter Green: guitar; Klaus Voorman: Fender bass; Jim Gordon: drums

"Blue Shadows" (5:11) (L.C. Glenn)

B.B. King: guitar and vocal; with Gary Wright: electric piano; the Mystery Shadow: organ; John Uribe: guitar; Klaus Voorman: Fender bass; Jim Keltner: drums

"Alexis' Boogie" (3:32) (Alexis Korner)

B.B. King: acoustic guitar; with Alexis Korner: acoustic guitar; Steve Marriott: harmonica; Greg Ridley: bass; Jerry Shirley: drums

"We Can't Agree" (4:52) (L. Jordan–W. Gray)

B.B. King: guitar and vocal; with Gary Wright: electric piano; The Mystery Shadow: organ; John Uribe: guitar; Klaus Voorman: bass; Jim Keltner: drums

"Ghetto Woman" (5:13) (B.B. King–D. Clark)

B.B. King: guitar and vocal; Gary Wright: piano; Jim Price: electric piano; Mac Rebennack: guitar; Klaus Voorman: bass; Ringo Starr and Jim Gordon: drums; strings arranged and conducted by Jimmie Haskell

"Wet Hayshark" (2:31) (Gary Wright)

B.B. King: guitar; with Jim Price: trumpet; Bobby Keys: tenor saxophone; Gary Wright: piano; Klaus Voorman: bass; Ringo Starr and Jim Gordon: drums

"Part-Time Love" (3:17) (C. Hammond)

B.B. King: guitar and vocal; with Jim Price: trumpet; Bobby Keys: tenor saxophone; Gary Wright: organ; Klaus Voorman: Fender bass; Ringo Starr: drums

"Power of the Blues" (2:19) (Pete Wingfield)

B.B. King: guitar and vocal; with Pete Wingfield: piano; Paul Butler: guitar; John Best: bass; Barry Ford: drums

"Ain't Nobody Home" (3:27) (J. Ragovoy)

B.B. King: guitar and vocal; with Jim Price: trumpets and trombone; Bobby Keys: saxophones; Gary Wright: organ; Dr. Ragovoy: piano; John Uribe and David Spinozza: guitars; Klaus Voorman: Fender bass; Jim Keltner: drums; Joshie Armstead, Tasha Thomas, and Carl Hall: vocals; horn arrangements by Jim Price

Live in Japan

ABC-LP (Japan), 1971; MCA, 1999

(Originally released as ABC-LP [Japan] 841, *Live in Japan*, as a double LP, 1971; portions of the original album were released in the U.S. and elsewhere on the *King of the Blues* box set (two songs) and on *How Blue Can You Get? Classic Live Performances 1965 to 1994* (four songs); U.S. release of entire double album, MCA, 1999.)

Recorded March 4 and 7, 1971, Sankei Hall, Tokyo, Japan

Reissue produced by Andy McKaie

Digitally remastered by Erik Labson, MCA Music Media Studio, North Hollywood, California

Musicians
B.B. King: vocals and guitar
Ron Levy: piano
Wilton Freeman: bass
Joseph Burton: trombone
John Browning: trumpet
Earl Turbinton: alto sax
Louis Hubert: tenor sax
Sonny Freeman: drums

Songs
"Every Day I Have the Blues" (2:10) (Peter Chatman)
"How Blue Can You Get" (5:17) (Jane Feather)
"Eyesight to the Blind" (4:03) (Sonny Boy Williamson)
"Niji Baby" (6:27) (B.B. King)
"You're Still My Woman" (5:56) (B.B. King–Dave Clark)
"Chains and Things" (5:41) (B.B. King–Dave Clark)
"Sweet Sixteen" (6:00) (B.B. King–Joe Josea)
"Hummingbird" (4:08) (Leon Russell)
"Darlin' You Know I Love You" (4:26) (B.B. King–Jules Taub)
"Japanese Boogie" (9:17) (B.B. King)
"Jamming at Sankei Hall" (9:35) (B.B. King)
"The Thrill Is Gone" (5:36) (Rick Darnell–Roy Hawkins)
"Hikari No. 88" (7:57) (B.B. King)

For his first studio album of the post–Bill Szymczyk era, B.B. employed a pair of producers close to Szymczyk, Ed Michel and Joe Zagarino (the latter had been an engineer on the "Well" sessions for the *Live & Well* album) and set up shop at London's Olympic and Command Studios from June 9 through 16, 1971. Despite B.B.'s stature among British blues musicians, this album was not to be a blues super-summit. The personnel was drawn from the Szymczyk template, being a mix of stalwart bluesmen—Alexis Korner and Fleetwood Mac founder Peter Green—surrounded by a cast of musicians of American and British extraction who came to the blues from a rock perspective (the lone exception to this rule, arguably, being Mac Rebennack, aka Dr. John, who would loom much larger in B.B.'s future than anyone knew at this time). These included keyboardist Gary Wright of Spooky Tooth (the odious "Dream Weaver" still lay a merciful few years ahead), Steve Marriott of Humble Pie and the Faces, Klaus Voorman of the Plastic Ono Band (and the artist of the Beatles' *Revolver* album cover); keyboardist Pete Wingfield; and topflight American session players David Spinozza (guitar), Jim Price (primarily a trumpet player, he also appeared on keyboards on one cut and arranged another), Jim Keltner (drums), and Bobby Keys (saxophone), among others. Not the least of the assembled cast was Beatles drummer Ringo Starr, who would play more blues here—and acquit himself admirably—than he had since his pre-Beatles days with Rory Storm and the Hurricanes.

The result was medium-cool. The album's oddity was the shambling boogie "Alexis' Boogie," featuring B.B. working out on acoustic guitar (and getting that same rich tone out of a borrowed instrument as he did out of Lucille on other cuts), and Marriott blowing some affecting harp. B.B.'s wrenching vocal on Lloyd Glenn's slow blues, "Blue Shadows," was a story unto itself. Side two had the big highlights, starting with its first cut, a B.B.–Dave Clark co-write, "Ghetto Woman," which became a No. 25 R&B single. Dark and foreboding, keyed by B.B.'s dramatic mise-en-scène opening guitar solo, the song's drama was heightened subtly by the restrained wash of strings in the background. A familiar name had returned to do the string arrangements here, in Jimmie Haskell, Rick Nelson's main man, back for another round after his exquisite contribution to *Indianola Mississippi Seeds*. On a cut featuring not only a grand performance by B.B., but also solid drumming by Ringo and Keltner, Haskell is the news. Locked into the lyrics, he came up with a string arrangement suited for a movie, augmenting and then heightening the drama as the story progresses to its denouement, deploying the instruments judiciously for maximum effect—a flash of pizzicato here, a swift, descending strike following the line, "the radio blastin' the news." Majestic in every way, those strings, and for Haskell his artistry here compares favorably to his most inspired work for Rick Nelson. The easygoing shuffle "Part Time Love" finds Ringo in a solid groove, Wright adding some sparkling organ fills, and B.B. delivering a personable vocal that alternates between shouts and softer, melismatic passages. The final cut on the album, Jerry Ragovoy's "Ain't Nobody Home," is modeled after *Indianola*'s take on Leon Russell's "Hummingbird," and it's almost as effective. A big Southern soul production, the arrangement is marked by soaring blasts of horns, the organ keeping things rooted in the church, and a gospel chorus comprised of Joshie Armstead, Tasha Thomas, and Carl Hall cooing and wailing, à la Szymczyk's Angelic Chorus on "Hummingbird." Vocally, B.B. doesn't have to be pushed to bring the power and the passion—the gospel foundation of his vocal style is amply displayed as he roots around in the lyrics.

In his radio interview with B.B., Spencer Leigh found his subject a bit testy in response to an offhand comment that on these sessions the bluesman had played with a Beatle. But B.B.'s retort also shed some light on what went on inside the studio.

"I would like to think [Ringo] played with me," B.B. said. "It was my album. We were making an album [in London] and we asked for some British musicians to sit in with us. There was Peter Green and a whole lot of people. When we heard from Ringo, I said, 'Oh, yes, please, the Beatles.' Some of the musicians had contemporary thoughts about what we should play and how we should play it, but Ringo wouldn't allow it. He would say, 'That's not B.B.,' and I was so happy because I didn't have to say it myself. [ABC] didn't put Ringo's name on the album when it first came out. There was a star where his face should be."[16] (Indeed, but Ringo is still easily identifiable, even with a star covering his face, as it was on the initial vinyl issue of the album.)

Of his acoustic recording, B.B. related that he recognized a familiar influence on Alexis Korner's style, and that perhaps made him bolder when Korner suggested the acoustic duet. "Alexis got a lot of things from Big Bill Broonzy," B.B. noted, "so I knew where he was coming from. He had two beautiful Martin guitars and he said, 'B, if you and I could do an acoustic thing on these guitars, I'd be the happiest guy in the world.' We fooled around a little bit and we recorded something called 'Alexis' Boogie.'"[17]

Nearly four months prior to the London sessions, though, B.B. had completed a successful tour of Japan, his first, that was captured on tape but not released in the United States until 1999. When he arrived in the Land of the Rising Sun, on February 23, 1971, he was on a hot streak. "The Thrill Is Gone" had catapulted him to the upper reaches of the pop chart and into the white-dominated mainstream, *Completely Well* had been his first Top 40 album, and both *Indianola Mississippi Seeds* and *Live at Cook County Jail* peaked at No. 26 pop, the latter notching an impressive 33-week chart run. He had also added to his veteran band a promising young blues piano player, Ron Levy, who became a fixture in B.B.'s onstage and studio lineups and also found time to launch his own blues label, Bullseye Blues.

The set list is standard fare for this period—"Every Day I Have the Blues," "How Blue Can You Get?", "Chains and Things," "The Thrill Is Gone," "Sweet Sixteen," "You're Still My Woman," "Eyesight to the Blind," "Darlin' You Know I Love You," and what to date has been the only live recording of "Hummingbird." (B.B. rushes through it, adds a perfunctory guitar solo, has the horns blaring prominently, and is without the services of the Angelic Chorus; the approach loses its gospel flavor and becomes instead more of a rock song, far less appealing than the glorious recorded version.) For this new audience, though, B.B. added three exhilarating instrumentals— the slow blues "Niji Baby," featuring a swinging, low-down dialog between Levy's piano and Lucille; a crowd-pleasing jump blues, "Japanese Boogie," nine minutes plus of sputtering sax, roadhouse piano, and Lucille in high dudgeon in a rollicking solo rife with fleet-fingered single-string runs, bent notes, pull-offs, and trills; a stomping, rhythmically formidable workout titled "Jamming at Sankei Hall"; and a boisterous set-closing near-eight-minute jam that pays homage to both T-Bone Walker and Elmore James in B.B.'s soloing. It was a set designed to give Lucille free rein, and over the course of the four instrumentals, B.B. essentially took her through a history of his influences and let her speak her own mind enough so that surely no one left the hall complaining that there wasn't enough guitar in the show. The album is drawn from shows recorded on March 4 and March 7 at Sankei Hall in Tokyo; on the tour B.B. performed eight shows for the local audience and another nine shows at U.S. Army bases. According to reissue producer Andy McKaie's liner notes, "the audiences' response was uniformly remarkable," so much so that during an afternoon show in Osaka more than a hundred fans jumped onstage to dance.

In retrospect, *B.B. King in London* (and the studio album that preceded it, the out-of-print *L.A. Midnight*, featuring Taj Mahal and some top-drawer session men in drummer Earl Palmer, sax man Plas Johnson, and bassist Red Callender, half of its tracks being instrumentals) and *Live in Japan* mark the end of the Bill Szymczyk era in B.B.'s history. The studio album shows him working the Szymczyk formula one more time, with mixed results without Szymczyk aboard, whereas the live album reflects the adjustments he was making in his live presentation as a result of adopting the sensibility Szymczyk had advanced in the studio—bringing new ideas about the blues into the mix by way of blues-influenced rock musicians. In concert the change wasn't drastic when compared to the show taped at the Regal (the show captured on *Blues Is King* is a world unto itself and not applicable to a conversation about where B.B.'s music was headed stylistically or even spiritually), but the rhythmic thrust is intensified and harder driving on *Live in Japan*. B.B. seemed to be in a good place with his music at this point, rooted in the blues but adding just enough contemporary flourishes to keep it in sync with current sensibilities. In 1980 he explained his modus operandi to *Living Blues* magazine, but he might as well have been talking about what he was doing nine years earlier.

"I think the blues have changed quite a bit," he said. "Something like life itself in a way. In fact to me blues is life, because it's the past, the present, and, believe it or not, quite a bit of the future. Basically I should say I'm still doing the same thing. I still feel '3 O'Clock Blues' when I sing. I still feel 'Sweet Sixteen' or 'Sweet Little Angel' or any of the tunes I made in the late

'40s, early '50s. But in order to get them on the radio today, I have to broaden them to whatever fad of music is being played at that time. I try to be smart enough to take my blues with the same basic feeling, but maybe change the beat just a little. If soul is big, I try to put a little bit of soul beat on it. If rock is on, you know, you put just a little bit of rock on it. But the basic blues are still there. And I don't think anything stays the same except change."[18]

Although it was 1988 when B.B. articulated the above philosophy, it applied to his post-Szymczyk studio recordings in the early to mid-'70s that teamed him with prominent non-blues musicians who pushed his music in new directions, or at least in the same direction but outside the 12-bar structure and with a bit more instrumental flair. At the same time, though, a new marketing strategy emerged from conversations between Sid Seidenberg and ABC, and a conscious effort was made to court B.B.'s older fans.[19] Within the context of that plan, B.B. embraced some aspects of funk, the latest trend in black music (which traced its roots back to James Brown's progressive rhythmic excursions in the '60s and to Sly Stone's ongoing rock 'n' soul fusions, which begat the hyperbolic, endlessly entertaining visionary George Clinton, leading his groovecentric troupe Parliament/Funkadelic), while keeping the blues as the bedrock of it all. The results of this revised game plan were mixed aesthetically, but in the long term near-disastrous commercially. This, despite a good start in 1972 with the Joe Zagarino–produced *Guess Who*.

Guess Who _____

MCA, 1972
Produced and recorded by Joe Zagarino, courtesy of Jimmy Miller
    Productions

Rhythm Musicians
B.B. King, Milton Hopkins: lead guitar
Cornell Dupree: rhythm guitar
Wilbert Freeman, Jerry Jemmott: bass
Ron Levy, Frank Owens: piano
V.S. Freeman, Bernard Purdie: drums

Horns
Joseph Burton, Garnett Brown: trombone
Edward Rowe, Ernie Royal, Steve Madaio: trumpet
Earl Turbinton, Bobby Forte, Gene Dinwiddie, Trevor Lawrence: tenor saxophone
Louis Hubert, Howard Johnson: baritone saxophone

Dave Sanborn: alto saxophone

Photography and design: Tom Gamache, Tom Gundelfinger, Philip Schwartz
for Scenic Overlook: a rare photo of B.B. showing some beefcake,
sprawled on the beach, on his back, his yellow shirt pulled up around his
chest, his feet bare

Songs

"Summer in the City" (3:20) (John Sebastian)

"Just Can't Please You" (4:30)

"Any Other Way" (4:30)

"You Don't Know Nothin' About Love" (4:20)

"Found What I Need" (2:50)

"Neighborhood Affair" (Joe Thomas) (3:15)

"It Takes a Young Girl" (3:23)

"Better Lovin' Man" (4:40)

"Guess Who" (Jo Anne Belvin) (4:05)

"Shouldn't Have Left Me" (4:00)

"Five Long Years" (Eddie Boyd) (5:19)

This mellow outing finds B.B. reaching back to re-record his 1953 version of Joe Thomas's blues ballad "Neighborhood Affair," updating his 1962 version of Jesse Belvin's 1959 love song "Guess Who" (which was released as a. single and charted at No. 21 R&B/No. 62 pop), and embracing rock 'n' roll's recent past by covering the Lovin' Spoonful's 1966 chart-topper, "Summer in the City," written by John Sebastian. The sound is centered south of the Mason-Dixon line, with a number of arrangements reflecting the influence of Muscle Shoals and Memphis, especially in the horn charts and grooves. "Any Other Way" is a classically styled soul stirrer (that bears some melodic and structural similarity to Gene McDaniels's 1962 hit "Point of No Return") featuring a pumping horn section, a propulsive rhythm section chugging straight on, and an amiable, crooning vocal reading from B.B. Atmospheric and swampy, the soul ballad "You Don't Know Nothin' About Love" pits a forceful B.B. vocal against a surging horn part and a sultry chorus of female singers sassing him. Ron Levy's delicate piano intro kicks off the swaying take on "Neighborhood Affair," supplanting the dreamy sax solo that introduced the original version, and B.B. luxuriates in a tender vocal plea for reconciliation with a woman he's been carrying on with, much to the neighbors' consternation. The arrangement builds to a boisterous climax, and B.B. plays his frustration for all it's worth, shouting the lyrics as the horns wail, crying out in an exasperated appeal to the woman to come back, and promising to invite all the nosy neighbors to watch their reunion. In "Summer in the City," an unlikely cover for B.B. (and one he loathed), the pace is slow, sensual, lazy, quite the opposite of the Spoonful's urgently rendered depiction of an intense, sweltering inferno populated by denizens wilting in the day's blistering heat. Nightfall brings a "different world" of skirt chasing and romance, which plays right into the sultry groove of B.B.'s version, its sensuality quotient boosted by a flirtatious female chorus chanting behind him and some tasty blues piano fills courtesy Ron Levy. Closing with the grinding blues of "Five Long Years," B.B. delivers a growling, gritty vocal, so forceful and righteously angry he seems close to straining his vocal cords. He's speaking to anyone who's been mistreated, telling a story of working "five long years" for a woman who then "had the nerve to put me out." He sings of toiling in a steel mill, "chunking steel like a slave," taking his pay home to her each week, implying that she spent it all. On alto sax, David Sanborn spits out a line that seems to mock B.B., as does a trumpeter playing a sarcastic, muted riff—in an overambitious horn chart, these cameos stand out for their brevity and punch. As the song churns to a heated close, B.B. reveals that the next time he marries, his bride has "got to work and bring in the dough." Herewith a new wrinkle in an old philosophy: she pays the cost for him to be the boss.

B.B. refers to *Guess Who* as "a big production album with a big band." He was especially fond of the title song, written by Jesse Belvin's wife Jo Anne. Remembering the Belvins as "a loving couple" who were both killed in a car crash in 1960, B.B. said the song "reminds me of their love for each other and of my love for my fans. I'm still singing it at concerts."[20]

No such affection is reserved for "Summer in the City," though. "The producer thought it'd be a good tune to cover," B.B. said. "It wasn't; it didn't fit my style and I wish I'd left it off."[21] Instances are rare of B.B. trashing any of his own recordings; apart from "Summer in the City" (which merits only the mild "it didn't fit my style" put-down), the other song he resolutely denigrates is his 1956 RPM recording of "Bim Bam," a stab at rock 'n' roll that has found considerable favor in England but not with B.B. "I hate it," he said to Spencer Leigh. "I didn't like it then and I don't like it now. That is the only record I ever did that I didn't like at all, even though we did a pretty good job on it. I only did it because one of the executives at the company asked me to do it for a friend. They thought they was getting into rock 'n' roll. No more favors for friends."[22])

A polished affair with some inspired moments, *Guess Who* found B.B. and Zagarino massaging the Szymczyk formula by bringing in noted session players such as rhythm guitarist Cornell Dupree, bassist Gerald Jemmott (from the *Live & Well*, *Completely Well*, and *Indianola Mississippi Seeds* sessions), drummer Bernard Purdie, tenor saxophonist Gene Dinwiddie, and alto saxophonist David Sanborn (and, inexplicably, another lead guitarist in Milton Hopkins), and blending in some key players from B.B.'s road band, including Ron Levy, drummer Sonny Freeman, tenor saxophonist Bobby Forte, and baritone saxophonist Louis Hubert. The course on which Szymczyk had set B.B. was nearing its end; the next year, 1973, would see it reach a logical, and successful, conclusion, when Stevie Wonder energized the sessions for *To Know You Is to Love You*. However, it would be another half decade before B.B. and those around him understood the need for a bold stroke to sustain his career at any significant level.

Lucille Talks Back

ABC, 1975
Produced by B.B. King
Arranged by Hampton Reese, Eddie Rowe, and B.B. King

Musicians
B.B. King: guitar, vocals

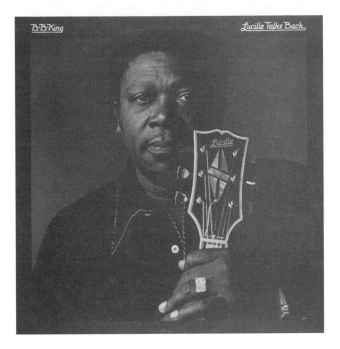

Rusty Aikels: bass
Marcus Barnett: percussion
Joseph Burton: trombone
Jess Daniels (Houck): rhythm guitar
Bobby Forte: baritone and tenor sax
Milton Hopkins: rhythm guitar
Ron Levy: synthesizer and piano
Eddie Rowe: fluegelhorn and trumpet
John Starks (Jabo): drums
James Toney: organ
Cato Walker III: alto sax

Songs
"Lucille Talks Back (Copulation)" (2:26) (B.B. King)
"Breaking Up Somebody's Home" (2:58) (A. Jackson–T. Matthews)
"Reconsider Baby" (2:53) (L. Fulson)
"Don't Make Me Pay for His Mistakes" (3:15) (M. Grayson–B. Lexing)
"When I'm Wrong" (6:11) (B.B. King)
"I Know the Price" (3:06) (B.B. King)
"Have Faith" (2:36) (Shirrell Sutton)
"Everybody Lies a Little" (3:43) (B.B. King)

Sandwiched between two live albums teaming B.B. with Bobby "Blue" Bland, both of which got B.B. back to his bedrock blues without the burden of funk affectations, *Lucille Talks Back* was as troubled as B.B.'s career at the time. In July 1975 Sid Seidenberg closed a deal giving his other client, Gladys Knight and the Pips, a national television show in the wake of the group's across-the-board success with "Midnight Train to Georgia." Feeling slighted by Seidenberg's attention to Knight, B.B. ended his association with the S.A.S. firm and opted to manage his own affairs. Debacle after debacle ensued, beginning with his band bus breaking down and needing an entire new engine to make it roadworthy again. Then B.B. decided to produce his next album himself. Released in 1975, *Lucille Talks Back* yielded one minor hit in the slow blues "When I'm Wrong" (No. 22 R&B in 1976), but in most other ways the album was ill-conceived, sloppy, and reeked of a desperate stab at hipness by an artist who in standing his ground as a bluesman over the years was the very embodiment of hip.

The problems began with the packaging. On the original black-framed cover (which was changed for the CD re-issue to feature a warmer photo), a sleepy-eyed, black-clad B.B. stares out morosely (actually, he looks more like Muddy Waters than himself in the cover photo), a dark black-green background behind him. Clutching Lucille in his left hand by the bottom of the headstock shows off his diamond-encrusted B.B. initial ring. On the back cover, WDIA's venerable Nat D. Williams penned liner notes that could have used the services of a good editor to reshape run-on sentences such as this closing sentiment: " . . . he did a beautiful job all the way until he earned an international reputation as one of the world's greatest Blues singers and we are happy to present to you B.B. King & 'Lucille' with some basics of the new blues tunes B.B. has created which have made him today, THE KING OF THE BLUES. . . ."

In the musician credits, the name of the outstanding New Orleans sax man Herb Hardesty is misspelled not once, but twice, as Herb Hardisty. There are no studio or engineer credits at all, an egregious oversight. Then and now, many studios relied on album credits as marketing tools to draw new business to their facilities, and when an artist of B.B. King's stature works at a recording facility, other musicians take note. Given that B.B. has made no public statements indicating he had a bad experience at the studio or found it unsuitable on some level, omitting its credit is at the least an insult, at the worst a puzzling disregard for a long-established common courtesy.

Once the record begins, more problems surface immediately on the first song, "Lucille Talks Back (Copulation)," an original B.B. instrumental that kicks off on a subdued note with an enervated wah-wah guitar solo and proceeds to go nowhere. Throughout the album B.B. is working the wah-wah pedal hard—

Lucille isn't heard without it—and it robs B.B. of his complementary voice and the lovely, breathtaking textures and shadings he coaxes out of that voice. Coming off the Philadelphia studio sessions for *To Know You Is to Love You*, B.B. sounds fatally infatuated with TSOP (The Sound of Philadelphia), which was both a band and a smooth, propulsive soul style that pointed the way to disco, neither of which suited the bluesman's temperament or musical voice. The wah-wah simply wreaks havoc here: the song "When I'm Wrong" begins with a dramatic guitar solo—bolstered by a surging blast of horns—that would have been captivating had the wah-wah been left in the gear bag.

Yet even a subpar B.B. outing has memorable moments. A take on Lowell Fulson's classic "Reconsider Baby" is defined by its ingratiating mellow mood, with James Toney sending up a steady, somber wash of moody chords on the organ, a horn section subtly deploying its commentary, Ron Levy adding some bluesy punctuation on piano, and B.B. bringing it home with a restrained, pleading vocal. By far this album's best moment, and one that would fit on many of his best albums, comes with the shortest song, Shirrell Sutton's beautiful "Have Faith." The arrangement, which wouldn't have been out of place on a Percy Sledge record, references gospel and Southern soul (not that there's much distinction between the two), and B.B. digs into its uplifting message of faith and prayer as a balm in a troubled world. "Do unto others as you would have them do to you," B.B. sings in the penultimate verse, "and there's a reward waiting somewhere for you." His gritty, shouting vocal is straight out of the church and sets up a triumphant crescendo of horns at the close. It's a stirring two minutes and 36 seconds of preaching and testifying, and the one time on the album when B.B. sounds fully engaged by the material. In a curious bit of sequencing, though, he follows "Have Faith" with his cynical, self-penned "Everybody Lies a Little," which posits the title philosophy as a fundamental truth about human nature. On the heels of a song that counsels faith and prayer as the best means to survive troubled times, endorsing the use of situational ethics in personal affairs (especially if they serve to "save your life or your home") is a dubious proposition. If B.B. seems confused about his moral code, then that's only fitting given the chaos in his professional life at the time.

Together for the First Time ... Live
B.B. King and Bobby Bland

MCA, 1974
Produced by Steve Barri
Recording engineer: Phil Kaye

Recorded at Western Recorders, Studio 1

Mixing and mastering at ABC Recording Studios

Musicians

Bobby Bland and B.B. King: vocals

B.B. King, Milton Hopkins: guitars

Melvin Jackson, Sonny Freeman, Mel Brown, Michael Omartian, Ben Benay, Milton Hopkins, Joseph Burton, Ron Levy, Cato Walker, Louis Hubert, Bobby Forte, Edward Rowe, Wilbert Freeman, Charles Polk, Tommy Punkson, Harold Potier, Jr., Theodore Arthur, Theodore Reynolds, Leo Penn, Joseph Hardin, Jr., Alfred Thomas

Introduction: Don Mack

Songs

Introduction

"3 O'Clock Blues" (3:15)

"It's My Own Fault" (4:13)

"Driftin' Blues" (5:10)

"That's the Way Love Is" (3:51)

"I'm Sorry" (9:55)

"I'll Take Care of You" (3:50)

"Don't Cry No More" (2:30)

"Don't Want a Soul Hangin' Around" (3:52)

Medley: "Good to Be Back Home"/"Driving Wheel"/"Rock Me Baby"/"Black Night"/"Cherry Red"/"It's My Own Fault"/"3 O'Clock Blues"/"Oh, Come Back Baby"/"Chains of Love"/"Gonna Get Me an Old Woman" (14:00)

"Everybody Wants to Know Why I Sing the Blues" (6:19)
"Goin' Down Slow" (5:16)
"I Like to Live the Love" (6:00)

Together Again ... Live
Bobby Bland and B.B. King

ABC Bluesway, 1976; MCA, 1990
Produced by Esmond Edwards
Horns arranged and conducted by Johnny Pate
Recorded at the Coconut Grove, Los Angeles
Principal engineer: Barney Perkins with Additional Engineering by Reggie Dozier, Howard Gale, and Stuart Taylor
Remix engineering: Barney Perkins and Geoff Gillette
Remote recording facilities provided by the Enactron Truck with additional recording at the ABC Studios, Los Angeles
Mastered at Kendun Mastering Labs, Burbank, California

Musicians
Bobby Bland and B.B. King: vocals
B.B. King, Milton Hopkins, Johnny Jones, and Ray Parker: guitars
Rudy Aikels and Louis Villery: bass guitars
Harold Potier and John Starks: drums
James Toney: organ
Robert Anderson: piano
Red Holloway: tenor saxophone
Jerome Richardson: baritone saxophone

Oscar Brashear, Albert Aarons, and Snooky Young: trumpets
Garnett Brown and Benny Powell: trombones
Viola Jackson: voice from audience on "The Thrill Is Gone"

Songs

"Let the Good Times Roll" (6:14) (Sam Theard–Fleecie Moore)

Medley: "Stormy Monday Blues" (Aaron Walker) / "Strange Things Happen"
 (Percy Mayfield) (6:41)

"Feel So Bad" (8:19) (Sam "Lightnin'" Hopkins)

Medley: "Mother-in-Law Blues" (Don Robey) / "Mean Old World" (Walter
 Jacobs) (5:55)

"Every Day (I Have the Blues)" (4:01) (Peter Chatman)

Medley: "The Thrill Is Gone" (Roy Hawkins–Rick Darnell) / "I Ain't Gonna Be the
 First to Cry" (Michael Price–Dan Welsh–Mitch Bottier) (12:54)

Upon his retirement in 1973, Don Robey had sold his Duke/Peacock label
to ABC, which brought Duke's reigning star, Bobby "Blue" Bland, into the fold,
now on the same roster with his buddy B.B. King. In 1974 ABC staff producer
Steve Barri put the two giants together to cut a live album in Los Angeles, at
Western Recorders' Studio 1, before an invited audience of family and friends
(including James Brown, who made a special trip to be in the audience for this
event). The result could hardly have been better. B.B. and Bobby kick it off with
a churning version of "3 O'Clock Blues," with Bland singing lead. B.B. makes
his presence felt initially via the stinging notes Lucille is spitting out in
advance of him growling his way through the second verse as the band stomps
into the action and the horns swell behind it all. "Ladies and gentlemen, nothing is planned tonight; we didn't plan anything," B.B. says in greeting the
audience, whereupon Bland cuts in to tell him, "Here's your beer."

B.B.: "So what I'm thinkin' is we just gonna pull something out of the hat,
you might say, and toss it up and get right into it."

"We'd like you to sit back and relax," Bland suggests, then moans, "It's
my own fault, darlin'. . . . "

The set is heavy on the "sexy blues" of Bland's legend (including his 1959
single, "I'll Take Care of You"; a 1960 single, "Don't Cry No More"; 1962's
"That's the Way Love Is"; and 1964's "Black Night") and B.B. monuments
such as "3 O'Clock Blues," "Everybody Wants to Know Why I Sing the Blues,"
"It's My Own Fault," and, included in a 14-minute medley, "Rock Me Baby"
(given a slow, earthy treatment that's right in Bland's wheelhouse) and
"Chains of Love." (One of the medley's many charms is an interlude during
a reprise of "3 O'Clock Blues," when B.B. and Bobby reminisce about their
early days in Memphis.)

No one's pulling rank; Bland often starts the song, B.B. comes in for the second verse, and they alternate from there, with, obviously, plenty of room left for Lucille. There's melancholy in the version of Charles Brown's "Driftin' Blues"; moony-eyed tenderness in "I'll Take Care of You"; a jaunty, celebratory R&B workout in "That's the Way Love Is," with its rousing horn chart; some lowdown blues in the song B.B. introduces as being about "a jealous man," "Don't Want a Soul Hangin' Around," which heretofore had always been titled "Don't Answer the Door." The difference between the two men as performers is evident even on disc: Bland is not shy about sparring vocally with B.B. or spurring him on, but is brief and even a bit remote (albeit jovial) in his remarks to the audience; whereas B.B. achieves an immediate intimacy with the assembled throng with his warm, welcoming, casual style. Between songs he chats and introduces new numbers as comfortably as if he were speaking to family. In short, Bobby Bland is Bobby Bland, B.B. King is B.B. King, and they found a way to make the twain meet and to make it electrifying—an object lesson in the blues as life. And on the theory that B.B.'s live albums are not without a greater purpose, the first outing with Bobby Bland, coming in the wake of the mellow, ornate blues of *Guess Who*, demonstrated to any doubters that what happens in the studio is one thing, but out on the boards, out there in the world, B.B. remained steadfastly a dedicated urban bluesman who hadn't lost his hard edge. Aesthetically the album was a winner, and commercially too—*Together for the First Time … Live* was certified platinum. Its success was sweet revenge for B.B.

"One critic for a national magazine … rode me and Bobby hard," B.B. recalled. "Said the album was a mess and called the music nothing. That bothered me. It's one thing if a critic says he doesn't like you, but another to call your music nothing, especially if he can't make music himself. I don't like arguing with critics, so I didn't. I waited. Waited to see the fans' reaction. Well, the fans loved it. [The album] went platinum. By then, I couldn't contain my emotions anymore, so I wrote the magazine, saying 'Please let the critic who criticized my album criticize all my albums. With the success of my record with Bobby Bland, the man is bringing me luck.' Never heard back from the magazine. But I did hear from ABC, who said they wanted me and Bobby to cut another album, which we did a couple of years later. So much for critics."[24]

Produced by Esmond Edwards, with horns arranged by Johnny Pate (his first work with B.B. since the *Live & Well* sessions) and recorded at the Coconut Grove in Los Angeles, B.B. and Bobby's second joint project, *Together Again … Live*, follows the same approach as their first get-together, the two artists quick to share the spotlight and to interject smart quips and energizing ripostes during each other's solo parts. The pair do a moving, sensitive turn on a medley of T-Bone Walker's "Stormy Monday" and Percy Mayfield's beautiful "Strange Things Happen," get the night off to a boisterous beginning with an exuberant rendition of Louis Jordan's "Let the Good Times Roll," and swing hard later on during an ebullient reading of "Every Day I Have the Blues." The highlight is the closing medley, keyed by a decidedly sexy, slinky version of "The Thrill Is Gone" (plus a taste of "I Ain't Gonna Be the First to Cry") that features B.B. and Bobby alternating bone-deep lyric readings, and some effective, stuttering interjections by a muted trumpet heightening the loneliness inherent in the story's subtext. A star cameo from an audience member, as startling as it was unplanned, is a sheer delight. Towards the end, Bland approaches a female patron who identifies herself as Viola (identified in the credits as Viola Jackson), who comandeers the mic and promptly proceeds to slay the crowd with some husky, Mavis Staples–style gospel-inflected, goosebump-inducing moaning redolent of sex.

Together Again ... Live did not follow its predecessor into platinum territory but, like the first album, was a reassuring and eloquent statement on B.B.'s part that the studio animal and the live performer operated independently of each other—the former might wander off the blues route at times to see what else was out there, but the latter never forgot whence he came, and made sure no one in his audience did either.

Whatever energy surge B.B. might have experienced in his second recording date with Bobby Bland did not carry over into a better studio album any more than it had after the first time, when the disappointing *Lucille Talks Back* followed *For the First Time*. In 1977 B.B. followed *Together Again* with *King Size*, featuring an agreeable version of Muddy Waters's "Got My Mojo Workin'" and a single, "Slow and Easy," which managed to scrape the lower reaches of the R&B chart, peaking at No. 88.

Chapter 10

"GIVE ME A THRILL, STEW"

tewart Levine knew something was amiss with B.B. when he saw him perform at the Village Gate in New York. A musician and producer himself, Levine was a long-standing friend of Sid Seidenberg, whom he had met through the auspices of Oscar Cohn, the heir apparent to Joe Glaser at Associated Booking. The Bronx-born Levine had entered the music business as a horn player working the circuit around New York City. While studying music theory at the Manhattan School of Music he had befriended a classmate, South African trumpeter-bandleader-arranger Hugh Masekela, and a fruitful partnership ensued. In the mid-'60s they founded their own label, Chisa, aiming to bring to a wider audience the music of Africa and other third-world countries. As Masekela's producer, Levine was behind the board for the artist's 1968 mainstream breakthrough album, *The Promise of a Future*. It contained the original instrumental version of the summery, exuberant, No. 1 (pop and R&B) version of "Grazing in the Grass." (The next year the Friends of Distinction's cover—with lyrics—went to No. 3 pop.) Masekela's unique mesh of American pop and South African rhythms heralded the commercial potential of a fusion that would not be fully realized until 1986, with the release of Paul Simon's *Graceland* album.

Joe Glaser had taken an immediate liking to the street-savvy Levine and the worldly, gifted Masekela, and a friendship blossomed. Glaser introduced the pair to others in his circle, including Seidenberg. Levine learned that Seidenberg had been doing some accounting work for B.B. King relating to his manager's financial dealings, and was considering the bluesman's request to become his manager.

When he went to the Village Gate, though, what Levine saw was not encouraging. "There was very little happening for [B.B.]," Levine remembers. "He was between careers."[1]

It was 1968. "Rock Me Baby" and *Live at the Regal* were four and five years in the past, respectively, and B.B.'s track record since signing with ABC in 1962 showed his only hit single to have been on the Kent label. He had moved to Manhattan, hoping to rejuvenate his career, with Seidenberg at the helm. Two years later, in 1970, now managed by Seidenberg and produced by the young rock and blues aficionado Bill Szymczyk, B.B. had cut "The Thrill Is Gone" and experienced the long-sought-after and career-altering crossover hit of his dreams.

Meanwhile, Stewart Levine had started his own label, Blue Thumb, and was working with a group out of Houston, Texas, called the Crusaders. In 1954 pianist Joe Sample had formed the band with his high school buddies Wilton Felder (a tenor saxophonist) and Stix Hooper (a drummer). This triumvirate fleshed out the lineup by adding flutist Hubert Laws, trombonist Wayne Henderson, and bassist Henry Wilson, and went out as the Modern Jazz Sextet. Come 1960, all the members save Wilson moved to Los Angeles and re-emerged as the Jazz Crusaders (Wilson's bass spot was a revolving door through which entered and exited several short-term Jazz Crusaders). A recording contract with Pacific Jazz in 1961 led to a productive decade of stu-

The Crusaders during their 1974 tour of Japan, with producer Stewart Levine at left.

dio albums that found the group experimenting with fusions of jazz, Memphis soul, and traditional R&B. In 1971 the band dropped the "Jazz" from its name and became simply the Crusaders, the implication in the name change being that the musicians were eager to venture out into other musical realms. The original members had also added an impressive young guitarist to their ranks in Larry Carlton, who fit right in with the new approach, and whose assured, melodic playing stood out among many strong performances on the band's acclaimed MCA debut album from 1971, *The Crusaders 1*, which yielded an R&B hit in the instrumental "Put It Where You Want It."

In 1974 Levine had a brainstorm to produce a music festival to coincide with the 1974 heavyweight title match between Muhammad Ali and George Foreman, in Zaire, South Africa. "The idea of it was really just to help create more consciousness about Africa, because I had been pioneering the South African music thing since 1964 and looking for any way to get it going," Levine said. "I had my own label, and by that time the Crusaders were with me and we were doing all right. I kind of came up with the idea and created this incredible albatross on my neck that became known as 'Zaire '74.'"

As depicted in the Academy Award–winning documentary *When We Were Kings*, the "incredible albatross" encumbering Levine was a wild, near-two-month ride featuring political intrigue, drug- and alcohol-induced madness (not evident in the movie), great music, the outsized ego of promoter Don King, the street theater of Ali, the dazed surliness of Foreman, and a stunning, electrifying title bout that forever altered both pugilists' futures. Well ahead of the fight preparations, Zaire's dictatorial, brutal president, Mobutu Sese Seko, in an effort to head off any violence, rounded up 1,000 of the usual suspects, imprisoned them in a cage below the stadium where the fight was to be held, and summarily executed 100 of their number as a warning to the others that their government and underworld connections would be of no use to them in this situation. Then the fight was delayed for six weeks after Foreman suffered a cut over his eye while sparring, which gave a restless Ali further opportunity to belittle his verbally outmatched opponent and to rally the locals to his cause by mingling in the neighborhoods and encouraging the natives' chant of "A-li, boom-ba-yea! A-li, boom-ba-yea!" Throughout this odyssey, Levine and his crew were ensconced in a luxury hotel in Zaire, operating under the impression that the government was covering all their expenses, which of course prompted the well-lubricated producer to encourage one and all to live it up and put it on the tab. When he checked out, he was presented with a bill for $80,000; unfazed, Levine produced his American Express card, said, "Charge it!" and retreated to the airport.

The concert featured an exciting mix of American R&B/soul artists and local favorites. James Brown was there, as were the Crusaders, the Spinners, and Miriam Makeba. Through his connection with Sid Seidenberg, and a casual friendship with B.B. through the years, Levine acquired the services of the King of the Blues too.

"Zaire was where I really got to know B.B.," Levine recalls. "He left Lucille, his guitar, in my room during the whole goddamn festival, and we always laughed about that. As precious as Lucille was, he put her in my room, which was ridiculous because I was bouncing off the walls in those days."

Despite all the insanity of Zaire, the concert was a triumph—albeit a bittersweet one for Levine, who returned to America dazed, weary, and disenchanted. He proceeded to sell his Blue Thumb label to ABC. "I said, Fuck this, I'm going to stop being an impresario and become an independent producer." It was a good move: right off the bat he produced a hit record for Minnie Riperton, and the Crusaders were still going strong. Life again was beautiful for Stewart Levine.

Not so for B.B. Since splitting with Sid Seidenberg in 1975, his only musical success had been fair to middlin', in the form of the second pairing with Bobby "Blue" Bland; lacking a big hit and having exhausted all the momentum from "The Thrill Is Gone," he found his drawing power on the road diminished, and his rate going down. He also moved back west, to Las Vegas, against the advice of Seidenberg, who thought it the worst possible nesting place for a compulsive gambler. By 1976 B.B. had to admit "things were getting a little loose. The touring wasn't so smooth, the scheduling wasn't tight, and I felt myself losing control. Little by little, I was falling into the kind of money messes I'd fallen into before."[2]

In a scenario reminiscent of the one that brought Bill Szymczyk into B.B.'s orbit before B.B. knew it, Stewart Levine was being approached at this time about producing B.B., without B.B.'s knowledge of any such strategy. George Greif, the Crusaders' manager, hatched the idea and ran it by Levine, whose initial response was, "What would we do? I just don't want to record straight-ahead blues."

But Levine knew he had some formidable resources at hand, especially in the Crusaders' Joe Sample, who was a superb piano player with a gift for writing intriguing melodies. Where, then, does the rest of the song come from? He set out to answer his own question, first by calling his friend Chuck Kay, the head of publishing at Irving/Almo Music, the publishing arm of Herb Alpert and Jerry Moss's A&M Records label. Kay in turn suggested an up-and-coming writer in his stable, Will Jennings, an east Texas native that Kay felt would be a good fit with the Houston-born Sample. Jennings's first break had come with writing re-creations of Motown-Stax mid-'60s pop soul for the 1976 film *The Commitments*, and in 1977 he had collaborated with composer Richard Kerr on Barry Manilow's No.1 pop hit "Looks Like We Made It." These would not seem the credentials necessary for writing songs for B.B. King, but Levine respected Kay's judgment and so set up a dinner meeting with Jennings and Sample. Jennings fit right in—"he's a very bright guy, Will," notes Levine—and the talk turned to concepts. Levine said the blues wasn't the answer, "but song forms that incorporated the feeling of the blues, the idea being that B.B. could read the phone book and it was still gonna be the blues, it didn't matter. And if we had songs that had like verse and chorus, why not look at it that way?"

Sample and Jennings agreed with Levine's premise and set out to compose a batch of songs for a B.B. King album. ABC endorsed the idea, feeling that the red-hot Crusaders might light a fire under a tepid B.B. King.

From his perspective, Levine saw the King of the Blues in a decidedly unregal state. "Incredibly cold," he says of B.B.'s career at the time. "No manager, managing himself, some other hustlers were around, and B.B. was shabby. He wasn't in great shape, he wasn't feeling good, he had big government problems and everything." But when the two met to discuss the idea of a joint project with the Crusaders, B.B. jumped at it, even though he was nervous about what Sample and Jennings were going to cook up for him. This reticence was one of Levine's first insights into B.B.'s artistic makeup: he was uncomfortable learning new material (which perhaps explains why he so assiduously recycled the past in his early years and, with equal vigor, had recycled himself since signing with ABC) and in essence needed to be walked through the process before he could get a handle on his role.

Picking up on this quirk, Levine suggested B.B. use a guidebook to his vocals; that is, he would have Sample and Jennings cut "primitive" demos of their songs—"In the case of 'Midnight Believer,' Joe played piano and he sang the songs in the most primitive of ways, and sometimes Will would sing them in the most primitive of ways"—and run those demos through B.B.'s headphones in the studio. "B.B. felt comfortable if he had a guide vocal in his headphones," Levine said. "He just knew where he was then, he could learn quicker. As hard as it is to believe, he's very tentative in the studio, needs help, wants help, and therefore is infinitely producible. You gotta help him along; you can't expect him to be a genius, which is what a lot of guys think—'Oh, B.B. King, he's gonna go in there and do it all by himself.' He likes the idea of having some idea of what the music is supposed to be like in its original form. He likes to hear the way it was meant to be sung, with the melody, and that's why he's so good at it. Because he basically learns it from somebody who's just singing the melody—not a professional singer, just somebody who wrote the song. When he gets that little idea in his head, he can interpret it. And when he sings it, it sounds entirely different."

And the Crusaders meshed perfectly with B.B.'s approach, which was no surprise to Levine. He knew the veteran band understood B.B.'s tradition and "had a pop sensibility."

At the same time, the producer had a clear vision of his assignment: make an album that connected with the public. "We weren't trying to win any blues awards; I was trying to get his price up. That's what he needed. He needed a record that could get him back on the radio and get him back to where he could be touring. I also spoke to Oscar Cohn, who said, 'Listen, it's going away, man.' 'The Thrill Is Gone' was it and then a couple of things happened after that, and his career was going the wrong way."

Midnight Believer

MCA, 1978
Produced by Stewart Levine and "Stix" Hooper, Wilton Felder, and Joe Sample
Engineered and mixed by Rik Pekkonen
Mastered by Bernie Grundman at A&M Studios, Hollywood, California
Recorded at Hollywood Sound Recorders, Hollywood, California
String and horn arrangements by Joe Sample

Musicians

B.B. King: lead guitar

Joe Sample: keyboards

Wilton Felder: bass on "World Full of Strangers" and "Midnight Believer"; tenor sax solo on "Never Make a Move Too Soon"

"Stix" Hooper: drums and percussion (all selections except "A World Full of Strangers," "Never Make a Move Too Soon," and "I Just Can't Leave Your Love Alone")

Robert "Pops" Popwell: bass (all selections except "A World Full of Strangers" and "Midnight Believer")

Dean Parks: rhythm guitar

Roland Bautista: rhythm guitar

James Gadson: drums on "World Full of Strangers," "Never Make a Move Too Soon," and "I Just Can't Leave Your Love Alone"

Horns: Steve Madaio, Charles B. Findley, George Bohanon, Dennis Quitman, Kurt McGettrick, Greg Herbig; horns on "I Just Can't Leave Your Love Alone": Abe Most, Dick Cary, Robert Enevoldsen, Eddie Miller

Julia Waters Tillman, Maxine Waters Willard, Luther Waters, Oren Waters: background vocals

Strings conducted by Sid Sharp

Songs

"When It All Comes Down (I'll Still Be Around)" (4:11)

"Midnight Believer" (4:59)

"I Just Can't Leave Your Love Alone" (4:18)

"Hold On (I Feel Our Love Is Changing)" (4:10)

"Never Make a Move Too Soon" (5:29)

"A World Full of Strangers" (4:23)

"Let Me Make You Cry a Little Longer" (5:49)

All songs written by Joe Sample–Will Jennings, except "Never Make a Move Too Soon" by "Stix" Hooper–Will Jennings

With the Crusaders' lineup bolstered by Robert "Pops" Popwell on bass, Dean Parks on rhythm guitar, Roland Bautista on rhythm guitar, and, on three cuts, James Gadson on drums, plus a six-piece horn section and the gospel-oriented Waters siblings providing background vocals, *Midnight Believer* sounds as right for its time as *Completely Well* did in 1970. Its seven songs (six written by Sample and Jennings, with "Never Make a Move Too Soon" credited to Stix Hooper and Jennings) advance a diverse array of moods and textures, embrace influences both contemporary and old school, have some wit to recommend them, and allow B.B. room to stretch a bit vocally while staying in a fairly sedate, sensuous groove. Sample's string and horn arrangements are as subtle or as grandiose as necessary without being ostentatious. The album opener, "When It All Comes Down (I'll Still Be Around)," sets the tone with a swaying groove and mellow vocal, which are soon bolstered by horns, strings, and a soothing gospel chorus, with Lucille filling in the spaces with some stinging commentary in a song about perseverance and staying power—themes designed to connect with B.B.'s own life. A funky, horn-laced mid-tempo groove defines the title song, with the strings rising sweetly after bursts of horns and B.B. turning saloon singer with a sensuous, crooning vocal. On a fanciful note, "I Just Can't Leave Your Love Alone" has a rollicking New Orleans feel, complete with a wailing clarinet line swirling around the arrangement, a Dixieland-style horn chart, the chorus chanting "hot-ta-cha-cha" during the breaks, and B.B. rising into a wry falsetto at the end of each verse. The party feel gets into gear on the stomping "Never Make a Move Too Soon," with B.B. announcing, "I'm just a man who sings the blues," as if that's not enough, and being goosed along by background handclaps, shouts, whistling, and lively chatter. B.B. gets into the mood and adds some shouts and laughter of his own to a philosophy he can certainly embrace, that timing is everything in life; at the end, as he's chanting, "do it, do it, do it," the crowd on the track bursts into cheers and applause. ("Never Make a Move Too Soon" was originally a Stix Hooper–penned instrumental titled "Greasy Spoon" on the Crusaders' *Southern Comfort* album. "Just a gutbucket thing," Levine termed it, to which Will Jennings wrote lyrics on the spot in the studio before B.B. and band cut it.) A cautionary blues about a woman who's leaving a relationship, "World Full of Strangers" features a spooky background chorus part, sharp bursts of warning horns, and tart retorts from Lucille as B.B. announces he'll still be around if the woman finds the outside world too daunting. An interesting construction job, the album-closing "Let Me Make You Cry a Little Longer" opens with only B.B. and the unadorned band in the first verse; then the strings rise gracefully, B.B. gets low-down vocally, and the musicians individually add extra flourishes. Becoming more baroque and funky with each measure, the arrangement features cascades of guitar lines, rolling piano lines, washes of strings, a chanting background chorus, and bursts of bluesy horns in an incremental expansion as impeccably designed as it is seductively insinuating.

On day one of the *Midnight Believer* sessions at Hollywood Recorders in Hollywood, California, B.B. drove in from his Las Vegas home at the appointed hour, but minus Lucille. He didn't think he'd be asked to play on a vocals session, because he doesn't play and sing at the same time—what Sam Phillips observed long ago in Memphis remained true in 1978 in Hollywood.

Seeing this, Stewart Levine, in his own words, "freaked out."

"B," he pleaded, "when you come tomorrow, man, bring Lucille. You're gonna play. I just don't want you to sing; I want you to *play*, man."

"I don't know," B.B. responded. "I usually put that on afterwards. I don't sing and play at the same time."

"Precisely," Levine countered. "I want to get a feeling. I don't want you just playing straight through the song. I want you to play the way you're gonna play."

B.B. looked around the studio and spotted a Fender Stratocaster propped up against a wall. "I'll play that," he said.

"B.B. King playing a fucking Strat? Are you kidding me!?" Levine exclaimed.

Everything they cut that night was trashed. *Midnight Believer* was under way.

As the album progressed, B.B. began to "smell it," in Levine's recollection. The sessions flew by—it took a little more than a week for tracking, overdubs, and vocals. One night when a session ended early and he was preparing to make the 300-mile drive back to Las Vegas ("insane," Levine said, "but he had a bad gambling problem then"), B.B. approached his producer.

"Stew," B.B. said (and Levine is quick to point out that B.B. "is one of the few people I'll allow to call me Stew"), "I feel something here."

Levine was surprised to hear B.B. taking him into his confidence, knowing that "B.B. ain't much about talking like that. He doesn't let his armor down too often."

He let it down further when he continued. "I think I made a terrible mistake with Sid. I really think I need Sid back on this one. This is one that could work."

Sensing that B.B. "knew he had something," Levine responded with a question of his own: "What are you tellin' me?"

"I don't know. It'd just be great," B.B. said.

"Do you want me to call Sid?" Levine asked.

B.B. let out a slight, nervous laugh. "Oh, I don't think Sid wants any part of me."

Apparently B.B. had not heard that Seidenberg and Gladys Knight had parted ways. The manager, once a big-time player, could use a high-profile client. When he received the call from Stewart Levine feeling him out about reuniting with B.B., Sid was pleased but surprised. "B said he'd like to see me?" Seidenberg asked. "I thought he wanted to do it himself. I wished him well."

"Listen, he's the one who asked me to make the phone call," Levine reported. "So, you know, if I were you I would come out and check it out, man. See what you think of the music."

A pause followed. "B really wants to see me?" an incredulous Seidenberg queried again.

"Yeah," Levine asserted.

"I'll be there tomorrow."

Seidenberg took the red-eye flight from New York and spent the next day at Hollywood Recorders with B.B. and Levine, listening to the new music and discussing the state of things. At the end of the day artist and manager were back in business together. And *Midnight Believer* became B.B.'s best-received studio recording since 1970's *Completely Well*.

Speaking to biographer Charles Sawyer shortly after reuniting with B.B., Seidenberg noted that the conventional music industry wisdom held that he had made a mistake in taking on an aging artist in a blues market that was cold. "I think I can heat him up again," Seidenberg stated. "He's got as much potential now as he had in 1968, when I first took him over. He's still got that appeal for young college kids. The old college kids that are grown up now— they'll still buy his records *provided he's promoted properly*."

He reiterated what he had told B.B. at the outset of their relationship: it's all about a plan. "If I hadn't had a master plan when I met B.B., he wouldn't be where he is now. The booking agency doesn't have a master plan; the record company doesn't have a master plan. That was B.B.'s mistake when he walked out on me three years ago; he thought he could continue to thrive without someone taking a deep personal interest in his career. Record company executives usually haven't the vaguest idea how to promote a record. *Someone* has to know and then has to get to the right people at the record company and threaten, cajole, sue them until they do what's necessary. If you don't do these things, nothing happens."[3]

"That Album Resonated"
Stewart Levine on the *Midnight Believer* Sessions

How far into Midnight Believer *were you when you called Sid Seidenberg and got him back together with B.B.?*

Just about finished. It didn't take very long. We did about three or four days of tracking, then maybe two or three days of overdubbing. Not long. I think we did the vocals kinda after. There was enough to play Sid, short a couple of overdubs and things.

Interesting thing about that record, aside from it doing extremely well, a lot of people thought it was a nice piece of work, including Chris Black-well at Island. He turned Steve Winwood on to it, and that's how Steve Winwood and Will Jennings got hooked up. [Author's note: Jennings collaborated with Winwood on the latter's acclaimed *Arc of the Diver* and *Talking Back to the Night* albums, from 1980 and 1981, respectively.] Chris was crazy about this record. I think people saw that there was something special about the song forms. They're real songs; they're just not 12-bar blues. At the same time they weren't bullshit pop songs. There was something different about it; it sat in between both worlds, I think. That album resonated; I still like that album.

With Will and Joe's songs, as you suggested, there's some meat on the bone there. In "When It All Comes Down," when you listen to what they're saying, it's about perseverance, it's about commitment, it's about staying power—it really says something about B.B.

The songs were all tailor-made. I didn't cast the songs, and I never did that with B.B. There was a point later on when I did on an album that's very obscure, *Love Me Tender*. But other than that, all of them were tailor-made for him and Will got into his head, man, and wrote things that would have reflected the way B.B. looked and felt about things.

"Never Make Your Move Too Soon" is a cool song that B.B. eats up. You've got handclaps, party sounds, whistles going off, the band is shouting encouragement to B.B., he's laughing—

Yeah, it was meant to do business, you know. Good feeling, good vibe, and I knew we had a good angle at R&B radio and I figured they'd play it. It was a good-time-feelin' record, man. So that was it. The sessions were beautiful. B.B. primarily played on the sessions; he very seldom records his vocals live. With his touring schedule, it's almost impossible for him to sit down and learn these things before the sessions start. So he basically plays along with a guide vocal, like I say, primitive as it be, then he right away does the vocal. That's how it works. He's more comfortable with it that way. Occasionally he'll feel comfortable enough about it to do it live, but quite honestly that's how they're made.

You mentioned how he needs to be walked through it, but in his autobiography he talks about those years when he was recording for the Biharis, and how much he liked working with them because they left him alone. And he could do what he wanted to do. Is that B.B. putting up a front? Or was it simpler back then?

I think it was simpler. I think also he had broken in things and prepared them on the road. I believe that to be the case. He was respectful of the quality of the musicians that were around him always and the quality of the material that was around him—none of which he contributed. It was a lot like him coming in and we have tailor-made suits for him; nothing off the rack. We knew what it was that he could and could not do, and we stretched him to do things he didn't think he could do, but it was always, I think, within his range and within the realm that he functions.

One of the big things is he really didn't have the time to learn these things; he just didn't have the time physically on the road to work them out. So we would work them out in the studio and he trusted us enough to guide him through the vocals. In terms of the playing, it was always magical, wonderful; there was nothing ever to say about anything. It didn't matter what chords we threw in front of him, because a lot of these songs had chords that were not blues chords; they were like song-form chords, and they never posed a problem for him at all. He used to say that early on he learned to play "common tones"; he always would tell me that. "Common tones" would get him through everything.

The production touches on this album are an interesting mix of familiar B.B. touchstones and interjections of some new ideas. The strings, obviously, had become kind of a trademark since "The Thrill Is Gone," although he had recorded with strings before "The Thrill Is Gone." Horns had been a staple of B.B.'s records from the beginning.

That was Joe Sample digging in again to the tradition. We were all very serious about trying to walk the line of bringing in elements of some sort of pop devices and R&B devices, but at no time did we want to do anything that would be disrespectful of the tradition that B.B. came from, because to a certain degree Joe came from the same place. They came up through the Don Robey–Houston thing, and they knew about that shit. So it was a challenge to us to try to walk that line of putting a little drama and glamour attached to it, which is what Bill Szymczyk did in a very wonderful and amazing way. It's the same thing Bob Thiele did when he did "What a Wonderful World" with Louis Armstrong. Sometimes a little small touch like that, which is thought of as being a no-no, is just what you need to highlight the other side of what the music is. Then you can drench yourself in schmaltz and go fuckin' wrong, too. Something I never did. I'm basically, if anything, a minimalist as a producer. My way of thinking, my style, if there is one, is totally artist-based. I want you to listen to the song and the artist first, and I want you to feel the groove. And then if there's something else we can throw in here and there, one other element, fine. My producing style comes down to the artist being the focus, and then have something that's interesting and fun and a little bit thought out sitting in the background.

You also made good use of a gospel-based background chorus on all of your albums with B.B. That style of gospel backgrounds is another element that can be traced back to Bill Szymczyk's work with B.B. But whereas he used it on only one song, "Hummingbird," you've got them on almost every song on every album you did with B.B.

I knew B.B. loved gospel. He traveled with his record collection and it had a whole lot of gospel. He and I shared a love of the Golden Gate Quartet, which is one of the first things we started to talk about. I knew that that was a big part of it. He also liked smatterings of jazz. He thought that was the intellect of the music, and gospel was the heart and soul of it. So somewhere, wherever we could, we brought that in. I'm glad you saw it there, because it was the other device—and the word is chosen properly—that was used, but it was natural, something that reflected his background, and he would love when he'd hear those things. It'd just knock him out. Even if he could sing these things live with the rhythm section, he'd always say to me, "Stew, get the picture right for me first, man, put the stuff on. Give me a thrill." He used to say, "Give me a thrill, Stew." And then he'd put the headphones on, we'd get him a perfect mix, and he'd sit down and sing the shit out of it.

What did you think about the quality of his singing throughout these sessions?

Well, you know, I thought he was a magician. At times you'd think he was unprepared, he didn't know the songs, and that's the beauty of it. Great records are made out of a sense of danger, you know what I mean? And when someone's sat with these things for days, weeks, months, you can lose the immediacy. You need to get performances relatively quickly—two or three takes, and there isn't a lot of comping. I don't comp things. I punch for notes I don't like. I don't do five or six vocals and combine them; never did. That way you get no performance. I don't have the patience; I don't think that's how you make records. So with B.B., he'd sing one down and when it felt good, that was it. A couple of words, if he didn't phrase it right or whatever, we'd punch in and get them on the run. But I thought that he understood the essence of the lyrics. He's a great reader. He's like an actor, you know. He's a great reader of a lyric; give him a great lyric, he's gonna sell it. I thought for the most part on all of these records that his performances always played back better to me than when I was doing them. It's because you were sweatin' out trying to get these things to where they belonged, getting them to sit right in the rhythm section and phrasing-wise, and I was involved in the process. Then when I'd hear it when we'd go to mix it, a day or two later, whenever it was, the fucking thing would sound right. When I was fishin' for it, I'd think, Ah, I wish he'd just come in and do it live. But when I heard them back, I think he did justice to everything. I do believe I had a very good relationship with

B.B. He takes direction as good as you could possibly do it. Again, like a fine, fine actor. He trusts you. I don't know that he does that to everyone, but he sure did it to me, man. I think he respected my background and he knew that I knew what I was talking about.

There are two cuts back to back on Midnight Believer *that really illustrate how effective a vocalist he is. Those are the title track, where he does this beautiful, sensuous, crooning vocal, and "I Just Can't Leave Your Love Alone," which has that rollicking New Orleans feel, and B.B.'s just selling it—he's shouting, and he can go from one end of the spectrum to the other. He can croon as well as anybody, and if he needs to be a blues shouter, well, he grew up listening to Roy Brown and he knows what it's all about.*

It is the part that's most underrated. He's a great singer. Great singer. Totally, totally unique. Unlike lots of other artists, you can't figure out where B.B. comes from. You know what I mean? All due respect to Ray, you listen to Charles Brown, and there's Ray Charles. Who you gonna point to and tell me where B.B. came from? So I agree. That's why, quite honestly, if you'll listen through all of the albums I did with him, I presented him as a singer. I take it for granted that he's gonna play when he has to; to me, that's not the issue. There's nothing I can do to cause that to be highlighted. He's just gonna play. So I spend all my time on the songs and the vocal performances.

Take It Home

MCA, 1979
Produced by Stewart Levine and Wilton Felder, "Stix" Hooper, and Joe Sample
Engineered and mixed by Rik Pekkonen
Mastered at A&M Studios by Bernie Grundman

Musicians
B.B. King: guitar
Dean Parks: guitar
Paul M. Jackson, Jr.: guitar
Wilton Felder: bass, sax solo on "Take It Home"
Joe Sample: keyboards
Stix Hooper: drums and percussion, all songs except "Happy Birthday Blues," "I've Always Been Lonely," and "Tonight I'm Gonna Make You a Star"
James Gadson: drums and percussion on "Happy Birthday Blues," "I've Always Been Lonely," and "Tonight I'm Gonna Make You a Star"
Paulinho da Costa: percussion on "Take It Home," "Better Not Look Down," "Same Old Story (Same Old Song)"

Horns
Steve Madaio: trumpet

Gary Grant: trumpet
Dennis Quitman: sax
Larry Williams: sax
Kim Hutchcraft: baritone sax
Jack Redmond: trombone
Charles Findley: trombone
Horns: all cuts except "Tonight I'm Gonna Make You a Star," "A Story
    Everybody Knows," and "Take It Home"
Julia Tillman, Maxine Willard, Luther Waters, Oren Waters: background vocals
all cuts except "I've Always Been Lonely," "Tonight I'm Gonna Make You a
    Star," "The Beginning of the End," "A Story Everybody Knows"

Songs
"Better Not Look Down" (3:22) (Joe Sample–Will Jennings)
"Same Old Story" (4:30) (Joe Sample–Will Jennings)
"Happy Birthday Blues" (3:16) (Joe Sample–Will Jennings)
"I've Always Been Lonely" (5:27) (Joe Sample–Will Jennings)
"Second Hand Woman" (3:20) (Joe Sample–Will Jennings)
"Tonight I'm Gonna Make You a Star" (3:25) (B.B. King–Will Jennings)
"The Beginning of the End" (2:21) (B.B. King–Will Jennings)

"A Story Everybody Knows" (2:47) ("Stix" Hooper–Will Jennings)
"Take It Home" (3:07) (Wilton Felder–Will Jennings)

There was no great conceptual leap on B.B.'s second teaming with the Crusaders. *Midnight Believer* had done the job of connecting with B.B.'s audience and bringing in some new fans, so, not wanting to mess with success, label and management wanted one more ride on the merry-go-round.

"We came back with the same cast of characters, the same formula," Levine says. "The idea was to develop the plot. We felt we had one more album in us that could be done as an extension of the last one. It's as simple as that. It really was part two, you know."

The album's nine songs included five Sample–Jennings collaborations, a Jennings collaboration with Stix Hooper on the wry "A Story Everybody Knows," and a Wilton Felder–Jennings co-write on what became the title song, "Take It Home." B.B. teamed with Jennings as well, co-writing "Tonight I'm Gonna Make You a Star" and "The Beginning of the End."

The most striking aspect at first about *Take It Home* is how airy B.B.'s voice sounds and how carefree it is. He even sounds younger than his years (which would become an issue, and humorously so, after the album was completed), and unburdened of a lot of cares, but certainly not without deep passion in his vocals. Moreover, the deep passion of *Take It Home* is enhanced by its deep grooves. The Crusaders and their accompanying musicians are locked into a profound rhythmic dialog that works with B.B.'s commanding persona to produce some stirring, even spiritual moments. The funky album opener, "Better Not Look Down," proffers some down-home philosophy advising forward momentum as the best way to avoid heartache, with B.B. speaking the verses in a rhythmical fashion (in a style somewhere between talking blues and the earliest forms of rap), then singing the choruses fully supported by horns and a chanting female chorus. One of the B.B. co-writes with Will Jennings, "The Beginning of the End," features a dramatic, sorrowful reading from B.B. of his story about lovers becoming friends, a development he sees as "the beginning of the end." Equally cynical is the Stix Hooper–Will Jennings mating game farce, "A Story Everybody Knows," which serves up, in a lighthearted manner, the usual litany of reasons a woman rejects a man's sexual overtures. "Second Hand Woman" is a potent, stomping blues, with B.B. shouting out the lyrics in loud, clear, impassioned terms as the arrangement takes on new layers: with the band rooted in its fierce stomp, a burst of horns follows the first verse, a female chorus buoys the second chorus, and the instrumental break is sparked by a feisty dialog between Lucille and Sample's piano. The album's most moving number is its closer, the title track co-written by Wilton Felder and Will Jennings. Cast in a deliberate, stately gospel style, the tender lyrics evoke the South of B.B.'s youth in nostalgic terms, and B.B., fully immersed in the gospel feel, pulls from way down in his soul a gentle, reflective vocal revealing his spiritual attachment to the place he'll always call home. In the end, the story of *Take It Home* is the story of B.B.'s spirit—the depth of the blues he delivers, the sass on "A Story Everybody Knows," the carefree testifying on "Better Not Look Down," and the soaring emotions and gospel touches in the title track. Less a revelation than *Midnight Believer*, *Take It Home* is a solid effort by master craftsmen who never let their technical mastery get in the way of imaginative vitality and expressive performance.

The backstory on "Take It Home," the song, is that it, like "Better Not Look Down," was a rewrite of a Crusaders hit, in this case "Way Back Home," which had been what Levine calls "a big, anthemic hit" as an instrumental off the first Levine-produced Crusaders album, *Old Socks, New Shoes*. It was also a song adopted as a theme by the murderous American terrorists who assembled as the Symbionese Liberation Army, a radical group of ex-cons and misfits who, in addition to cold-blooded homicide, made headlines for kidnapping Patty Hearst. "They used it as their theme song," Levine recalls, "and this caused great problems in the Jehovah's Witness church, which Wilton Felder belonged to, but that's another movie. One day we were in the studio and some newspeople come around and tell us the Symbionese Liberation Army is using the song. What the fuck is this Symbionese Liberation Army? So we let that go by, and a couple of years later, again looking for material, I suggested that Will write a lyric for 'Way Back Home.' And he designed it to reflect an experience in B.B.'s life.

"That one," Levine states with authority, "was a beauty."

Take It Home included two rewrites of earlier Crusaders tunes, the second being the groove-happy philosophy of "You Better Not Look Down," which evolved from a Joe Sample instrumental, "Don't Let It Get You Down," off the band's *The Second Crusade* album. Levine makes no bones about the unabashedly commercial nature of his quest in "looking for something that had a party feel to it that could do some business at radio, particularly on that second album; we had to follow something up. Will wrote a lyric reasonably on the spot. We really just recut that groove and put a vocal on top of it, and it was a big hit, that one. That did big business for B.B."

But the story of "Better Not Look Down" didn't end with *Take It Home*. Ten years later the song caught the attention of someone in Hollywood, and it was in the original script of *Thelma & Louise* as the music to be played over

B.B. at the height of the success of "The Thrill
Is Gone."

the closing scene when the title characters, played by Susan Sarandon and
Geena Davis, launch their car off a cliff. Levine had been sent a script, and
after seeing that the final two pages contained nothing but the lyrics to "You
Better Not Look Down," had called director Ridley Scott, "who was a delight,
and I'm a big fan of *Alien* and all this shit, so I agreed to do it."

Reconvening in 1991, Levine and B.B. ("he got paid a lotta dough; had
quite a nice payday to do this movie, because it was the end title theme")
recut a "very straightahead version" of the song, "almost the same, you
know," and sent it off to Ridley Scott.

In a phone call to Levine, Scott praised the song, saying "it's great, except
one thing: B.B. sounds older on the original." It was now 12 years after the
original recording was made.

"What are you pointing to?" Levine asks.

Scott stammers and finally says, "Maybe you could—"

"You want me to call him and ask him if he could do it again and try to
sound *older*?" Levine said. "Fuck, you guys are somethin' else again. All

right, I'll do it." At the very least, he figured, B.B. would get a kick out of the phone call.

"So I called B, he says, 'God, I don't believe it. Stew, do you remember what kind of shape I was in when we did that? I had the government up my ass, I had a divorce, I was a mess! Now I'm happy, everything's cool. If I sound younger, I don't wanna sound older!' He's laughing! I said, 'Okay, forget it.' I get back to Ridley Scott and tell him, 'I have a way to do this. I'll fly in his vocal from the old tape.'

"I call the studio, it was right down the street, and sure enough they still had the multitrack masters. I had them sent over and I told [the movie people] it was a lot harder than it really was. I just transferred his vocal to a piece of two-track and dropped it in line by line. Took a couple of hours, and gave them B.B.'s old vocal on the new track. And everyone was happy.

"I see the film, I realize something ain't right here. At the end they've got some bullshit score piece and they've cut the whole ending, it's different. In the script the girl drives over the cliff and they play 'Better Not Look Down' for two minutes. After what I saw, I see Ridley Scott, and I say, 'What happened, man?' He's got his head down and says, 'You know they previewed it and people were confused with the ending.' He gets quiet and I say, 'Man, you're Ridley Scott. What the fuck you talkin' about? You let them do that?' He just shook his head. I said, 'Fuck it, man,' and walked away. And that was it. So it didn't end up being what it was supposed to be, but it's interesting that the song penetrated far enough for them to use it in the screenplay."

Even more successful than *Midnight Believer*, *Take It Home* sold upwards of half a million units and furthered B.B.'s artistic and commercial revival. But the string was playing out with the Crusaders. It was harder to come up with songs for the sequel, hence the co-writes with B.B. (and, Levine points out with a gravelly laugh, "it was time he got a little bit of publishing, and management had moved in a bit").

"We did as well as we could at that moment in time with that album" is Levine's assessment of the *Take It Home* sessions. "It had some big high points but was not quite as consistent as *Midnight Believer*. Which led me to believe, when [the label] came *again*, for us to do the next record, I felt that little plot had played itself out and we couldn't do any more with the Crusaders. Felt that that whole thing had been great and they were on to doing what they were doing and it was time to rethink it."

Chapter 11

WHAT'S UP, DOC?

n New York City, Doc Pomus was emerging from a decade's hiatus as a songwriter, a time when he too decided "it was time to rethink it." He had gone into self-imposed retirement in 1965 "because I didn't like what was happening."[1] Up to that point, though, he and his partner Mort Shuman had established themselves in the top tier of rock 'n' roll songwriters, on a par with Jerry Leiber and Mike Stoller. They had amassed a stunning catalog of hits written for the Coasters, the Drifters ("Save the Last Dance for Me" among several elegantly crafted and breathtakingly produced—by Leiber and Stoller—love songs bearing the Pomus–Shuman copyright), Dion and the Belmonts ("Teenager in Love"), Ray Charles ("Lonely Avenue"), Bobby Darin, Andy Williams, plus more than two dozen songs for Elvis Presley, including "Viva Las Vegas," "Little Sister," "(Marie's the Name) His Latest Flame," "A Mess of Blues," and "Suspicion." Pomus was a true urban romantic, his lyrics being both streetwise and tenderhearted, mirroring the man himself.

A big man with a big heart, born June 27, 1925, Pomus, né Jerome Felder, was a Brooklyn native (as a toddler he was voted Brooklyn's Most Beautiful Baby) and an early convert to the blues as sung by Big Joe Turner, his favorite number being "Piney Brown Blues." While still in his teens he began playing local clubs (afflicted with polio at age six, he walked and performed on crutches), modeling his rugged singing style after Big Joe's. In his late teens he hung out at George's Tavern in Greenwich Village, where Frankie Newton's band held forth. Eventually he wrangled a singing gig at the club, simply in order to stay in the place.

219

"What was really interesting was the fact that I didn't know any blues," Pomus said. "I just knew one or two, and I started singing in the place because I saw the owner was about to throw me out for hanging around the bandstand. So I told him I was a singer, and Frankie Newton, a great trumpet player and a really nice fellow, told me to sit in with the band. I knew one blues at that time, 'Piney Brown Blues,' and I did 'Piney Brown,' and when they asked me to do an encore, I did 'Piney Brown' again. I really was not so much a blues fan then, but a Joe Turner fan. I didn't start collecting records of my favorite singers till I was in my twenties."[2]

Pomus built up a repertoire and a reputation as a solid blues shouter and talented writer, and by 1945, at age 19, he was making his first recordings as a solo artist, for the Apollo label. He assembled a number of bands over the years, invariably drawing premier players into his fold, including, at one time in the same group, both saxophonist King Curtis and guitarist Mickey Baker. He recorded for several different labels over the next ten years, but his only hit came in 1955, when his song "Heartlessly," for the Dawn label, was championed by pioneering rock 'n' roll disc jockey Alan Freed and became a local hit. RCA bought the master recording, intending, Pomus believed, to break it nationally. Instead, for reasons that were never explained to him, the label killed the single and, with that, Pomus's career as a solo artist.

"We never knew what happened," Pomus said of the demise of "Heartlessly." "As soon as the record started opening up in New York, it got killed. But Alan Freed had stayed on the record for several weeks straight and was real excited about it, swore it was a hit. In those days Alan was never wrong. It depressed me so much that eventually I stopped singing, because I thought that was my big chance.

"I had been so poor all my life and now it just didn't seem to be going anywhere. It looked like ultimate disaster to me, so I packed it in.

"I was barely surviving with that. Then I said I would be a songwriter exclusively. Then I started thinking that the best thing to do is to write a lot of songs; you can't survive writing a few songs as a songwriter. So I found this kid who had been hanging out with my cousin at parties and I broke him in. I let him stay in the room when I wrote a song and every time he was there I would give him like 10 percent of the song, or 15 percent. This went on for years. Finally one day years later I said, 'You're my partner,' and from then on he got 50 percent of the songs. But he went through like an apprenticeship with me for years. Just for being in the room I'd give him 10 percent, 15 percent, 20 percent. That was Mort Shuman, and eventually we became full-time partners and eventually we were very successful."[3]

Doc Pomus, New York City, 1980s:
"I always figured I am the quintessential
person — in other words, what I feel is
what a lot of other people out there feel.
I always write that way."

Very successful indeed, right up to the moment in 1965 when, discouraged by the direction popular music was taking, he broke up the partnership. What never left him, though, was his love of the blues and of blues artists, not only Big Joe Turner, who had become his close friend, but T-Bone Walker, Little Jimmy Scott, B.B. King, Ray Charles—their records dominated his extensive collection. Despite all the hits bearing the Pomus–Shuman credit—none of which he disavowed—the music that continued to speak to him on intimate terms about his life was the blues.

In the mid-'70s he had become acquainted with Mac Rebennack, the gifted and charismatic New Orleans guitarist-keyboardist known professionally as Dr. John, an alter ego Rebennack assumed in 1967. Dr. John, in fact, was a real New Orleans character, a root doctor who, according to Rebennack, "was preeminent in the city for the awe in which he was held by the poor, and the fear and notoriety he inspired among the rich"; later in life Rebennack learned that the real Dr. John and a lady named Pauline Rebennack, whose relationship to Mac Rebennack remains uncertain, were arrested for running a voodoo operation and a whorehouse.[4] The modern-day Dr. John, originally christened as Dr. John the Night Tripper, turned his concerts into spiritual, mystical, hallucinatory, and rhythm-bound N'awlins celebrations, with the master of ceremonies decked out in resplendent, colorful plumes, symbolic face paint, beads, and walking sticks (one sported a shrunken head), all the while advancing some seriously deep grooving music born of those infectious Crescent City second-line rhythms. If Dr. John's entire presentation seemed informed by drugs and drug culture, well, that part wasn't necessarily a show: Rebennack had been using narcotics since his early teens and was introduced to heroin, his drug of choice, around his fifteenth year. It could be said with some degree of accuracy that his highs informed his art. Image aside, though, he was a supremely gifted musician, dedicated to his craft and serious in his musical explorations. He was still in junior high school when he sold some of his original songs to the Specialty label, for Little Richard, who periodically came through town to record, and to Art Neville, then working in a local band; also as a teenager, he began sitting in on guitar on sessions with some of the great names in New Orleans R&B.[5] In 1965 he moved to Los Angeles and became an in-demand session player (working with Phil Spector, among others) before he started his solo career in earnest. Although never a major pop artist, he did have a Top Ten hit in 1973 with the slinky "Right Place Wrong Time," one of the last mainstream chart incursions of New Orleans–influenced pop.

Pomus and Rebennack hit it off both personally and professionally. Producer Joel Dorn, a quadruple Grammy winner whose impressive résumé ranges from Bette Midler to Roberta Flack ("Killing Me Softly" was a Joel Dorn production), from Roland Kirk to the Neville Brothers, put the two together to write a song, "a new national anthem," according to Dr. John, for a movie he was backing.[6] The movie project failed to materialize, but the two doctors forged a deep bond and good memories from their aborted first collaboration. "I've still got a fond spot in my heart about that project," Dr. John said, "because Joel used to talk about having Fathead Newman, one of my closest partners, dribbling a basketball with one hand and playing his sax with the other during this national anthem."[7] The friendship blossomed commercially in 1978 and 1979 when they teamed to write most of the songs on Dr. John's *Tango Palace* and *City Lights* albums (both of them co-produced by Rebennack's buddy and B.B. session veteran Hugh McCracken). In that same time frame Pomus had ventured tentatively back into the rock world by writing three songs for Willie DeVille's *Le Chat Bleu*, which was released in 1980 and wound up winning an Album of the Year citation from *Rolling Stone* magazine.

All of these more recent songs demonstrated the growth in Pomus's writing. The urban settings were still there, but the emotions were more complex;

no more teen dramas or fears of the other guy stealing his girl, but rather an internal monolog about survival, within a relationship, within the context of getting through a day, and serious thought as to the meaning of love, the quest for love, the necessity for love—themes that illuminated Pomus's life, in fact and in song.

One night in the mid-'80s, while suffering with a toothache, Doc was trying to find something on late-night TV to distract him from his pain. Lo and behold, there was Charlie Rose hosting the talk show "Nightwatch" on CBS. His guest was B.B. King. What Pomus saw inspired him to reflect on his *raison d'être* as a songwriter in his later years, and those ideas were already in place at the moment Stewart Levine was rethinking the approach to B.B.'s next album.

"As usual the interview was very interesting because B is so articulate and always finds new things to say and he's so gracious," Pomus said. "After the interview ended, out of the clear blue, Charlie asked him, 'What's your favorite song?' So he said, 'I have two favorite songs. One of them is a song Willie Nelson recorded called 'Always on My Mind,' and the other is a song Johnny Adams recorded called 'A World I Never Made.'"

Pomus was shocked, because the Johnny Adams song was one he had written, and he had no idea B.B. had ever heard it, much less liked it.

"The thing that really moved me about it was that this is one of the songs I've written in the last few years, and these represent to me a different approach to writing. This is one of those songs that I've written that I write to an older audience. When I was writing 20, 25, 30 years ago a large part of the thrust of my writing was geared towards young people. But today the thrust of my writing is to older people, and I think I went back to my roots. Originally when I started writing songs—and at that time I was writing by myself—I was writing to an adult audience, blues or rhythm and blues. The audience at that time was adults mostly, and some young people bought records incidentally. So here I'm going back again to those kinds of roots, to people who are out there stumbling in the night, but they're all adults doing that. I think basically they're kind of lost, have a lot of problems—problems with women, problems with finances, problems with just trying to figure out who they are, and mostly trying to get through the night. You're out there at night and there's a world surrounding you, and it looks cold and it looks distant. You don't feel like you're really a part of it. At least I always figured I am the quintessential person—in other words, what I feel is what a lot of other people out there feel. I always write that way.

"I think young people have some of those same feelings, but they haven't lived the years in this world to experience a lot of those things to the depth, and the feelings aren't as extended as they are with older people. After all, I'm 63 years old; I'm operating with a wide, wide range of experience."[8]

B.B. needing a new direction, and his contemporary Doc Pomus focused on writing songs that addressed issues and feelings common to older adults, seemed to Levine to be a good place to start a new album. Over the phone the producer described for Pomus what he was looking for, and about a month later, in the fall of 1980, a cassette arrived in his mailbox. When he played it, he was "absolutely stunned" by what he heard.

"I put [Mac and Doc] on assignment to write, and they handed me the whole fucking album," he said. "And they made these demos that were unbelievable at the piano. I think they did them right there in Doc's apartment. They were outrageous. It was a gorgeous cassette, man. They were beautiful. I thought these songs were masterpieces."

But he wasn't sure B.B. could pull them off. And when B.B. heard the demo, he wasn't sure he could either. He thought it sounded like a Ray Charles album. Levine agreed. "If you heard Mac's demos of the songs, at the Wurlitzer piano, phrasing them the way he did, they really did sound like they would have been right for Ray Charles and maybe not right for B.B. A lot of that was just the way Mac sounded. It took me a lot of convincing to get B.B. to agree to it."

Another problem surfaced: B.B. was, in Levine's words, "very put off by Dr. John." Despite having used him on his 1971 *In London* album, and no matter that the offstage Dr. John was a fairly sedate, and sedately attired, Mac Rebennack, pianist par excellence, B.B., Levine said, "knew him as an artist, and he knew him as a character, but he didn't really know him as a musician. He was intimidated by Mac."

Intimidated, as it turned out, by the excellence of Mac's artistry on the demo tape. As guide vocals he was used to hearing Joe Sample and Will Jennings, untutored singers to put it mildly. When he heard their voices in his headphones during the recording sessions, "they were horrible, and therefore he felt comfortable, because all they were there for was to tell the story," Levine said. "Now you get demos that are good. Mac makes them sound a little too learned and a little too Ray, and B.B. starts to think they were not made for him. It was a superficial response; at that point he wasn't even really listening to them."

Levine urged B.B. to take the demo, go away somewhere, and listen to it alone, absorb it, and consider what he'd do with it.

After a week of silence, Levine got a call from B.B.

"Whatever you think, Stew," he heard B.B. say. "I'll be there. I trust you, whatever you think. I don't know if I can do these. Now I've heard 'em and there's some beautiful words here."

"'Beautiful words,'" Levine recalled. "That's what he said."

Then B.B. fretted some more. "I'm really worried about it, because he sounds so good doing 'em."

"About a dozen times," in Levine's estimation, B.B. worried aloud as to whether he could pull it off. "He was insecure at that point" is Levine's assessment of B.B. going into the album sessions at the Hit Factory in New York in November 1980.

There Must Be a Better World Somewhere _____

MCA, 1981
Produced by Stewart Levine
Executive producer: Sidney A. Seidenberg
Engineered and mixed by Rik Pekkonen
Recorded at the Hit Factory, New York City
Assistant engineer: John Smith
Re-mixed at Hollywood Sound Recorders
Mastered by Bernie Grundman
Cover illustration: Ron Kriss

Musicians
B.B. King: lead guitar and vocals
Dr. John: keyboards
Pretty Purdie: drums
Wilbur Bascomb: bass
Hugh McCracken: rhythm guitar

Horn Section
Hank Crawford: alto sax
David "Fathead" Newman: tenor sax
Ronald Cuber: baritone sax
Tom Malone: trombone
Waymon Reed: trumpet
Charlie Miller: trumpet
Horns arranged by Hank Crawford
Donny Gerrard, Carmen Twillie, and Vennette Gloud: background vocals on "More, More, More"

Songs
"Life Ain't Nothing but a Party" (6:25) (Doc Pomus–Dr. John); alto sax solo: Hank Crawford

"Born Again Human" (8:31) (Doc Pomus–Dr. John); alto sax solo: Hank
   Crawford; tenor sax solo: David "Fathead" Newman
"There Must Be a Better World Somewhere" (5:37) (Doc Pomus–Dr. John)
"The Victim" (6:19) (Doc Pomus–Dr. John); tenor sax solo: David "Fathead"
   Newman
"More, More, More" (4:38) (Hugh McCracken–Jay Hirsh)
"You're Going with Me" (4:32) (Doc Pomus–Dr. John)

A lilting, minor-key blast of horns, with Crawford's alto sax murmuring
down low as Lucille gets in a few quick cries, opens "Life Ain't Nothing but
a Party," the first song on *There Must Be a Better World Somewhere*, on a note
that recalls nothing so much as a Maxwell Davis arrangement. A beautiful
intro settles into a mellow groove, and B.B. handles the lyrics tenderly, rising
to a growl only near the end, and only for a fleeting effect. The key lyric, "Life
ain't nothin' but a party / Tomorrow too soon is yesterday / If you live it that
way / And don't give it away / The party still goes on and on and on,"
reflects exactly what Pomus meant about bringing a life's experience to bear
on his writing. He had learned to savor that which persisted in his world—
the friends, the family, the music he loved—and felt, in his sixties, a sense of

triumph over the follies of his younger years. B.B. handled the vocal with the proper avuncular touch, and closed out the song with a sweet, angular commentary from Lucille.

The same generosity of spirit informs the second number, the eight-and-a-half-minute "Born Again Human," which kicks off with a three-minute-fifteen-second instrumental intro featuring David "Fathead" Newman blowing a spirited tenor sax solo that sets up another deliberate vocal on B.B.'s part, he entering with the generous sentiment, "You taught me how to bend and never break / You showed me how to give and never take / There was no sacrifice too great for you / Sweet, sweet woman, can't you see what you mean to me / Born again human…"; at the end he sings, "…through your love / I rejoined the human race." The track is steady and a bit somber, reflective, drummer Bernard Purdie adding a hi-hat–cymbal flourish here and there, B.B. giving Lucille free rein to moan throughout, and Dr. John settling in below it all with some trebly right-hand blues runs.

The thoughtful mood is sustained in the album's signature and title song, a meditation on persistence in the face of adversity, set to the tune of an old hymn Rebennack had heard in his youth in New Orleans titled "This Earth Ain't No Place I'm Proud to Call Home." "Flying high / some joker clips my wings / just because he gets a kick / out of doing those kinds of things / I keep on falling in space / Or just hanging in mid air / But I know, oh yes, I know / There's got to be a better world somewhere," B.B. sings with a gospel feel, going on to describe the woes of being mistreated by women along the way, but always coming back to the abiding theme that "there must be a better world somewhere."

Although not originally conceived as such, the first three songs form a literary and musical cycle, a metaphysical survival guide to getting through the battle, no matter the obstacles. Bad women, bad breaks, a shallow appreciation of the moment—commonplace woes all, but in Pomus's mature worldview, nothing that a big heart, real love, and a positive outlook can't overcome. So it's only fitting that a rollicking song titled "The Victim" should follow this philosophical trifecta. It opens with Dr. John's rolling piano lick that summons the ghost of Jelly Roll Morton and settles into a stomping groove as B.B. relates a tale of being "a victim of every girl I meet." Its party atmosphere and Fathead Newman's intense tenor sax solo provide a buoyant lift to what had been a noirish mood. The album's closer, "You're Going with Me," opens with a thumping round of rhythm courtesy Purdie and Wilbur Bascomb's prominent ostinato bass riff, and the rest of the band slides into the groove, with a sharp, stinging Lucille solo out front as the horns pump and Purdie stays hard on the backbeat. The whole thing chugs almost to a stop near the end, and then cranks right back up to a brisk shuffle as B.B. intones, "You goin' with me, you goin' with me" at the fade.

The only song not composed by Pomus and Rebennack is a co-write by rhythm guitarist Hugh McCracken and Jay Hirsh. Titled "More, More, More," it's a gospel-styled hosanna to unbridled self-indulgence, in which B.B. sings of giving up wine and women at age 18, only to return to taking "all I can get." With an urgent female chorus shouting behind him, he sings of wanting "more, more, more," and Dr. John rolls off some dramatic arpeggios to heighten the intensity. Philosophically the song is at odds with the Pomus–Rebennack material, but its dark mood seems to suggest that the young man is destined to pay a price for his shameless hedonism—which is more or less the backstory of the album's opening triptych.

The story of the songs and their performance is but part of the tale, however. Levine deliberately stripped down the instrumental support to a basic band to suit Pomus and Rebennack's narratives. In addition to Rebennack on piano, he brought in the veteran session drummer Bernard "Pretty" Purdie, bassist Wilbur Bascomb ("A pain in the ass," Levine said. "I didn't like him, man. He and I had bad tension between us."), and on rhythm guitar Hugh McCracken, who had first played with B.B. on the Bill Szymczyk–produced sessions in 1969 and 1970. For the six-piece horn section (three saxes, two trumpets, and a trombone) he deliberately sought out and hired two former mainstays of Ray Charles's band, alto saxophonist Hank Crawford (who arranged the horns) and tenor sax man David "Fathead" Newman. "I rubbed it in with Hank and Fathead," Levine said, "because B.B. was talking about how 'Ray' these songs were. I said, 'Fuck it, I'm going right into it. He gave me the idea.' I went and got Hank and Fathead. I just felt B.B. was up to it, to handle that territory that Ray no longer possessed."

Recording at the Hit Factory in New York, scene of his triumphs with Szymczyk, B.B. fell in with a wild bunch the likes of which he had never encountered in a studio environment. The troupe worked from eight at night until four in the morning for about two weeks straight, several of the key players laboring under the influence of various pharmaceuticals and libations.

"Oh, what sessions these were, baby," Levine recalled, at once laughing and shuddering at the memory. "There was a mood about them; I think Doc's lyrics permeated the air, and that's one of the reasons the mood was what it was. I think we were all aware of it. My memory is that it was very, very intense, very musical, and very heavy. You can't say it was a good time. It was serious, you know what I mean? Everyone was at the top of their game, playing as well as they could. But there wasn't too much communication between people, 'cause Mac was out of it, I was kinda having to be in charge of things, and I was drinkin' too much, Purdie was off in his world. Somehow it all came together. It was dark, and it fit the music, man. Sometimes you gotta make these things make themselves. The mood creates the music. And this record had a real mood. It was just heavy."

Serving notice that these were not going to be routine dates, Bernard Purdie showed up for the start of sessions without his drum kit. He said he would use the studio's kit, only to find out the studio didn't have a full kit. Levine's mixer-engineer, Rik Pekkonen, found some drums in a closet and set them up. "Purdie hit 'em a couple of times and there it was. Unbelievable. We had nothin', and we just taped 'em up, put the mics up, and the fuckin' thing sounded great. It was weird, man; it was a fuckin' crazy session."

The lack of a proper drum kit was the least of Levine's problems. Mac was "a bit of a mess; Mac was incommunicado," according to Levine. "Mac was fucked up, he was nodding out, and B.B. didn't really enjoy his presence that much; he just loved the way he played. He was in bad shape."

It goes on.

"And I was at the end of my alcoholism and for the first time really drinking in the studio. I was drinking three, four, five bottles of white wine a night—and I never even drank wine. It was delirious. Mac was on methadone and mixing it up with other stuff; Purdie was weird; the bass player was weird; Hank Crawford was fucked up, drunk and stoned." Hugh McCracken was called in not only because of his history with B.B., but because "he was very, very close to Dr. John, and I needed someone in there that could try to keep it going.

"Mac, Hank, and I were basically in the same place, and we were getting along perfectly. Hank and I were gettin' juiced and gettin' high, and we were locked in; it was very, very musical. You know what I mean? It wasn't at all frivolous because we were stoned. I don't want to say it to make a point of, like, in favor of drugs or alcohol, but it does come to a point where, just ask Charlie Parker and a lot of other people, why the fuck you think they did all that shit? It does zone you in sometimes, and it zones you out other times. But we were on the same level and we were very on the mood. That's one record I really feel like where we got the tone, the fabric of the songs comes through. And it's the same old instrumentation. We ain't got nothin' on that record. It's stripped down, very sparse."

With all this, Levine managed to put to use some lessons he had learned along the way. Early in his career an arranger had told him that a singer should be set up with either an arpeggio or "five minutes." For the song "Born Again Human," Levine had the musicians jamming before he started rolling tape. For three minutes and fifteen seconds, it's a jam, then B.B. enters vocally. "When he comes in, that's a real jazz record," Levine said. "The irony of it was that with Hank being around it really wasn't a jazz band. The joke was that we had the Jazz Crusaders being with B.B. on two albums and we do one thing; then we have Dr. John and these other guys who are not jazz players, and we make what's essentially a jazz album. It was beautiful."

The drama didn't end with the last notes recorded, though. When Levine and Pekkonen arrived at Hollywood Sound Records to mix the album, they found that the high end on the recordings kept going away. Upon further inspection, they found that the oxide was peeling off the back end of the 16-track tapes. "Because it was the blues, we had to stop every 12 bars, clean the tape heads, and then mix the next section. We pieced that album together in mixes 12 bars at a time. The whole album. It was a bad batch of tape, and when it went to play, it kept coming off on the heads.

"It was ridiculous. It was one of those records that had pain written all over it, you know?"

Postscript: Levine tells the story of the making of *There Must Be a Better World Somewhere* with a sense of awe and wonder at what transpired at the Hit Factory in the wee, small hours of those November mornings in 1980. But the message in Doc Pomus's songs sank in, and once the album was complete he got sober and has stayed that way ever since. "I said, Okay, this chapter's over, man. I hear what he's talking about. I better go get it together."

A year after its release, *There Must Be a Better World Somewhere* won a Grammy Award as Best Traditional Blues Album. At a party after the ceremony, B.B. wanted to make a champagne toast to his producer. He poured a glass for Levine, who politely declined, saying, "No, B, I ain't doin' it anymore. I had to cut it loose."

Surprised by this revelation, B.B. was rendered speechless for a moment. "Really!" he said at last. "Stew, I didn't know you had a problem."

Most of all, Levine took pride in learning that Doc Pomus was pleased with the finished product. Pomus's daughter Sharyn Felder would later tell Levine that her father considered the album one of the high points of his later life. "I always felt a lot better that Doc thought I was okay," said Levine, *sotto voce*. "Made me think I was a little better than I had planned to be, the fact that he thought I was cool and we did justice to this music. Doc was not impressed by much. 'How are you, Doc?' 'Same old shit.' And he loved this record."

Love Me Tender _____

MCA, 1982
Produced by Stewart Levine
Executive Producer: Sidney A. Seidenberg
Tracks recorded at Music City Music Hall, Nashville
Engineer: Bill Harris
Asst. Engineer: David DeBusk
Horns recorded at Muscle Shoals Sound Studios, Muscle Shoals, Alabama
Engineer: Gregg Hamm
Asst. Engineer: Pete Greene
Strings and Vocals recorded at the Hit Factory, New York City
Engineer: Joe Ferla
Asst. Engineer: Brian McGee
Mixed at the Hit Factory, New York City
Engineer: Joe Ferla
Asst. Engineer: Brian McGee
Mastered by Jack Adelman

Rhythm Accompaniment
David Briggs: keyboards
Reggie Young: guitar
Sonny Garrish: steel guitar
Larrie Londin: drums
Dale Sellers: guitar
Bob Wray: bass
David "Fathead" Newman: saxophone solos
Rhythm and Strings arranged by David Briggs
Patti Austin, Vivian Cherry, Casey Cisyk: vocal backgrounds

Muscle Shoals Horns
Harrison Callaway: trumpet
Ben Cauley: trumpet
Ronald Eades: baritone sax
Harvey Thompson: tenor sax
Walter King: alto sax
Charles Rose: trombone
Horns arranged by Harrison Callaway
Gene Orloff, Alfred Brown, Sanford Allen, Marvin Morgenstern, Lewis Eley, Paul Gershman, Gene Lumia, Elena Barbere, Max Ellen, Winterton Garvey, Richard Sortomme, Kenneth Gordon, Marilyn Wright, Emanuel Vardi, Julian Barber, Sue Pray, Frederick Zlotkin, Kermit Moore: strings

Songs
"One of Those Nights" (4:58) (Conway Twitty–Troy Seals)
"Love Me Tender" (3:28) (Elvis Presley–Vira Matson)
"Don't Change on Me" (4:35) (James Holiday–Edward Reeves)
"(I'd Be) A Legend in My Time" (2:52) (Don Gibson)
"You've Always Got the Blues" (4:57) (Mickey Newbury)
"Nightlife"/"Please Send Me Someone to Love" (4:30) (Willie Nelson; Percy
    Mayfield)
"You and Me, Me and You" (3:05) (Will Jennings–Troy Seals)
"Since I Met You Baby" (4:30) (Ivory Joe Hunter)
"This Is a Thief" (5:26) (Mickey Newbury)
"A World I Never Made" (5:13) (Doc Pomus–Dr. John)

After completing *There Must Be a Better World Somewhere*, Stewart Levine retreated to his Woodstock, New York, home to "clean up and get it back together," with no intention of returning to the studio anytime soon. But MCA was calling, wanting another album to follow up the success of *There Must Be a Better World Somewhere*. Levine, though, didn't sense the stars to be in proper alignment for him to dive into another B.B. project.

"I was living in upstate New York, slightly lost and not really knowing what the fuck to do," Levine said, "but I really didn't want to make another record with B.B. because I didn't have any angle. Had done the Crusaders, I had done Doc, I had played my hand out. Will Jennings, who was living in Nashville, had run dry; he had nothing; he couldn't think of anything to do; Mac and Doc couldn't come up with anything because Mac was so fucked up. It's not as easy as it looks, in terms of the way I felt you had to make records with him, which is not a bunch of isolated songs strung together. It needed some sort of cohesive angle."

Jennings came up with an angle of sorts: he suggested Levine pay a visit to Nashville, and check out the music scene with an eye towards doing a record with B.B. there. Levine, who had no affinity whatsoever for country music, scoffed at the notion of working in Music City. Ask him about country music and he relates an anecdote about the volatile jazz giant Buddy Rich, who, prior to a surgical procedure, responded to a question about any allergies he had by saying, "Only country and western music." But upon further reflection Levine began to appreciate the whimsy of Jennings's epiphany, and soon enough was Nashville bound.

"One of the things I've done right through my little career is when someone asks me to do something and I don't understand what it is or why they asked me, if I decide that maybe I got a shot, I go and do homework. So that's what happened with this and I had a fuckin' ball in Nashville. I stayed about three or four days and I came home with a shitload of fuckin' songs. I called B.B. and said, 'Listen, B, I got an idea for the record.' He says, 'What's that?' I said, 'That Memphis is only 150 miles from Nashville, man, and there you are and there are worlds between you. So why don't we make a record that's based on country songs, not like what Ray did, but I got a bunch of country songs, and what do you think of it?' He said, 'I'd love it, man.' Straight out. 'I love country music,' he said. It might've been him that said Memphis is only 150 miles away. I thought it was a profound remark, so it's probably him that said it, 'cause I never said no profound shit like that."

On the surface, there seems to be no "angle" to the album that became *Love Me Tender*. It does have the strongest country influence of any of B.B.'s albums by far, but it's not totally a country album, although it features well-crafted songs by Conway Twitty and Troy Seals, Don Gibson, Mickey Newbury, and Willie Nelson. A case could be made that it's a countrypolitan outing, thanks to Levine's exquisite deployment of strings that recalls nothing so much as a masterful Billy Sherrill production. It certainly isn't a blues album, despite the presence of that Doc Pomus–Dr. John gem, "A World I

Never Made," closing the festivities, and B.B. handling the two Newbury tunes in a blues vein. It would seem to be what Levine said he could never do with B.B., an album of unrelated songs strung together.

B.B. articulated an angle, however, in a few words he penned on the back cover of the striking Milton Glaser–designed package. "This is the greatest album I have recorded in my 35 years in the music business," he wrote, a statement he had made before and would make again. "It represents my life-time dream in expressing my feelings through music and song and puts together all my roots and influences from blues to country and everywhere else. It is something different but yet the same."

Overview, then, is one angle. From the Conway Twitty–Troy Seals team came "One of Those Nights"; from Don Gibson came "(I'd Be) A Legend in My Time," a poignant rendition of a song that had already been a No. 1 country single for Ronnie Milsap, his third in a string of 40 chart-topping singles; from Willie Nelson came "Nightlife," a country classic B.B. had performed on his incendiary live album from 1967, *Blues Is King*. Will Jennings and Troy Seals had combined on a funky number titled "You and Me, Me and You" that would not have been out of place on either of B.B.'s collaborations with the Crusaders. Two evergreen R&B ballads were present in Percy Mayfield's socially conscious "Please Send Me Someone to Love" (which B.B. makes the second half of a medley leading off with "Nightlife") and Ivory Joe Hunter's "Since I Met You Baby." And the final cut is a deep blues ballad from Doc Pomus and Dr. John, originally recorded by Johnny Adams and cited by B.B. as one of his favorite songs (in the "Nightwatch" interview Pomus had stumbled upon during his toothache crisis), "A World I Never Made." The title tune, "Love Me Tender," adds both a pop element to the tune stack and the more subtle angle of this production: Elvis Presley looms all over the album. Unintentionally, *Love Me Tender* is the moment when the King of Rock 'n' Roll meets the King of the Blues.

For one, songwriter Mickey Newbury, represented on the album by two songs, penned one of Elvis's greatest late-career recordings, "American Trilogy," which became both a hit single and a show-stopping concert piece. The exceptional keyboard work, as rich as it is understated, is supplied by Muscle Shoals native David Briggs, who as a 23-year-old had filled in for Floyd Cramer at a 1966 Elvis recording session in Nashville and immediately became one of the King's favorite and oft-employed studio sidemen. Guitarist Reggie Young, also a veteran studio picker, had added fire and subtlety to Elvis's epochal 1969 Chips Moman–produced Memphis sessions that yielded monuments on the order of "Suspicious Minds" and the *From Elvis in*

Memphis album. From the pen of Doc Pomus had come some of Elvis's legendary hits. With Briggs taking a major role in the production by not only playing keyboards but also arranging the rhythm and strings, and Levine employing the Muscle Shoals horns and a gospel-styled female chorus, *Love Me Tender* at points sounds like it came not from Nashville but from producer Chips Moman's American Studios in Memphis, circa 1969–'70.

The Elvis link is made right at the start of the first cut, the Twitty–Seals number, "One of Those Nights," when the strings gently introduce the song and the soaring female gospel chorus enters later. The sumptuous strings dominating the soundscape of "Love Me Tender" recall the arrangement Elvis used in his televised 1968 comeback special. The Newbury songs, "You've Always Got the Blues" and "Time Is a Thief," find a host of latter-day Elvis touches—strings, gospel piano, forthright blasts of horns—underpinning B.B.'s sensitive country-blues ballad vocals. And much as Elvis's producers did, Levine, to B.B.'s delight no doubt, employed the pedal steel (played here by Sonny Garrish) discreetly, precisely enough to give Newbury's "Time Is a Thief" a traditional country tinge in the midst of an R&B-styled arrangement. Briggs is sensational throughout in supporting B.B. with an immaculate touch on the keyboards, from the spare lines he plunks at the opening of "Nightlife" to the expressive commentary he lends to the lilting take on Ivory Joe Hunter's beautiful "Since I Met You Baby."

Heavy on mordant strings and given added poignance by a stinging, bristling Lucille solo as it fades out, the Pomus–Rebennack number "A World I Never Made" could properly have been part of *There Must Be a Better World Somewhere*, save for its depressive nature. B.B. handles the lyrics deliberately and with moving tenderness, investing the frightful narrative ("I'm a stranger and afraid / In a world I never made") with the overwhelming, aching loneliness of a man whose path keeps leading him to dead ends ("there's no way I can win") until he's completely isolated not only from other people but also from the earth itself.

Levine thoroughly enjoyed himself during the *Love Me Tender* sessions, which had none of the tension of the sessions for *There Must Be a Better World Somewhere* but an equally elevated caliber of musicianship, "the finest I had ever encountered," he said. "These guys were un-fucking-believable. The demos on that record were outrageous, because Troy Seals was singing his ass off, man. They were unbelievable—and that didn't scare B.B. He liked that. Troy sang all the guide vocals live, because B.B. was really in over his head on this shit. There were no demos; [Troy] sang the guide vocals. He sat in the fuckin' booth and he sang while everybody else played, and he was just absolutely stunning. We had David Briggs, Reggie Young; Larrie Londin, who had to be—pardon the expression because he was so fat—pound for pound one of the greatest drummers I ever worked with. David Briggs was wonderful and accompanied the hell out of B.B. We had a great time. We came up to New York and [Briggs] wrote some beautiful string arrangements, and we cut those in New York; went to Muscle Shoals and did the horns there. And everyone hated the record. No one understood that it was the real thing. 'Cause country was dead, man. It's not like we were trying to ride no bandwagon. We weren't tryin' to do anything. I got infatuated with the music and musicians, I felt it was a comfortable place, I felt there was a link between Tennessee and that shit, and B.B. liked it. B.B. loved the record! And it was a zero—the record company didn't have a clue what to do with it.

"I love that record, man. It's obscure, but I rate it among the best things I've ever done in my life."

That the spirit of Elvis had permeated the project is no mere critic's construct. During the first night of work at the RCA Studios, Levine sensed "a certain kind of strange spirituality going on in the studio. I can't explain it; I thought it was B.B. and them all being there and B.B. was in heaven, loving it. He asked for a steel guitar player and Sonny Garrish, one of the great players, came over and we did 'Love Me Tender.'"

But something was in the air that night, and Levine could sense it. When the night's work had ended, drummer Larrie Londin told Levine he wanted to "apologize for everybody."

Puzzled, Levine wondered what in the world there was to apologize for. The session had been amazing—"It was a great selection of songs." Londin then informed Levine that he bore a strong physical resemblance to Elvis's long-time producer Felton Jarvis, and there were a bunch of Elvis's boys in the studio not quite believing what was going down.

"You look just like Felton Jarvis, and your mannerisms are the same," Londin told Levine. "We did all those records with Elvis in this room, and we're all spooked. Everything about you is the same—the way you speak, the way you treat the musicians, the way you get the work done, and the way you look."

Felton Jarvis had made some of Stewart Levine's favorite Elvis records, "records that I love." Dumbstruck, Levine tried to take it all in.

"Fuck me, man," he said after a long pause.

Chapter 12

CONSOLIDATING THE GAINS

Blues 'n' Jazz

MCA, 1983
Produced by Sidney A. Seidenberg
Arranger: Calvin Owens
Engineer: Peter Darmi
Assistant Engineer: Doug Grama
Recorded at M&I Recording, New York City, and Rivendale Recorders, Pasadena, Texas
Mastered by Bill Kipper at Masterdisk, New York City

Musicians
B.B. King: guitar, vocals
Lloyd Glenn: piano
James Bolden: trumpet
Arnett Cobb: tenor saxophone
Also: Woody Shaw, Don Wilkerson, Fred Ford, Major Holley

Songs
"Inflation Blues" (4:12) (L. Jordan–A. Alexander–T. Southern)
"Broken Heart" (2:43) (B.B. King)
"Sell My Monkey" (3:02) (B.B. King)
"Heed My Warning" (L. Jordan–H. Bowman)
"Teardrops from My Eyes" (5:05) (Rudolph Toombs)
"Rainbow Riot" (3:37) (Andy Gibson–Angelyne Carlington)
"Darlin' You Know I Love You" (4:44) (Jules Bihari–B.B. King)

"Make Love to Me" (4:15) (A. Copeland–P. Mares–W. Milrose–W. Norvas–B. Pollack–M. Stitzel)
"I Can't Let You Go" (3:48) (B.B. King)

Over four consecutive albums B.B. and Stewart Levine had raised the musical and aesthetic ante, and the result was a revivified artist. Levine and B.B. would work together again, but not for another eight years. And a case could be made that come their next project together, B.B. was again in need of the direction and vision Levine could supply, just as he was in 1977—not to the degree that he needed it in 1977, but at the outset of the '90s B.B.'s '80s successes seemed what they were: intermittent bursts of inspiration or recognition, rather than the products of a coherent, systematic vision.

Such criticism does not apply, however, to 1983's *Blues 'N' Jazz*, which credits Sid Seidenberg as producer. B.B.'s bandleader and arranger Calvin Owens, a Bill Harvey protégé hired by B.B. in 1979, more than earned his keep in the studio with several scintillating big-band arrangements that betray Maxwell Davis's influence, in addition to a beautiful small-combo arrangement on the album-closing "I Can't Let You Go" that could hardly have been better conceived or more tastefully executed.

Released in 1983, with Reaganomics in full flower, *Blues 'N' Jazz* opens with a swaying, big-band arrangement of Louis Jordan's "Inflation Blues," with B.B. shouting out at the start, "Hey, Mr. President, all you congressmens too," and "I'm tryin' to make a livin' / I can't save a cent / It takes all of my money / just to eat and pay the rent." He goes to bemoan the devalued dollar as a "low-down dirty shame." Given the temper of the times, and "Inflation Blues" being the lead song on the album, it seems a conscious rebuke of a failed policy that was doing the most damage to those who could least endure it. The robust tenor sax solo that deepens the blues most likely comes from Arnett Cobb. Another Jordan tune pops up later on, a mid-tempo blues titled "Heed My Warning," with a punchy horn arrangement, some voluble piano retorts from Lloyd Glenn, and from B.B. a most engaging, even comedic vocal turn. Rudy Toombs's "Teardrops from My Eyes" is done as a finger-poppin', mellow jazz groove number, its arrangement notable for the atmospheric ostinato guitar riff throughout, a bright vibraphone solo, and B.B.'s gently swaying, warmhearted vocal, giving a sad theme a genial gloss. "Rainbow Riot," an instrumental, is a hard-driving workout showcasing Lucille in a spitfire dialog with the exuberant horn section, as the arrangement incorporates stop-time passages to set up electrifying solo spots for the vibes and then the sax.

Arguably the feature piece of the album, "Darlin', You Know I Love You" is an update of B.B.'s 1953 chart-topper for RPM, his first charting single post–"3 O'Clock Blues." The original was a dirge-like blues lacking any audible guitar soloing, heavy on a droning sax solo, with Ike Turner spotting up on piano, adding some low-down right-hand runs and trills to bolster one of B.B.'s most fully realized early vocals, piercing and warm all at once, a real crooning clinic. Revisited 31 years later, the tune is brighter; the droning sax remains but is buried deep in the orchestral mix. What was a sax solo in the original recording is now a trumpet solo, which adds a keening, anxious quality to the atmosphere as opposed to the sax's earthy, moody attitude. B.B. then lets Lucille make her entrance with a responsive, tart solo. At 4:47 this cut is more than a minute and a half longer than the 1952 version, and from the 2:18 mark to the end it's all instrumental. B.B.'s vocal, which flits by, is tender and sincere, ascending to an affecting falsetto at the end of the verses and in the chorus. Lloyd Glenn on piano gets far less play than did Ike Turner, and a wisp of vibes can be heard down in the mix as well.

As the title implies, there's a dichotomy at work here, in that the songs all feature ample portions of instrumental interplay and solos in a jazz style, but in the end the album is a most effective showcase for B.B. the blues singer. The depth of feeling he delivers on the blues numbers, especially "Darlin', You

Know I Love You," "Broken Heart" (a vocal rife with melismatic effects and low-register gospel moaning, every bit as tortured as his performance on "Don't Answer the Door"), and "I Can't Let You Go," rank with any of the high points of his recording career, both before and since.

"I Can't Let You Go" opens with a tender, tearful confession by Lucille, supported by Glenn's sympathetic blues piano, before B.B. enters with an anguished, shouted query, "What did I do wrong, baby?" A muted trumpet rises at the end of the first verse, Glenn sends up a series of rolling notes, as if in protest, and the muted trumpet answers back poignantly as B.B. cries, "I just can't let you go!" It's after-hours in the club, a small combo is playing soft and blue for broken hearts in a smoke-filled room, the lights are down low, and so are spirits. Fade to black.

Blues 'N' Jazz won a Grammy Award in the Best Traditional Album category, puzzling B.B. who calls it "one of my least traditional albums."[1] If it wasn't traditional in some academic sense of the term, though, the album was traditional in the B.B. King sense—that is, it spoke the language the artist had been speaking since his time with the Biharis, both in the big-band arrangements and the small-combo numbers, but with a modern twist, as exemplified by the updated "Darlin', You Know I Love You." Half a dozen of one, six of the other, and a Grammy well deserved, whatever the category.

Six Silver Strings _____

MCA, 1985
Produced by David Crawford
Executive producer: Sidney A. Seidenberg
"In the Midnight Hour," "My Lucille," "Memory Lane" produced by John Landis
    and Ira Newborn
Tracks recorded at The Studio, Hialeah, Florida
Engineer: Freddy Stonewall
Mastered by Greg Fulginiti at Artisan Sound
"Six Silver Strings," "Big Boss Man" remixed by Louis Silas, Jr.
Remix engineer: Tavi Mote

Musicians
B.B. King: guitar, vocals
David Crawford
Luther Dixon
Nathaniel Seidman
Julio Ferrer
Larry Dermer

Robert Caldwell
Willie Covington
Paul Mullen

Songs
"Six Silver Strings" (4:23) (Luther Dixon–David Crawford)
"Big Boss Man" (4:46) (Luther Dixon–Al Smith)
"In the Midnight Hour" (3:22) (Steve Cropper–Wilson Pickett)
"Into the Night" (4:10) (Ira Newborn)
"My Lucille " (3:42) (Ira Newborn)
"Memory Lane" (4:38) (Luther Dixon–David Crawford)
"My Guitar Sings the Blues" (3:38) (Luther Dixon–David Crawford)
"Double Trouble" (5:12) (Luther Dixon–David Crawford)

In the time that had passed between the release of *Blues 'N' Jazz* and *Six Silver Strings*, a new kid in town sparked a renewed interest in the blues the likes of which had not been seen since the early '60s. Among the generation of blues guitarists who came of age in the early '80s, only Robert Cray approached the elusive combination of skill, influence, and heart that Stevie Ray Vaughan possessed in abundance. (Vaughan's brother Jimmie sneaks in there as well on the strength of his powerful work with the Fabulous Thunderbirds.) To be sure, though, Vaughan, the latest in an estimable and influential line of Texas-born and -bred guitar slingers dating back to Blind Lemon Jefferson, kick-started a blues revival in the early '80s with his first two albums, 1983's *Texas Flood* and 1984's *Couldn't Stand the Weather*, which became unlikely best-sellers in the midst of a rock market being consumed by glossy, frigid techno-pop.

Texas Flood pays its debts to traditional Texas blues and R&B, sounding a tad muddy, the better to savor the slice-and-dice solos Vaughan delivers so fluidly. Stylistically, Vaughan was a true eclectic whose hard-driving, steely sound achieved individuality while incorporating quotes from Hubert Sumlin, Buddy Guy, T-Bone Walker, Lonnie Mack, Albert Collins, B.B. King, Elmore James, and Jimi Hendrix. That's a broad palette, but it also illustrates how artfully Vaughan built on the best of what had come before to express the emotional extremes described in his lyrics and instrumentals.

Couldn't Stand the Weather finds Vaughan broadening out a bit beyond R&B to include a stirring rendition of Hendrix's "Voodoo Child" and bringing a Charlie Christian–Kenny Burrell flavor to the jazz-tinged "Stang's Swang." Out of a troubled time for Vaughan in 1985, the album *Soul to Soul* represented Vaughan and his band Double Trouble's great leap forward. First the additions of keyboardist Reese Wynans and sax man Joe Sublett expanded the sound, adding textural possibilities that heightened the shifting moods of Vaughan's original material and, as best exemplified by his contribution to a version of Hank Ballard's "Look at Little Sister," revealed previously hidden wells of feeling in the impeccably chosen cover versions. By this time Vaughan was showing more facility with melody in his songwriting, producing his first outstanding ballad in "Life without Love." Vaughan had a tender side that he could express effectively with either a delicate vocal or wailing guitar solo. Perhaps the most amazing fact about *Soul to Soul* is that it exists at all and happens to be standing the test of time rather well. SRV was deep in the throes of drug addiction during the recording sessions, often showing up hours late and indulging his habit within the confines of the studio during sessions. It's not his most consistent album, but the sum of the parts adds up to an assured move towards re-energizing his sound while remaining rooted in the hard Texas blues he loved.

B.B. and Stevie Ray forged a strong bond of friendship, the latter always deferring and paying respect to the former as the master he sought to become. Vaughan was steeped in tradition and followed B.B.'s lead in paying tribute to those blues artists of yore who paved the way for him. B.B. saw a fellow traveler, and immediately sized him up as being the real deal.

"I loved him," he said of SRV. "Stevie came through in the early '80s, just after Mike Bloomfield died an early and tragic death. I remember thinking that another white boy nurtured by black music was going to keep the faith. Stevie did more than that. He played with such incredible technique and genuine soul that he became the boldest guitarist of his generation. He was a superstar with the potential of Elvis. What Elvis did for rock 'n' roll, Stevie might have done for the blues.

"When his brother Jimmie, another great guitarist, introduced us, Stevie said, 'B.B., I feel like I've known you my whole life.' He treated me like a son treats a father. And I came to love him as I had Mike Bloomfield. These *were* my sons, these were the children who'd not only learned my craft, but improved upon it. They could play everything I played—and much more. They brought the blues to a new generation of fans. They spread the word wider than I could ever have spread it myself."[2]

B.B. didn't respond to the harder blues Vaughan was championing on either *Blues 'N' Jazz* or *Six Silver Strings*. The latter is more in a pop mode than any other B.B. long-player to this point, but not at the expense of the female choruses or Lucille's need to speak out eloquently on behalf of the blues. But the arrangements reflect a sense of the times in incorporating some discreet hip-hop rhythmic touches—in the most unlikely of places, such as a reworking of Jimmy Reed's "Big Boss Man" that sounds like it was inspired by "Beat It" on Michael Jackson's *Thriller* album rather than any big-beat blues from back in the day—and adding more overt contemporary pop flourishes to several of the songs.

Three of the songs on *Six Silver Strings* were from the soundtrack to the John Landis–directed film *Into the Night*, in which B.B. both sang and had a minor onscreen role as himself. One tune was a rousing cover of Wilson Pickett's "In the Midnight Hour," with B.B. delivering a credible shouting vocal; two others, the urgent, keyboard-heavy title song and a driving, uptempo pop-blues, "My Lucille," were written specifically by Ira Newborn under specific instructions from the director to "compose a motion picture score to feature a particular player and not compromise his unique talents or the integrity of the movie," as Landis wrote in his liner notes for the soundtrack album. Predictably, the movie tunes are glossier, and more cliché-ridden, fare than the other tracks, but winning in their own way thanks to B.B.'s convincing vocal performances.

For the other five tracks, Sid Seidenberg booked the recording sessions in Florida, at The Studio in Hialeah. Then he tracked down Dave Crawford, the former ABC staff producer who had worked with B.B. on the *To Know You Is to Love You* album in 1973. All the songs but one were co-written by Crawford with Luther Dixon, and Dixon was a co-writer on "Big Boss Man" with Al

Smith. In Crawford Seidenberg teamed B.B. with a producer well versed in both contemporary soul and B.B. King's style of blues. In Dixon, he had a visionary songwriter-producer who had made his mark in the '60s with his beautifully crafted work for Florence Greenburg's Scepter label, most notably for the Shirelles. At Scepter, Dixon's studio savvy translated into memorable, sophisticated productions unlike the typical teen fare of the day, especially in his use of horn sections playing robust, soulful choruses that prefigured both the Memphis soul sound and the gospel-soul pioneered in Chicago by Curtis Mayfield. Moreover, Dixon brought his own considerable songwriting skills to bear on the Shirelles' repertoire, and he proved himself capable of being as fanciful ("Boys," later covered by the Beatles) or as dramatic ("Tonight's the Night") as any of the more heralded tunesmiths in the Shirelles' camp. On the strength of these songs, the Shirelles were mainstays on the pop charts for five years, from 1958 through 1963, and in that time were rarely out of the Top 40—indeed, the group's singles often rose into the Top Ten. At a time when female groups were rarely heard from more than once, and when pop music was far more male-dominated than it is now, the Shirelles' longevity spoke volumes, both for the viability of girl groups as an artistic entity and for the legitimacy of the distaff point of view in rock 'n' roll. How critical was Dixon to the Shirelles' success? The record shows that after 1963, when he moved to the Capitol label, the Shirelles had no more hits, despite having an indisputably great lead singer in Shirley Alston.

The tunes Dixon and Crawford penned for *Six Silver Strings*, while not being the sort of landmarks Dixon had penned for the Shirelles, were captivating, pop-influenced items, with intoxicating, gospel-style byplay between B.B. and a female chorus on the lilting "Six Silver Strings," and a gentle, swinging reading of a tenderhearted love song with a lovely melody, "Memory Lane," that brings out the best of B.B.'s romantic side and is further enriched by bright bursts of horns and celebratory backing choruses. Dixon hadn't been heard from in years, but his work on *Six Silver Strings* bespoke a writer who still had the touch. Crawford had a different story: *Six Silver Strings* for him was basically a rehab job with a tragic postscript. What Seidenberg found when he finally located Crawford in Florida wasn't a pretty sight. "David was out of the business," Seidenberg recalled. "He wasn't doing too well—financially in very bad shape—and he was working with a guy named Luther Dixon, who was an old writer that I knew many, many years ago. For that *Six Silver Strings* album, David was really broke and I gave him another shot. Then in '87 or '88 I got a phone call that David had overdosed, and that was the end of Mr. Crawford."[3]

Crawford's and Dixon's last hurrah was a slow-grinding, mean-woman blues, "My Guitar Sings the Blues," very much in the style of the re-energized blues on the "Well" side of B.B.'s Bill Szymczyk–produced *Live & Well* album. Cognizant of B.B.'s history and smart writers to boot, the team modeled the song on "Why I Sing the Blues" and even reprised one of that song's key lyrics at one point, when B.B. asserts with a gravelly shout, "I've really paid my dues, people!"

"My Guitar Sings the Blues" won a Grammy in 1985 for Best Traditional Blues Recording, a category B.B. was coming to own but for one night shared with two deserving veterans, one of whom, Dixon, had never been recognized for the monumental work he had done in the '60s but finally had a moment to savor in being recognized by the industry he had helped build.

King of the Blues, 1989 _____

MCA, 1988
Various producers and studios
Executive Producer: Sidney A. Seidenberg

"(You've Become a) Habit to Me," "Can't Get Enough," "Standing on the
    Edge," "Go On," "Undercover Man"
Produced by Jerry Williams
Engineered by Chris Green; assistant engineers: Charlie Brocco, Tom Beiner;
    guitar programming by Jimmy Hotz
Recorded and mixed at The Village Recorder, Los Angeles

"Drowning in the Sea of Love," "Let's Straighten It Out"
Produced by Al Kooper/Partners in Crime
Engineered by Richard "Fast Fingers" McIntosh and Rick Delana
Assistant engineer: Chris Steinmetz
Recorded in "The Slammer," North Hollywood, California
Guru for Partners in Crime: Charles Colello

"Change in Your Lovin'," "Business with My Baby Tonight"
Produced by Trade Martin
Mixed by Trade Martin
Rhythm tracks and mixes: Doug Conroy at Waterfront Studios, New Jersey
Horns, Vocals and Strings: Roger Rhoads at Media Sound, New York City

"Lay Another Log on the Fire," "Take Off Your Shoes"
Produced by Frederick Knight
Engineers: Robert Jackson, John Fleskes, Roosevelt Green, Pete Green
Recorded at Memphis Sound, Ardent Studio, and Muscle Shoals Sound,
    Alabama

Remixed and additional production by Courtney Branch and Tracy Kendrick at Baby O Studios, Hollywood, California

Musicians

"(You've Become a) Habit to Me": Jerry Williams: drum machine programming, keyboards, background vocals

"Can't Get Enough": Mick Fleetwood: drums; Jerry Williams: rhythm guitar, keyboards, drum programming; Marty Grebb: saxophone; Stevie Nicks: background vocals

"Standing on the Edge": Mick Fleetwood: drums; Steve Cropper: rhythm guitar; Jerry Williams: keyboards, drum machine programming, background vocals; Tom Scott: saxophone; Loralei Wehba: background vocals

"Go On": Jerry Williams: drum machine programming, keyboards; Bonnie Raitt, Loralei Wehba: background vocals

"Undercover Man": Mick Fleetwood: drums; Steve Cropper: rhythm guitar; Jerry Williams: drum machine programming, keyboards, background vocals; Chris Mancini: background vocals

"Drowning in the Sea of Love," "Let's Straighten It Out": all instruments played by Al Kooper except for the left-side lead guitar, played by Riley B. King; the Jim Gilstrap Singers: background vocals

"Business with My Baby Tonight," "Change in Your Lovin'": Trade Martin: all rhythm instruments; Rodney Kelly: computer programming; Randy Brecker: horns and reeds; Alan Rubin: horns, reeds, trumpets; James Pugli: trombone; Ronald Cuber: baritone saxophone; Robert Magnuson: alto and tenor saxophones; Lou Marini: tenor saxophone; Joseph Malignaggi (concertmaster), Ethel Abelson, Ann Barsk, Maura Giannini, Anthony Posk, Carmel Malignaggi: violins; Trade Martin, Alfa Anderson, Liliana Pumpido, Joe Amato, Luci Martin, Alfredo Rios: background vocals

"Take Off Your Shoes": Michael Toles: guitar; Michael Spriggs: guitar; Ray Griffin: bass; James Robinson: drums; Harrison Calloway: horn arrangement; The Muscle Shoals Horns; Carson Whitsett, Clayton Ivey, Earnest Williamson: keyboards; Jewell Bass, Catherine Henderson, Tomasine Anderson: background vocals

Songs

"(You've Become a) Habit to Me" (4:45)
"Drowning in the Sea of Love" (4:36)
"Can't Get Enough" (4:50)
"Standing on the Edge" (5:19)
"Go On" (3:50)

"Let's Straighten It Out" (5:35)
"Change in Your Lovin'" (3:25)
"Undercover Man" (5:38)
"Lay Another Log on the Fire"
"Business with My Baby Tonight" (3:35)
"Take Off Your Shoes" (5:31)

"I been out here so very long / I done lost my direction," B.B. sings in "Drowning in the Sea of Love," and those words may well be the succinct review of the misguided *King of the Blues, 1989*. Recorded in eight different studios in New York, the Los Angeles area, and Memphis, the album suffers from the same ailment afflicting most endeavors employing multiple producers (in this case, four, or six, counting two who are credited for remixing and additional production): a lack of a consistent vision. The result is scattered and unfocused, its workmanlike execution betraying a pronounced lack of commitment to the least distinguished collection of songs B.B. had ever committed to a long-player. Although B.B. throws himself into each performance with his usual brio, it's all for naught when he's singing such shallow lyrics. The idea of teaming B.B. with musicians from outside the blues realm dates back, of course, to the Bill Szymczyk sessions in 1969–'70 and had been employed by B.B. periodically over the years. Not that the cast assembled here was inferior: Al Kooper, Mick Fleetwood, Steve Cropper, Tom Scott, Stevie Nicks, and the Muscle Shoals Horns. Two cuts steered by Trade Martin—a funky ditty called "Change in Your Lovin'," and the penultimate tune, the soul workout "Business with My Baby," which inspired a fiery, shouting vocal from B.B., his most effective on the album—feature robust horn and string sections. The problem is that this cast changes almost from cut to cut, whereas Szymczyk, for instance, used the same basic configuration over the course of an album, and when another joined that crew the conceptual vision and the approach remained consistent—witness the triumph of *Indianola Mississippi Seeds*. Here it's all over the map, with the Trade Martin tracks hearkening back to B.B.'s big-band days, Frederick Knight's Memphis-based sessions (the evidence here indicates Knight should have done the entire album, as B.B. sounds most inspired, and most at ease, on "Lay Another Log on the Fire" and "Take Off Your Shoes") summoning the portentous mood of some of the Szymczyk-era recordings, and the Jerry Williams–produced sides seeming to aim for the the dance audience, what with the pronounced—and jarring—use of drum machines.

As events go, 1989 produced a major one in B.B.'s career when the Irish rock band U2 teamed with B.B. in the studio on a cut lead singer Bono had written expressly for the King of the Blues after meeting him backstage at the bluesman's Dublin concert a year or so earlier. The song, "When Love Comes to Town," was a pumping, driving blues rocker, and Bono gave B.B. plenty of room on the recording to do some of his most aggressive shouting, while the horn section behind him was engaged in a riotous assault on the whole track, featured on the band's mega-hit album *Rattle and Hum*. A video of the song went into heavy rotation on MTV and ultimately won a Video Music Award, and for three months B.B. toured as an opening act for U2, which brought him once again to the attention of a younger generation that hadn't even come of age when "The Thrill Is Gone" vaulted B.B. into the mainstream. And as he had found when touring with the Rolling Stones in 1970, the audience welcomed him as a friend.

"In every concert, I felt a new energy coming from audiences who brought with them a fresh appreciation of the blues," B.B. said. "I'll never know how many new fans I made on that tour. But I believe my music was heard by still another new generation of young people who seemed to feel the same thing I'd felt when I first heard the blues sung by my Uncle Jack hollering in the cotton fields outside Indianola—raw emotion."[4]

Two live albums appeared in 1990 and 1991, respectively *Live at San*

Quentin and *Live at the Apollo*. The former, recorded at two shows at the infamous California penitentiary, finds B.B. in a rambunctious mood and singing and playing with fiery authority, as well as joking with the audience and engaging them on a personal level with his between-songs patter. It's a great set—well-worn versions of "Let the Good Times Roll," "Every Day I Have the Blues," "Sweet Little Angel," and "Rock Me Baby" sound as fresh and vital as ever, thanks to B.B.'s energy and enthusiasm and a seven-piece band that cooks mightily. The one anomaly, and a curious one it is, is the version of line producer Trade Martin's topical "Peace to the World," which was recorded in a New York studio with patently overdubbed audience applause and the addition of a gospel-style backing chorus otherwise absent on the album. Sequenced between a swaggering rendition of "The Thrill Is Gone" and a slow, grinding version of "Nobody Loves Me but My Mother," "Peace to the World" sounds plain weird in this context.

On August 26, 1990, Stevie Ray Vaughan and his band Double Trouble performed at a concert at Alpine Valley, Wisconsin, part of a lineup that included Buddy Guy, Eric Clapton, and Robert Cray. After his set, SRV boarded a helicopter that was to fly him and three members of Clapton's entourage back to Chicago. Shortly after midnight on August 27, the helicopter crashed into a hillside, killing all on board. At Vaughan's funeral in Dallas in August 31, more than 3,000 fans gathered outside the chapel to pay their respects, along with the likes of Dr. John, Bonnie Raitt, ZZ Top's Billy Gibbons, Ringo Starr, and other luminaries.

The news of Stevie Ray's death "devastated" B.B., who felt like he had "lost part of myself" in the tragedy as well. "The world had lost the man destined to become the greatest guitarist in the history of the blues. I still miss Stevie—and miss Mike [Bloomfield]—and wish both boys could have lived long, prosperous lives. They deserved kinder fates."[5]

The pain of Vaughan's passing was eased somewhat when B.B. met then-eighteen-year-old Kenny Wayne Shepherd, a hotshot blues guitarist who opened some shows for B.B. "The boy could play the blues, and after my show he told me how his idol had been Stevie Ray. It was beautiful to see Stevie Ray's legacy living through a teenager. Just as I like to think T-Bone's legacy is living through me."[6]

In the fall of 1990 B.B. toured internationally with a 17-piece big band assembled and sponsored by the tobacco industry behemoth Philip Morris and billed as the Philip Morris Super Band. This conceit, which was repeated

B.B. performing with Bono of U2, 1989.

in 1991, found B.B. in the company of some topflight players in the jazz world: among the musicians on board were guitarist Kenny Burrell ("my favorite jazz guitarist," according to B.B., who said listening to Burrell play every night "was a like a lecture from a great university professor"[7]), Harry "Sweets" Edison on trumpet, George Bohannon and Urbie Green on trombones, Jerry Dodgion on alto sax, and Plas Johnson (who had played on B.B.'s *L.A. Midnight* album) on tenor sax, with conductor Gene Harris doubling on piano. On November 10 the troupe landed at Harlem's famed Apollo Theatre for a date that was recorded and released as *Live at the Apollo*. On the evidence of the recording the night was joyous and jumping, and B.B. seems to have found the fountain of youth. His exuberant "yeah, yeah, yeah, yeah" shouts that open "When Love Comes to Town" are echoed with equal fervor by the audience, and from there he digs in to shout the first verse exuberantly as the band flat-out rocks behind him. The second verse is followed by a scorching, stuttering sax solo from Plas Johnson that goes from the bottom end to an exciting stretch for high notes in the instrument's upper register. B.B. then closes things out with a concise single- and double-string solo, the end of the song met with thunderous applause, whistles, and shouts from the audience. A 7:20 version of "Sweet Sixteen" follows and casts a mellow, lonely, late-night ambiance, with B.B.'s quavering vocal, part crooning, part shouting, meshing beautifully with the quiet, rising horns. This turns out to be the ideal setup for a moody rendition of "The Thrill Is Gone," the title sentiment being greeted with a burst of excited shouts when B.B. cries it out for the first time. The heart of the set captured on the disc is a powerful ballad sequence towards the end, beginning with a cool, swaying take on Willie Nelson's "Nightlife," which had now become, in B.B.'s repertoire, permanently attached to a plaintive reading of Percy Mayfield's "Please Send Me Someone to Love," bolstered by an elaborate, layered chorus of horns pushing the vocal forward. This is followed by a gently rocking rendition of Ivory Joe Hunter's "Since I Met You Baby" done with a pulsating horn part and keyed by B.B.'s smooth, plaintive crooning, with Lucille adding some sharp retorts along the way. The set proper closes with B.B. thanking the assembled multitudes—band, audience, technical and behind-the- scenes crews—and then offering a searching, tender reading of "Guess Who," from the 1972 album of the same name, that has all the intimacy of a cabaret number, thanks both to the warmth of B.B.'s vocal and to the bright arpeggios pianist Gene Harris sprinkles throughout the number. If, indeed, B.B.'s live albums were not mere filler but done with an express purpose in the wake of studio projects, then the San Quentin and Apollo albums ought to be seen as B.B. serving notice after the folly of *King of the Blues, 1989* that he was still in good fighting form and advancing his stock-in-trade bedrock blues. With that job done, he returned to the studio. It had been five years since his last credible studio album, *Six Silver Strings*, and though his dalliance with U2 had boosted his profile internationally, that one-shot, its subsequent tour, and the San Quentin and Apollo live albums didn't amount to much of a statement artistically but were more like holding patterns despite both winning Grammy Awards as Best Traditional Blues Recording of 1990 and 1991, respectively. For some new juice he turned again to Stewart Levine.

Chapter 13

DOC: *DUM SPIRO SPERO*

There Is Always One More Time

MCA, 1991

Produced by Stewart Levine

Executive producer: Sidney A. Seidenberg

Engineered and mixed by Daren Klein at Conway Studio, Los Angeles

Assistant engineer: Marnie Riley

Mastered by Bernie Grundman at Bernie Grundman Mastering, Hollywood, California

Musicians

B.B. King: lead guitar and vocals

Joe Sample: piano

Neil Larsen: organ and keyboards

Jim Keltner: drums

Freddie Washington: bass

Michael Landau: guitar

Arthur Adams: guitar

Lennie Castro: percussion

Paulette Brown, Valerie Pinkston-Mayo, Bunny Hull: background vocals

Songs

"I'm Moving On" (4:15) (Joe Sample–Will Jennings)

"Back in L.A." (5:00) (Joe Sample–Will Jennings)

"The Blues Come Over Me" (5:13) (Joe Sample–Will Jennings)

"Fool Me Once" (4:18) (Joe Sample–Will Jennings)

"The Lowdown" (4:10) (Joe Sample–Will Jennings)

"Mean and Evil" (4:20) (Arthur Adams)
"Something up My Sleeve" (4:27) (Arthur Adams)
"Roll, Roll, Roll" (5:56) (Arthur Adams)
"There Is Always One More Time" (8:24) (Doc Pomus–Ken Hirsch)
This album is dedicated to the late and great "Doc" Pomus. There is always one more time.

Some eight years had passed since the completion of *Love Me Tender* and Stewart Levine crossing paths with B.B. again. In 1984 the producer had moved to England, where he had a lucrative run producing pop hits for, among others, Simply Red. In '87 he had returned to the States and "carried on what I was doing in England." In '89 he had met up with B.B. to re-record the vocal for "Don't Look Down" for the *Thelma & Louise* soundtrack. A conversation had ensued at the time, with B.B., Levine, and Sid Seidenberg contemplating another B.B. album of Joe Sample–Will Jennings songs.

In contrast to the artist he had met a dozen years earlier, a man who was "fraught with lots of problems when we started on *Midnight Believer*," Levine now encountered a man who was at ease with himself and with his life. "He became much more comfortable as the years went on. He seemed to grow into his own stature. By '91 he started to believe what was going on. Rather than not believing the success he was having, he was feeling wonderful about it.

He's a fucking great cat, man. He's absolutely beautiful. He's so special. He never gave me a hard time and I really treated him with kid gloves all the time. I always made it very, very comfortable for him."[1]

When approached by Levine about writing some new material with Joe Sample, Will Jennings was enthusiastic but wary; uncertain as to whether he and Sample had gone to the well once too often, he suggested they could get four songs together. With some coaxing from Levine, the duo delivered six songs. Guitarist Arthur Adams, fast making a name for himself as a blues artist, brought in two tough original songs that made the cut, "Mean and Evil," a blues with a rock edge excoriating a two-timing woman, and a brisk-paced R&B-tinged number, "Something up My Sleeve," a song of conciliation and seductive pleasures. Calling on Doc Pomus again, Levine received a tape of Pomus–Rebennack songs, some new, some pieced together from older fragments. These latest offerings didn't arouse the same degree of excitement and awe as had the demos for *There Must Be a Better World Somewhere*. They weren't nearly as good, a fact Levine attributed to Rebennack's increasingly disabling heroin addiction. The only song Levine liked had a title similar to a new Jennings song, "Roll, Roll, Roll," and Jennings's "Roll" was the superior of the two. Immediately, Levine found himself in the throes of an existential crisis. He expected he would use several Pomus–Rebennack tunes on the album, not only because of their merit, but also because he had some inside information that Pomus, recently diagnosed with lung cancer, was in a New York hospital, failing fast.

"The things Doc sent me felt good, but not great, which can happen, you know, particularly with the shape Mac was in," Levine said. "But the one that felt good was this thing with the word 'Roll' in it. But Will and Joe had already written this other thing. I remember it was a very uncomfortable moment with Doc, trying to explain to him that the song he presented had a similar title and the song wasn't as good as the one Will had written. It was fucking hard, man. I was walking around for days going, What the fuck, man, is it worth it? I remember it was an interesting moment for me because was it worth telling a guy that was dying that I wasn't using one of his songs, because it wasn't very good and I had another song that was pretty good? I came out of it in a place where I said, Well, I can't do this to the artist and to myself, because the guy's sick. All I could think about was Doc Pomus and how I had let him down in not recording any of these new songs. But they just weren't great. It was twofold: I didn't want to have B.B. not represented the best I could, and I didn't want to have Doc not represented the best I could."

At that point, an epiphany. Several years earlier Levine had produced an album on Joe Cocker that included among its tunes a poignant reflection on faith and perseverance, "There Is Always One More Time," penned by Pomus and his late-life writing partner Kenny Hirsch. "We recorded a beautiful version with Joe Cocker. I thought B.B. could do it, and when I played it for him, he loved it."

Crisis averted, Levine assembled the band for the sessions: Joe Sample on piano; Neal Larsen on organ and keyboards; stalwart session drummer Jim Keltner, who had played on B.B.'s *In London* album; bassist Freddie Washington; guitarists Michael Landau and Arthur Adams; and Lennie Castro on percussion; and a gospel-style female chorus featuring Paulette Brown, Valerie Pinkston-Mayo, and Bunny Hall. Sessions convened at Conway Studios in Los Angeles, with Daren Klein engineering and mixing.

"That record was well cast," Levine said, "and there was a good vibe about it. The rhythm section was great—Keltner was a killer. Crusaders were over with, you know, it wasn't like we had to go back to that. I'd been working with Keltner a little bit; I'd known him since we both came to California in '66, and that was the year we did a couple of records together. I had heard Keltner play behind some blues guys; at the Grammys or something he played in a rhythm section behind a whole bunch of blues guys, and he just played the shit outta that stuff. And I love Freddie Washington, he's my favorite bass player, and Joe loved him. Arthur Adams had been a mainstay in our rhythm section with the Crusaders on all the records we made in the early '70s. He's a wonderful rhythm guitar player who turned into a really good blues artist. B.B. loved Arthur, loved the way he sang and the way he played. He did all the demos and he sang the guide vocals on the spot, so he was a great spirit to have in the studio."

In contrast to the drama that had attended the making of *There Must Be a Better World Somewhere*, the sessions at Conway were free- and high-spirited, in a natural way. "Those sessions were very, very bright, kind of business as usual, straightahead, very bright studio in Hollywood, with sunlight coming in, very relaxed, nothing to prove," is Levine's recollection. "Just very comfortable and almost like we had all earned the right to go make a fuckin' record, you know. I think the record company, they were just thankful I was making it. And because I was making all these fuckin' pop hits at the time, they thought I was gonna come up with some massive track—Will had just come off a bunch of hits too. So I think they decided I would come up with something clever, and I decided I didn't want to be clever. There's nothing on the record that's attempting to get on radio; it has none of those qualities about it, none of the intent of the first two albums to have something that could really do well for B.B. He was doing well, he had had that record with

U2, and he was starting to become what Sid had always wanted him to become. He wanted him to become Louis Armstrong, you know. But I didn't want to make 'What a Wonderful World.' I wanted to make just a pretty comfortable record. In fact, at the end the record was just about what I wanted it to be. Nobody needed it to do any more than it was, you know what I mean? It didn't have any agenda. The first three I did with B.B. I definitely had an agenda, man. The first one was, We gotta get this guy back. The second one was, We gotta keep him going. The third one was, We gotta make an important record. *There Must Be a Better World Somewhere*, we gotta make something that shows his artistry. This one, there was no fuckin' point of view, man; it was a day off."

For "a day off," *There Is Always One More Time* contains a lot of good music and a B.B. King who sounds completely relaxed and in splendid harmony with his bandmates. Apart from the above-mentioned Arthur Adams gems, which brought out the best in B.B. the dramatic vocal stylist, the swinging R&B kiss-off song, "I'm Moving On," has an ingratiating gospel feel courtesy Neal Larsen's burbling organ lines and the cooing female chorus, and a carefree vocal from B.B., the aggrieved party who is getting on with his life without looking back. "Back in L.A." is a foreboding minor-key blues with the female chorus shouting a warning about the dark side of the City of Angels and its sinister allure, as B.B. wearily evokes the frustration of an ex-con who's returning to the scene of his crime and strapping in for the ride, "working on another line." Another unsettling narrative, "The Blues Come Over Me," is a steady, mid-tempo number in which B.B. confesses to doing wrong by his woman "when the blues come over me." In his most plaintive, crying tone—the way he stretches out the word "blue" in the chorus is heartwrenching—he describes an inner darkness that descends and upends, leaving him feeling useless, enumerating symptoms a psychologist would have a field day analyzing. The strings ride in on a slow cresting wave, Larsen vamps away on the keyboard, and Lucille stings and sings, redoubling the pain B.B. reveals in this most penetrating Sample–Jennings lyric. Both "Fool Me Once" and "The Lowdown" lift the clouds: the former is a blues stomp with the bass drum pounding, a tambourine shaking frenetically, and B.B. spicing the adventure with some razor-edged bottom-string soloing; the latter is a gently swaying bit of blues-based philosophizing on the subject of perseverance ("when they hit you / just get up and go another round," B.B. growls), as the piano and Lucille engage in a scintillating, sensitive dialog throughout. A halting gospel piano riff introduces "Roll, Roll, Roll," setting the stage for Lucille to enter with tart, trebly cries in what is a mid-tempo reflection on good times and, at once, a pledge to keep 'em coming that takes an intimate turn when B.B. sings, "Right there in the music is where I belong." He goes on to imagine his arrival in heaven, with music in hand, and being introduced to an inquisitive God who wants to know more about his band. Midway through, B.B. offers up a punchy solo that plays off Larsen's insistent chording and then gives way to the piano man for a vivid, rolling solo that engages most of the 88s.

All of this is mere prelude to the unqualified masterpiece that closes the album, "There Is Always One More Time." All of the gospel flourishes Stewart Levine has brought to the other songs leading up to this moment seem a setup for this powerful performance, rooted squarely in the church, and clocking in at eight minutes and 24 seconds total, with the final 3:30 minutes being a roiling, soul-shaking instrumental sparring match between a piercing Lucille, a vibrant, pumping organ courtesy Neal Larsen, Joe Sample's glory-bound gospel piano, and thunderous percussion, as if the heavens had opened up. But before that, all is quiet and somber, as Sample's soulful, stately gospel piano intro, announcing itself like a hymn of invitation and echoing too many such songs for its source even to be identified, precedes B.B.'s vocal entrance and establishes the proper introspective ambiance. The band enters, discreetly, on the second verse, B.B. hits a couple of anguished, sustained notes, and Sample rumbles down the gospel highway. Initially B.B. sings with deliberate conviction, his voice deep and somber, heavy on the vibrato; when he gets to the chorus, he soars, with power and gripping intensity, so deeply invested in the lyrics he's taken the performance to another plane, delivering house-wrecking drama of Mahalia Jackson magnitude. Pomus's lyrics, Hirsch's music, Levine's vision, and the musicians' commitment to the text and to the moment brought B.B. to the pinnacle of his vocal artistry, which says it all about how the song affected him on a fundamental, spiritual level. The eternal optimism informing Pomus's point of view is a quality B.B. had nurtured from his youth, even before Luther Henson had promised the young black children in his Delta school class that a better day was coming for people of color. In B.B.'s case, Henson's lesson had insinuated itself into the fabric of his soul and marked him as a man as surely as had the patience and tolerance his mother preached to her dying breath. Now, in Doc Pomus's lyrics, he found himself.

If your whole life somehow | wasn't much till now | and you've almost lost your will to live | no matter what you do | long as there's breath in you | there is always one more time.

And if your dreams go bad | every one that you've had | that don't mean that some dreams | can't come true | 'cause it's funny about dreams | as strange as it seems | there is always one more time.

And if we meet one day | please don't walk away | 'cause there's always one more time . . . whoa! | there is always one more time.

In New York, late February 1991, Doc Pomus, weak and bedridden, was laboring for breath. Cancer was eating him alive. He was on oxygen, unable to speak. When he had been able to talk to family and visitors, his standard line had gone from "Same old shit" to "Can you believe this shit?"

At the beginning of March, Levine flew into New York. To Pomus's bedside he brought a recording of the track of "There Is Always One More Time" with Arthur Adams's guide vocal on it. Pomus listened through headphones and weakly nodded his approval. Jetting immediately back to L.A. for what was "a very emotional afternoon," Levine witnessed B.B., fully aware of Pomus's condition, open his heart fully, investing the lyrics with the weight of his own history and a reverence for every shade of meaning in the haunting lyrics. When the song was completed, Levine called Pomus's hospital room. Raoul Felder, Pomus's brother, answered and held the phone to Doc's ear. B.B. said a few words to his friend, and then Levine rolled the tape.

Doc Pomus died on March 14, 1991, B.B.'s performance of "There Is Always One More Time" being the last music he heard in his life.

Upon hearing from Levine of Pomus's terminal condition, B.B. cried. "He loved Doc," Levine said. "B.B. really related to Doc because of who Doc was and what he had been through and his whole take on life. So B.B. was very taken by Doc as a person, very knocked out by the work he had done for him. B.B. felt really honored to have had that album [*There Must Be a Better World Somewhere*] written for him; he always thought of that song, 'There Must Be a Better World Somewhere,' as the most perfect song he had ever recorded, he told me.

"B.B. loved Doc, and when he heard Doc was dying and then spoke to him that day, he was just torn up. And I knew I had to do it in the sequence of letting him sing first and then letting him talk to him, because it couldn't have been the other way around."

Sitting alone with only engineer Daren Klein at Conway Studios after hanging up the phone, B.B. and Levine stared in complete silence at nothing in particular. After some time had passed, Klein quietly left the room. "I don't know how long we sat there," Levine said. "Didn't talk. I think I got up and said something stupid and we went on with it."

Postscript: Mac Rebennack reclaimed his life before the decade was over, thanks largely to the support of Doc Pomus, and has since been more productive and more in demand than at any other time in his long and storied career. At Pomus's funeral in 1991, Rebennack paid stirring tribute in eulogizing the great songwriter, telling teary-eyed mourners, "I stand before you a guy who used to be a scumbag dope addict, and Doc Pomus used to say, 'Why don't you get off them narcotics? Why don't you get down to the real work?' He was a real man. Doc was one of them spirited cats from the old school, but he didn't fit the old school. He was a progressive thinker, musician, songwriter, and a bad-ass sumbitch."

Chapter 14

AUDITING THE REGENCY

"The Most Gracious Man in Show Business"

King of the Blues

MCA, 1992

Ultimately the four-CD box set *King of the Blues* provides the most sweeping survey of B.B.'s remarkable blues odyssey. Its 77 tracks begin with "Miss Martha King," which at the time was unavailable on any domestic release, and goes on to trace the high points with RPM, Kent, ABC/Bluesway, and MCA, concluding with a 1992 version of "Since I Met You Baby" cut for Gary Moore's *After Hours* album. To some, the importance of B.B.'s Modern output and the influence it had on blues artists of his own time and on succeeding generations demands and deserves more attention than the eight tracks contained here. Despite problems with obtaining licenses for some of that material, and considering that B.B. had spent more time with ABC and MCA than he had with the Biharis' various labels, the eight titles on Disc 1, *1949–1966*, do honor the key moments of the artist's Modern affiliation even if they don't provide a wider view of what B.B. was doing stylistically on his Crown albums. Certainly that period's commercial highlights at least are well represented by "She's Dynamite," "3 O'Clock Blues," "Please Love Me," "You Upset Me Baby," "Every Day I Have the Blues," "Rock Me Baby," and "Recession Blues." To the set's credit, though, it includes 30 other tracks that at the time of release had never made it onto CD before. (Some have since shown up on other releases, such as two live

performances from B.B.'s 1971 tour of Japan, "Niji Baby" and "Eyesight to the Blind," which saw the light of day again in 1999 when MCA issued an entire set as *Live in Japan*, one of B.B.'s most exciting live albums.) Seven cuts were previously unavailable in any form, including a boisterous "Goin' Down Slow," a live cut that didn't make it onto the vital *Blues Is King* album, and, from the Bill Szymczyk–produced sessions for *Completely Well*, a fine mid-tempo blues grinder, "Fools Get Wise," showcasing a powerful horn chart, a searing Lucille solo, and a pleading vocal from B.B. that ranks with his most impassioned efforts from those sessions. One of the rarities uncovered for the set is the 1966 recording of a Jimmy Rogers barnburner titled "Sloppy Drunk," a rousing big-band number with an energetic horn section sputtering out exclamations all over the place, an overactive tambourine providing comic relief, an organ comping wildly down in the mix, and B.B. shouting out a joyous vocal extolling the pleasure of his inebriated state. No producer or personnel could be found for this track, but it has all the earmarks of a Johnny Pate–produced and –arranged session, and remains one of the real finds in this box.

The idea for *King of the Blues* originated with Andy McKaie, now senior vice president, A&R, Universal Music Enterprises. An aficionado of all types of roots music, McKaie began his career as a respected music writer in New

York, then joined the publicity department of the fledgling Arista Records label founded by Clive Davis. During his time at Arista, he began exercising his interest in the roots of rock 'n' roll by publicizing anthologies of vintage blues and R&B licensed from the Savoy label, notably in the double-vinyl *Roots of Rock* collection that featured the likes of Big Maybelle, Sam Price, the Ravens, and Johnny Otis, among other pioneers. After joining MCA's West Coast publicity department in September 1983, and then moving into catalog A&R in 1986, he steered important reissues of the Chess material MCA owned, producing acclaimed box sets on Muddy Waters, Howlin' Wolf, Bo Diddley, and Willie Dixon in addition to Buddy Holly (not a Chess artist, obviously, but rather a Coral artist, a label absorbed by MCA in the 1960s), as well as single-disc series of Chess blues recordings and the reissue and retooling of Holly's catalog not only to give it a proper chronology but also to restore the recordings to their original state, before the horror of posthumous overdubs had obliterated Holly's vision of his music.

To the best of McKaie's recollection, it was 1990 when he engaged Sid Seidenberg in conversations about the box set idea; during the next year they were joined by B.B. and music historian and author Colin Escott. (Escott contributed a solid biographical essay for the accompanying booklet, and teamed with McKaie on an interview with B.B. that was published in the first person and reads like a blueprint for B.B.'s award-winning 1996 autobiography.) They agreed on the scope and content of the project and on a late-1992 release date, that being a year when B.B. had no plans for another studio album release. *King of the Blues* remains the definitive overview of B.B.'s post-Modern years; eight years later, Ace Records would fill the gaps in the early years in spectacular fashion on the exhaustively researched four-CD collection of Modern recordings, *The Vintage Years*, spearheaded by John Broven with substantial contributions from Colin Escott on the editorial side and Roger Armstrong and Duncan Cowell on the technical side of researching and mastering the original tapes.[1]

How *King of the Blues* was assembled is a fascinating story that McKaie discussed at length for this book.

Where did the idea for the box set originate?

B.B.'s a great, historical artist that we all have a great deal of respect personally for. I talked to the president of MCA, Richard Palmese, and we both thought it was a good idea, because even though B.B.'s a current artist, he's had a legendary career and he wasn't going to have a new album that year. After I approached Sid, B.B. got involved, and not just to say yes. He really wanted a couple of tracks on there that we hadn't listed, and we agreed.

Was it a hard sell with Sid and B.B.?

No. They were amenable pretty quickly. They understood what we were doing and respected the other boxes that I had already done. And they realized it would be a great thing to encapsulate B.B.'s career in a box set. Sid told me he would also make sure he would help get some of the earlier tracks that either Virgin or Ace or Jazz Interactions in Japan had the right to.

I had started to go through the vaults. I pulled every B.B. King tape that we owned, and gave them their own storage area. I went down into the vault, and spent most of a full day just hand-sorting through the tapes, not checking that we had every tape but looking for unusual things, looking for things that were a little different that struck me as possible rarities and things I hadn't heard. I went through the tapes fairly methodically, and we found maybe 20 reels or so that were interesting suspects.

I assume the vault contained the entire B.B. catalog, even the out-of-print recordings.

Oh, yeah. When it comes to B.B., it's pretty complete. It's got all the ABC albums, singles, edits, all the MCA material, everything he's done for those two labels.

So I brought up the suspects and I went through them, and noted the multitracks that I thought were interesting. I booked some time in a small studio near the office, and I went there with the multitracks and riffled through, say, a live session like *Blues Is King*. I went through the multitracks for that and found "Goin' Down Slow," which hadn't been mixed even. So I did a rough mix on it and brought it back with me, and went through some other tapes, methodically going through all the tapes that contained something that might be an intriguing rarity, because, obviously, this is one of the places for them to give people a little bit different picture of the artist and then to elaborate on the career. I found a two-track work tape and on it I found him doing "Sloppy Drunk," for instance. So I took some of those with me.

B.B. was going to go on the road, so we had to do the interview pretty quickly, as I recall. Colin Escott and I went to his house in Vegas on January 9, 1992, and we did the interview, which was wonderful—he was very open and together about it. After the interview, we went into his bedroom, where he has a huge stereo setup, and he wanted to play us some things, a couple of suggestions for the tracks. He pulled out a 78 and played us "Don't Get Around Much Anymore," which he had recorded with the Duke Ellington Orchestra. He said he'd like it on the box and we said, "Of course," it was great. Then I played him "Sloppy Drunk," and when he stopped laughing, he said, "I didn't know I had recorded that!" He almost fell on the floor; I mean, he was roaring. Every time he would hit the chorus he would just fall apart. So I said, "You mind if we put this on the box?" And he said, "No, that's fine! That's cool!" And he laughed. I played him a few more things, and he played us a few things, and we went back and forth and talked about it. Then we ate dinner and left.

We went back and I drafted up another version of the box for his and Sid's approval, as far as the content went.

You must have had, at the outset, a rough idea of how many CDs you wanted in the box.

Oh, I knew I wanted four. In fact, to be honest, I wanted more Virgin tracks, more tracks from the first ten years than we ended up getting. But there was a licensing problem. When I went to them initially they ignored us and turned us off. But we had also gone to Ace and we went to Jazz Interactions in Japan, and we got them all to sign off on what I wanted; then with Virgin, they were saying no, they were going to be doing something.

One of the owners of Ace is a friend of mine as well as a great musical person, Roger Armstrong. He's really into music and he's into doing things right. I called him and told him about the problems we were having. He and his partner Ted Carroll talked to Virgin, and we got the vast majority of the tracks we wanted.

Was B.B. more interested in, say, one phase of his career than another? Did he have any specific instructions to you about what was closest to his own heart?

If I recall correctly he wanted the song "Six Silver Strings" on the package. And he wanted "Don't Get Around Much Anymore." Now one is from the late '80s and the other is from the '60s. No, he respected the whole thing, liked the concept, liked what we were doing. When he heard the mastering, he was very excited. He told Paul Atkinson, who was the head of A&R, that it was the best he's ever sounded. He was very encouraging and very helpful, and he has been right through the subsequent 13 years that I've gotten to know him. He's been just tremendous. He doesn't look at anything in the short run; he respects his entire career. He respects what people do for him.

I wrote in the liner notes for *Blues Summit* that he's the most gracious man in show business. I'll stand by that. He was an absolute gentleman the whole time, encouraging, grateful, thankful—I should say appreciative—appreciative of what we were doing for him.

Does he have a good perspective on the whole arc of his career?

Oh, yeah, and he remembers it, too. Totally respects it. In fact, we came to him with a bunch of tracks and we didn't know who the personnel were, and we asked him and he told us. He has that kind of recall. He's absolutely remarkable.

How long did you spend foraging through all those master tapes in the vault?

I listened to everything. I know that Colin did too. Generally it takes a month or two to go through everything, minimum. B.B.'s career is of such substance that it may have taken longer. There's obvious things you want; you start with that and start sketching it out that way and start filling in the blanks thereafter. That's generally what I do with these. I'm one of those people who just listens to everything. I sit in my office, I have a nice deck in my office, now it's a TASCAM reel-to-reel. But I'd sit there and listen to everything. Anything I found of interest I'd run a cassette of it and then I'd live with that cassette. And if the song lived with me, if the performance lived with me, I put it on the list. But many of the rehearsal tapes weren't worth using because they were incomplete or he'd stop and talk about something. This wasn't like a Chuck Berry, Howlin' Wolf, Chess Blues package, where you went for mostly familiar things; this had a lot more depth. So I spend time, and after a couple of months of doing this, as well as taking notes and deciding which tracks have to be on, which ones are alternates or possible tracks, and going through all that and listening to all these other tracks, you start to formulate in your head what the vision of it should be. Having a partner like Colin, who also has his own opinion and knows the catalog as well as I do, is a marvelous thing. You reach a compromise with each other because your visions are not exactly the same, but they're close. I mean they were real close.

How about your and Colin's vision with respect to Sid's and B.B.'s ideas about what should be on there?

It was pretty close. The narrowing-down process was pretty good. Sid and B.B. came back with, as I recall, two or three tracks, one of which we said, "Of course." They said, "This is great except for these three tracks," is how I recall it went. The other two we said, "Well, we don't know." Then Sid and B.B. sort of held their ground [*laughs*], and we came back and said, "'Six Silver Strings,' we'll include that," and they were fine with that. Sid sent me tapes of unreleased material that he had, including the song "Many Miles Traveled." He sent me a session he had that was never released. I've subsequently used that session a couple of other times too. But they went along—I think it might have been three tracks that they submitted that they felt we were missing. One we accepted immediately, the other two we didn't, and then we compromised and took one of the two. With that, they were onboard.

Then I started pulling tapes and gathering sources. I had a disc transfer of my own done for "Miss Martha King," 'cause they didn't have a source as to who owned it. We found a source and we had a transfer done and cleaned up.

Those vault tapes you went through in making your selections, how much audio restoration did they require?

There was some cleanup. But they were in pretty good shape. ABC wasn't the best in taking care of their vault, but the artists they seemed to care about they kept better than the others. They didn't have the storage facility back in the old days—the storage facility for ABC was Belkins, and I don't know how good that was; I have a feeling it wasn't very good. But subsequently the tapes were with us, and we had one good storage facility and two adjacent ones that weren't very good. B.B.'s were all in the good one; and in '99 we built, in conjunction with the film company, a monstrous airplane hangar–like facility that's state of the art and still is. Literally, if the people who run it come in in the morning and something happened to it overnight, a computer will tell you what went wrong or if there were fluctuations in the temperature, whatever, the humidity. The curious thing about those kinds of facilities, when they're good enough, they actually seem to have a positive effect on the tapes even if they weren't stored in the best ways in the past. And B.B.'s tapes were generally in fairly decent shape, compared to much of the ABC stuff. They were in pretty good shape. There's a few things missing here and there.

Did you use a CEDAR system on the audio restoration?

Yeah, we used it on "Miss Martha King." I didn't use it much. The original intro and outro of "Sweet Sixteen," when they made the tape for an album, they cut those out. So we started to restore them. We found the original 45 of "Sweet Sixteen" and took the intro and the outro of a two-sided single, beginning on the first side, ending on the second side, and cleaned it up the best we could with CEDAR and then edited together with a tape master we inherited from ABC. And then on "Miss Martha King" we found a 78 rpm; Chris Strachwitz did it. When we were doing "Miss Martha King," we couldn't find it, most collectors didn't have it, but Strachwitz had it and agreed to do a transfer for us. He has his own label—Arhoolie—and he's good at that stuff. I mixed, along with an engineer named John Strother, "Rockin' Awhile" and "Goin' Down Slow." "Rockin' Awhile" I think was from a four-track, and "Goin' Down Slow" was from an eight-track. "Help the Poor," "Fools Get Wise," "Slowly Losin' My Mind," were remixed from threes, fours, and eights, I think, by Bill Inglott.

Obviously you and I could listen to B.B.'s records and get different things out of

the same song. That's the subjective nature of music. In going through B.B.'s catalog,
what really touches you about his art?

In the '60s, first time I saw him, I was amazed by his guitar, by his voice—
his voice has always been a powerful instrument in and of itself—the way he
projects a song. You know, B.B. speaks from the heart. I can feel it. He understands his songs. That's one of his great strengths—he understands the material he's dealing with; he won't do certain kinds of songs unless he feels comfortable with them. He's just a great artist. Between the guitar and the voice
and the songs he selects and the approach—

And his own writing.

His own writing. He has some unique ideas. He's just a great artist, a great
blues artist who's passed the test of time and who periodically makes a great
record. He went through two or three decades where he couldn't do much
wrong. As you get older you start repeating yourself; you know, it gets harder
and harder, and times change, and it's harder and harder, and he's managed to
make it through those times and had success at virtually every stage.

On almost every album you're guaranteed that there will be a couple, three
moments that are going to stay with you forever.

Right. I agree 100 percent. And as I went through the catalog I found that.
Now some of the albums were very hard for me to break down and say "no"
here and "yes" there. I had an idea of what songs I wanted early on, for sure,
and I just had to figure out which versions. In some instances I got what I wanted, in some instances I didn't. The version of "Please Accept My Love," I actually wanted the original version, but I couldn't get it. That was one of the tracks
I couldn't get from the Modern/Kent era. So, you know, Colin and I were talking about it, and he said, "Listen to the live version again," and there it was.
That's not a bad version at all. With B you want to make sure you get the right
combination of things, because you want to reflect all the different sides and his
roots as much as possible. So sometimes if there was a choice, it was the roots
versus something else. But B wanted, like I said, "Six Silver Strings," which is
certainly not roots. It's an interesting attempt at something. On the other hand,
I was looking at making sure some of the duets got on. I thought that was a cool
thing to do to show the latter part of his career, and there's nothing wrong with
some of those duets either. It actually laid itself out reasonably quickly for me
once I got through everything. The hardest part was deciphering which of the
rarities to spice it up with. Later on I did a rarities package for Hip-O called *Here*
and There, and that was the rest of the stuff we were considering, plus some
other things. Really, that's what it boiled down to.

Chapter 15

SUMMITRY OF A HIGHER ORDER

Blues Summit

MCA, 1993
Executive Producer: Sidney A. Seidenberg
Produced by Denny Diante, three selections produced by Denny Walker
Album Concept and Co-producer: Andy McKaie
Mixed by John Hampton at Ardent Studios, Memphis; assisted by Skidd Mills

Additional recording:
Conway Recording, Hollywood, California (engineered by Gil Morales, assisted
     by Paul Lundin)
Trax Recording, Hollywood, California (engineered by Vincent "Vini" Cirilli,
     assisted by Liz Magro)
Crosstown Recording, Memphis (engineered by Rusty McDaniel)
Ardent Recording, Memphis (engineered by Jeff Powell, assisted by Jeffrey
     Reed)
Mastered by Bernie Grundman at Bernie Grundman Mastering, Hollywood,
     California

The Memphis Sessions
Recorded February 15–19, 1993, at Ardent Studios, Memphis
Recorded by Tom Harding, assisted by Skidd Mills and Jeff Powell
B.B. King: vocals and guitar

B.B. King Orchestra
Leon Warren: rhythm guitar
Calep Emphrey, Jr.: drums

James Toney: keyboards
Michael Doster: bass
Tony Coleman: percussion
James Bolden: trumpet
Melvin Jackson: sax
Walter King: sax, horn arrangements, musical director

Songs
"Since I Met You Baby" (Ivory Joe Hunter) Katie Webster: piano, vocal
"Something You Got" (Chris Kenner) Koko Taylor: vocal
"There's Something on Your Mind" (Cecil James McNeely) Etta James: vocal
"Little by Little" (Amos Blakemore) Lowell Fulson: guitar, vocal
"Call It Stormy Monday" (Aaron T. Walker) Albert Collins: guitar, vocal
"We're Gonna Make It" (Gene Barge–Billy Davis–Raynard Miner–Carl Smith)
　　Irma Thomas: vocal
"You're the Boss" (Jerry Leiber–Mike Stoller) Ruth Brown: vocal
"I Pity the Fool" (Deadric Malone) Buddy Guy: guitar, vocal
"I Gotta Move Out of This Neighborhood"/"Nobody Loves Me but My Mother"
　　(B.B. King) performed by B.B. King and Orchestra

The Berkeley Sessions
Recorded March 8–12, 1993, at Fantasy Studios, Berkeley, California

Recorded by Eric Thompson, assisted by Richard Duarte

B.B. King: vocals and guitar

Songs

"Playin' with My Friends" (Robert Cray–Dennis Walker)

The Robert Cray Band—Robert Cray: guitar, vocal; Kevin Hayes: drums; Jim
    Pugh: keyboards; Richard Cousins: bass; Robert Murray: rhythm guitar

"Everybody's Had the Blues" (Joe Louis Walker)

Joe Louis Walker and the Bass Talkers—Joe Louis Walker: guitar, vocal; Paul
    Revelle: drums; Mike Eppley: keyboards; Jeff Lewis: horns; Tim Devine:
    horns; Henry Oden: bass

"You Shook Me" (Willie Dixon–J.B. Lenoir)

John Lee Hooker: guitar, vocal; Robert Cray: guitar; Roy Rogers: slide guitar;
    Kevin Hayes: drums; Jim Pugh: keyboards; Richard Cousins: bass

Sidemen

Kim Wilson: harmonica on "You Shook Me," "Little by Little," "I Pity the Fool"

Lee Allen: saxophone solo on "We're Gonna Make It" and "Something You Got"

Maxine Waters, Julia Tillman Waters, and Maxayne Lewis: background vocals
    on "We're Gonna Make It" and "Something You Got"

Randy Waldman: string synthesizer on "There's Something on Your Mind"

Antoine Salley: percussion on "Something You Got"

Vasti Jackson: rhythm guitar on "Since I Met You Baby"

Nancy Wright: saxophone on "Since I Met You Baby"

The Memphis Horns: "Playin' with My Friends," "Call It Stormy Monday," and
    "We're Gonna Make It"

Ben Cauley: trumpet on "You Shook Me," "I Pity the Fool," and "I Gotta Move
    Out of This Neighborhood"/"Nobody Loves Me but My Mother"

Robert Cray: rhythm guitar on "Something You Got"

Joe Louis Walker: background vocals on "Little by Little"

Mabon "Teenie" Hodges: rhythm guitar on "I Pity the Fool" and "We're Gonna
    Make It"

Tony Coleman: percussion on "You Shook Me" and "Everybody's Had the
    Blues"

Walter King: baritone sax on "Something You Got"

B.B.'s Horns: "You Shook Me"

Recorded in February and March of 1993, *Blues Summit* not only brought
B.B. back to Memphis to record, but also found him energized by the concept—on his first studio album since *There Is Always One More Time*, his
singing and playing were full of life, and the women who joined him in this

271

project were welcomed by their host with open arms and a naughty mind, much to all parties' delight, apparently. Not to diminish the efforts of the stalwart bluesmen onboard, but the blueswomen carry the day here. Their cuts bring out the best in B.B., and all of them engage him on a personal level, flirting with him, sassing him, cajoling him into come-on mode, whereas with the male artists B.B. is often heard shouting encouragement without much in the way of return banter. But then using their singing voices is what the women here do best—powerful and personable, Ruth Brown, Etta James, Katie Webster, and Irma Thomas are formidable stylists; the men by and large are best known for their instrumental prowess, with only Fulson (and, some might argue, Robert Cray) highly regarded as vocalists.

Following the stage-setting opener, a celebratory, freewheeling reworking of Louis Jordan's "Saturday Night Fish Fry" titled "Playin' with My Friends," Ivory Joe Hunter's graceful, pop-influenced love ballad "Since I Met You Baby" gets a reconsidered treatment as a slow, grinding blues, thanks to B.B. and the no-nonsense Katie Webster. Ivory Joe surely would have appreciated the transformation in his song. B.B.'s gravelly shouts give way to Webster's forceful declaiming (which elicits supporting responses from B.B.) before B.B. cuts loose at one point with an electrifying solo, working the bottom strings at the bottom of the guitar neck, pulling off and bending notes while Webster interjects with forceful piano chording. The opening repartee suggests the convivial mood among the principals.

"You know, B.B.," Webster begins.

"Yes, baby," B.B. answers softly.

"Life is hard being out here on the road by myself all the time. . . . "

"Yeah, I know it."

" . . . and I'm just getting tired."

B.B. queries: "How do you spell it, baby, how do you spell it?"

"T-i-d-e, tired," Webster answers straight-faced.

"Sometimes it makes me feel like I wanna clean up my act," she announces, adding " . . . but they always told me that something worth having is worth waiting for, and I have definitely been waiting a long time. But you know, B, since I met you, I feel like all my strifes and troubles are all over in life. . . . "

"Yes, they are, baby, I'm here with ya. . . . "

" . . . because I feel like you are the man . . . someone who will treat me like the queen I am, the swamp boogie queen."

Koko Taylor gets B.B. going on "Something You Got," Chris Kenner's straightforward love song done at a mid-tempo pace with a funky New

Orleans groove and a crooning female chorus answering the vocalists' verses. Koko and B.B. engage in flirty dialog throughout, culminating in her telling him, "B.B., you know I love you," prompting B.B. to offer encouragement: "All right, Koko, talk to me. . . ."

" . . . and I don't put nobody above you. . . ."

B.B.: "You better not, baby, you know I'm a pretty big guy."

Koko coos, seductively, "Yeah, baby," prompting a cool response from B.B., "Yeah, talk to me." Koko suggestively offers, "Awww, I like it that way," B.B. retorts, "I like it too, baby, can't have it no other way," and the song's fadeout begins, the diminishing sound saying everything about where this verbal *pas de deux* is headed.

Big Jay McNeely's blues ballad "There's Something on Your Mind" features Etta James gently exploring the opening lyric line as B.B. lets Lucille speak for him in high, keening notes. When B.B. comes in vocally, he's in the pulpit delivering a sermon, giving advice on the proper response to an unfaithful mate— "You just pack your clothes, turn around, and slowly walk outta the door / look over your left shoulder as you go out, then you hang your head and you say, 'Ooooh, please don't try to tell me . . . '" When B.B. starts singing he bursts forth with power, crying out his lines, Lucille interjecting a comforting phrase here and there, setting up another pulpit moment for B.B. during which he offers some rather startling advice to the aggrieved party: grab a baseball bat, go back home, kick down the door, and "beat the hell outta everybody that you can see, everybody that come through the door." Etta returns with a pleading, conciliatory verse as the big band modulates to a low roar, the horns blaring behind Etta and B.B.'s shouts. Co-producer Andy McKaie reveals in his liner notes that James and B.B. "changed the song for her duet the night before the session, so she and B.B. learned, rearranged, and even rewrote portions of 'There's Something on Your Mind' on the spot," thus accounting for B.B.'s dramatic advice to the lovelorn, a wrinkle McNeely had not included in his smooth, yearning original version, which posits infidelity as a fait accompli with the singer in resigned acceptance of a love affair's end.

Ruth Brown makes her entrance with "You're the Boss," a saucy Jerry Leiber–Mike Stoller number originally recorded in 1961 by the Ravens' great lead singer Jimmy Ricks and the imposing R&B legend LaVern Baker but better known as a saucy duet by Elvis Presley and Ann-Margret for the *Viva Las Vegas* soundtrack (it did not appear in the film). Brown, however, supplants Ann-Margret's sex-kitten sultriness with a mature, sassy sensuality, and B.B. responds with sly, seductive crooning, the two veterans singing conversationally before they start in on the suggestive repartee.

"You get better lookin' every day," Brown says, and B.B., naturally, responds, "Yeah, I know that, I know that." Then Brown draws out the word "Beee Beee," and pauses long enough for B.B. to answer in the affirmative, "Yes, that's me. . . .," after which Brown picks up from where she left off and takes it to a whole other level as the song winds down, even having some fun at the expense of B.B.'s big hit: " . . . look out, I'm closin' in! I didn't make my move too soon, did I? Is the thrill gone? Go back to the source, baby. You sure you named that guitar right? Shoulda been called Ruth!" Feigning disdain, she signs off muttering in mock-bitterness, "Lucille!" Both parties are reduced to laughter at the fade.

"We're Gonna Make It" (co-written by arranger Gene Barge, among others) spotlights Irma Thomas on a cool, classic soul workout with a positive message of riding out hard times on the strength of love and friendship. It features an energetic female background chorus and Thomas and B.B. trading genially phrased verses, B.B. adding a punchy solo, Melvin Jackson soaring with a blustery sax solo, the horns rising high and triumphant, and the entire cast falling into a repetitive gospel shout of "We're gonna make it!" for the last half-minute.

A song that became a monument for B.B.'s buddy Bobby "Blue" Bland, "I Pity the Fool," with Buddy Guy, features tasty solo duets between the two guitarists between verses, with James Toney's insistent chording on the piano standing out. The song fades out with B.B. and Guy shouting verses at each other, as if the song couldn't possibly end yet.

Willie Dixon's "You Shook Me," with John Lee Hooker, pairs two blues giants with distinctly different styles. Still, they find common ground that accommodates Hooker's dark, turgid riffing in a stark setting and B.B.'s more expansive approach featuring horns.

"Little by Little" teams B.B. with Lowell Fulson, the artist whose "3 O'Clock Blues" put B.B. on the map. Here, on an Amos Blakemore tune, Fulson joins the man who rode his song to the top of the blues pantheon on an engaging shuffle, Fulson's warm, weathered baritone and B.B.'s husky-voiced emoting proving a good fit. Fulson cuts loose with a lively solo, and B.B. comes back later with a swinging workout on the lower neck.

T-Bone Walker's "Stormy Monday" finds B.B. giving the Iceman, Albert Collins, ample room to establish the mood with a piercing solo run ahead of B.B.'s gruff, moaning plea of a vocal as the band grinds it out. Toney again steps out on piano and engages Collins in a spirited dialog before Collins adds a nasal vocal and a darting, steely guitar solo that prompts B.B. to shout, "Yeah, do it one more time!"

B.B. and his Orchestra work out on a slow, mournful blues written in the studio, "I Gotta Move Out of This Neighborhood," paired with "Nobody Loves Me but My Mother." The new tune recounts a misstep—fooling around with another man's wife, prompting her husband to take knife in hand to settle matters—that has forced the narrator to relocate to safer turf. The number features a rich, trilling solo from B.B. and an evocative horn chart by Walter King marked by steady washes of ensemble brass and swaying, ascending passages in which James Bolden's trumpet makes a forceful statement. The self-pitying warhorse "Nobody Loves Me but My Mother" is done at a stately, dirge-like pace that allows B.B. considerable latitude for a solo that's minimalist by his standards in that he lingers on single notes and lets each one sink in. The oddest moment is during the guitar solo, when it sounds as if B.B. sneezes while he's playing. Undeterred and unfazed, he continues with his solo. (Questioned about this, producer Andy McKaie said he had no recollection of B.B. sneezing during this recording, but he added that he had not listened to the track in some time.)

With Joe Louis Walker and his band, B.B. closes the album with Walker's jump blues "Everybody's Had the Blues," a lively turn marked by Walker's high-pitched vocals and stinging, distortion-rich guitar solos, with B.B. adding some angular runs up the neck and a gruff vocal, on the album's least effective track.

"The project was also virtually a lovefest from beginning to end," McKaie concluded in his liner notes. "From the artists to the producers, once asked to sign on, the response was unanimously something like, 'If B.B. wants me, tell me when and where!' The King of the Blues himself, possibly the most gracious man in all music, then treated each guest like royalty.

"It was a remarkable few weeks. Whether we captured that elusive musical magic on tape or not, each listener will have to decide for themselves. We think we did pretty darn well. One thing for sure, no one involved will soon forget these sessions."

"They Came with Bells On"
Andy McKaie on the Making of *Blues Summit*

Blues Summit won a Grammy Award in 1993 in the category of Best Traditional Blues Recording. The project was the idea of Andy McKaie, senior vice president, A&R, for Universal Music Enterprises, who suggested it to the then head of A&R at MCA, Paul Atkinson (since deceased; Atkinson was the original lead guitarist in the Zombies in his younger years), who encouraged not only the idea but also McKaie as the producer. When McKaie hedged—

"I've never done anything like that," he told Atkinson, "I'd be a fish outta water"—Atkinson assigned the project to Denny Diante, a versatile producer whose credits also included Barbra Streisand's *Broadway* album. "He was a handyman kind of guy; he could produce anything and work with anybody," McKaie says of Diante.

McKaie pitched the idea to B.B. on a visit to the artist's Las Vegas home. McKaie already had a lengthy list of potential songs and guest artists at hand, and B.B. embraced the idea from the start, even to the point of recommending they do a cut with one of his favorite younger players, Joe Louis Walker. With Sid Seidenberg's blessing, the project began to come together in late '92. Diante gave McKaie hands-on instruction in creating a recording budget and in some of the particulars of production, invites went out to the guest artists, and the decision was made to record in Memphis, B.B.'s career ground zero, but, owing to schedule conflicts, three cuts were recorded at the Fantasy Studios in Berkeley, California.

In an interview from his MCA office, McKaie looked back on the *Blues Summit* sessions with fondness and discussed the particulars of the recording process.

How were the songs selected for this project? You had so much material to choose from.

I was getting ready to do the box set with B.B., and I had this idea to do a duets album, but a duets album with blues people. The original idea was to do old blues songs that B.B. had never done and match him up with his peers or younger artists. He asked about songs, and we talked about that a little bit. Most of the songs were agreed upon very early and we started working on arrangements. B.B. decided he wanted to do one of his own songs as an extra song, but just with his band, and that was pretty cool because it fit well. Etta James showed up in Memphis, didn't like her song, so overnight we had to rearrange everything, which was fine. Etta was great; she just didn't like her song, that's all. She said, "I don't know who committed me to this song." I said, "Your manager." She said, "Well, he shouldn't have, because I don't want to do this song." I said, "Great, what song do you want to do?" We talked about it, and we ran out, found a CD with "There Is Something on Your Mind" on it, brought her to the studio and ran through it with the band—

Had anybody suggested that Jay McNeely song? Or did you just pull it out of a hat?

Pulled it out of a hat the night before she showed up. By the time she showed up, we had it rehearsed. The band was rehearsing the songs all along.

We'd send songs to B.B., and B.B. would have the band rehearsing; by the time they got to the studio they knew the songs. Then the artists would show up, and B.B. was always around the studio; for the most part he hung in the studio, he'd only leave every once in a while. He was like the master of ceremonies. He would greet and meet people, talk, try to make them feel comfortable, and they'd sit down and work out the duets. It was all pretty much improvised in the studio as far as the duets go. We had ideas, and sometimes the artists showed up with ideas. Katie Webster came in and said, "I know what we're gonna do. I just love this song, I know exactly what to do." She sat down at the piano and showed us the whole song, and the band, B.B., the producers all stood around and watched her and heard what she had to say, and decided, okay, that's cool, let's do that. That's a little different than we thought it was gonna be, but that's cool. And the band fell into place.

Most of the stuff was done in a short amount of takes, finished takes anyway, and pretty much live in the studio. There were some overdubs afterwards—B.B.'s voice went at one point—

There is a huskiness to his voice on a couple of cuts that's not there on others. I was wondering if he was a bit under the weather.

Yeah, his voice went at one point. We had already booked a week to mix the album and to do overdubs. We went about a week and a day in Memphis, came back to L.A. and took a week off, then we went to Fantasy, did a week there where we were recording Cray, Joe Louis Walker, and John Lee Hooker. Cray was in both places; Cray came to Memphis to the jam ["Playin' with My Friends"]. So the three of them did their tracks there, but also we had some overdubbing still left to do, and they did some of the overdubbing; they volunteered on the spot. We'd say, "Yeah, we need a rhythm guitar on this," and Walker says, "So, I'm sitting here. I could do that." Okay. We'd run through it. We did some overdubs with Teenie Hodges down in Memphis—B.B.'s voice went on Thursday for only a day or so, so those vocals had to be replaced. But overdubs were relatively rare; most of it was live in the studio, it was an absolutely terrific, fun week. Irma Thomas had a birthday while we were in the studio. We found out the day before she showed up, and we had arranged to get a birthday cake. We had the cake hidden in a refrigerator, and B.B. said, "Who's the birthday cake for?" When he found out it was Irma's birthday, he said, "That's wonderful. Let me take care of it." So Irma shows up and they cut their track, and B.B. disappears suddenly. He comes back, walks in with the birthday cake and sang "Happy Birthday to You," and Irma almost cried. "B.B. King sang 'Happy Birthday' to me!" It was a lovefest, as I said in the liner notes; it really was. Then Buddy Guy showed up. And Buddy Guy, he has this reputation as this swaggering, hot guitar slinger, and you think he's got ego and self-assurance out the door. He shows up and we start running through the track, and he's sitting way behind B.B. on the guitar, waaayy behind. When he starts to sing he's singing softly. So I walked over to him and said, "What's going on?" He said, "Well, this is B.B.'s record. I don't wanna intrude on his record." I said, "This is a duet. It's you and B." He said, "But this is B.B. This is my idol." So we had to pump him up in the studio until we got him to the point where he was unloading and rocking and getting into it. And he got into it, but it took a while. I don't know if he was intimidated by the circumstances; I wouldn't say that. But he was certainly overwhelmed by them in a certain respect, and he showed a side of him I never knew existed. He was very sweet. Very nice man. Everyone was. Etta maybe played the prima donna a little bit by not liking the song she had been assigned, but she was the sweetest and funniest person. She was great. And her and B.B. had so much fun in the studio doing that song together.

Everything you're saying about the spirit in the studio comes through on the record. And B.B. sounds energized by what's going on here; there's an enthusiasm to his presence—and it's not like it had been a while since he'd made a good record—but he just sounds up on every single cut.

He had a great time. There were a couple of very funny things that happened too. Koko Taylor wanted to sing in a booth, so we set up a booth for her, because that's how she was used to singing. B.B. was out in the studio with everyone else, but she's back in the booth, which is fine. When she started to sing, the needle went off the dial. The engineers were leaping at the board, trying to pull back. It was hysterical. She was so powerful a singer, she just blew out everybody. It was hilarious. The whole place started roaring. This was just rehearsal, so it didn't matter.

And when we were at Fantasy, John Lee Hooker came in late. We had ordered some food, so we called up and ordered more food. He was with Roy Rogers, the slide player. We all sat around—and Joe Louis and Robert Cray were there that night, too—they hung out the whole time; they both showed up for the rehearsals at Fantasy and stayed the whole time, to the end. They didn't leave. So we sat around in this big room outside the studio, where you can eat and relax. And B.B. and John Lee sat next to each other and started telling stories. Here we are, the clock's on, and we sat there for close to three hours listening to stories from John Lee and B.B. It was hilarious. They were telling stories back and forth at each other, and the place was in absolute hysterics.

As you mention in your notes, the meeting of B.B. and John Lee had some his-

*torical resonance in that these two premier bluesmen of their times had totally differ-
ent styles and had never met in the studio before. What was B.B.'s reaction to having
Hooker involved?*

He was thrilled. But we had a tough time trying to figure out a song that
would work. "You Shook Me" I came up with, and I guess it sorta works.

The arrangement strikes a nice balance between Hooker's style and B.B.'s.

That's what I thought. I suggested it and everybody agreed. And B.B. had
signed off on a bunch of songs early on, about 25 songs. Then we went to the
duet partners and tried to make it work together. "You Shook Me," the recording of that was pretty funny too. After we got done eating our lunch and hearing these stories, we knew we needed to go in and record—we're spending a
lot of money here—and so we went inside, and they lined up. The band went
on one side, and four guitar players—John Lee, B.B., Cray, and Roy Rogers—
they lined up like an offensive line in football, with guitars right across them,
John Lee next to B.B., and started staring at us in the booth. In the booth we
got everything set, the mikes and all, and we just get back in the booth, the
engineer sits down and John Lee starts, and the whole band picks up, and
they're off, playing the song. So we missed the beginning. They play the
whole song through and it's perfect. It was tremendous, absolutely great.
Everything fell into place. The finish and John Lee's [growls like Hooker], "All
right, that's it," and he starts to unplug his guitar. I'm standing in the window
waving my arms, and we're hitting the intercom button going, "No! No!" And
B.B. leaps in front of John Lee as they're leaving and says, "I think they want
another one." I say, "Yeah, we want another one. We missed the beginning."
And John goes [growls], "No, that was a good one, don't need another one.
That was a good one." And B.B.'s going, "No, let's do another one. We started and they weren't quite ready for us." John Lee goes, "No, that was a good
one." So John Lee sits down and they nail the beginning and then the air goes
out of the tire. They did the rest of the song, but the second take was … well,
John Lee had no interest in being there then. He had done it. He wanted out.
One take, that was it, you got it. At the end of the second take he got up,
packed his guitar, and left. With Roy Rogers in tow. And we all sat there roaring. So what we did was take the intro of the second take and overdub it onto
the first take. Then we had ourselves a full take.

*One of the distinguishing features about the songs with the female artists is this
repartee between B.B. and the women. Did they plan that?*

No, it happened on the spot. They had a blast. Ruth Brown, who's flirtatious from way back—I've known her for years—she's a piece of work, she's
loads of fun. She came in all sassy, and I knew she and B would have a good

time. They started as soon as she walked in. I mean, from the minute she walked through the door they were at each other. I think Denny Diante said, "Save it for the record!" The two of them were hilarious together.

That song is interesting, because it was by Leiber and Stoller, most famously done by Elvis and Ann-Margret.

I love that song. I thought it was so cool. It was early Leiber–Stoller, which they repeated later on with Elvis. I had the Jimmy Ricks version, and I played it for everybody and everyone loved it. We had to go to Leiber and Stoller because we changed the lyrics. We played it for them and they thought it was great. B.B. rewrote some of those lyrics and changed some in "There Is Something on Your Mind." He didn't want to shoot somebody, as it says in Jay McNeely's original version. He would hit 'em with a baseball bat, but he didn't want to shoot anyone. He just felt like shooting was a bad thing. Hit 'em with a baseball bat. I said to him, "If you're going to do this song, you're mad and you're going to go after this person, so you'll have to do something pretty dangerous." We were going back and forth trying to figure out what he should do, he was in the studio, I was in the control booth, and we were working on the lyrics. One of us came up with that. And then we redid it to make it work that way. That song was improvised, a lot of it, on the spot.

You have that incident, where he talks about taking a baseball bat to somebody, and in "I Gotta Move Out of This Neighborhood" he talks about a man showing up at his door with a knife in his hand.

Yeah, I know. But he didn't want to talk about guns. What can I say? B has his own set of values in that respect.

It was wonderful to work with him. He was so amenable to trying things, whatever we came up with. And his band was terrific. Walter King, who is his nephew, was the arranger for this whole thing, and he was great.

When we were mixing, we all got together and mixed it together. B.B. sat in for every mixing session, and he listened to everything. He'd make a suggestion, but he really wasn't interfering. He wanted to be there and hear how it was going. He was very proud of it, very happy with it. We were fortunate that everything worked out so well. It really was like, let's have a party. I'm gonna throw a record party; let's all come together and do this. We had real professionals doing it, Walter King supplying great arrangements, B.B. King being such a gracious host to everyone, I don't know. It was a very hard, grueling week. But totally improvised, totally together.

I've listened to this over and over, trying to figure out if it is what I think it is. On "Nobody Loves Me but My Mother," does he sneeze during one of his solos?

[Laughs] Not that I know of. I don't know. I'd have to listen again.

He sneezes, but he keeps going, and it sounds like he stifles another sneeze—you can hear him sniffling like he's trying to keep from doing it again.

I think that was the full second take, so if he did, we didn't catch it. I don't think so, though.

There were things about it that we had to improve upon and work on, but it was mostly live in the studio, and yeah, there are some blemishes there, you can hear 'em. But the notion was to capture this music the way it came down. We were very fortunate that it worked as well as it did, that it was received as well as it was. To that point it was B.B.'s best-selling album in a while, like a decade or so. Then *Deuces Wild* was wildly successful.

Were there artists you wanted to get but couldn't?

Yeah, it didn't work out for Little Milton and Bobby Bland to make it. But everybody else we invited was there. And they came with bells on and were there for B.B. and anxious to record with him. It was an absolute blast.

Heart to Heart
Diane Schuur and B.B. King _____

GRP, 1994
Produced by Phil Ramone
Executive producers: Dave Grusin and Larry Rosen
Engineered by Dan Hahn
Additional engineers: Brian Ehrlich, Dann Wojar
Recorded at Capitol Studios, Hollywood and Power Station, New York City
Mixed by Charlie Paakkari and Phil Ramone at Capitol Studios, Hollywood,
    California
Assisted by Brian Ehrlich
Digital editing by Michael Landy at The Review Room, New York City

Musicians
Dianne Schuur: vocals, piano ("No One Ever Tells You," "It Had to Be You")
B.B. King: vocals, guitar solos
Randy Waldman: piano
Chuck Berghofer: bass
Paul Viapiano: guitar
Vinnie Colaiuta: drums
Doug Katsaros: synth on "No One Ever Tells You"

Songs
"No One Ever Tells You" (4:57) (Carroll Coates–Hub Atwood)
"I Can't Stop Loving You" (4:28) (Don Gibson) Bashiri Johnson: percussion;

Doug Katsaro: synth; Diva Gray, Vaneese Thomas, Karen Kamon, Jill Dell'abate: background vocals; horns conducted by Patrick Williams; Gary Foster and Daniel Higgins: saxophones; George Graham and Warren Leuning: trumpets; Richard Todd: French horn; George Roberts: bass trombone

"You Don't Know Me" (3:54) (Eddy Arnold–Cindy Walker) Randy Waldman: synth, string arrangement

"It Had to Be You" (3:17) (Isham Jones–Gus Kahn) Tom Scott: tenor saxophone; Doug Katsaros: synth; Dianne Schuur: additional arrangement

"I'm Putting All My Eggs in One Basket" (3:33) (Irving Berlin)

"Glory of Love" (3:50) (William Hill) Patrick Williams: horn arrangements; Gary Foster and Daniel Higgins: saxophones; Warren Leuning: trumpet; Richard Todd: French horn; George Roberts: bass trombone

"Try a Little Tenderness" (4:28) (Jimmy Campbell–Reginald Connelly–Harry Woods)

"Spirit in the Dark" (5:01) (Aretha Franklin) Doug Katsaros: piano; Bashiri Johnson: percussion; Diva Gray, Vaneese Thomas, Karen Kamon, Jill Dell'abate: background vocals

"Freedom" (4:44) (Lotte Golden–Tommy Faragher) Doug Katsaros: synth; Bashiri Johnson: percussion; Diva Gray, Vaneese Thomas, Karen Kamon, Jill Dell'abate: background vocals

"At Last" (5:13) (Harry Warren–Mack Gordon) Dianne Schuur: additional arrangement

All songs arranged by Doug Katsaros, except "Glory of Love," arranged by
Patrick Williams

The pairing of B.B. with then-rising young jazz vocalist Diane "Deedles"
Schuur appears to have been an idea sprung from Sid Seidenberg's desire to
see his artist embraced by the audience that worshiped at the altars of great
classic American pop singers such as Frank Sinatra and Tony Bennett.[1] To
steer the project, which was released on the label Schuur recorded for, GRP,
producer Phil Ramone, who had engineered B.B.'s *Live & Well* sessions in
1969, was enlisted as producer. Ramone came with an enviable track record.

A classically trained violinist who studied at the Juilliard School of Music,
Ramone rebelled during his school days and began playing jazz on his electrified instrument. While working clubs around New York City, he was hired
as an assistant at JAC recording studio, where he began learning the art of
recording. One of his early assignments was doing the sound for President
John F. Kennedy's infamous birthday party, at which Marilyn Monroe
famously cooed a salacious version of "Happy Birthday." He went on to do
special events for the Kennedy, Johnson, and Carter administrations. As a producer, he had a bead on New York–based or –identified artists, and he made
wonderful records with them—Paul Simon, Barbra Streisand, Frank Sinatra,
and, most notably, Billy Joel, with whom he had a decade-plus run of multi-
million-selling albums. Influenced as a producer by his friend Quincy Jones
and, like most modern producers, by the fifth Beatle, George Martin, Ramone
developed a philosophy of his role that put him in the artist's shadow, his contribution transparent.

"Producers are way in the back," he told *Billboard*'s Paul Verna in a 1996
interview. "If our names were on the front cover, it would be different. I don't
think the record-buying public go to the Phil Ramone section in Tower
Records. They just don't. So you have to put your ego where it belongs: with
the artist, the song, and the crew you put together. If you think you have a
style and you perpetrate that onto people, you're hurting the very essence of
their creativity. The reward of producing comes when someone inside the
record company who has a lot to do with what's going on actually calls you
and says, 'Boy, this record really came out great.' Or when other artists call
you and want to work with you."[2]

In his liner notes for *Heart to Heart*, Ramone wrote that when he first
heard B.B.'s and Schuur's voices coming through the console, he realized this
session was going to spotlight a side of B.B. that few fans knew well—that
being the "great balladeer." That's an arguable point, given the powerful ballad

performances B.B. had been committing to tape since the early '50s and with "The Thrill Is Gone" having become his signature song, but it's also true that of his latter-day albums, *Heart to Heart* keeps the focus strongest on the ballad side. Despite a rousing interpretation of Aretha Franklin's "Spirit in the Dark" (with the gospel element most pronounced in the swinging arrangement and a female background chorus chanting and shouting as if they were recorded in the choir stall) and a funky to-do on "Freedom," the eight other songs are cool and mellow. The artists wisely avoid emulating Ray Charles's arrangement of "I Can't Stop Loving You" and instead treat it as a lush pop ballad; ditto for another country standard, the poignant Eddy Arnold–Cindy Walker evergreen "You Don't Know Me," with B.B. and Schuur trading sorrowful vocals with a subtle synth-and-strings backing. "It Had to Be You" swings here and there, and it's mostly a showcase for Schuur's reedy, Dinah Washington–like voice. B.B. delivers a warm, pleasant reading of Irving Berlin's fanciful "I'm Putting All My Eggs in One Basket," and both "Glory of Love" and "Try a Little Tenderness" are done in a dreamy, romantic style with small-combo backing and subtle, soothing horn arrangements fleshing out the soundscape.

Judging from Ramone's account of the sessions as detailed in his album liner notes, *Heart to Heart* is the result of deliberate pre-production planning, followed by a laissez-faire approach once the tape started rolling. Ramone and arranger Doug Katsaros spent three days at Schuur's house, "checking ideas, picking places for harmony or exchanges between B.B. and Diane. Tapes went off to B.B. and the process began." On the first day of sessions at the Capitol studios in Hollywood, Schuur and the band were rehearsing some arrangements when B.B. arrived and energized the room with his very presence. He asked Ramone if he could hang out in the control room while Schuur and the band rehearsed "I Can't Stop Loving You."

"Diane was warming up and just blowing everyone away with her vocal and musicianship," according to Ramone. During a break, she came in to meet B.B., which Ramone describes as "the first of many affectionate, fun moments to come, as they joked and hugged. B.B. said to me, 'I wonder about keeping up with her.' I assured him that this vocal marriage would work."

Schuur did another reading of "I Can't Stop Loving You," then shouted at Ramone, "Play that f***er back!" After he had stopped laughing, B.B. said to Schuur, "Oh, baby, you just made me feel at home!"[3]

There is indeed good camaraderie between B.B. and Schuur, but not the warmth that comes through in his *Blues Summit* duets with Katie Webster, Etta James, Koko Taylor, and Ruth Brown. For starters, Schuur, effective though she is at times, is not in a league with the great R&B and blues singers B.B. had been teamed with a year earlier. For B.B.'s part, it sounds like another day at the office—his singing is engaging, even beautiful on occasion, but it's also studied, technically impressive but only rarely emotionally compelling.

But it worked commercially. *Heart to Heart* topped the jazz chart, making one of B.B.'s most ordinary studio efforts his first-ever No. 1 album.

Deuces Wild

MCA, 1997

Produced by John Porter, except "Dangerous Mood," produced, engineered, and mixed by Chris Lord-Alge

Executive producer: Sidney A. Seidenberg

Recorded and mixed, except as noted, by Joe McGrath

Mixed at Sound Castle Studios, Silverlake, California, except "Dangerous Mood," mixed at Image Recording, Los Angeles

Digital editing by John Porter

Additional engineering by Steve Holroyd and Ron Black

Assistant engineers: Joe Brewer, Gabe Chiesa, Mike Dy, Matt Gregory, Dino Johnson, Aaron Lepley, Barbara Lipke, A. Mixdorf, John Nelson, Jay Reynolds, John Sorenson, and Aya Takemura

Mastered by Bernie Grundman at Bernie Grundman Mastering, Hollywood, California

Songs and Musicians

"If You Love Me" (Van Morrison) with Van Morrison. B.B. King and Neil Hubbard" guitar; Paul Carrack: keyboards and Hammond B3 organ; Jools Holland: piano; Pino Palladino: bass; Andy Newmark: drums; Phil Marshall: string arrangements and conducting; Sid Page (concertmaster), Bruce Dukov, Arman Garabedian, Berj Garabedian, Norman Hughes, Tamara Hatwan, Kenneth Yerke, and Andrea Byers: violins; Robert Becker: viola; Larry Corbett, Marston Smith, and Dane Little: cello. Recorded at Westside Studios, London, and Sound Castle Studios, Silverlake, California

"The Thrill Is Gone" (Ray Hawkins–Rick Darnell) with Tracy Chapman. B.B. King, Johnny Lee Schell, and Neil Hubbard: guitar; Tommy Eyre: Wurlitzer piano; Paul Carrack: Hammond B3 organ; Reggie McBride: bass; Tony Braunagel: drums and percussion; Lenny Castro: percussion; Martin Tillman and Miles Tackett: cellos; Joe Sublett: tenor sax; Darrell Leonard: string and horn arrangements, and trumpet; Yvonne Moriarty, Daniel Kelley, and Kurt Snyder: French horns. Recorded at Conway Studios, Cherokee Recording Studios, Hollywood, California, and Townhouse Studios, London

"Rock Me Baby" (Joe Josea–B.B. King) with Eric Clapton. B.B. King and Eric Clapton: guitar; Pino Palladino: bass; Paul Carrack: Hammond B3 organ; Simon Climie and Paul Waller: progamming; Paulinho Da Costa: percussion. Recorded at Townhouse Studios, London, and Sound Castle Studios, Silverlake, California

"Please Send Me Someone to Love" (Percy Mayfield) with Mick Hucknall. B.B. King and Neil Hubbard: guitar; Chris Stainton: keyboards and piano; Paul Carrack: Hammond B3 organ; Pino Palladino: bass; Andy Newmark: drums; Phil Marshall: string arrangements and conducting; Sid Page (concertmaster), Bruce Dukov, Arman Garabedian, Berj Garabedian, Norman Hughes, Tamara Hatwan, Kenneth Yerke, and Andrea Byers: violins; Robert Becker: viola; Larry Corbett, Marston Smith, and Dane Little: cello. Recorded at Westside Studios, London, and Sound Castle Studios, Silverlake, California

"Baby I Love You" (Ronnie Shannon), with Bonnie Raitt. Sir Harry Bowens, Terrence Forsythe, and Vincent Bonham: backing vocals; B.B. King, Bonnie Raitt, and Hugh McCracken: guitar; John Cleary: piano; Leon Pendarvis: organ; Pino Palladino: bass; Steve Jordan: drums. Recorded at Avatar Studio, New York City, Cherokee Recording Studios, Hollywood, California, and Westside Studios, London

"Ain't Nobody Home" (Jerry Ragovoy) with D'Angelo. B.B. King and Hugh McCracken: guitar; D'Angelo: keyboards; John Cleary: Wurlitzer piano;

Leon Pendarvis: organ; Pino Palladino: bass; Steve Jordan: drums; Lenny Castro: percussion; Wardell Quezergue: horn arrangements and conducting; Brian Murray and Jamil Sharif: trumpet; Joseph Saulsbury, Jr.: tenor sax; Carl Blouin: baritone sax. Recorded at Avatar Studio, New York City, Cherokee Recording Studios, Hollywood, California, Boiler Room Studios, New Orleans, and Westside Studios, London

"There Must Be a Better World Somewhere" (Doc Pomus–Mac Rebennack) with Dr. John. Randy Jacobs: guitar; Billy Payne and Tommy Eyre: keyboards; James "Hutch" Hutchinson: bass; Jim Keltner: drums; Lenny Castro: percussion; Wardell Quezergue: horn arrangements and conducting; Brian Murray and Jamil Sharif: trumpet; Joseph Saulsbury, Jr.: tenor sax; Carl Blouin: baritone sax. Recorded at Ocean Way Recording, Hollywood, California, and Boiler Room Studios, New Orleans

"Confessin' the Blues" (Jay McShann–Walter Brown) with Marty Stuart. B.B. King and Marty Stuart: guitar; Billy Payne: keyboards, Hammond B3 organ; James "Hutch" Hutchinson: bass; Jim Keltner: drums. Recorded at Ocean Way Recording, Hollywood, California

"Paying the Cost to Be the Boss" (B.B. King) with the Rolling Stones. Mick Jagger: vocals; B.B. King, Keith Richards, and Ron Wood: guitar; Tommy Eyre: keyboards; Darryl Jones: bass; Charlie Watts: drums; Mick Jagger: harmonica; Joe Sublett: tenor sax; Darrell Leonard: trumpet. Recorded at Ocean Way Recording and Cherokee Recording Studios, Los Angeles

"Dangerous Mood" (Kevin Moore–Candy Parton) with Joe Cocker. C.J. Vanston and Tommy Eyre: Hammond B3 organ; Chris Stainton: piano; Dean Parks and Michael Landau: guitar; James "Hutch" Hutchinson: bass; Kenny Aronoff: drums. Recorded at NRG Studio and Image Recording, Los Angeles

"Keep It Coming" (Heavy D–B.B. King) with Heavy D. B.B. King and Hugh McCracken: guitar; John Cleary: piano; Leon Pendarvis: organ; Pino Palladino: bass; Steve Jordan: drums; Lenny Castro: percussion. Recorded at Avatar Studio, New York City, Cherokee Recording Studios, Hollywood, California, and Westside Studios, London

"Cryin' Won't Help You" (B.B King–Sam Ling) with David Gilmour and Paul Carrack. Paul Carrack: vocals; Sir Harry Bowens, Terrence Forsythe, and Vincent Bonham: backing vocals; B.B. King, David Gilmour, and Neil Hubbard: guitar; Paul Carrack: keyboards and organ; Chris Stainton: piano; Pino Palladino: bass; Andy Newmark: drums. Recorded at Westside Studios, London

"Nightlife" (Willie Nelson–Paul Buskirk–Walter Breeland) with Willie Nelson. Randy Jacobs: guitar; Billy Payne: keyboards; Tommy Eyre: Hammond B3 organ;

James "Hutch" Hutchinson: bass; Jim Keltner: drums; Mickey Raphael: harmonica. Recorded at Ocean Way Recording, Hollywood, California

To some, B.B.'s second album of duets, *Deuces Wild*, betrays a good idea having run its course. *Blues Summit* had a gripping intensity, and it was B.B. in his element—the blues, nothing but—and paired with fearless stylists who brought fire and personality to their numbers and ignited the same passion in B.B., who engaged his guests fully on every artistic level. *Deuces Wild* seems more an exercise in making a point that musical genres are separated from the blues by the thinnest of boundaries and that through the blues different generations of artists can find common ground. The former conceit can be both supported and disputed by musicologists, but the latter, on the basis of the performances here, suggests an abyss between the young guns of the day and the veteran artists. Heavy D (who at least has some humorous moments), D'Angelo (except as a pianist), and Mick Hucknall seem inadequate, whereas Dr. John, Bonnie Raitt, Marty Stuart, Van Morrison, Joe Cocker, and Willie Nelson all acquit themselves admirably. The oddity in the bunch is the Rolling Stones accompanying B.B. on a swinging version of "Paying the Cost to Be the Boss" and sounding like an anonymous small combo (B.B.'s Tympany Five?), despite Mick Jagger's incendiary, wailing harmonica solo near the end. That said, the album is pleasant enough, mostly because B.B. does something interesting every time he enters.

"If You Love Me" features Van Morrison crooning his own R&B-flavored tune with sweet, swaying strings, a churchy organ, and B.B. interjecting languid solo lines throughout and in a solo passage, but not singing. The arrangement of "The Thrill Is Gone" echoes that of the Bill Szymczyk–produced classic of 1970, but the tension comes not from the mood, but rather from the contrast between Tracy Chapman's trembling vocal style and B.B.'s rough-hewn, throaty singing, which adds drama simply on the strength of its aged quality—where Chapman sounds fearful, B.B. sounds defiant; where Chapman sounds fragile, B.B. sounds strong. B.B.'s first recorded venture with Eric Clapton, a reprise of "Rock Me Baby," features a mid-song shootout between the two guitar masters, serviceable vocals, and an odd, cavernous sound, as if it had been recorded in an empty club or a basement. A mellow take on Percy Mayfield's "Please Send Me Someone to Love," with lush strings and atmospheric Hammond B3 fills by Chris Stainton, is essentially an object lesson in the difference between an artist and an artisan: when B.B. digs into one of Mayfield's socially conscious lyrics, his voice brings the weight of history to bear on the words he sings; when Mick Hucknall sings lyrics such

"I find that the pop songs, the country songs, jazz tunes, the blues, all seem to have a very close tie." Captured between takes at Ocean Way Recording in Hollywood, B.B. takes a break with his partners in swing on a re-imagined version of Jay McShann's classic "Confessin' the Blues" recorded for the *Deuces Wild* album. Back row, from left, are: Jim Keltner (drums), Bill Payne (keyboards), Marty Stuart (guitar, vocals), Joette Phillips (project assistant), producer John Porter, project coordinator Tisha Fein, Mickey Raphael (harmonica) and Marty Stuart's manager, Bonnie Garner. In the front row, from left, are Tommy Eyre (keyboards), Randy Jacobs (guitar) and B.B.

as "peace will enter when hate is gone," he sounds like he's reading from a broadside rather than feeling it deep down. B.B. doesn't croon this beautiful ballad, as Mayfield did; rather, he attacks it as a gospel warrior, selling every heartbreaking sentiment to the hilt. A gospel chorus, Leon Pendarvis's tasty organ, a stinging guitar solo by B.B., and a sizzling slide guitar retort by Bonnie Raitt fuel a rendition of "Baby I Love You" that starts at a slow boil and reaches a roiling state as the last few bars come in sight. Jerry Ragovoy's mid-tempo R&B lament, "Ain't Nobody Home," tries to walk the line between the more macho style of testifying of B.B.'s generation and the wimpy, falsetto whining of Prince-style R&B. B.B. takes the gold for expressiveness, but D'Angelo, like Mick Hucknall earlier, sounds emotionally distanced from the material. D'Angelo's contemporary, rapper Heavy D, fares better on the fluffy "Keep It Coming," which finds B.B.'s Lucille in the context of a shuffling hip-hop arrangement, B.B. doing little more vocally than singing the title sentiment, but

Heavy D adding some levity by coming on to Lucille as if the instrument is a real live female ("he been fondling you for years," he quips at one point). Genial it is, but B.B.'s taut, single- string solo near the end is more captivating stylistically than anything the hip-hop arrangement has to offer. More like it is a new version of the Doc Pomus–Mac Rebennack gem "There Must Be a Better World Somewhere," with Dr. John bringing his New Orleans funk to bear on his own co-write and pitching in with a randy vocal that plays well off B.B.'s shouting, the two artists engaging each other and believing in what they sing, even to the point of improvising witty banter as the song fades out. (Clearly B.B.'s early wariness of the good doctor had worn off by this time.) This, the highlight of the album, is followed by another outstanding performance, with honky-tonk advocate Marty Stuart giving as good as he gets on a stomping take of a chestnut close to B.B.'s heart, "Confessin' the Blues." Stuart navigates his vocal parts with aplomb and passion, finding the tonk within the R&B groove, contributing a sizzling, serpentine guitar solo before yielding to B.B.'s single-string excursions, and generally sounding right at home with the King of the Blues, whose early affinity for country appears unabated. The honky-tonk state of mind informs the last song on the album as well, a languorous, convivial version of Willie Nelson's "Nightlife" that features alternating guitar solos by B.B., his electric piercing and soaring, and Nelson, plucking flurries of notes on his gut-string acoustic, as keyboardist Billy Payne sneaks in here and there with some exciting honky-tonk piano runs. A reprise of "Cryin' Won't Help You Baby" is done at a steady, mid-tempo pace rather than as a funk-driven workout as it was on *Completely Well* (when it was titled "Cryin' Won't Help You Now"). As such it's fairly undistinguished, with guests Paul Carrack and Pink Floyd guitarist David Gilmour making their respective marks with less conviction than the uncredited background chorus and B.B.'s own lively soloing. On "Dangerous Mood," the urgent vocal interplay between B.B. and Joe Cocker on the slow blues grind is invigorating—Cocker's gravelly voice and commitment to his part is matched by a similar level of engagement on B.B.'s behalf, and behind them Chris Stainton is a whirlwind on the piano, drummer Kenny Aronoff is rock solid, and B.B.'s overdubbed guitar solos are laced throughout the tight ensemble sound.

"Have I done the best I can do? Can I do a little better?"
An Interview with B.B. King

The following interview with B.B. King was conducted on February 14, 1998, at the Trump Plaza in Atlantic City, where B.B. was appearing for two nights. On assignment for *Rolling Stone*, I questioned B.B. about his new album of duets, *Deuces Wild*, and solicited his opinions on some other issues relating to his career and the blues as a genre and as a cultural statement. As is evident from some of his answers, the then-72-year-old King of the Blues was still driven to better himself as an artist, was still unsatisfied with the progress he had made over the years as a musician, and remained a bit self-conscious about his lack of formal education. In short, many of the insecurities that drove him as a young man to work harder at his art, and simply to work harder in general, continue to spur his artistry. Witty, informed, self-deprecating, perceptive, humble, serious—B.B. manifested all these qualities during the course of a near-hour-long conversation, and never seemed bored with a question, although surely he had heard some of them many times over. As always, he was most gracious about the contributions his collaborators made to *Deuces Wild*, but clearly stung by some negative critical responses to the project—so much so that he opened the interview by addressing his critics, even though he wasn't asked to. Who better to set the record straight, though, than the man himself? Beloved internationally, a true ambassador of the blues, B.B. King can talk back to anyone he wants. With or without Lucille.

I don't know that Deuces Wild *is as intense an experience as* Blues Summit, *but it mostly holds up on repeat listenings. Lots of good interchanges between you and the guest artists.*

Thank you. We're happy about it. Some of my critics have said it's the same old soup. But how can it be the same old soup if you got the Rolling Stones doing it, if you've got Dr. John doing it?

You have an interesting array of artists. Blues Summit *was exactly that—you and some other premier blues artists making no bones about it: you were singing the blues. But for* Deuces Wild *you've assembled artists from across the musical spectrum.*

That's right. And that's why I don't let [the criticism] bother me. So some of the songs were originally recorded some time back. It's funny how I think about it. I never hear anybody say too much about "Satin Doll." They just say play it. "Satin Doll." They say play "Sophisticated Lady." And they play it. So only the good tunes, as far as I'm concerned.

The greatest we've ever had, like Benny Goodman, Duke Ellington, Count Basie, you can name Lionel Hampton, many others, the songs like they played in jazz, pop, they play 'em over and over and over, 'cause they're great songs. I think some of the blues songs are great songs too. So I don't mind whenever they criticize me about playing some of them.

The collection of artists you have on here are categorized as something other than blues artists. You've got Marty Stuart and Willie Nelson, who are different genera-

tions but from the same spectrum of country; Heavy D and D'Angelo, same genera-
tion but different spectrums of contemporary R&B; got veteran artists like Joe Cocker
and Bonnie and Van Morrison, who have always made blues a touchstone of their
music but added other elements to it. Were you trying to make a point that there's
only a thin line separating these genres from blues, if there's any line at all?

It may have crossed my mind a bit. May have crossed my mind a bit. But
I'm a firm believer that music is a family. It's a country and there's the many
different styles you mentioned, but it's still a family of music. I tell you the
truth. I read music, but slowly. I learned to read by getting books from Sears
Roebuck. There used to be a guy called Nick Maniloff, a guitarist. He'd have
the guitar books in the Sears Roebuck catalog. The point I'm trying to make,
the first song I ever learned to play musically was "Oh my darling / oh my
darling / oh my darling Clementine"—that was in the book. And several others. So I learned that long before I knew "3 O'Clock Blues." Long before that.
And even today, some of the best country songs, the lyrics make good blues
songs. So I find that the pop songs, the country songs, jazz tunes, the blues,
all seem to have a very close tie.

Interesting collaboration with Heavy D on there. That was certainly unexpected.
I thought it was very gallant of you to let him bust a move on your guitar there. He
was coming on to Lucille pretty heavy.

But you know, he's a very talented person. I knew of him. I had heard
some of his work. I didn't know him very well. But he put that together right
there in the studio, right on the spot.

Making up the lyrics as he went along?

He may have had some ideas about it before we came; I didn't ask him.
But I've been against certain words in songs. It's sort of like going to see a
movie. There might be nude scenes in it, but in my opinion if it's nude scenes
just to sell the movie, I'm not really for that. If I want to see a porno, I just go
and get one. Well, the same thing I think usually about songs. If it calls for four-
letter words—I mean really calls for it and you put it in there, then I can take
it. But if it don't, some of the words I wouldn't feel comfortable taking my children or grandchildren to a concert to hear it. That's been my stand ever since
I've listened to music. Suggestive, yes. We've all done tunes that are suggestive. You know, for example, "My sweet little angel / I love the way she spread
her wings," you know what I mean. But generally we don't come out with it.

But Heavy D was very respectful to me. I don't know if he'd heard my
thoughts along those lines, but he asked me in the studio, he asked me, "Do
you mind if I use the word 'ass'?" And I said no, I don't mind at all. I hear it
on the radio and TV all the time, so why not, yes. And that's the only word

B.B. and Lucille, 1994.

that he used that might be a little different than what I normally use. I was really grateful to him for being so respectful to me. And I enjoyed working with him; had a ball.

Well, Lucille really talked back to him on that song. I think Lucille put him right down.

Yeah, well, Lucille like younger men anyhow.

I was wondering if she might have preferred an older man, the way she was protesting.

Most young girls stay with older men because of the work. Older men don't mind working; they don't try to pimp the girls at all. Lucille likes that. She can use her six strings, no problem. All the girls seem to like younger men for some good reasons.

A couple of songs on the album also remind me of another aspect of your life and career. You did the Percy Mayfield song "Send Me Someone to Love" and the Doc Pomus–Dr. John song "There Must Be a Better World Somewhere." Percy had an elegant way of insinuating social commentary into a beautiful love song. And Doc, when he was writing the songs for that album, told me was trying in a subtle way to make a statement about the things he was seeing going on around him and from the perspective of a man more experienced in the world. I know you were a friend of Martin Luther King; you play the Medgar Evers benefits—

Every year for the last 25 years.

You've very subtly made causes part of what you do as an artist. And you've made a statement in that way. Do you feel that's important for you to do that as an artist, and what would you say to young artists who are wondering if they should get involved, if they should take a position on an issue?

I would say to them, kind of like I thought. I'm not a politician, and I'm not very good at doing some of the heavy protest things like some of the people have. I work, though; I work for any movement that's good for mankind. Any movement that's good for mankind, I'll work for it. Like during civil rights, I didn't do a lot of marching like everybody, but I worked and made money to help out the causes. And I would do that today.

I could probably never write a song like "Blowin' in the Wind." I could never do that. But the guy that wrote it wrote it so beautifully that anyone that's listening could pay attention: "The answer, my friend, is blowin' in the wind." There are many others that are great songs that didn't put anybody down but just tell it like it is, in a nice way.

Would you, or do you, encourage young artists to get involved in things beyond just music and pursuing the dollar?

Sure I do. But I also tell them, you don't break the camel's back, of course, that you need to get your financial aid from. But you still stand up for your principles, you stand up for what you think is the right thing to do. And if you're good at doing it, if you're good at writing a song, performing the songs or whatever, do it. But only if this is what you want to do. Don't do it simply because somebody else think you should do it. Do it if you want to do it. The world is still a good place, but it can be a better place.

You know, you were speaking about Heavy D and having heard some of his music, and your position on lyrics and that sort of thing in popular culture. I know that you've been something of a musical historian and archivist. You have or had a massive record collection; you've given a lot of material to the University of Mississippi. You started as a DJ and you've seen the whole spectrum of popular music evolve in this country. Do you see any connection between rap and the early blues? Obviously the environment it's coming out of is different, but in terms of lyrical content and the sort of things they talk about, if you think about Robert Johnson's "32-20 Blues," Jelly Roll Morton has a seven-part "Murder Ballad" that's about as brutal as anything we've ever heard from a rapper.

That one I missed. But I am familiar with people like Blind Lemon Jefferson, for example. In one of the songs he did, he said in so many words, "black people picking and talking about collard greens / white people in the parlor having ice cream," so these little things, just little things like that, which is not much, but that was a way of showing there was a difference.

Blues has always been revealing of its culture.

Yes. I think that most of the blues singers at that time, including Memphis Slim and a few others, wrote about things but in a light way. They didn't come down real hard like a lot of the rap does today on certain issues. But it's hardly been any that didn't say some words. If you trace back you'll find, even Lonnie Johnson—I love to think of myself trying to be like him somewhat—but he still would say little things, there was things he said in some of his songs. A lot of times when we mention, for example, a lady, we would use the word, we wasn't always talking directly about a lady. We had certain other issues in mind that we talked about. But we didn't dare to say 'em out. But the smarter people generally figured 'em out anyway.

I think it's good for the young people to take leads on some of the things along those lines. I think it's good. And a lot of the kids do. You don't have to encourage them; they'll do it anyway. I believe personally that the younger generation are more outspoken and honest than a lot of us were when we were coming up. Because they were never put down.

I'll give you an example. Growing up in the South and a segregated society—and believe me, I had white friends; had it not been for some of them a lot of us wouldn't be around today. That was one of the nice things, and still is one of the nice things about the Southern people, black or white, their word usually means more to them than anything else. I could walk into a store today in Indianola, my hometown, and if a white or black person told me they would do something, they would do it. They would do it. And if they said they wasn't gonna do it, look out! They wasn't gonna do it. I think what I'm trying to say is that while growing up you would find water fountains, one had written on it white, the other written colored. The restrooms, generally, if there was one for black people, there'd be white men, white ladies, and colored. I'm trying to tell you that I grew up with this, and it was sort of like a brainwashing. And when everything was integrated, I still wasn't comfortable. Even now I go to some of the places and it's almost like, No, check this out first. I'm trying to say it takes me a while to be comfortable.

I think it's been the same thing along the line in the music business. A lot of us blues singers, when we were growing up, didn't rock the boat. Some of 'em did. But then look what happened to some of 'em. So the others didn't rock the boat because we didn't want to offend anyone. And we didn't rock the boat so much. I think I made one or two songs during the civil rights movement—one, "I'm gonna sit in / till you give in / and give me all your love," "Sit In" is what it's called. I wasn't thinking so much about the lady as what it implied. But that was a time when the sit-ins was around, so I didn't get a lot into that. Like I say to many people today, especially when you're traveling around the world, you go out of this country to other countries and always somebody want to ask you how is the race relations. And it usually bugs me sometimes, because I've gone into many countries where there was one race of people and they're killing each other and doing all this, and I say to myself, How can you ask me that? Here in the U.S. we got 100,000 different-ent cultures; in other words, we can't go to war today without fighting some of our people somewhere in the world. We go to Iraq, we got people here from Iraq; we got people here from you name it. We kill each other, but not as much as a lot of them do when it's one people! So that part bothers me sometimes. And usually everybody want to ask me about race relations, and I say I think we doing good. Compared to a country where it's just one race of people and they have different religions and they kill each other because of that. We don't do that. You see what I'm saying.

Another sort of homecoming on this album is that Rolling Stones cut because you have a history with them. In 1970 you opened a few dates for them on their U.S. tour and that was important in expanding your audience right after "The Thrill Is Gone" was a big hit. What was it like seeing them again?

It's always fun, it's like old homecoming. You see, legendary people like the Rolling Stones, they are there. They've stood the test of time; they are there. And to work with them, they're so professional. Oh, man, nobody more professional than they are.

Was it easy to get the take on the song?

Oh yeah. I don't have the European version of the album, but there's a few other songs more on the European version of the CD than on the U.S. version. Dionne Warwick, for example, is on it. We do "Hummingbird," which is to me one of my favorite cuts. And there are a couple of others that we did that are not promoted in the U.S. Some very good takes that you don't hear.

We hardly did more than two to three takes of anything on the whole album. That just shows you how professional these people are. They are professionals. And working with the Rolling Stones, and Keith Richards, you know, he always want to cut my head with the guitar [*laughs*]. We're good friends. He's terrific. And wasn't drinking. That day we did these he wasn't doing anything, nothing. I tell you that day he played, and had fun with me, 'cause he always plays things I can't and he knows it.

You know they're on this massive world tour and there's obviously another couple of generations finding them. I wonder if by having them on your album, some younger generations are going to find you. You'll be rediscovered. Again.

I hope so. That's one of the great things about having these giants in the business. When I was with U2 that opened up a whole new avenue for B.B. King. I was surprised, Van Morrison, you know I had a couple of black ladies tell me, "God, I'm so crazy about that guy. You got him?!" In other words, they were fans of his long before. And I'm telling myself, Black chicks doing this? And the song was, you know, "If I loved you, I'd do all of this," and I'm saying, My God, this is not only opening a new avenue as far as the world is concerned, but black people that hadn't paid any attention to me. He was so good, that's why I didn't try to sing on it. What we decided to do was, John Porter the producer, he said, "B.B. what do you think?" I said, "I guess I'm thinking the same thing you are—leave it alone. I'll just play on it." I felt very comfortable playing on it.

You still go down to Mississippi, you're from there, I'm sure you're aware of what's going on there with the casinos coming in. I spend a lot of time down there too, and I notice in the southern Delta a lot of the cotton fields, the soybean fields are disappearing. The motel chains are coming in there, buying up the land, and it's being paved over to accommodate the casino crowd. I wonder if it concerns you in some way to see the fields disappearing. A lot of music has come out of that connection. But in that part of Mississippi generations will be growing up never knowing the land in an intimate way. No one mourns the demise of sharecropping and the inequities, financial and otherwise, that came with it. But what about losing that spiritual connection to the earth beneath your feet? Waking up to find that the earth has been cemented over to accommodate gas marts and parking lots.

I think of it like an old saying: Nothing is ever destroyed, it's just changed into something else. For example, when I was growing up cotton was king. Nothing more than cotton. In fact, in a lot of the areas, we didn't have that much corn crops because cotton took it up. Then later on it became peanuts and then soybeans and so on.

I'm thinking that we'll always have plantations and we'll find something to raise on them that's good. Work as a whole has been something that most of us take pride in, because it gives you freedom. Even though the slaves, a lot of them, the reason they sang blues wasn't because of the work, but you took my woman, you sold my family—that's what hurt me. So that's what I'm singing about.

You can always have that. I personally believe that blues has to do with people, places, and things. And as long as you got people, they gonna have something to argue about, one way or the other. And the argument is, I get more rice than I want, or I don't get enough molasses—something! And if it has to do with the environment, we're concerned about many things and we sing about them.

Each new generation seems to find the blues, no matter the other musical trends. Musical trends come and go, the blues endures. New generations find you, find artists who came before you, they find newcomers like Jonny Lang, they found Stevie Ray Vaughan. What's the source of the blues' enduring appeal?

I wish I knew. I have an idea. For one thing, it's not so sophisticated. Blues is subtle; it's simple. People use the word simplistic, but everybody can't do it. It's like an ingredient to pecan pie or something. Many people like it, but not too many people can make it.

Blues is also honesty. You can say what you're gonna say with a minimum of words. Of course, most of us would like to do like the great singers—Frank Sinatra, Nat Cole—and paint this beautiful picture. The lady, I can see her now, down in the meadow—what the hell is a meadow?—but there is this pretty lady you see with this negligee kind of dress on. So you can see this pond not far from her. And all of us can picture this; all men that love women can see all this. But then this guy wants to make it with her, so he paints all these beautiful pictures of her in this song. When a blues singer will go and say, "Baby, I'm crazy about you. I sure wish I could keep you tonight." One of those. To some women, they would understand it and wouldn't be offended, 'cause they know you comin' from the heart. Some might smack your face, but most of them would not. Because that's the way we are as a people. And I think the kids get that—not the sexual part, that's not it; I'm talking about the honesty part. Just coming direct. I think that helps in a lot of cases.

From a personal standpoint, what is the challenge for you now? You've achieved so much in your life and career—wealth beyond anything you could ever imagine, material goods, heads of state change their schedules to meet you when you come to foreign countries. I wonder, how blue can you get?

[*Laughs heartily*] Mighty blue sometimes. I remember reading something once where the Hertz rental car company was saying "We're Number One." And Avis said, "We're Number Two, But We Try Harder." Well, once you get to be 72 years old, and you have a lot of people always praising you, you have to watch to keep your head from inflating—keep punching holes in it every once in a while to deflate it—but after a while you start to believe that people are for real and they're praising you because they're doing it because they want to; they don't have to. I start to think, Have I done the best I can do? Can I do a little better? Do I really deserve some of these things that the people have given me?

This is not false modesty. Because after a while you start to saying—and people sometimes seem to do this to you—after you make a certain name, get to a certain place, they seem to want to pick on you then. You know, "He does the same old thing all the time." So you had to work hard to get there. I think what I'm trying to tell you now is that any day I don't learn something new is a day lost. I'm not trying to compete with anyone anymore but myself. Only me. And I know my limitations. I hear these people playing—George Benson, Kenny Burrell—and wherever they got these guitars from, those notes ain't on my guitar.

And then I don't feel so bad. They didn't have airplanes during the days of Jesus Christ. But we do have 'em today. But it shows, to me, between that time and now, we've made some progress. But God, I've got a long ways to go. Long ways to go. All that practicing I still can't find them notes, so I think they cheated me on my guitar.

So a lot of times—I'd like to share this with you—you're with a bunch of people, especially young people who ask you a bunch of questions and half of 'em I don't know. But luckily I got a computer now and a CD-ROM, so if they ask me something I don't know, I sneak back in and try to find it. There's so much I don't know. But you do get a lot of knowledge in 72 years. Get a lot of knowledge. There's so much I don't know that I want to know. There's not a day passes, if I don't learn something—I don't care if it's only a word—but just that little bit, that may not mean much to most people, but to me it means a hell of a lot. Because I didn't finish high school. I had to walk five miles to school each day. But I could've done better; I could've done better; I could've done much better than what I've done.

As you said, I've made money, I've done very well lately. It took me years and years before we started to make any money. But today I could retire right now, and would never have to work any more the rest of my life. And could live pretty good. I'm not a rich man, but we've made good investments, so I could live. But as I travel around the world, I meet all these great people, and I always miss the education that I didn't get. I've heard that money can't buy love; maybe it can't, but it can buy you a lot of things that will teach you a lot of things. And that has been good for me, as far as tutoring myself in many ways. But it still don't take the place of that education that I should've had. And I think most of us that didn't have it always live each day trying to get your nose up a little bit further out of the water, because you know your limitations. People praise you and do all these things that swell your head in some ways, but if you're like me you deflate it right quick. You know everybody means well, but you know you can't do this—I know. I have talent, yes, I play guitar pretty well. But I never thought about it until I heard John Lennon, in an interview, someone asked him what he'd like to do and he said, "Play guitar like B.B. King." When I read that I almost fell out of my chair.

Because to me it was just having fun. Having fun, trying to make a living. But when somebody as great as John Lennon said B.B. King, I said, Oh my God, I can't believe it. Then I started to pay more attention. So now, each night when I hit the stage, I don't know what young person might like B.B. King, but believe me, I do the best I can do. A lot of times the best is not as good as I'd like it to be, but you believe me—it was the best that I could do. Each night. I don't care feeling good or bad. When I hit the stage, I feel good. When I get off I may feel like dying [*laughs*]. But I'm serious, because to me that means the most.

A year or so ago I found a little bit of footage of one of my idols, T-Bone Walker. I found a little footage of Lonnie Johnson that they did on him while he was in Canada. Two of my great idols. I'm happy to say that when I die my fans won't have to worry about that. They will read much about me, they'll get a chance to know me almost as well as I know myself. That's another reason I play as hard each night. People say I do the same thing over and over; maybe so, but it's the best I can do, over and over. Just hoping that my fans won't have to go through what I've had to go through trying to find things on people. Wished I could've seen Blind Lemon play. Wished I could've seen Django Reinhardt play. Finally found a little bit; they've got a video where they're talking about him, but there's about two or three minutes maybe of him playing. That to me is like heaven. Never did get a chance to see Charlie Christian play. But loved him.

I would like to say I'm happiest at this time as I've ever been in my life. Happiest I've ever been in my life. I know where I can get me a room tonight. I know where I can eat tomorrow. And I got a good guitar. Lot of friends. Lot of people I believe care about me, and a lot of people I love. So I'm very happy.

Note: Deuces Wild *sold more than 700,000 copies in the United States, more than 1.4 million worldwide, making it B.B.'s best-selling album to this point.*

Chapter 16

SIMPLIFY, SIMPLIFY, SIMPLIFY!

Blues on the Bayou

MCA, 1998
Produced by B.B. King
Executive producer: Sidney A. Seidenberg
Recorded by Tony Daigle at Dockside Studios, Maurice, Louisiana
Engineer assistant: Jim Watts
Mixed by John Porter at Sound Castle, Los Angeles; mix engineer: Joe McGrath
String arrangements: Phil Marshall
Mastered by Stephen Marcussen at Precision Lacquer, Hollywood, California

Musicians
B.B. King: guitar
James Bolden: bandleader, trumpet
Walter R. King: contractor
Tony Coleman: percussion
Calep Emphrey, Jr.: drums
Melvin Jackson: saxophone
Leon Warren: guitar
Michael Doster: bass
James Sells Toney: keyboards
Stanley Abernathy: trumpet

Songs
"Blues Boys Tune" (B.B. King)
"Bad Case of Love" (B.B. King)

"I'll Survive" (B.B. King–Sam Ling)
"Mean Ole' World" (B.B. King)
"Blues Man" (B.B. King)
"Broken Promise" (B.B. King–Sam Ling)
"Darlin' What Happened" (B.B. King)
"Shake It Up and Go" (B.B. King–J. Taub)
"Blues We Like" (B.B. King)
"Good Man Gone Bad" (B.B. King–J. Taub–F. Wash)
 "If I Lost You" (B.B. King–J. Taub)
"Tell Me Baby" (B.B. King–Sam Ling)
"I Got Some Outside Help I Don't Need" (B.B. King–D. Clark)
"Blues in 'G'" (B.B. King)
"If That Ain't It I Quit" (B.B. King)

Regardless of their commercial success, *Blues Summit*, *Heart to Heart*, and *Deuces Wild* were something akin to novelty items, with generous amounts of bonhomie among the participants, good spirit, and, in some instances, some outstanding music. But it was time again for something deeper, a statement, and for this B.B. ventured to the Deep South, to Maurice, Louisiana, about six miles from Lafayette, where he set up shop at

Dockside Studios. The facility had been recommended to him by an MCA executive who had scouted it out as a location for the next Cowboy Mouth sessions. Located on a 12-acre, 30-year-old plantation, the studio is owned by Steve Nails and his wife Wish and rests in a bucolic setting dotted with 500-year-old trees and sporting a large, fully stocked fishing pond. Steve Wish is a former guitarist now wheelchair bound as the result of an accident a few years ago. His studio has become a drawing card on the strength of its vintage gear.

"All vintage equipment," Steve says. "I'm using a 1978 discrete Neve console, and there's no IC chips in the whole board. It's completely the old stuff. The first *Rocky* movie was made on this Neve board. It's the very first Neve board by Rupert Neve with no IC chips. I have all vintage mics, and Steve Doerr TAD monitors."

Of B.B., who recorded two albums at his facility, Steve echoes most other people's sentiments: "He's a gentleman, a total gentleman. He's the nicest person I've ever met in the music business."

But did he go fishing?

"No, he didn't fish," Steve says, chuckling. "But he ate it."[1]

Blues on the Bayou also marked, for the first time since 1975's *Lucille Talks Back*, B.B. taking a producer credit on an album, and the first time he had recorded in the studio with his road band since 1985.

"Over the past five decades I've enjoyed having others produce my music," B.B. writes in his liner notes. "Many of those producers were great, and many of those productions led to hits.

"But recently I've felt the urge to go back to basics. Maybe it's my age— I'm turning 73 this year—or maybe my conviction that this current band is my best ever. Whatever the reason, I wanted to simplify. And this was my simple idea: go to a studio and, without a lot of fanfare, cut B.B. King songs with B.B. King's band under B.B.'s supervision.

"Well, it worked."

He describes the setting at Dockside as "kicked back," the feeling "downhome."

"Me and the fellas had a ball. No one was telling us what to do. No one needed to tell us what to do. After all, this is the band I travel with—play with, live and die with night after night, 225 nights a year."

The song selection was a typical blend of old and new, "I'll Survive," "Broken Promise," "Darlin' What Happened," "Shake It Up and Go," "Good Man Gone Bad," "If I Lost You," "Tell Me Baby," and "I Got Some Outside Help I Don't Need" being pulled from the vault and reconfigured in striking terms.

In an impressive show of strength and sensitivity by the band, keyboardist James Sells Toney has another momentous outing. He has the first word on the album opening "Blues Boys Tune," with an urgent blast of organ chords before Lucille enters crying the blues and takes over the instrumental showcase. His rolling fills on "Blues Man" add a murky atmosphere to the lament that B.B. sings so soft and quizzically. The powerful "Broken Promise" is keyed by the full-bodied sound of Toney's organ humming along behind B.B.'s edgy, shouting vocal. The reworked "I'll Survive" finds B.B. shouting the lyrics but caressing the title sentiment, investing it with powerful, sad feeling, as if he doesn't believe his own vow to overcome the heartbreak of a breakup; when he cries out "God bless you!" in the second verse, he allows his anger to surface fleetingly, and as it does the strings rise gracefully and Toney once again lays on the blues hard with discursive right-hand trills, arpeggios, and blocks of chords. "Blues We Like" is another slow, surging instrumental showcase for Lucille charged up by an orchestral crescendo about midway followed by a heated blast of horns before it settles back into its meditative groove—though Toney's insistent right-hand runs threaten to raise the temperature a bit. Towards the end the horns break out in a swaying to-and-fro riff lifted (not for the first time on a B.B. King recording) from Ray Charles's "Night Time Is the Right Time." Two old songs back to back, "Good Man Gone Bad" and "If I Lost You," inspire B.B. to his most moving ballad treatments here. The latter is the killer number of the two, a string-laden pledge of love and devotion from a man who does not present himself as wronged but rather as flawed. Deeply devoted to his long-term partner but lamenting "all the lies I told you," such as "giving you the stars," buying her minks, diamonds, two brand-new cars each year, he sounds not a little bit awed at the woman's commitment to him. He's contrite to the nth degree, the polar opposite of the man who raked a high-maintenance woman over the coals in "Every Day I Have the Blues" for scorning the good things he brought to her ("I bought you a ten-dollar dinner / you said thanks for the snack"). All in all, it's an interesting choice for him to have reworked in his 73rd year, although he has hardly abandoned mean-woman blues, on record (a fierce version of the merciless "I Got Some Outside Help I Don't Need") or in concert. Balance is everything.

Some of the most positive reviews in his career greeted the release of *Blues on the Bayou*, and B.B. came back to Dockside two years later, again behind the board, to cut *Makin' Love Is Good for You*. Prior to that, though, he had another date with Stewart Levine, for a project close to his heart, and the fulfillment of a dream long deferred.

Let the Good Times Roll
The Music of Louis Jordan

MCA, 1999

Produced by Stewart Levine

Executive producer: Sidney A. Seidenberg

Engineered and mixed by Rik Pekkonen

Assistant engineer: Al Sanderson

Recorded and mixed at Cello Recording Studios, Hollywood, California

Mastered by Bernie Grundman at Bernie Grundman Mastering, Hollywood, California

Musicians

Dr. John: piano; vocals, "Is You Is, or Is You Ain't (My Baby)"

Earl Palmer: drums

Russell Malone: rhythm guitar

John Heard: bass

Neil Larsen: Hammond organ; piano, "Saturday Night Fish Fry"

Hank Crawford: alto sax

David "Fathead" Newman: tenor sax

Marcus Belgrave: trumpet

Lenny Castro: percussion

Horns arranged by Hank Crawford

Rhythm charts by Neil Larsen

Songs
"Ain't Nobody Here but Us Chickens" (2:51) (Joan Whitney–Alex Kramer)
"Is You Is, or Is You Ain't (My Baby)" (3:22) (Billy Austin–Louis Jordan)
"Beware, Brother, Beware" (3:07) (Morry Lasco–Dick Adams–Fleecie Moore)
"Somebody Done Changed the Lock on My Door" (3:28) (William Weldon)
"Ain't That Just Like a Woman" (3:30) (Claude Demetrius–Fleecie Moore)
"Choo Choo Ch'Boogie" (2:37) (Vaughn Horton–Milton Gabler–Denver Darling)
"Buzz Me" (2:52) (Danny Baxter–Fleecie Moore)
"Early in the Mornin'" (4:47) (Leo Hickman–Louis Jordan–Dallas Bartley)
"I'm Gonna Move to the Outskirts of Town" (4:49) (William Weldon–Andy Razaf)
"Jack, You're Dead!" (2:09) (Walter Bishop–Dick Miles)
"Knock Me a Kiss" (2:40) (Mike Jackson–Andy Razaf)
"Let the Good Times Roll" (2:39) (Sam Theard–Fleecie Moore)
"Caldonia" (2:17) (Fleecie Moore)
"It's a Great, Great Pleasure" (2:38) (Louis Jordan–William Tennyson, Jr.)
"Rusty Dusty Blues (Mama Mama Blues)" (4:17) (J. Mayo Williams)
"Sure Had a Wonderful Time Last Night" (3:07) (Claude Demetrius–Fleecie Moore)
"Saturday Night Fish Fry" (4:24) (Ellis Walsh–Louis Jordan)
"Nobody Knows You When You're Down and Out" (4:34) (J. Cox)

Out in Pacific Palisades, California, B.B. King was on Stewart Levine's mind. He was thinking about how B.B. had told him his two dream albums would be a gospel record and a tribute to Louis Jordan. Levine knew B.B. had recorded Louis Jordan tunes over the years, but never an entire album devoted to the jump-blues master's music. Lo and behold, MCA called, asking him to do another B.B. album, another duets album, a "big album with a big budget," to capitalize on the success of Frank Sinatra's *Duets*. Most of the artists had already been confirmed, and when Levine read the lineup, he declined, not so politely, to wit: "Fuck you, man. Not interested."[2]

But Levine couldn't get the Louis Jordan tribute idea out of his head. MCA was intrigued, and an A&R executive scheduled a lunch with Levine to discuss the concept. Levine found the repast to be on the far end of the horrific scale.

"The A&R people at the record company, by this time there were all these aliens, you know what I mean? Some English guy, he was just alien," Levine recalled. "I had breakfast with him, and he didn't know anything, nothing. Didn't have basic language skills. I walked away and said, 'Goddamn, man, I hope they just let me make this and we'll hope for the best.' Well, they did let me make it and I didn't hope for the best, and it was the ultimate secret release." (About which more later.)

Levine promptly pored over a multi-disc Louis Jordan box set that had been released by the German Bear Family label. He whittled the song selection down to 25 numbers, all short songs that Levine wanted to record as close to the original versions as possible, all "salient, the ones that were known." Then he assembled a dream team of a band.

"I got in touch with Hank Crawford, who I thought had to play the part of Louis Jordan, and he was way up for it. Then Mac, Dr. John, came in—I love this rhythm section—and I got Earl Palmer out of mothballs and he came out to play. And John Heard, a great, great bass player out of L.A., played upright. Russell Malone played guitar—I found out Russell loved Louis Jordan and loved B.B. and he could comp that way. Neil Larsen played some organ and he wrote the rhythm charts. It was a fuckin' good band. I put together the original Ray Charles band with Marcus Belgrave and Fathead Newman. It was a killer. The budget was there to do it nice; everybody got paid well. And B.B. really did his homework on that one. His eyesight was failing by that time. He'd had some kind of surgery with cataracts or something had happened."

The side trip on this album was a movie MCA had commissioned on the making of the Louis Jordan tribute album. On the first day of shooting, Levine walked into the studio to find B.B. bathed in huge lights so bright he couldn't see a foot in front of him. Levine threw the crew out of the studio and called a friend of his in England, Lol Creme, who had been part of the '70s British pop band 10 cc and, along with his partner Kevin Godley, a pioneering music video auteur.

The result was, in Levine's estimation, "a shockingly great piece of work. Lol came down to the studio, just on his own, with a handheld Steadicam type of thing and filmed the whole making of this record, and edited it into a one-hour documentary. Fantastic, man. Black and white, a real covering of a real recording session. And they were going to get it placed on the A&E channel and all this shit. And when the record came out it was a complete secret release, because they were preparing for B.B. to do this record with Clapton. I don't know what the politics were behind it, why they would let us make it, then barely release it, and then didn't do anything with this film, which is a killer. This guy shot it over three days with a camera himself, just one of those little $1,000 things, and cut it together in a brilliant way, put interviews on it. It really gives you the feeling on the inside of the making of that record, 'cause there were no lights or anything."

Let the Good Times Roll is a gem. First, it's a meaty fest, clocking in at close to an hour and a half of music, 18 songs in all. Second, the vibe on the album is captivating; the band takes things at a steady pace, never overplaying or blasting the blues, but rather reining in the volume in favor of a sumptuous mood, late-night but spirited, celebratory, life-affirming. Vocally B.B. is at the top of his game, swinging through uptempo movers such as "Jack, You're Dead!" and crooning with feeling on the likes of "Early in the Mornin'." Jordan wrote vivid, clever lyrics, and B.B. sounds like he's having the time of his life with the propulsive rhythms and hot jive on "Saturday Night Fish Fry."

Levine: "The end of the story is fantastic. My daughter Sophie wasn't even two yet. She came running into this big studio, Ocean Way Studios in L.A., and I had a microphone, which was like a talkback, you know, and a Shure 57, a vocal mic. She came running up to me and takes the microphone and holds it in her hand like she's going to sing. But she holds it sort of underneath the way a singer does—how the fuck did she know? This guy who made the film made a still of it and it's a gorgeous photograph.

"So now it's about three months later, and I've gone to see B.B. at the North Sea Jazz Festival in Holland, would have been July of 1999. Had a very poignant hour with B.B. Got there early and he hadn't gone on yet, and we were alone in the dressing room. We got down with each other, and he told me some really wonderful things, man, some honest shit about life on the road, his life and all that shit. It was beautiful. Just as he was ready to go out, I took out the snapshot of my little daughter at the studio with the microphone in her hand. Beautiful picture. He just looked at it for a while and shook his head. 'Unbelievable,' he said. He went out on stage and he did an hour. Sat down, as he does now. There was 16,000 people there. And I wanted to get out, didn't want to hang out after hours, which is why I went to see B.B. first, you see. So I'm standing on the side of the stage. As he comes off I'm gonna say, 'Nice set, B,' and give him a big hug. He's sweatin' like a pig. He gives me a big hug. I said, 'I'm gonna run off now.' He looks at me and says, 'You know, Stew,' pulls his head back and says, 'the whole time I was up there I was thinkin', "How's Sophie know how to hold that microphone like that?"' I kinda just looked at him and said, 'I don't know, B, it must be in the genes or some shit.' I walked off and thought to myself, This motherfucker just sang for an hour and he tells me the whole time he's up there he's thinkin' about that. So there's something in that story.

"That was the last time I saw B.B."

One of the ironies of *Let the Good Times Roll* is that it was nominated for a Grammy for "Is You Is, or Is You Ain't (My Baby)" in the category of Best Pop Vocal Duo by a Male or Female. "Now the record had come out and nobody even knew it was out," Levine said. "This was like eight months later or something.

"My wife said to me, 'They'll probably give it to B.B. because he's an old man,' and Mac said, 'B.B. ain't ever gonna be old enough to get that fuckin' award, you know.' So I didn't even watch the Grammys that year. I had some health issues and wasn't in great shape. Mac called me the next morning from the airport and said, 'The muthafucker won the Best Pop Vocal award at the Grammys.' The hypocrisy of the whole thing is that nobody heard that record and voted for it. It was just the name seemed like a better choice than the next guy. I didn't want to make records for three years after that. It pissed me off; what happened to that record really made me angry. I took a little time off."

Then Levine asked how many albums he had done with B.B. Told the number was six, he laughed. "God bless, man. I'm happy about that.

"Maybe there's one more left."

A Conversation with Stewart Levine
"Records are snapshots. They're still photographs. They should be made quickly and they should have a certain kind of danger. That's the magic of them."

You're one of the few producers B.B.'s worked with who basically put him in the studio with new songs. And you did that on all the records, Louis Jordan being the exception, but that was a concept piece. No one had done that to the degree you did it.

There's a couple of reasons no one had done that. It's hard to find songs. If you don't find them, you have to make them, and you have to have somebody who's writin' them who understands a whole lotta shit—you gotta understand him, you gotta understand the tradition he comes from and be able to pull off writing new songs. Not an easy task. You gotta remember, I went to some brilliant guys. Joe Sample and Will Jennings understood exactly what it was that I was looking for or that was necessary. And obviously Doc Pomus understood it as well or better than anybody. That was it. I didn't go any further—if it wasn't for those guys I wouldn't have had nothin'. So that's part of what I felt I needed to do if I was gonna take on this responsibility of making these records, that we introduced him to new music and the challenge of making them. What was great about his performances on these records is that they were new to him. I remember Smokey Robinson telling me, "You know, when you record 'My Girl' the first time, you never dream you're gonna sing it for thirty fuckin' years. You just kinda go in there and it's three minutes of your life and it's a new moment." I always believed records are snapshots. They're still photographs. They're not movies, you know what I mean? They should be made quickly and they should have a certain kind of danger, and that's the magic of them. It's not just me that thinks so. If you follow the history of recording, you'll see from the early recordings straight through, the great records of Motown and the Beatles and everybody else, no one fucked around with these things. They went in, got 'em done, they were prepared, and they went home. There was something about the tension of not knowing—that the audience doesn't even know this, but the artist is discovering these things just a little bit before they do. That's why when you re-record things that have been done and you're so familiar with, they become really difficult to do. Because what are you going to bring that's new to them, you know? So that's what we tried to do. I'm quite proud of these records. I like them all, and the ones that didn't do as well as the others, I like as well as any of them. I think we did well by him.

Regardless of sales figures, musically they're good records.

And you know that's all that's really necessary. With a guy who's had 75, 80 albums, it's not necessary, it really isn't, to have hits each time out or for them to do really well. Even the record company, as much as I put them down, they know that. They know you just have to continue to make records that have some integrity. It would be really bad now, with an 80-year-old guy, for them to try to find one more trick for him. I don't know that—who the fuck knows? Maybe he should be making another one. There is one record left in him, and that's the gospel record.

I'm sure at some point you developed a notion of what the producer's role is vis-à-vis an artist. Do you have to become the artist's friend? Who are you as the producer relative to the artist?

The audience. I'm the guy they gotta get past. They got to turn me on. They gotta get past me. In terms of the performance, I try to be the judge and jury. You gotta get me, man. You gotta be honest, you're gonna have to do a good piece of work, and you're gonna have to ring my bell, man. I have no predisposed idea of what it should be, I just want to enjoy it. So if I'm not enjoying it, no one else is gonna enjoy it. Although I'm a musician, and rather cultured in that way, when I'm producing I try to walk that line between knowing technically what it's all about and musically what it's all about, and then trying to be, as they say in England, the punter. I try to be the guy in the street who's gonna listen to it. And not a dummy in the street, but somebody who has a predisposed reason to want to like it. So I try to make the artist feel, create an environment where they're comfortable, and then I expect them to do their very best work and not feel like they're in an isolated situation, the cold thing that happens in recording. I try to make it a warm environment and let them know in fact you're not singing to one person, but this is your whole audience. I represent everybody, so knock me out, man. That's kinda it.

My premise is, it's the artist, and it comes from being an old-fashioned arranger, that if you made the artist sound good, the singer sound good, they call you back and pay you again [*laughs*]. Yeah.

Another feature that was part of all your B.B. productions was the gospel feel, through the music, the singers, or both. "There Is Always One More Time" has that Joe Sample piano intro that's right outta the church. You never let go of that gospel thing.

I felt it was really where his heart was, where his soul was. To be honest, B.B. has been my only exposure to making blues records. I'm fairly knowledgeable about the blues, but it's not an area I spend a huge amount of time in. I was a straightahead jazz guy, then I got into rhythm and blues, then a lot of world music, a lot of this, a lot of that. I was obsessed with Lightnin' Hopkins early on and the real blues, I always liked it.

But I always felt B.B. had the blues, man. That's not what I was there to bring to it. I came to it from a place of being more like a fan, if you know what I mean. And I tried to dig into the things that people didn't know about B.B.'s taste, and I knew that included the sophistication of jazz and the heart and soul of gospel. So I kept jazz guys around him. And if you look at his bands, he always had good jazz guys playing with him, from George Coleman straight through. B.B. loved the idea intellectually of being around players that he felt were high-class and—I'm quoting him—superior to him. Stupid fucking remark, you know, even though he made it.

Riding with the King _____

Reprise, 2000
Produced by Eric Clapton and Simon Climie
ProTools: Simon Climie
Engineer: Alan Douglas
Assistant Engineer: Tom Sweeney
Tracks 2, 3, 5, 8, 9, 10 mixed by Alan Douglas
Tracks 1, 4, 6, 7, 12 mixed by Mick Guzauski

Songs

"Riding with the King" (4:23) (John Hiatt) B.B. King: guitars, vocals; Eric Clapton: guitars, vocals; Andy Fairweather Low: guitar; Doyle Bramhall II: guitar; Nathan East: bass; Steve Gadd: drums; Tim Carmon: Hammond organ; Joe Sample: piano, Wurlitzer; Susannah Melvoin, Wendy Melvoin: backing vocals; Paul Waller: drum programming

"Ten Long Years" (4:39) (Riley B. King–Jules Bihari) B.B. King: guitars, vocals; Eric Clapton: guitars, vocals; Andy Fairweather Low: guitar; Doyle Bramhall II:

guitar; Nathan East: bass; Steve Gadd: drums; Tim Carmon: Hammond organ; Joe Sample: Hammond organ; Paul Waller: drum programming

"Key to the Highway" (3:40) (William Broonzy–Charles Seger) B.B. King: guitars, vocals; Eric Clapton: guitars, vocals; Nathan East: bass; Steve Gadd: drums; Tim Carmon: Hammond organ; Paul Waller: drum programming

"Marry You" (5:00) (Doyle Bramhall II–Susannah Melvoin–Craig Ross) B.B. King: guitars, vocals; Eric Clapton: guitars, vocals; Andy Fairweather Low: guitar; Doyle Bramhall II: guitar; Nathan East: bass; Steve Gadd: drums; Tim Carmon: Hammond organ; Joe Sample: Wurlitzer; Susannah Melvoin, Wendy Melvoin, Doyle Bramhall II: backing vocals; Paul Waller: drum programming

"3 O'Clock Blues" (2:55) (Riley B. King–Jules Taub) B.B. King: guitars, vocals; Eric Clapton: guitars, vocals; Nathan East: bass; Steve Gadd: drums; Tim Carmon: Hammond organ; Joe Sample: piano

"Help the Poor" (5:06) (Charles Singleton) B.B. King: guitars, vocals; Eric Clapton: guitars, vocals; Andy Fairweather Low: guitar; Doyle Bramhall II: guitar; Jimmie Vaughan: guitar; Nathan East: bass; Steve Gadd: drums; Tim Carmon: Hammond organ; Joe Sample: Rhodes; Susannah Melvoin, Wendy Melvoin: backing vocals

"I Wanna Be" (4:46) (Doyle Bramhall II–Charlie Sexton) B.B. King: guitars, vocals; Eric Clapton: guitars, vocals; Andy Fairweather Low: guitar; Doyle Bramhall II: guitar; Jimmie Vaughan: guitar; Nathan East: bass; Steve Gadd: drums; Tim Carmon: Hammond organ; Joe Sample: Rhodes; Susannah Melvoin, Wendy Melvoin: backing vocals; Paul Waller: drum programming

"Worried Life Blues" (4:26) (Maceo Merriweather) B.B. King, Eric Clapton: guitars, vocals; Nathan East: bass; Steve Gadd: drums; Paul Waller: drum programming

"Days of Old" (3:00) (B.B. King–Jules Taub) B.B. King: guitars, vocals; Eric Clapton: guitars, vocals; Andy Fairweather Low: guitar; Doyle Bramhall II: guitar; Nathan East: bass; Steve Gadd: drums; Tim Carmon: Hammond organ; Joe Sample: Rhodes; Susannah Melvoin, Wendy Melvoin: backing vocals; Paul Waller: drum programming

"My Heart Beats Like a Hammer" (7:08) (B.B. King–Jules Taub) B.B. King: guitars, vocals; Eric Clapton: guitars, vocals; Andy Fairweather Low: guitar; Doyle Bramhall II: guitar; Nathan East: bass; Steve Gadd: drums; Tim Carmon: Hammond organ; Joe Sample: piano; Paul Waller: drum programming

"Hold On I'm Coming" (6:21) (Isaac Hayes–David Porter) B.B. King: guitars, vocals; Eric Clapton: guitars, vocals; Andy Fairweather Low: guitar; Doyle Bramhall II: guitar; Nathan East: bass; Steve Gadd: drums; Tim Carmon: Hammond organ; Joe Sample: piano; Paul Waller: drum programming

"Come Rain or Come Shine" (4:11) (Johnny Mercer–Harold Arlen) B.B. King: guitars, vocals; Eric Clapton: guitars, vocals; Andy Fairweather Low: guitar; Doyle Bramhall II: guitar; Nathan East: bass; Steve Gadd: drums; Tim Carmon: Hammond organ; Joe Sample: piano; Paul Waller: drum programming; Arif Mardin: string arrangement and orchestration

B.B. and Eric Clapton's long-discussed collaboration was a huge, multi-platinum success, but a mixed bag musically. It opens with a churning, gritty version of John Hiatt's "Riding with the King," with Clapton's stinging guitar lines soaring around all over the track, but not much of any statement from Lucille. Clapton cedes the vocal spotlight entirely on a tough rendition of a B.B. chestnut from the Modern era, "Ten Long Years." A longtime standard in Clapton's repertoire, Big Bill Broonzy's "Key to the Highway" features the two electric bluesmen going acoustic (B.B. for the first time on record since 1971's "Alexis' Boogie," on *Live in London*) and engaging in some convivial call-and-response towards the end of this slow, deliberate treatment with Delta overtones. Apart from its impressive sustained dark mood, the eight-

and-a-half-minute rendition of "3 O'Clock Blues" here is most remarkable for B.B.'s performance—a lengthy, serpentine guitar solo gets more expressive with every snarling note, and his gruff, weary vocalizing is profoundly affecting—and especially for Joe Sample's exceptional evocation of Johnny Ace and Ike Turner in his cascading rolls of right-hand runs. Big Maceo's "Worried Life Blues," a No. 48 R&B single for B.B. in an overdubbed version released in 1970 on the Kent label, is here transformed from the hymn-like take on the single (complete with organ and female background chorus) to a slow, mournful acoustic blues with the two titular artists accompanied only by bass and discreet drums; vocally, Clapton and B.B. alternate verses and complement each other beautifully in their measured phrasing and downcast attitudes. Another B.B. chestnut from the Modern era, "Days of Old," is a roiling jump blues with a swinging, shouting vocal by B.B., a sassy female chorus chanting back at him, and ferocious electric guitar soloing. Following this mayhem comes another early B.B. tune, a slow, churning blues titled "When My Heart Beats Like a Hammer" that gets down and gritty for more than seven minutes of Lucille crying to the skies, Clapton answering with robust riffs, and Sample filling in the gaps with pungent blues piano punctuations. A funky workout on the Isaac Hayes–Dave Porter Memphis soul classic "Hold On I'm Coming" is more Clapton's vocal showcase, and the clunky arrangement fulfills its destiny of undermining the subtleties in B.B.'s performance. In a nice closing touch, the album ends with an exquisite Arif Mardin orchestral arrangement of the Johnny Mercer–Harold Arlen standard, "Come Rain or Come Shine," its blues-based shadings tailor-made for B.B.'s nuanced, heartfelt vocal and evocative guitar fills. By contrast, Clapton seems out of his element vocally, phrasing clumsily and growling inappropriately and unconvincingly (an affectation, not an effect) in a show of falsely rendered angst. Despite some missteps, *Riding with the King*'s inspired moments endure—many artists would love to have back-to-back moments as convincing as "Worried Life Blues" and "Days of Old"—and render the album more than a curiosity piece in B.B.'s catalog.

"An unplugged dynamic, a contemporary dynamic, and a live blues dynamic"
Eric Clapton on *Riding with the King*

Riding with the King was the realization of a dream both artists had held close since meeting in the late 1960s. The occasion of their introduction was a show at a Greenwich Village nightclub in New York City, when Clapton, then with Cream, went to see the inaugural gig of his friend Al Kooper's new band,

B.B. and Eric Clapton in 2004, performing at the Crossroads Guitar Festival, Dallas, Texas.

Blood, Sweat and Tears. Also in the audience: B.B. King. The two were introduced, and stayed after hours, and after all the customers had left, to jam with the house band "for a couple of hours," according to Clapton.

"We kind of always tried to repeat that situation," Clapton said. "Whenever they were in the same town on the road or something, we'd try to get together and play."

Time moved on, and B.B. and Eric kept up a dialog about someday making a record together. Sincere though he was, Clapton figured it was "something we'd say, kind of like a promise that would never be kept."

In late 1998 Clapton had, in essence, an epiphany: "I thought, I really like this man, and I don't know how many opportunities we're going to have. But it seems to me I'm really going to have to make time, because otherwise it just becomes like BS, you know; you talk about these things, and I don't want to be known as a BS-er."

He asked B.B. about his plans for early 2000. B.B. was uncertain of his schedule but said, "Let's set time aside." At that point planning for the album got under way. "It takes a long time, believe it or not, to set something like this for the future," Clapton said. "I usually have to plan something like this a year in advance. And we got to it. By the time we got into the studio, we were so psyched up that it was a really quick job. We probably could have done the album even quicker than we did, but it was a fairly quick process. And I'm really pleased with the result."

For one of the few times in his career, B.B. engaged in an extensive pre-production period before getting into the studio. For a week he and Clapton worked out songs and ideas using acoustic guitars only. The next week they started in on contemporary songs, "and then when it was getting difficult, just as a moment of light relief, we'd do something from B.B.'s past," according to Clapton. "In terms of material, some of it was going to be new and some of it was going to be covers and some of it was going to be ancient B.B. material. I mean, I really wanted him to visit his own past.

"Nothing was really routine. You know, there are some situations when we'd go into the studio where a certain amount of time is set aside in advance to rehearse material. I had kind of compartmentalized what I thought we could approach, which was kind of like an unplugged dynamic, a contemporary dynamic, and a live blues dynamic. And I wanted to create a good environment for each of those sort of concepts."[3]

Makin' Love Is Good for You _____

MCA, 2000
Produced by B.B. King
Executive Producers: Floyd Lieberman and Sidney A. Seidenberg for Sasco
    Productions, Inc.
Recorded by Tony Daigle at Dockside Studios, Maurice, Louisiana
Engineer Assistant: Jay Burton
Mixed by John Porter for World's End America at Cello Studios, Hollywood,
    California
Mix Engineer: Joe McGrath
Second Engineer: Bill Kingsley
Coordinator for World's End America, Inc.: Martie Kolbl
Mastered by Stephen Marcussen at A&M Mastering, Hollywood, California

Musicians
B.B. King: guitar
James Bolden: bandleader, trumpet
Walter R. King: contractor, saxophone
Calep Emphrey, Jr.: drums
Melvin Jackson: saxophone
Leon Warren: guitar
Michael Doster: bass

James Toney: keyboards
Stanley Abernathy: trumpet

Additional Overdubs by:
Joe Sublett: tenor sax
Darrell Leonard: trumpet
Tommy Eyre: keyboards
Tony Braunagel: percussion
John Porter: guitar

Songs
"I Got to Leave this Woman" (Jackson)
"Since I Fell for You" (Buddy Johnson)
"I Know" (Barbara George)
"Peace of Mind" (B.B. King–J. Josea)
"Monday Woman" (Willie James Mabon)
"Ain't Nobody Like My Baby" (B.B. King)
"Makin' Love Is Good for You" (Tony Joe White)
"Don't Go No Farther" (Willie Dixon)
"Actions Speak Louder Than Words" (B.B. King)
"What You Bet" (George Taylor–George Williams)
"You're on Top" (B.B. King–S. Ling)
"Too Good to You Baby" (B.B. King)
"I'm in the Wrong Business" (A.C. Reed)
"She's My Baby" (B.B. King)

To close out the century, B.B. returned to Dockside Studios in Maurice, Louisiana, near the end of 1999 with his band and four new songs in tow. Reaching back to the past, as usual, he revisited "Peace of Mind" and "You're on Top" from the Modern era, and selected an interesting crop of covers, including the 1963 Lenny Welch hit "Since I Fell for You," Barbara George's "I Know," Willie Dixon's "Don't Go No Farther," and two humorous blues workouts, Willie James Mabon's "Monday Woman" and A.C. Reed's wry "I'm in the Wrong Business." Of the new songs, the slow blues "Ain't Nobody Like My Baby," brings out the shouter in B.B. as he trumpets the virtues of his woman's "sly way of lovin'." On the other hand, aggrieved shouting is the order of the day in B.B.'s "Actions Speak Louder Than Words," which percolates along on the strength of a winding, writhing Lucille solo, James Sells Toney's aggressive support on piano, and stuttering blasts of horns. A familiar curlicue phrase from Lucille kicks off "Too Good to You Baby," Toney bangs away on the keys, the horns hum smoothly, and B.B. muses, in a voice heavy with both regret and irony, on the deleterious effects of his material gifts on a "wanderin', cheatin' woman"—"I was too good to you / I gave you everything I owned," he laments, as if he can't believe how blinded by love he had been. The album closes with the fourth new B.B. original, a lilting blues balled titled "She's My Baby," a song praising a good woman, fueled by Lucille's persistent, serpentine commentary and Toney's rich, gospel-styled wash of organ chords. In a measured vocal performance, B.B. offers up praise for the woman who treats him like a king; the reportorial nature of his reading as he reels off virtue after virtue is genuinely affecting, and doubly so when he closes out a lyric line with a gruff shout followed by a low, moaning tone for added effect. It's his most soulful performance on a disc abundant in soul.

A Christmas Celebration of Hope _____

MCA, 2001
Produced by B.B. King
Executive producer: Floyd Lieberman
Recorded by Tony Daigle at Dockside Studios, Maurice, Louisiana
Assistant engineer: Jay Burton
Mixed by John Holbrock at Soundtrack Studios, New York City, except "Merry Christmas, Baby," produced by Michael Abene; tambourine by Tony Coleman
Recorded and mixed by Josiah Gluck at Sound on Sound and Unique Studios, New York City
Assisted by Devin Emke, Ken Quartarone, and Rich Costey

Musicians

James Bolden: bandleader, trumpet

Walter R. King: contractor

Calep Emphrey, Jr.: drums

Melvin Jackson: saxophone

Leon Warren: guitar

Michael Doster: bass

James Sells Toney: keyboards

Stanley Abernathy: trumpet

The Nashville String Machine appears on "To Someone That I Love," "Please Come Home for Christmas," and "Christmas in Heaven"

Songs

"Please Come Home for Christmas" (Brown–Redd)

"Lonesome Christmas" (Glenn)

"Back Door Santa" (Carter–Daniel)

"Christmas in Heaven" (Ward)

"I'll Be Home for Christmas" (Gannon–Ram–Kent)

"To Someone That I Love" (Brown)

"Christmas Celebration" (B.B. King)

"Merry Christmas Baby" (Cavanaugh–Smalley)

"Christmas Love" (B.B. King)

"Blue Decorations" (Gillespie)

"Christmas Comes but Once a Year" (Milburn–Shubert)

"Bringing in a Brand New Year" (Brown)

"Auld Lang Syne" (arranged by B.B. King)

It's remarkable, really, the warm spirit infusing the sessions for B.B.'s first Christmas album, recorded at Dockside Studios in June 2001. Taken individually, the performances on the album are ingratiating enough, appropriate to the season, some treated in a lighthearted manner, a couple of blues getting down into rich wells of poignant feeling; but when it's all over, a spell lingers. There's something special about the imprint B.B. puts on these songs—the conviction in his voice, the personality he projects throughout, Lucille's sunny tone—and when that's coupled to his road band's high-spirited accompaniment, the end result is a model yuletide blues album that sneaks up on you. Produced by B.B., *A Christmas Celebration of Hope* believes in itself, and its optimism burrows into a soul as surely as did the lessons Scrooge learned on that fateful eve. In fact, the project bears a kind of Dickensian pentimento in that all its profits were donated to the City of Hope, a biomedical research and treatment center engaged in advanced research into treating and finding cures for catastrophic illnesses such as diabetes (which B.B. has), HIV/AIDS, and cancer. Among the facility's notable achievements was the development of synthetic insulin, which has helped diabetics lead fruitful lives. Gene therapy, T-cell therapy, and the development of cancer drugs are among its front-burner priorities. Without trying to overstate the case for this album's humanity, its guiding philosophy seems to have been purloined from Jacob Marley's ghost, who enlightened a startled Scrooge as to an afterlife epiphany: "The common welfare was my business; charity, mercy, forbearance, and benevolence, were, all, my business. The dealings of my trade were but a drop of water in the comprehensive ocean of my business!"

This album recognizes a larger purpose for its music, and knowing that, B.B. and his fellow musicians bring it home with a mellow, comforting vengeance.

An in-the-pocket mid-tempo blues, Lloyd Glenn's "Lonesome Christmas," features a swaggering vocal from B.B., a rousing horn chart, and a couple of tart solo turns by Lucille in an arrangement that's more cheerful than lonesome. Clarence Carter's suggestive yule classic, "Back Door Santa," gets a horn-rich, driving treatment, although it would be fair to say that B.B. doesn't quite inhabit the song with the same gusto as Carter does in his original version, which doesn't make it any less enjoyable. A sumptuous love song, "Christmas in Heaven" gives B.B. a chance to croon a tender lyric about love and devotion, complete with surging horns and lush strings rising behind the vocal to add to the romantic atmosphere, an approach that works to equally compelling effect on the tender sentiments in "To Someone I Love." Whereas B.B. could have doubtless delivered an affecting vocal on the seasonal favorite

"I'll Be Home for Christmas," he opts instead to cast it as a cool, jazzy instrumental, with Lucille caressing the melody line before stepping aside to allow James Sells Toney to add some Jimmy Smith–inspired variations on that same melody before Lucille returns to pick up the main line with only a bent note here or a brief crying note there to alter the linear attack. The difference between the 1960 and the 2001 versions of "Christmas Celebration" (apart from the latter's engaging horn-and-guitar dialog near the end) is in B.B.'s approach: on the earlier cut his cynical pose rendered the title ironic, at the very least; a more mature B.B. sings with engaging sincerity to a woman with whom he shares a cherished history. Charles Brown's Christmas blues classic "Merry Christmas Baby" affords B.B. a chance to shout and growl the blues, and Toney hits those rolling piano notes with panache in an arrangement that affords Lucille an opportunity to get her lick in and play off Toney's inspired work on the 88s, as B.B. keeps upping the ante vocally to the point where he goes out with a roar, and gives Lucille one last quote, a taste of "Jingle Bells," as the horns ascend and slowly fade out. A B.B. original written for this project, "Christmas Love" is an instrumental blues for a small combo, languorous and tender, designed for late-night cuddling by the fire, Lucille whispering sweet nothings throughout the track. The album closes with a jubilant rendering of "Auld Lang Syne," rich in rhythmic thrust, celebratory horns, a burst of organ, and a robust Lucille interpolation of the melody line, all of it coming together beautifully at the big, booming end, a most fitting close to a hearty exercise in Christmas bonhomie.

"It has been my longtime dream to produce an album of Christmas music," B.B. said in a prepared statement that accompanied the album's release. "In addition, it is with pleasure that I dedicate this album to City of Hope in support of their hard work to bring hope and healing to all people who suffer from life-threatening diseases everywhere."

Honored with two Grammy Awards (for Best Pop Instrumental Performance for "Auld Lang Syne" and for Best Traditional Blues Album), *A Christmas Celebration of Hope* filled one of the few remaining gaps in B.B.'s life in music, even as it revealed a soul ever more grateful for what it knows of love.

Reflections

MCA, 2003

"I've long loved the R&B and pop standards on this package, and now I've finally had the opportunity to record these great songs. Despite everything, it certainly can be a wonderful world." —B.B. King

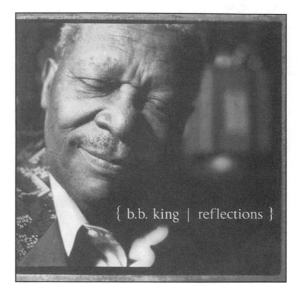

Produced by Simon Climie
Executive Producer: Floyd Lieberman for Lieberman Management LLC
Recorded by Don Murray at Record One, Sherman Oaks, California
Mixed by Mick Guzauski at Barking Doctor Studios, Mount Kisco, New York
Mix Assistant: Tom Bender
Assistant Engineer: Tom Sweeney
Pro Tools: Simon Climie, Jonathan Shakhovskoy
Recorded on Pro Tools HD with the Sony Oxford Plug-ins
Mastered by Bob Ludwig at Gateway Mastering, Portland, Maine
Production Coordinator: Debbie Johnson
Strings and brass recorded by Alan Douglas at Olympic Studios, London
Strings arranged and conducted by Nick Ingman
String leader: Gavin Wright
String coordinator: Isabel Griffiths
Brass leader: Derek Watkins

Musicians
Joe Sample: acoustic piano, Wurlitzer (on tracks 5, 13), and Fender Rhodes (on
    Tracks 1, 3, 7, 10)
Nathan East: bass
Abe Laboriel, Jr.: drums
Doyle Bramhall II: guitar
Tim Carmon: Hammond B3, acoustic piano (on track 7)
Toby Baker: Fender Rhodes (on tracks 11, 12), Wurlitzer (on track 6)

Songs
"Exactly Like You" (3:21) (Jimmy Mchugh–Dorothy Fields)
"On My Word of Honor" (3:22) (Jean Miles–Katherine Harrison)
"I Want a Little Girl" (2:48) (Billy Moll–Murray Mencher)
"I'll String Along with You" (3:31) (Al Dubin–Harry Warren)
"I Need You So" (3:03) (Laury Steve Bruce–Ronald Irwin Satterfield)
"A Mother's Love" (2:58) (Clyde Otis)
"(I Love You) For Sentimental Reasons" (3:30) (William Best–Deek Watson)
"Neighborhood Affair" (4:26) (B.B. King–Jules Bihari)
"Tomorrow Night" (3:35) (Lonnie Johnson)
"There I've Said It Again" (3:28) (Redd Evans–Dave Mann)
"Always on My Mind" (3:35) (Johnny Christopher–Wayne Thompson–Mark
    James)
"Cross My Heart" (4:28) (Don Robery–David Mattis)
"What a Wonderful World" (3:57) (George David Weiss–Bob Thiele)

Reflections represents the realization of another long-deferred dream for B.B., and that was to record an entire album of romantic ballads, sort of a *My Kind of Blues* dressed up for the ball. Produced by Eric Clapton cohort Simon Climie, who had co-produced *Riding with the King*, this outing re-teamed B.B. with some of the musicians from the Clapton collaboration, and Climie made elaborate use of his string and brass sections to weave the pop embroidery throughout. Lucille surfaces infrequently, Doyle Bramhall II seeming to be the guitarist of choice here, although B.B. does have a sweet solo moment in "Cross My Heart" and cuts loose with a startling wail of notes in the tender-hearted ballad "On My Word of Honor," from the Platters' canon. B.B.'s voice, never lacking for feeling, is, however, sounding all of its 78 years. But if he doesn't shout with the grit of old, or croon with the same velvet touch he employed back in the day, he can still turn a phrase with the master stylists, and that gets him through quite well.

He seems to luxuriate in the happy sentiments of the Dorothy Fields–Jimmy McHugh evergreen "Exactly Like You," to open the album on a swinging note, just as he burrows into the Platters' love pledge, "On My Word of Honor," with a feisty, shouting attitude that underscores the determination in his vow. The weathered quality of his voice works to his advantage more so than not, especially on the gently surging version of one of his favorite songs, "Always on My Mind," when its vibrato tails off rather than sustains and the energy B.B. pours into maintaining it is both endearing and poignant, appropriate to both the song and to his years.

The tune stack is representative of B.B.'s wide-ranging taste. The swinging big-band treatment of "I Want a Little Girl" comes by way of a 1967 T-Bone Walker recording. The dreamy Dubin–Warren love song "I'll String Along with You" dates back to 1934, when it was recorded by Dick Powell and Ginger Rogers for the film *Twenty Million Sweethearts*. "(I Love You) For Sentimental Reasons," a gorgeous love song, was a No. 1 hit for six weeks for one of B.B.'s musical touchstones, Nat King Cole, in 1946–'47. "There I've Said It Again" dates back to 1941 and was first recorded by Benny Carter and His Orchestra, followed by three hit versions in 1945 alone (Jimmy Dorsey and His Orchestra, Vaughan Monroe, and the Modernaires with Paula Kelly), a Nat King Cole hit treatment in 1948, and Bobby Vinton in 1964. The album concludes with a spare treatment of Louis Armstrong's enduring 1967 *tour de force* of balladeering, "What a Wonderful World," featuring B.B.'s quavering voice in a cool recitative over a small band, until the strings rise briefly in the chorus and he matches their intensity with some of his own before tempering it again—a lovely, touching performance. He also revisits three songs he had recorded previously in his career: Clyde Otis's winsome "A Mother's Love," Lonnie Johnson's "Tomorrow Night," and "Neighborhood Affair," which he first recorded in 1953 and here performs in a slow, funky groove redolent of his collaborations with the Crusaders.

Typically self-deprecating, B.B. told *Mix* magazine reporter Chris J. Walker that he had many songs he'd been wanting to record, and added: "Sometimes I think I like them because the person that did them prior to me was so good with them. And in my case, after you try them, they don't sound too good." According to Climie, the initial song list for the project numbered some 2,500 songs that was then reduced to 60, before picking 20 to record, with 13 making the final cut.[4]

Recording at Record One in Los Angeles in mid-December 2002, B.B. and Climie opted to cut the sessions live with the artist in the studio. "It's always fun for me to see what everyone else is doing and be able to feel them. I do a better job then," King told *Mix*.

Climie elaborated, explaining that B.B.'s approach to recording is "'Here I am.' So we just went through it, track by track. He did his thing, and that's what it was, and when it was great he just moved on and didn't question it. There are a lot of people who like the rather more indulgent recording process where you try every possibility. . . . With B.B. it's a totally emotionally driven thing. He loves the feeling in a song, and we spent more time focusing everyone, changing the key, and working on tempo. Suddenly, you'd get this incredible perform-ance and you have to be in 'record.' If you missed it, you wouldn't get it again."

Engineer Don Murray, who had worked with B.B. as an assistant engineer

B.B., circa 2002.

on the *Lucille Talks Back* album recorded at Philadelphia's Sigma Sound Studio in 1974, found that in late life B.B. had as much stamina as he'd exhibited almost thirty years earlier. "He would sing [live] all day long and just not lose energy," Murray said. "I guess he's used to it because he's on the road a lot. He didn't really play guitar live; he did that later as overdubs. He really wanted to concentrate on his vocals and we set a Sony C12 mic in the studio with the rhythm section. There was no isolation. He was in the middle of the band, literally ten feet from the drums. It produced a nice ambient sound that went well for this record. For this type of music and for B.B., I think it's more exciting to hear the songs as if you were in a club, rather than having everything isolated and pristine. I also set up a couple of room mics to capture even more ambience."

Like other producers who have worked with B.B. over the years, Climie found the experience as pleasant as it was informative. "There's not a lot of phenomenal music around at the moment," he observed, "and we did get to choose from the best songs in the last 50 years. That's got be a great inspiration for anyone."

Still very much the vital artist, B.B.'s take on *Reflections* pretty well summed up the attitude he had taken out of every recording session he had been in since 1949, and indicated his sense of mission, unabated even at age 78. "I still have a lot of songs I'd like to try," he reported.

EPILOGUE

In May 2000 SASCO Productions, Sid Seidenberg's company, issued a press release announcing Seidenberg as the new chairman, and his associate of 35 years, Floyd Lieberman, as president and CEO. As for the chain of command, Seidenberg would remain active "in all areas of management," with Lieberman assuming control of "all the day-to-day responsibilities." Another long-term employee (of 20 years), Tina France, was named vice president, with responsibilities "in all aspects of artist development."

It was, in effect, Sid Seidenberg's retirement announcement. In ill health and unable to attend to B.B.'s affairs as rigorously as he once did, he turned the reins over to Lieberman and moved to Florida. Lieberman picked up where Seidenberg left off, though, and in the years since B.B. has become an in-demand pitchman and, more to the point, a beloved and respected American musical ambassador to the world, exactly as Seidenberg had envisioned.

In 1994, when B.B. played sold-out shows in South America, opened the Hard Rock Cafe in Beijing, and had his first No. 1 album in *Heart to Heart*, Seidenberg reflected on what the Blues Boy from the Mississippi Delta had become. "B.B. is now as well known as Mick Jagger or Bob Dylan," he told Sebastian Danchin. "B.B. is in the movies in America, we've had a syndicated radio show throughout the '80s, we're on popular television in America, we're doing children's programs, we're doing lectures at universities as a leading authority on blues, and we get paid the same as celebrity people who go on lecture tours at universities. So we've reached a lot of levels on a lot of different markets with B.B. See, B.B. is an industry with, like, 20 different divisions. Rather than me have 20 acts, I have one act with 20 divisions—seven people who work all of the time on B.B.'s career. Twenty-five years it took us to get here! But it was part of our plan from the start."[1]

The awards and accolades keep piling up. B.B., his legs not as strong as they once were, now plays concerts sitting on a stool, but never betrays any physical infirmity. The voice is showing its age—*Reflections* proved that—but has lost none of its expressiveness; being a great stylist, B.B. knows how to use nuance and shading effectively to get the emotional content of a song across. And Lucille? Still crying, still laughing, still as feisty as ever, aging most gracefully, a grand doyenne of the guitar world.

Fittingly, given Lucille's critical role in B.B.'s legend, the Arkansas town of Twist, from whence the guitar's name sprang from a juke joint brawl and fire back in 1949, is going to recognize B.B.'s contribution to the state with a

$5,000 monument in his honor. Funding was pushed through by State Senator Steve Bryles, who felt B.B.'s connections to Arkansas were too little recognized, and that honoring them might help boost tourism.

In 2004 B.B.'s dream of leaving something worthwhile behind began to take shape in his hometown of Indianola, Mississippi. On January 5 it was announced that a development team was at work on plans for the B.B. King Museum and Delta Interpretive Center, with a groundbreaking scheduled for June 10, 2005, and a projected opening date in 2007. A $10 million facility encompassing 15,000 square feet, the museum will not only tell B.B.'s life story but will also be, according to a report on www.bbking.com/news, "designed for an interactive and educational experience. It will serve as a unique regional and national learning resource, committed to the creation of an innovative curriculum for K-12 and Lifelong Learning modules. Lesson plans and outreach initiatives will be created to encourage primary, secondary, and continuing education groups from the region to visit the B.B. King Museum for tours and educational opportunities."

A cutting-edge idea, the notion of the museum as an extension of and supplement to formal schooling struck a responsive chord in B.B., who has always regretted his lack of education. It's a way of giving back, of fulfilling an obligation he's felt since his ascension from the Delta cotton fields to the pinnacle of mainstream popularity. As he reaped the rewards of that success, he never forgot the disenfranchised, whether that meant playing prison concerts and founding the FAIRR organization or returning to Mississippi every year to play, for free, an annual benefit concert in the memory of his friend, the slain civil rights activist Medgar Evers.

"Can you change peoples' hearts?" he asks. "Can you erase centuries of blind hatred and ignorance? I've tried to stand for something, tried to let people see I'm a human being with human feelings just like everyone else, but have I made any real difference in the grand scale of things?"[2]

These existential questions of B.B.'s are not necessarily answered by brick-and-mortar monuments to a life's work, or by honorary degrees from Yale University, by legislation, or by anything in the corporeal world. Somewhere, though, someone's cueing up a B.B. King record, or seeing him live in concert, or hearing him on the radio, and they're feeling better about themselves. Maybe understanding their partners better, indeed, themselves too. Being moved to tears, or to healing laughter. Feeling the spirit, making a connection, moving to higher ground. *Feeling alive*. B.B. moans, Lucille cries, and the wind picks up the sound and lifts it into the ether, where on a lonely mountain road, out there in the world, a weary traveler tunes it in, *a single beam from out of the sky, vibrational energy, a wave again trapped before beginning its second stellar flight,* and everything changes.

From the beginning B.B. King heard a bigger blues. A bolder and brassier, if not brasher, blues. A blues that *sang,* sang in celebration of our every breath, sang in celebration of life lived with a passion.

Quoth Stewart Levine, on behalf of all who have been touched by this legacy: "God bless, man.

"Maybe there's one more left."

ANTHOLOGIES AND OVERVIEWS: A BUYER'S GUIDE

Consumers can choose from a dizzying number of B.B. King collections, from both major labels and from smaller outfits that have licensed certain material, packaged it shoddily, and are trying to make a buck with minimum effort. This guide focuses then on the better packages out there. When shopping for B.B. anthologies, a good rule of thumb (especially with online retailers that tend to offer the whole kit and kaboodle of B.B. product) is to go with the name brands—domestically, MCA (and its Hip-O subsidiary) and Flair/Virgin. Note that this list includes only U.S. releases; the indefatigable folks at Ace Records in England have several first-rate anthologies of B.B.'s Modern recordings, all of which trump most everything on the list below, and the Japanese P-Vine label also has several meritorious collections in its catalog, most superior to the U.S. releases. The dates in parentheses indicate the original year of release, followed by the label and year of reissue.

His Best—The Electric B. B. King (1968; MCA, 1988)

A solid 11-track overview of some Johnny Pate–produced ABC sides such as "Tired of Your Jive," "Don't Answer the Door," and "Paying the Cost to Be the Boss," plus two Quincy Jones–produced tracks from the film *For the Love of Ivy*, "The B.B. Jones" and "You Put It on Me."

The Best of B.B. King (1973; MCA, 1987)

Only nine tracks here (one of which is the 37-second introduction of B.B. at the Cook Country Jail), and even though the material is choice—"The Thrill Is Gone," "Hummingbird," "How Blue Can You Get," "Sweet Sixteen," "Why I Sing the Blues," "Nobody Loves Me but My Mother"—even at a discount price better collections can be had.

Back in the Alley: The Classic Blues of B.B. King (MCA, 1973)

A slight, nine-song budget album of B.B. standards such as "Sweet Little Angel," "Don't Answer the Door," "Sweet Sixteen," "Paying the Cost to Be the Boss," "Please Love Me," and—making its only appearance to date on an anthology—the ten-minute-plus monolog in blues produced by Bob Thiele, "Lucille," which perhaps makes this one worth the price of admission. Not really.

Great Moments with B.B. King (1981; MCA, 1990)

Now this is more like it. A reissue produced by Leonard Feather, *Great Moments with B.B. King* lives up to its title on a single-disc, 23-track collection of everything from "Waitin' on You," "Nightlife," "I Know What You're Puttin' Down," "Paying the Cost to Be the Boss," "Cherry Red," and others. Real bang for the buck here.

The Best of B.B. King, Vol. 1 (1986; Flair/Virgin, 1991)

Twenty tracks of choice B.B. from the Modern era, marred only by perfunctory liner notes and no session info. Still, for those seeking a sit-in with the early B.B., the classics here include "You Upset Me Baby," "Every Day I Have the Blues," "Sweet Little Angel," "3 O'Clock Blues," parts 1 and 2 of "Sweet Sixteen," "Please Accept My Love," "Blues at Sunrise," and "Please Love Me," among others. So close, this one, to being a must-have overview of the formative years.

The Fabulous B.B. King (Flair/Virgin, 1991)

Think of it as the budget-priced version of *The Best of B.B. King, Vol. 1*— that is, classic tracks, but only a dozen, rather than the latter's tasty 20. "3 O'Clock Blues," "You Upset Me Baby," "Sweet Little Angel," "My Heart Beats Like a Hammer," "Every Day I Have the Blues," "On My Word of Honor"— the selections are choice, every one of them. But for a couple of bucks more, a better overview can be had.

Do the Boogie! B.B. King's Early '50s Classics (Flair/Virgin, 1988)

Imagine a collection that touts itself as *Early '50s Classics* but doesn't include "3 O'Clock Blues," the biggest classic of them all. So it's not exactly what it claims, but it's close. "Woke Up This Morning (My Baby's Gone)," "Please Love Me," "Dark Is the Night, Parts 1 & 2," "Crying Won't Help You," "Every Day I Have the Blues," and the first rendition of "Why I Sing the Blues" pretty much qualify as classics in B.B.'s repertoire. Good liner notes by Ray Topping, but points are deducted for lack of a sessionography.

Spotlight on Lucille (Flair/Virgin, 1991)

Wonderful stuff here in a collection of recordings from 1960 and 1961, all instrumental, in a variety of styles from slow blues to jump blues to flat-out rockers and tender ballads, plus a liner booklet containing some priceless vintage photos of young B.B., one showing him beside an equally young and flashily attired Elvis Presley. Not essential, this, but a good one to have in the archives. No sessionography whatsoever—shame, shame.

Heart & Soul: A Collection of Blues Ballads (Pointblank/Virgin, 1992)

A powerful disc arguing for B.B.'s supremacy as a blues balladeer, and winning converts right and left. The 20 tracks, all from B.B.'s Modern catalog, are simply beautiful, from the avuncular treatment of Duke Ellington's "Don't Get Around Much Anymore" to the powerful, gospel-styled testifying on "On My Word of Honor." Great stuff and essential for its tight focus on one towering aspect of B.B.'s vocal artistry.

My Sweet Little Angel (Flair/Virgin, 1992)

Alternative takes and previously unissued takes dot this 20-song overview of the Modern years that includes the title song and some other monuments (such as "Please Accept My Love," "Recession Blues," and "Ten Long Years"), as well as some tasty instrumentals (one to check out: the previously unissued "String Bean"). Also offers well-researched liner notes by Ray Topping, but no sessionography.

How Blue Can You Get? Classic Live Performances 1964 to 1994 (MCA, 1996)

As anthologies go, this one's essential: two CDs, 29 live tracks from across three decades, with serviceable liner notes by Mark Humphrey, thorough sessionography, and a host of powerful live tracks, including four cuts from the powerful *Blues Is King* live album from 1966, four from *Live at the Regal*, and four from the Bill Szymczyk era. That's disc one. Disc two features three performances recorded live in London with the Crusaders that appeared only on that group's *Live in London* album, as well as a version of Percy Mayfield's "Please Send Me Someone to Love" not from an LP but from an HBO special, "A Night of Red Hot Blues," and two live tracks from the Blues Summit Concert at B.B.'s Memphis nightclub, including the irrepressible Ruth Brown coming on to B.B. on "Ain't Nobody's Business." It's rounded out with tracks from *Live at Cook County Jail*, *Live at San Quentin*, *Live at the Apollo*, and a previously unreleased 1994 treatment of "Rock Me Baby" recorded at The Rosengarten in Mannheim, Germany. Endlessly entertaining, frequently moving, this collection shows B.B. firmly in his element, reigning supreme over all he surveys.

Greatest Hits (MCA, 1998)

A good mix of the predictable—"Every Day I Have the Blues" (a live cut), "The Thrill Is Gone," "Paying the Cost to Be the Boss," and the like—with unexpected selections such as "There Must Be a Better World Somewhere,"

"Better Not Look Down," and "Never Make a Move Too Soon" with the Crusaders, and Leon Russell's "Hummingbird" from the brilliant *Indianola Mississippi Seeds* album.

Best of B. B. King: 20th Century Masters (MCA, 1999)

At a mere ten familiar tracks, this 20th Century Masters entry hardly seems worth the effort. The tracks are from the '60s and '70s (save for the 1985 movie theme song "Into the Night") and are unsurprising choices—"The Thrill Is Gone," "Guess Who," "Paying the Cost to Be the Boss," and so forth. For the extremely budget-minded only.

The Vintage Years (Ace Records, 2000)

What artist would not want his or her recorded legacy to be treated as honorably as Ace Records has done with B.B. King in the momentous box set *The Vintage Years*? A true team effort that brought together A&R consultant John Broven, award-winning writer Colin Escott, ace managing director Roger Armstrong (who pored over the Ace archive of 2,000 B.B. King master tapes from the Modern era to pin down not only the best recordings, but the correct ones), Duncan Cornwell at Sound Mastering Ltd. (who is responsible for the sparkling audio restoration), B.B. himself, and a number of avid collectors and historians. The aim was to get it right, "it" being the arc of B.B.'s '50s and '60s work for the Biharis' various labels, thus illustrating the remarkable musical journey of his formative years. Four discs spotlight specific aspects of B.B.'s artistry, beginning with Disc 1, *The Great B.B.*, which gathers 24 of his defining hits, such as "Three O'Clock Blues," "Rock Me Baby," "Downhearted" (aka "How Blue Can You Get?"), and other monuments. Disc 2, *Memphis Blues 'n' Boogie*, illustrates an artist en route to shaping a distinctive style; 28 early-'50s tracks take B.B. from Memphis (the Sam Phillips sessions are here) to Houston and feature hard-driving boogie on the order of "She's Dynamite" to brooding blues such as the original "Neighborhood Affair" (from 1953) to heartfelt pleas that showcase B.B.'s growing confidence as a balladeer ("Please Help Me"). Disc 3, *Take a Swing with Me*, documents the arrival of Maxwell Davis as B.B.'s arranger, the decline of the blues market, and B.B.'s and Davis's subsequent forays into R&B, pop balladry (the beautiful "On My Word of Honor," from 1957), jazz (Duke Ellington's "Don't Get Around Much Anymore"), and gospel ("Precious Lord," from B.B.'s lone gospel album, *B.B. King Sings Spirituals*). Also included among this disc's 28 tracks is the previously unissued ballad "Why Not," which featured the first use of strings on a B.B. King recording, more than a decade before "The Thrill

Is Gone" was credited with that distinction. Disc 4, *King of the Blues*, spotlights the latter years of B.B.'s affiliation with the Biharis, with most of the 26 tracks having been released on the Kent label after B.B. had signed with ABC. This one's a mixed bag, containing the folly of "Mashed Potato Twist" and a few tepid performances, but the good parts—and they do outnumber the less-inspired takes—are wonderful: the first version of "Christmas Celebration," a previously unissued version of "Baby Please Don't Go," the delightful "Beautician Blues," and the urgent "Five Long Years." The icing on the cake is a superb 74-page booklet (sourced many times in this book) of thoroughly researched, clearheaded, and non-didactic appraisal of B.B.'s musical legacy. John Broven contributes a most revealing interview with Sam Phillips, who spoke often and colorfully in his lifetime about Elvis, Carl Perkins, Jerry Lee Lewis, Johnny Cash, and the rockabillies who came through his studio, but was rarely queried about the specifics of the pre-Elvis years or, even more specifically, about B.B. King's work in his studio. He does so here, and it's riveting history. Broven also spoke at length with Joe Bihari of Modern Records, and the story of Modern Records thus gets the fleshed-out treatment it deserves (actually, on the evidence of Broven's essay on the Biharis and Modern Records, it sounds like there's a whole book yet to be written on that unique label). Escott pens an incisive history of B.B.'s life and early years as a professional musician in the essay "The Blues Every Day" and adds track-by-track commentary, citing not only the relevant information about the recording session that produced the songs, but also, when it applies, the historical antecedents of earlier songs on which B.B. built his original tunes—all in all, a remarkable exhibition of investigative musicology. Not the least of the booklet's virtues is what Broven calls a "user-friendly" discography that he gathered with his colleague Peter Gibbon, a chart of B.B.'s late-'50s tours as well as vintage and contemporary photos of some of the chitlin' circuit clubs where the King of the Blues began his ascent to regency. This is what a box set should be, and it's a measure of B.B.'s importance to 20th-century music that he has two of them in his catalog, the earlier MCA four-CD set (detailed in these pages) *King of the Blues* being mostly focused on his ABC and MCA work. Simply put, no one who claims to be a serious fan of B.B. King and of the blues can afford to be without either box set.

Anthology (MCA, 2000)

Thirty-four prime-time tracks from the ABC/MCA years on two discs. No real surprises in the choice of tunes, but "I Got Some Help I Don't Need" is the single edit, the version of "When Love Comes to Town" with U2 is the seven-inch mix, and there's an unedited version of "Call It Stormy Monday" with Albert Collins from the *Blues Summit* sessions. Mark Humphrey's liner notes are first-rate—comprehensive, concise, insightful all at once—and the sessionography is thorough. An excellent package all around.

Here and There: The Uncollected B.B. King (Hip-O/MCA, 2001)

A terrific off-the-beaten-path collection of B.B.'s work assembled by MCA's Andy McKaie, this single-disc set includes such rarities as "T'Ain't Nobody's Business (If I Do)," from the *King of Comedy* soundtrack; a tough blues with Arthur Adams, "Get You Next to Me," that illustrates why B.B. thinks so much of this impressive bluesman; and a low-down duet with Willie Nelson on "The Thrill Is Gone" that reinvigorates B.B.'s signature song.

Classic Masters (Virgin, 2002)

A dozen classic tracks from the Modern years, in 24-bit digitally remastered sound, sparsely annotated but hitting the high points, such as "3 O'Clock Blues," "You Upset Me Baby," the beautiful ballad "On My Word of Honor," "Sweet Sixteen, Parts 1 & 2," "Sweet Little Angel," etc. Another solid single-disc set, albeit a severely abridged look at B.B.'s formative years with the Biharis. No match for any of the Ace collections or Flair's *The Best of B.B. King, Vol. 1* (see above).

Martin Scorsese Presents The Blues: B.B. King (Hip-O/MCA, 2003)

A companion CD to the PBS series *The Blues*, this 12-song, single-CD collection is essentially a concise, well-considered greatest hits–type package of mostly obvious B.B. standards—"3 O'Clock Blues," "Every Day I Have the Blues," "How Blue Can You Get?," "The Thrill Is Gone," "Don't Answer the Door," "Paying the Cost to Be the Boss," etc. The time frame covers 1953 ("3 O'Clock Blues") to 1998 (the reworking of 1960's "I'll Survive" from *Blues on the Bayou*) and shows B.B. in small-combo to big-band settings. Not a bad choice for a single-disc collection. Note: Liner notes for this collection were written by this author.

ENDNOTES

1. Delta Born, Delta Raised, Delta Scarred

1. King, B.B., with Ritz, David, *Blues All Around Me* (New York: Avon Books, 1996), 7-8 (hereafter cited as *Blues All Around Me*)
2. Ibid., 10
3. Ibid., 10
4. Ibid., 11
5. Ibid., 12
6. Ibid., 13
7. Ibid., 13
8. Ibid., 16
9. Ibid., 17
10. Ibid., 17
11. Ibid., 17
12. Ibid., 18
13. Ibid., 19
14. Ibid., 19
15. Ibid., 19
16. Ibid., 19
17. Ibid., 19
18. Ibid., 20
19. Ibid., 23
20. worldblues.com, 03/30/04
21. *Blues All Around Me*, 24
22. Ibid., 24
23. Ibid., 23
24. Ibid., 24
25. Ibid., 25
26. Ibid., 26
27. Ibid., 25
28. Ted Drozdowski, "B.B. King: Ramblin' Gamblin' Man," *Guitar World*
29. Ibid.
30. Ibid.
31. "Interview with Blues Legend B.B. King, Part II," musicianshotline.com, March/April 2002
32. *Blues All Around Me*, op. cit., 27
33. Ibid., 28
34. Swenson, John, editor, *The Rolling Stone Jazz & Blues Album Guide* (New York: Random House, 1999)
35. Drozdowski, op. cit.
36. Ibid.
37. *Blues All Around Me*, op. cit., 33
38. Ibid., 36
39. Ibid., 36
40. Ibid., 36
41. Ibid., 41
42. Ibid., 42
43. Ibid., 43-44
44. Ibid., 44
45. Ibid., 44
46. Ibid., 44
47. Ibid., 53-54
48. Ibid., 52
49. Ibid., 51-52
50. Ibid., 52-53
51. Ibid., 54
52. Ibid., 58
53. Ibid., 55
54. Ibid., 59
55. Ibid., 64
56. Ibid., 62
57. Ibid., 62
58. Ibid., 65
59. Ibid., 65-67
60. Ibid., 68
61. Ibid., 67
62. Ibid., 69
63. Ibid., 69-70
64. Ibid., 64
65. Ibid., 70
66. Ibid., 70
67. Ibid., 72
68. Ibid., 71
69. Ibid., 78
70. Ibid., 79
71. Ibid., 79
72. Ibid., 80
73. Ibid., 80

74. Ibid., 82
75. Ibid., 82-85
76. Ibid., 91
77. Ibid., 98
78. Ibid., 101

2. Memphis: Arrival, Retreat, Return

1. Booth, Stanley, *Rythm Oil* (New York: Pantheon Books, 1991)
2. Davis, Francis, *The History of the Blues* (New York: Hyperion, 1995), 43
3. Guralnick, Peter, *Last Train to Memphis: The Rise of Elvis Presley* (New York: HarperCollins, 1994), 52
4. Ibid., 5
5. Ibid., 7
6. American Roots Music, www.pbs.org/americanrootsmusic/ pbs.arm.oralh.bbking.html, 2001
7. *Blues All Around Me*, 104
8. Ibid., 103
9. Ibid., 106
10. Ibid., 107
11. Ibid., 106
12. Ibid., 109
13. Swenson, John, editor, *The Rolling Stone Jazz & Blues Album Guide* (New York: Random House, 1999), 567
14. *Blues All Around Me*, 110
15. Ibid., 111
16. Ibid., 111
17. Ibid., 112
18. Ibid., 112
19. Ibid., 112
20. Ibid., 114
21. Ibid., 115
22. Ibid., 116
23. Ibid., 116
24. Ibid., 117
25. Ibid., 120
26. Weinraub, Bernard, "Spinning Blues into Gold, the Rough Way," *New York Times*, March 2, 2003
27. *Blues All Around Me*, 126
28. Bowman, Rob, Richardson, Jerry, "A Conversation with B.B. King, King of the Blues," *The Black Perspective in Music*, 1989
29. *Blues All Around Me*, 126
30. West, Rebecca, *Blues On Stage*, April 20, 2000
31. *Blues All Around Me*, 131
32. Ibid., 131
33. Ibid., 131
34. Weinraub, op. cit.
35. *Blues All Around Me*, 132
36. Weinraub, op. cit.
37. *Blues All Around Me*, 127
38. Ibid., 127
39. Ibid., 128-129
40. Ibid., 130
41. Ibid., 132
42. Ibid., 133
43. Ibid., 133
44. Ibid., 134
45. Ibid., 134
46. Ibid., 137
47. Ibid., 137
48. Liner notes, *I Pity the Fool: The Duke Recordings, Vol. One*, MCA, 1992
49. *Blues All Around Me*, 137
50. Welding, Pete, *Bluesland* (New York: Dutton, 1991), 197
51. Ibid., 198
52. *Blues All Around Me*, 73
53. Ibid., 142
54. Lee, Peter, *Guitar Player*, July 1991
55. Clayton, Rose; Engle, Bob; Ferris, Bill; Newman, Mark; O'Neal, Jim; Steel, Suzanne, "B.B. King," compiled by Mary Katherine Aldin and Peter Lee, *Living Blues*, May/June 1988
56. Ibid.
57. Escott, Colin, "The Blues Every Day," liner book, *The Vintage Years*, Ace Records 2000
58. *Blues All Around Me*, 138

59. Ibid., 140
60. Ibid., 139
61. Escott, op. cit.

3. The Modern Age

1. Broven, John, "B.B. King's Record Company," liner book, *The Vintage Years*, Ace, 2000
2. Ibid.
3. Escott, Colin, with Hawkins, Martin, *Good Rockin' Tonight: Sun Records and the Birth of Rock 'n' Roll* (New York: St. Martin's Press, 1991)
4. Danchin, Sebastian, "Sam Phillips, Recording the Blues," *Soul Bag*, Winter 1986
5. Danchin, Sebastian, *'Blues Boy': The Life and Music of B.B. King* (Jackson, MS: University of Mississippi Press, 1998)
6. *Blues All Around Me*, 143
7. Ibid., 143
8. Escott, Colin, "The Blues Every Day," liner book, *The Vintage Years*, Ace Records 2000
9. *Blues All Around Me*, 144
10. Interview with author, 08/19/04
11. Broven, John, "A New and Different Sound: Sam Phillips of Sun Records," liner book, *The Vintage Years*, Ace Records 2000
12. Ibid., 25
13. Ibid., 26
14. McGee, David *Go, Cat, Go! The Life and Times of Carl Perkins, The King of Rockabilly* (New York: Hyperion, 1996)
15. Broven, op. cit., 26
16. Broven, op. cit., 26
17. Leigh, Spencer, "An Audience With the King," spencerleigh.demon.on.uk/ bbking/htm, 2000
18. *Blues All Around Me*, 144
19. Interview with author, 08/19/04
20. *Blues All Around Me*, 145

21. Interview with author, 08/19/04
22. Ibid.
23. Escott, Colin, "The Blues Every Day," liner book, *The Vintage Years*, Ace Records 2000
24. Broven, John, "A New and Different Sound: Sam Phillips of Sun Records," liner book, *The Vintage Years*, Ace Records 2000
25. Danchin, op.cit.
26. *Blues All Around Me*, 148-149
27. Ibid., 155
28. Danchin, op. cit.
29. *Blues All Around Me*, 160
30. Ibid., 161
31. Ibid., 140-141
32. Interview on pbs.org/american-rootsmusic, 2001)
33. Danchin, op. cit., 44-45
34. *Blues All Around Me*, 172

4. Pre-Album Singles: An Artist Revealed

1. Danchin, op. cit., 52
2. *Blues All Around Me*, 174
3. Ibid., 175
4. Escott, Colin, "The Blues Every Day," liner book, *The Vintage Years*, Ace Records 2000
5. Ibid., 41

5. The Crown Albums

1. *Blues All Around Me*, 199
2. Ibid., 200
3. Ibid.
4. Ibid.
5. Danchin, op. cit., 54
6. Escott, Colin, "The Blues Every Day," liner book, *The Vintage Years*, Ace Records 2000, 13
7. Ibid., 13
8. Broven, John, "B.B. King's Record Company," liner book, *The Vintage Years*, Ace 2000, 19
9. Escott, op. cit., 12
10. Interview with author, 08/19/04

6. 'Ain't Nothing but a Business'

1. Danchin, op. cit., 48-49
2. Dixon, Willie and Snowden, Don, *I Am the Blues* (Quartet Books, 1989), 207
3. *Blues All Around Me*, 206
4. Ibid., 211
5. Clayton, Rose; Engle, Bob; Ferris, Bill; Newman, Mark; O'Neal, Jim; Steel, Suzanne, "B.B. King," compiled by Mary Katherine Aldin and Peter Lee, *Living Blues*, May/June 1988
6. Interview with author, 08/19/04
7. Ibid.

7. Drifting Blues

1. Guralnick, Peter, *Sweet Soul Music* (New York: Harper & Row, 1986) 231
2. Ibid., 233
3. Ibid., 235
4. Ibid., 235
5. Palmer, Robert, "James Brown," *The Rolling Stone Illustrated History of Rock & Roll* (New York: Random House, 1980)
6. Guralnick, op. cit., 244
7. Gillett, Charlie, *The Sound of the City: The Rise of Rock 'N' Roll* (New York: Dell Publishing Company, 1970)
8. *Blues All Around Me*, 210-211
9. Ibid., 211
10. "B.B. King," *Living Blues*, May/June 1988
11. *Blues All Around Me*, 213
12. *The Vintage Years* box set booklet, 44
13. *Blues All Around Me*, 224
14. Danchin, op. cit., 67
15. *Blues All Around Me*, 224
16. Ibid., 224
17. Ibid., 225
18. Ibid., 219
19. Ibid., 232
20. Ibid., 231-232

21. Ibid., 230
22. Sawyer, Charles, *The Arrival of B.B. King: The Authorized Biography* (New York: Doubleday, 1980)
23. *Blues All Around Me*, 227
24. Ibid., 230

8. Manhattan Transfer

1. Danchin, op. cit., 73
2. Sawyer, op. cit., 108
3. Danchin, op. cit., 74
4. *Blues All Around Me*, 238
5. Ibid., 239
6. Danchin, op, cit., 74
7. *Blues All Around Me*, 245
8. Ibid., 233
9. Ibid., 233-234

9. Rebirth

1. Unless otherwise noted, all quotes from Bill Szymczyk in this section are from an interview with the author, 06/20/04
2. Sawyer, op. cit., 163
3. *Blues All Around Me*, 235
4. Ibid., 236
5. Danchin, op. cit., 79
6. *Blues All Around Me*, 75
7. Liner notes, *The Thrill Is Gone*, Roy Hawkins, Ace Records, CDCHD 754, 2000
8. Ibid.
9. *Blues All Around Me*, 251
10. Ibid., 252
11. Ibid., 252
12. Sawyer, op. cit., 110
13. *Blues All Around Me*, 268
14. Wheeler, Tom, "B.B. King—Playing the Guitar Is Like Telling the Truth," *Guitar Player*, September 1980
15. Danchin, op. cit., 88
16. Leigh, Spencer, "An Audience With the King," spencerleigh.demon.on.uk/bbking/htm, 2000

17. Ibid.

18. Clayton, Rose; Engle, Bob; Ferris, Bill; Newman, Mark; O'Neal, Jim; Steel, Suzanne, "B.B. King," compiled by Mary Katherine Aldin and Peter Lee, *Living Blues* (May/June, 1988)

19. Danchin, op. cit., 85

20. *Blues All Around Me*, 262

21. Ibid., 262-263

22. Leigh, Spencer, op. cit.

23. *Blues All Around Me*, 264

10. "Give Me a Thrill, Stew"

1. All quotes from Stewart Levine are from an interview with the author, 08/23/04

2. *Blues All Around Me*, 271

3. Sawyer, op. cit., 21

11. What's Up, Doc?

1. Doc Pomus, liner notes, *Send For the Doctor: The Early Years*, 1944-55 (Whiskey, Women, and …, 1983)

2. Ibid.

3. Interview with author, 1978

4. Dr. John (Mac Rebennack) with Jack Rummel, *Under a Hoodoo Moon: The Life of the Night Tripper* (New York: St. Martin's Press, 1994), 142

5. Ibid., 36

6. Ibid., 229

7. Ibid., 229

8. All Doc Pomus quote from interview with author, published in *BMI Music World*, 1988

12: Consolidating the Gains

1. *Blues All Around Me*, 279

2. Ibid., 297-298

3. Danchin, op. cit., 94

4. *Blues All Around Me*, 283

5. Ibid., 298

6. Ibid., 298

7. Ibid., 294

13. Doc: Dum Spiro Spero

1. All Stewart Levine quotes from interview with author, 08/23/04

14. Auditing the Regency

1. All details about the making of *The King of the Blues* box set and all quotes from Andy McKaie are from an interview with the author, 04/23/04

15. Summitry of a Higher Order

1. Danchin, op. cit., 100

2. "A Tribute to Phil Ramone", *Billboard*, May 1996

3. Liner notes, Phil Ramone, *Heart to Heart*

16. Simplify, Simplify, Simplify!

1. Quotes from Steve Nails from interview with author, 08/24/04

2. All Stewart Levine quotes from interview with author, 08/23/04

3. All quotes from Eric Clapton from AOL Online Chat, 07-24-00

4. All quotes from B.B. King, Simon Climie, and Don Murray from "B.B. King," by Chris J. Walker, *Mix*, January 1, 2004

Epilogue

1. Danchin, op. cit., 101

2. *Blues All Around Me*, 300

BIBLIOGRAPHY

Books

Booth, Stanley. *Rythm Oil*. New York: Pantheon Books, 1991.

Danchin, Sebastian. *"Blues Boy": The Life and Music of B.B. King*. Jackson, MS: University of Mississippi Press, 1998.

Davis, Francis. *The History of the Blues*. New York: Hyperion, 1995.

Dr. John (Mac Rebennack) with Jack Rummel. *Under a Hoodoo Moon: The Life of the Night Tripper*. New York: St. Martin's Press, 1994.

Escott, Colin, with Martin Hawkins. *Good Rockin' Tonight: Sun Records and the Birth of Rock 'n' Roll*. New York: St. Martin's Press, 1991.

Gillett, Charlie. *The Sound of the City: The Rise of Rock 'n' Roll*. New York: Dell Publishing Company, 1970.

Guralnick, Peter. *Last Train to Memphis: The Rise of Elvis Presley*. New York: HarperCollins, 1994.

King, B.B., with David Ritz. *Blues All Around Me*. New York: Avon Books, 1996.

Kostelanetz, Richard, ed. *The B.B. King Companion: Five Decades of Commentary*. New York: Schirmer Books, 1997.

McGee, David. *Go, Cat, Go! The Life and Times of Carl Perkins, The King of Rockabilly*. New York: Hyperion, 1996.

Palmer, Robert. *Deep Blues*. New York: Viking Penguin, 1981.

Sawyer, Charles. *The Arrival of B.B. King: The Authorized Biography*. New York: Doubleday, 1980.

Sigafoos, Robert J. *Cotton Row to Beale Street: A Business History of Memphis*. Memphis, TN: Memphis State University Press, 1979.

Swenson, John, ed. *The Rolling Stone Jazz & Blues Album Guide*. New York: Random House, 1999.

Welding, Pete. *Bluesland*. New York: Dutton, 1991.

Whitburn, Joel. *The Billboard Book of Top 40 Hits*. New York: Billboard Publications, 2000.

—. *Pop Memories 1890-1954*. Menomonee Falls, WI: Record Research, 1986.

Articles

Bowman, Rob, and Jerry Richardson. "A Conversation with B.B. King, King of the Blues." *The Black Perspective in Music*, 1989.

Broven, John. "B.B. King's Record Company," liner book, in *The Vintage Years*, Ace Records, 2000.

—. "A New and Different Sound: Sam Phillips of Sun Records," liner book in *The Vintage Years*, Ace Records, 2000.

Clayton, Rose; Bob Engle; Bill Ferris; Mark Newman; Jim O'Neal; Suzanne Steel. "B.B. King," compiled by Mary Katherine Aldin and Peter Lee, *Living Blues* (May/June, 1988).

Danchin, Sebastian. "Sam Phillips, Recording the Blues." *Soul Bag*, Winter 1986.

Escott, Colin. "The Blues Every Day," liner book, in *The Vintage Years*, Ace Records, 2000.

Hinckley, David. *Parade*, October 20, 1985.

Lee, Peter. *Guitar Player*, July 1991.

Leigh, Spencer. "An Audience with the King," online at spencerleigh.demon. on.uk/bbking/htm, 2000.

Walker, Chris J. "B.B. King." *Mix*, January 1, 2004.

Weinraub, Bernard. "Spinning Blues into Gold, the Rough Way." *New York Times*, March 2, 2003.

West, Rebecca. *Blues On Stage*, April 20, 2000.

Wheeler, Tom. "B.B. King—Playing the Guitar Is Like Telling the Truth." *Guitar Player*, September 1980.

ACKNOWLEDGMENTS

I n a sense the place to start thanking those who helped bring this book to fruition is with B.B. King. I was not granted access to B.B. for this project, but in the sheer quantity and quality of the man's music, and the extensive documentation of his life and career, he exerted his presence in my life. I did have one meeting with B.B., in 1996, while on assignment for *Rolling Stone*, and that interview is reprinted here in its entirety. We went longer than scheduled, as B.B. got on a roll talking about the issues around the blues. In warming to the challenge of answering some new questions, I could see what John Broven articulated in my interview with him for this book: "Another thing I noticed, when I interviewed him, was what an intelligent man he is. You can just see it in his eyes. He may have come out of the country, but he certainly is very sophisticated. And it's that supreme intelligence that has enabled him to be a great guitar player and to absorb everything that's gone on around him." I cherish my one personal encounter with B.B., and hope there will be others—after all, there is always one more time. But if our paths never cross again, I will count myself fortunate for being able to see for myself that this great ambassador of the blues does indeed possess all the dignity, humility, and keen intelligence others have attributed to him. It's all over his music, and it's all over the man. I hope that comes through in this portrait of a momentous life. Thank you, B.B.

In addition to B.B.'s autobiography, *Blues All Around Me*, written with David Ritz, both Charles Sawyer (*The Arrival of B.B. King*) and Sebastian Danchin (*"Blues Boy": The Life and Music of B.B. King*) have penned excellent biographies of B.B. that proved invaluable to me in reconstructing the artist's life and career and that are duly attributed as sources throughout. Sawyer's and Danchin's are true biographies that examine the social conditions and extra-musical issues of their subject's life and career as well as the music; my book touches on those subjects, for the sake of context, but keeps the focus more intensively on the evolution and making of the music through the years. I hope music historians to come will find all of our efforts worthwhile and essential to the B.B. literature. In that spirit, this book offers the first in-depth interviews with two of B.B.'s most important producers, Bill Szymczyk and Stewart Levine, who together account for ten of the artist's most important albums. To Bill and Stewart, thank you for the privilege of documenting your exemplary work with B.B., and for your candor in discussing the man and the making of these albums.

For helping me locate Bill Szymczyk, I am indebted first to Robert Clyne, president of Neilson Clyne Public Relations in Nashville. Robert is a valued and trusted friend of long standing who used his connections to get me to Bill's and Stewart's front doors, figuratively speaking. To the estimable engineer Elliott Scheiner, thank you for believing Robert's hype about me and putting in a good word; to Chuck Leavell, many thanks for believing in this project and paving the way for my first contact with Stewart.

Ultimately, in tracking down Stewart, connections formed through my friendship with the late, great songwriter Doc Pomus proved invaluable and once again brought home the fact of how those of us who were in Doc's inner circle are always ready to help one another, no questions asked. To that end, Joel Dorn, who will never realize his ambition to play for the Brooklyn Dodgers, but can sink a Max Koslofsky set shot with the best of 'em, and has four Grammy-winning productions of his own to boot, gave me the high sign that provided access to Stewart, another Doc ally. At the end of the journey, Doc's daughter, Sharyn Felder, and her husband Will Bratton, read and fact-checked the Stewart Levine sections of the manuscript and verified the accuracy of specific details about Doc's life and his role in two important Stewart Levine–produced B.B. albums. It seems I've known Sharyn and Will forever, and at this point maybe we'll just say that's been the case. Their friendship and support over the years is what Doc's was: reason enough to keep on keepin' on. Thank you, Sharyn and Will.

Robert Clyne wasn't the only person at Neilson Clyne who played a key role in my efforts to document B.B.'s music. Robert's trusted associate Corey Walthall surrendered part of his Labor Day weekend to scour the Great Escape in Nashville for a vinyl copy of *Love Me Tender*, which he found and mailed to me undamaged. I salute him, and owe him one.

A big tip of the hat goes to the staff of Ace Records, and especially to A&R consultant John Broven for generous assistance in supplying me with copies of the label's reissues of B.B.'s Modern recordings. John also sat for an interview about the assembling of Ace's indispensable four-CD box set of the Modern-era work, *The Vintage Years*, and was always quick with an e-mail response to follow-up questions. Few know B.B.'s early work as thoroughly as John, and it was most gracious of him to share his insights. Lunch is still on me, John.

Andy McKaie, now senior VP of A&R at Universal Music Enterprises, where he has been deeply immersed in B.B.'s music for well over a decade now, has been a trusted friend almost since the start of our respective careers. Andy understood the concept of this book from the git-go and was supportive throughout, in addition to giving me the inside story on the assembling of MCA's essential four-CD box set, *The King of the Blues*, and his production work on the powerhouse *Blues Summit* album. I hope the accounts here do him as much justice as he's done B.B. over the years.

Many thanks as well to Michael Powers of Yellow Dog Records in Memphis, who's doing yeoman work to keep the flame alive, for setting up my instructive interview with Calvin Newborn; to Calvin Newborn, for his reflections on B.B.'s first recording sessions, on the young B.B., and on the curative powers of Noni Juice, all of which make sense to me; to Steve and Wish Nails of Dockside Studios in Maurice, Louisiana, for their reminiscences about B.B.'s work at their facility, a first-rate studio at which B.B. clearly feels at home; to my colleague and softball partner Ashley Kahn, for his constant encouragement, especially when the going was tough, and for some interesting ideas about B.B.'s ABC years; to recording industry icon Chris Stone, for a riotous account of his Zaire experience with Stewart Levine; to David Goggin, Mr. Bonzai, for all the kind words over the years and for providing a fine photograph of B.B. in the studio; to Laura Fissinger, for her selfless and poorly remunerated work for me in going deep into the bowels of the Internet and the Lincoln Center Library for the Performing Arts searching for articles on B.B., and coming up with a treasure trove of invaluable information.

Once again, Sarah Lazin proved me correct in my assertion that she's the best literary agent in New York. To have someone of her intellect believe in you is a high every writer ought to experience, and to have her as a friend as well is maybe more than a fellow should expect in a lifetime. Much love to you, Sarah.

At CMP Information, Martin Porter was the first to see my proposal for this series of books titled Lives in Music. He believed in it, he championed it to the folks at Backbeat, and he kept tabs on my progress up to his last day with CMP. That this book exists at all is due in large part to his support, and for that, as well as a treasured friendship of some three decades now, I am humbled and grateful. May our paths cross again, and soon.

At Backbeat, Matt Kelsey and Richard Johnston earn my undying respect not only for seeing the value of this idea and green-lighting it, but for selecting from a long list of potential subjects one B.B. King with which to kick it off. Their choice could not have been better, and I am the recipient of their good judgment and their support throughout. Thank you, again. Also, Nancy Tabor, Gail Saari, and Amy Miller did the legwork in production to make a striking package out of my manuscript, and Nina Lesowitz and Kevin Becketti and their sales and marketing team were most enthusiastic and aggressive in anning their marketing strategy, much to the author's delight. This has been most satisfying experience at every level of the process.

Speaking of the process, a big hug and deeply felt thank you to my ʌvorite copy editor, Patricia Romanowski, who labored over the computer ˡes and once again, as she did on my biography of Carl Perkins, made it all ʌainless for me. I don't even want to think about what I would have done had she not been available. Would you consider a lifetime contract, Patty?

Then there are the constants in my life. My sons Travis and Kieran are always with me, even when they're not physically present. Both continue to inspire me, and they're good guys, too. I love you both, to the bone and through the bone.

Not least of all, my beautiful bride Mary Lenore, who not only survived my writing this book, made sure I didn't get eaten up by it, never failed to tell me how good it was going to be, then went above and beyond the call of duty: she even became my publicist, using all the resources of her company, BopStar-PR, to get the word out about *There Is Always One More Time*. It's a long-term project, like our marriage. Having crossed oceans of time to find you, Mary Lenore, I will always love you.

—*David McGee*

ABOUT THE AUTHOR

New York City–based author and music historian David McGee is the author of *Go, Cat, Go! The Life and Times of Carl Perkins, The King of Rockabilly*, a finalist for the 1996 Ralph J. Gleason Award. He began writing for *Rolling Stone* in 1975 and remains an occasional contributor. He has contributed to all four editions of the *Rolling Stone Album Guide*; written the closing chapter of *American Roots Music*, the companion volume to the PBS series of the same name; and written liner notes for albums by B.B. King, Dr. John, and for four Chieftains reissues. He is the editor of trade show publications at CMP Media, and also writes for *Acoustic Guitar* and *The Absolute Sound*. He has also served as an assistant curator for the Rock and Roll Hall of Fame and Museum.

PHOTO CREDITS

INDEX